POLICING PREGNANCY

For Bryony

Policing Pregnancy
The Law and Ethics of Obstetric Conflict

SHEENA MEREDITH

ASHGATE

Published by
Ashgate Publishing Limited
Gower House
Croft Road
Aldershot
Hants GU11 3HR
England

Ashgate Publishing Company
Suite 420
101 Cherry Street
Burlington, VT 05401-4405
USA

Ashgate website: http://www.ashgate.com

British Library Cataloguing in Publication Data
Meredith, Sheena
 Policing pregnancy : the law and ethics of obstetric
 conflict
 1.Obstetrics - Law and legislation - Great Britain
 2.Obstetrics - Law and legislation - United States
 3. Informed consent (Medical law) - Great Britain 4.Informed
 consent - (Medical law) - United States 5. Pregnant women -
 Legal status, laws, etc. - Great Britain 6.Pregnant women -
 Legal status, laws etc. - United States 7.Pregnant women -
 Treatment - Decision making 8. Medical ethics
 I.Title
 344.4'10412

Library of Congress Cataloging-in-Publication Data
Meredith, Sheena.
 Policing pregnancy : the law and ethics of obstetric conflict / by Sheena Meredith.
  p.   cm.
 Includes bibliographical references and index.
 ISBN 0-7546-4412-X
 1. Obstetrics--Law and legislation--United States. 2. Informed consent (Medical
law)--United States. 3. Pregnant women--Legal status, laws, etc.--United States. 4.
Obstetrics--Law and legislation--England. 5. Informed consent (Medical law)--England.
6. Pregnant women--Legal status, laws, etc.--England. 7. Pregnant women--Treatment--
Decision making. 8. Medical ethics. I. Title.

   KF2910.G94M47 2005
   344.7304'12--dc22

                                                                                2005011780

ISBN-10: 0 7546 4412 X

Printed and bound by Athenaeum Press, Ltd
Gateshead, Tyne & Wear.

Contents

Preface

In the past two decades, a series of high-profile court cases in both the UK and the US have highlighted a novel problem for both medical law and society. In intervening in situations when pregnant women and those charged with their care do not agree on management options or appropriate behaviour, the law has been forced to try to reconcile the often competing demands made in the name of foetal 'rights', maternal autonomy and medical authority. Society's interests, for instance in preserving life and safeguarding future citizens, may also be brought to bear.

This book examines the legal and ethical background to such cases and attempts to give an overview of the development of the law as it affects pregnant women; the current legal position, and potential future complications.

In addition to assessing those cases that have come before the courts, and the ensuing ramifications, it examines the legal principles underpinning such aspects as medical care in pregnancy and during childbirth, patient autonomy, foetal status and potential maternal liability, as well as the operation of these principles at the practical level of the doctor's office, clinic or obstetric ward. It discusses the varying ethical viewpoints about foetal rights and maternal duty, assesses the interaction between medicine and the law in this area, and examines those factors – medical, legal, ethical and social – that may in the coming years pose even further challenges within the already complex relationship between pregnant women and their health care providers.

Although many of these issues are heavily influenced by prevailing social mores, their underlying significance may pose intensely emotive questions, often at the difficult intersection of ethics with morality, which touch on fundamental beliefs about the meaning of the human condition, and have potential impact and importance for the nature of the society in which we wish to live.

In this context it should be noted that the book does not attempt to discuss the vast subject of abortion law *per se*, nor the enormous ethical questions it poses, except insofar as it relates, directly or indirectly, to issues arising when a pregnant woman and her medical advisers are in conflict over appropriate intervention or behaviour in pregnancy. Similarly, while there is much to be said concerning the complex issues raised by 'workplace protection' policies applied to pregnant or potentially fertile women, they do not represent an example of such direct conflict and will not be addressed specifically.

I have tried to give an overview of the many and varied opinions that have been expressed on the issues underlying what I have chosen to call 'obstetric conflict' (for reasons explained in Chapter 3). I am grateful to all those whose opinions and judgements are here quoted or analysed. The presentation of facts however is my own selection, and the opinions expressed mine except where I have made clear that I am citing the viewpoints of others. The responsibility for any errors is entirely my own.

In deference to my English roots, British spelling and terminology have been used throughout, except where I have quoted from original sources that use the American versions. I hope that this will not be overly jarring for my American readers. To forestall any accusations of inconsistency, readers should also note that whilst the standard English 'judgement' is used with its general meaning, I have used 'judgment' to represent court decisions, as appropriate in a legal context.

As the majority of cases that have arisen in this area have occurred in either the US or the UK, the discussion concentrates largely on the law as it applies in these jurisdictions – both based on common law (with the exception of the US state of Louisiana, which operates the French Civil Code). Yet while the basic legal principles of patient autonomy have developed in parallel between the two countries, the approach to the application of these principles when pregnant women are involved has diverged considerably. In addition, the legal position may vary between individual states in the US.

As to the fundamental question of whether a pregnant woman is entitled to the same rights of self-determination and bodily integrity as other adults, courts on both sides of the Atlantic have in some instances decided that she is not. The implications of such decisions are wide-ranging and their future development of great importance both for individual women and their families, and for society as a whole.

Cases cited

Airedale NHS Trust v Bland [1993] AC 789.

Angela MW v William Kruzicki et al 209 Wis 2d 112, 561 NW2nd 729 (1997).

Application of the President & Directors of Georgetown College Inc. 331 F.2d 1000, 1006-07 (DC Cir), cert. denied, 377 U.S. 978, 84 S.Ct. 1883, 12 L.Ed.2d 746 (1964).

Attorney-General's Reference (No.3 of 1994) (1997) LTL 25/7/97; TLR 25/7/97; (1997) 3 WLR 421; (1997) 3 AER 936; ILR 1/10/97; (1998) CAR 91.

Bonte v Bonte 136 N.H. 286, 289 (1992).

Bowditch v McEwan [2002] QCA 172.

Brinkley v State 322 S.E.2d 49 (Ga. 1984).

Brown v Shwarts 968 S.W.2d 331 (Tex. 1998).

Bruggemann and Scheuten v Federal Republic of Germany [1977] 3 EHRR 244.

C v S (1988) QB 135.

Collins v Wilcock [1984] 3 All ER 374.

Commonwealth v Cass 467 N.E.2d 1324 (Mass. 1984).

Commonwealth v Lawrence 536 N.E.2d 571 (Mass. 1989).

Conroy, In Re (1985) 486 A.2d 1209.

Crawley v South Carolina 523 U.S. 1145 (1998).

Crawley v Catoe U.S. 4th Circuit Court of Appeals, decided 16 July 2001.

Crouse Irving Memorial Hospital Inc v Paddock (1985) 485 NYS.

Cruzan v Director, Missouri Department of Health 497 U.S. 261 (1990).

Cullotta v Cullotta 287 Ill. App. 3d 967, 969-70, 678 N.E.2d 717, 718 (1997).

Curlander v Bio-Science Laboratories 165 Cal. Rptr. 477 (1980).

Endresz v Friedberg 24 NY 2d 478 [1969].

Ferguson v City of Charleston [2001] 99-936 (Supreme Court of the United States); (1999) 186 F.3d 469 (U.S. 4th Circuit Court of Appeals); [1998] CA-93-2624-2-12 (U.S. 4th Circuit Court of Appeals).

Fidelity Financial Services Inc. v Hicks 267 Ill. App. 3d 887, 890, 642 N.E.2d 759, 761 (1994).

Fosmire v Nicoleau 75 N.Y.2d 218, 227, 551, N.E.2d 77, 81-82, 551, N.Y.S.2d 876, 880-81 (NY 1990).

Grodin v Grodin 102 Mich. App. 396, 400-401, 301 N.W.2d 869 (Mich. Ct. App. 1980).

Hamilton v Fife Health Board (1992) TLR 28/01/92 [Lawtel]; on appeal [1993] SLT 624.

Harnish v Children's Hospital Medical Center 387 Mass. at 154-155, 439 N.E.2d 240 (1982).

Hughes v State 868 P.2d 730 (Okl.Cr. App. 1994).

In re Baby [Boy] Doe 260 Ill. App. 3d 404, 632 N.E.2d 326-335 (Ill. App Ct 1994).

Acknowledgements

This book would never have been started but for the urging of Colin Gavaghan, Course Director at the Institute of Law and Ethics in Medicine at the University of Glasgow. I am profoundly grateful for his support and encouragement, as well as for the immense amount of time and effort he has taken in helping me to present my earlier efforts coherently and in discussing many of the ideas herein.

I would like also to express my appreciation and admiration for Professor Sheila McLean, Director of the Institute, whose clarity and integrity of thought are a shining example. It was a great privilege to study at Glasgow, and I thank the whole team for their excellent teaching and organisation.

I am grateful to all those whose words or studies are mentioned herein, and to the many people who willingly gave their time to engage in constructive discussion or to offer helpful information during the preparation of the book. Particular appreciation goes to those whose apt comments I have quoted on occasion, for expressing my conclusions so eloquently that I did not attempt to put it better myself.

Much though I owe them all a profound debt, none of these individuals bear any responsibility for the content of this book, other than their direct quotes, or for the presentation of any facts, opinions or errors within.

I would also like to express gratitude to all the women whose experiences have unwittingly provided the case material for discussion here. Their own words have too rarely been heard as others have battled for control of their bodies, yet many have shown great courage in pursuing justice, which may help to make the experience of pregnancy and birth less threatening for women in future.

On a personal level, I thank Steve and Tania Potts for their hospitality in Australia during the final throes of writing, and Jacqui Christensen and Joy Carbines for their friendship and support there. I would like to note my affection and gratitude to Cathy Earle and Valerie Clifton, two remarkable women among many Americans whose welcome and friendship have sustained me on my travels there. In the UK, special thanks to Liz Anfield for her unfailing friendship over many years; to Myrtle Smith and Paula Rice for 'being there', and to Jill Unwin and Dawn Dingwall for everything they do and for being who they are.

I also thank my parents for their unquestioning support, especially at moments of crisis, and for tolerating my infuriating persistence and perfectionism for so long.

Most of all, thank you to my daughter Bryony, whose utter lack of patience and resentment of every moment I spent writing has continually reminded me that there are other priorities, and whose delightful company and exuberance make it all worthwhile.

Sheena Meredith, 2005

Introduction

Pregnant Women in Court

The first reported case of court-ordered Caesarean section occurred in Colorado in the US in 1979. A woman described as 'obese, angry and incooperative' by her treating physicians refused to consent to the Caesarean section they recommended for, *inter alia*, foetal hypoxia (insufficient oxygen reaching the foetus). A juvenile court hearing convened in the patient's hospital room later that day found that the foetus was dependent and neglected, and ordered the Caesarean to be performed to safeguard the life of the unborn infant.[1]

A steady stream of similar cases followed in the US – although quite how many have occurred remains unknown, since information is readily available other than in the local courthouse only for those cases going to appeal or recorded because they are regarded as setting a precedent. The vast majority of such cases are decided rapidly, and without much publicity, by local courts.[2]

However by 1987 there had been sufficient numbers in the US for the outcome of a series of cases to be assessed[3] – and for questions to be raised about the quality of evidence presented to secure such orders.[4] Since then there have been several American cases that have garnered national and international attention, including one in which a young woman dying of cancer was forced to have a Caesarean against her wishes, even though it was accepted that this would hasten her death – and in the event, the foetus died too – an order vacated on appeal[5] and an outcome that some commentators have compared, morally, with murder (see Chapter 6). Although this case led to a firm statement by the American Medical Association that such legal intervention is inappropriate,[6] a position upheld by the American College of Obstetricians and Gynecologists,[7] at local level a variety of similar judgements attempting to override maternal autonomy continue to the present day.[8] They have also included attempts to control behaviour deemed inappropriate for pregnant women, such as drug-taking or alcohol use. This has involved a variety of sanctions ranging from court orders to incarcerate the woman until birth, to subjecting the foetus to wardship proceedings or seizing the neonate at birth, and even imposing upon women criminal penalties for adverse pregnancy outcomes alleged to be their 'fault'.

In the UK, an early case based on a wardship application for the foetus appeared to establish definitively that a woman could not be detained during pregnancy (in this case, with a view to compelling her to give birth in hospital).[9] Yet, in a series of emergency court hearings seeking declaratory relief to overrule refusals of consent, Caesarean sections were enforced upon unwilling women. These hearings were characterised by, *inter alia*, deficits in due process, perfunctory competence assessments, minimal evaluation of evidence and lack of representation for the woman. When some of these cases went to appeal, the courts repeatedly stated that a competent pregnant woman has, like all other adults, an absolute right to refuse treatment, even if medical evidence is that this places her foetus at risk.

On both sides of the Atlantic, the various attempts that have arisen to compel treatment against pregnant women's wishes have been permeated by endeavours to evade this conclusion.

The Impetus for Conflict

Such disputes have arisen since, and largely as a consequence of, the advent of medicalised pregnancy and hospitalised childbirth. Until very recently, the foetus was substantially inaccessible to medical surveillance; generally, the pregnant woman was the one to impart limited information about its movements, and about her own well-being, and it was she who was the focus of attention. Midwives and doctors did their best to ensure a normal delivery and a healthy baby largely via promoting the mother's health and guarding her as best they could against any complications of pregnancy and childbirth.

However, the development of techniques for imaging, testing and treating the foetus has now yielded a medical view of the foetus as a separate entity,[10] and of pregnancy as involving two 'patients' in one body,[11,12] – a viewpoint that encourages physicians to see pregnancy as inherently involving a conflict of interests between the woman and the foetus she is carrying.[13] Such developments have also prompted an unprecedented degree of 'quality control' over pregnancy outcome, supplemented in most Western countries by ready availability and *de facto* state preference for termination of pregnancy in cases of severe foetal abnormality. In parallel, pregnancy and childbirth have become increasingly medicalised, supervised and subject to technological input.

Such developments have arguably enhanced (healthy) foetal status at the expense of pregnant women's rights to self–determination and control over their own bodies. Inevitably, instances have arisen where medical staff and mothers have disagreed on what is appropriate intervention and, having achieved in the UK and US the almost universal removal of childbirth to the hospital arena, those in authority have often been in a position to attempt to enforce compliance with medical recommendations, most noticeably in the spate of court-ordered Caesarean sections on both sides of the Atlantic. In the UK the use of this type of court case appears, at present, to have ceased; in the US, attempts to use the law to enforce obstetric procedures and, in some cases, behavioural supervision, continue to the present day.

Such prominent clashes have led to widespread debate about the extent to which maternal autonomy should be compromised in the name of foetal safety. As early commentators noted, 'the missionary zeal of physicians, judges, and society to save the at-risk fetus at times violates the competent woman's right to make decisions about the integrity of her body'.[14] It also raises wider issues about medical paternalism and social control of women – as Douglas puts it, the implication is that childbirth is 'too important to be left to women'.[15]

The resulting conflict has created profound quandaries in medicine, ethics and the law, and has been described as 'passionate and seemingly irreconcilable'.[16]

Notes

1 Memorandum in Support of Petition and Order. Unborn Baby Kenner, #79JN83, Juvenile Court, City and County of Denver and State of Colorado, 6 March 1979, reported by Irwin S, Jordan B. Knowledge, Practice, and Power: Court-Ordered Cesarean Sections. *Medical Anthropology Quarterly* 1987; 1(3):319-334.

2 Irwin S, Jordan B. Knowledge, Practice, and Power: Court-Ordered Cesarean Sections. *Medical Anthropology Quarterly* 1987; 1(3):319-334.

3 Kolder VEB, Gallagher J, Parsons M.T. 'Court-ordered obstetrical interventions'. *N Engl J Med* 1987; 316: 1192-6.

4 Irwin S, Jordan B, *op cit.*

5 *In re AC* 573 A.2d 1235 (DC Ct App 1990).

6 American Medical Association Board of Trustees. Legal Interventions During Pregnancy. Court-ordered medical treatments and legal penalties for potentially harmful behaviour by pregnant women. *J Am Med Assoc* 1990; 264: 2663-70.

7 American College of Obstetricians and Gynecologists. *Informed refusal.* Committee Opinion No 237, June 2000.

8 See, for example: Weiss D. Court Delivers Controversy. *Times Leader Northeastern Pennsylvania* January 16, 2004 (see further Chapter 2).

9 *In Re F (in utero)* (1988) TLR 5.2.88 : (1988) 2 AER 193 : (1988) 2 WLR 1288 : ILR 10.2.88 : (1988) FCR 529: (1988) 132 SJ 820 : (1988) 18 FAM LAW 337 : (1988) 138 NLJ 37 : (1988) 152 JPN 538 [Lawtel].

10 John A Robertson. *Children of Choice. Freedom and the new reproductive technologies.* Princeton University Press, New Jersey 1994, at pp 10, 174.

11 Flagler E, Baylis F, Rodgers S. 'Bioethics for clinicians: 12. Ethical dilemmas that arise in the care of pregnant women: rethinking "maternalfetal conflicts"'. *CMAJ* 1997 Jun 15;156(12):1729-32.

12 Bright HL. 'Safe havens for addicted mothers'. *CMAJ* 1997; 157: 1201 (letter).

13 Mackenzie TB, Nagel TC, Rothman BJK. 'When a Pregnant Woman Endangers Her Foetus'. *Hastings Center Report* 1986; 16(1):24-25.

14 Justin RG, Rosner F. 'Maternal/fetal rights: two views'. *J Am Med Womens Assoc* 1989;44(3):90-5 [Medline].

15 Gillian Douglas. *Law, Fertility and Reproduction.* Sweet & Maxwell 1991, at p171.

16 Thorpe LJ. 'The Caesarean Section Debate'. 1997 *Family Law* 663.

Chapter 1

Pregnant Women and the Law

Court cases in which medical staff seek to impose treatment on unwilling pregnant women represent a unique legal situation. Even in those instances where the hospital or physician is apparently acting in the pregnant woman's best interests, as well as those of the foetus, the very possibility of a health care provider instituting legal action aimed at overriding a patient's wishes is in many ways an extraordinary development, especially since such cases have proceeded even when it is perfectly clear that the woman concerned is legally competent to take her own decisions. A prime purpose of seeking the court's approval to proceed with the unwanted treatment, either by an injunction forbidding the woman to refuse intervention or by declaratory relief stating that intervention without consent is not unlawful, is in order for medical staff to avoid later sanctions that might otherwise ensue.

This, in turn, implies an unprecedented degree of antagonism and suspicion on both sides of the physician-patient relationship. Whilst such a combative medical stance may be seen partly as a response to the increasingly litigious – and less compliant – nature of the modern patient, particularly perhaps the obstetric patient, it has functioned to draw the law, and wider society, into what was previously a highly private, privileged and in many ways intimate relationship. Introducing the possibility of legal conflict and potential compulsory treatment transforms the confidence, trust and support supposedly inherent in medical interactions and dramatically alters traditional notions of physician-patient relationships in the case of pregnant women.

The 'two patient' model of mother and foetus[1] has played a substantial role in this shift and, although lacking legal standing in the UK and, to an extent, in most parts of the US (*vide infra*), undoubtedly has emotive power affecting judicial emphasis, as will be discussed. Especially where conflict arises around the time of birth, applications to sanction forced intervention are likely to require a rapid decision – often outside normal working hours – prompting disregard of normal procedural rules and heightening the emotive force of potential foetal damage with the threat of escalating risk due to delay.

The impetus for such haste is likely to stem from the medical party to the case, and the decision to be based on medical evidence supplied by the same protagonist(s), with little time for detailed consideration or adequate representation for the woman. Such actions are, of course, predicated on the notion that the medical view of the situation is the correct one, as well as on a view that physicians (or hospital administrators, or social workers) have a greater claim to having the foetus's best interests at heart and to safeguarding foetal well-being than does the woman carrying the foetus. They assume, furthermore, that the statements of the treating physicians in individual cases represent an absolute body of factual medical knowledge not subject to debate or to differences of opinion or variations in practice – a notion that has been repeatedly demonstrated to be inaccurate.

As will be discussed, the courts have tended to take medical evidence in such cases at face value, even though the situation is clearly very different from the assumed usual dispassionate role of the medical expert witness – and generally there are no witnesses appearing for the other side who might take a contrary view. In many cases in both the US and the UK, the court was not put in full possession of all the facts, medical pronouncements were often highly subjective and the woman was effectively left in the position of an unrepresented (and often unnotified) defendant; yet the unwanted procedure for which the order was sought was to be carried out by the party seeking the declaration.

Perhaps unsurprisingly, the initial outcome of such cases has often been a summary decision based on the alleged medical facts. Even if retrospective examination of the legal principles subsequently allows more considered judgment, by the time of any appeal, it is too late – 'it must be scant comfort to a woman to know that she was wronged when the wrong has already happened', as Maclean puts it.[2] Moreover, whilst court cases in the UK have been numerically insignificant, the ramifications have been widespread – as perhaps even more so in the US against its background of both an increased number and broader scope of such actions.

Legal Background: The Right to Consent to Medical Treatment

On the face of it, the legal position appears straightforward. Self-determination is a basic human right firmly entrenched in and protected by the common law in both the UK and the US, as well as recognised as fundamental to the standards of civilised society:

> The only purpose for which power can rightfully be exercised over any member of a civilised community against his will is to prevent harm to others. His own good, either physical or moral, is not a sufficient warrant.[3]

Common law in the US has long recognised the vital importance of bodily integrity, as expounded as long ago as 1891 when the court refused to force someone to submit to surgical examination:

> No right is held more sacred, or is more carefully guarded, by the common law, than the right of every individual to the possession and control of his own person, free from restraint or interference of others, unless by clear and unquestionable authority of law.[4]

Even those accused of a crime cannot be subject to forced invasion of the body in order to recover evidence.[5] As applied to medicine, in Judge Cardozo's famed explanation:

> Every human being of adult years and sound mind has a right to determine what shall be done with his own body; and a surgeon who performs an operation without his patient's consent commits an assault, for which he is liable in damages.[6]

The US position has been further refined by the doctrine of informed consent, which requires that not only must a patient freely and voluntarily consent to any proposed medical procedure, but also that this consent be given with an appropriate understanding of the circumstances, based on sufficient knowledge of the risks, benefits, burdens and reasonable alternatives. This, in turn, places on the physician a legal onus of adequate disclosure of 'sufficient information to enable the patient to make an informed judgement whether to give or withhold consent to a medical or surgical procedure',[7] meaning the risks and benefits that a reasonable person in the patient's position would want to know in order to make an informed decision.[8]

Not only must the physician impart details of the diagnosis; the nature, purpose and risks of the proposed treatment, and the alternatives thereto; but also he or she must be satisfied that the patient comprehends the information and has decisional capacity. Any patient who is a competent adult has the right to decide whether a particular medical treatment is in his or her own best interests. 'The law protects [an individual's] right to make her own decision to accept or reject treatment, whether that decision is wise or unwise'[9] – indeed, it was said in *Matter of Conroy* (1985) that:

> If the patient's right to informed consent is to have any meaning at all, it must be accorded respect even when it conflicts with the advice of the doctor or the values of the medical profession as a whole.[10]

Moreover the right of refusal has been explicitly upheld even when the proposed procedure was of potential major benefit to another. In *McFall v Shrimp* (1978), a man with a rare bone marrow disease sought a court order to compel his cousin, the only compatible donor, to submit to a bone marrow transplant. The court refused, commenting:

> For our law to compel the Defendant to submit to an intrusion of his body would change every concept and principle upon which our society is founded. To do so would defeat the sanctity of the individual and would impose a rule which would know no limits.[11]

Exceptions for Emergencies and Incapacitated Patients

Other than with minors, there are two general exceptions to the rule of informed consent under US law. If consent cannot be obtained in an emergency because the patient is unconscious or otherwise incapable, and no surrogate (*vide infra*) is immediately available, the treating physician is entitled to *presume* consent for procedures that are immediately vital and cannot be postponed until capacity is regained, based on the presumption that the patient would consent to such treatment if able to do so. This rule would also apply in the case of a patient undergoing surgery in whom the need for a more extensive procedure arises during the course of the operation, provided again that need is critical and cannot be postponed, including until a surrogate decision-maker can be found. The presumption can however be rebutted by evidence that the patient would not want such intervention, for example a living will stating advance refusal of consent for life-prolonging treatment, or an advance refusal of blood transfusion by a Jehovah's Witness.

The other exception is in the non-emergency situation of a patient judged incompetent or incapable of taking his or her own decisions. In such cases, *vicarious* consent may be given on behalf of the patient by a surrogate. This stands in marked contrast to the position under UK law, under which (at the time of writing) no-one else is entitled to make decisions for an adult except under mental health legislation (*vide infra*).

In the US, the laws on health care proxies vary from state to state, but typically specify that the patient can appoint someone to take his or her health care decisions in the case of incapacity (although pregnant women are often excluded – see Chapter 4). If no appointment has been made, the traditional position was that only immediately necessary treatment could be given until a court order could be obtained authorising other procedures. However many states have now enacted legislation that provides for the automatic appointment of a relative once the patient is judged incompetent – for example, under Illinois law[12] the proxy would be, in order of priority: the guardian, spouse, any adult child(ren), either parent, any adult brother or sister, any adult grandchild(ren), a close friend, or the guardian of the person's estate. In some cases if no-one else is legally nominated, entitled or available, a doctor may act as surrogate decision-maker. In addition any person – even someone who is legally (or actually) a complete stranger – is entitled to petition the court requesting that a guardian be appointed for an individual who cannot manage his or her own affairs. Any such order granted by the court takes precedence over any other authority, including any surrogate who may have been nominated by the individual whilst competent.

The standards of surrogate decision-making are regulated by both federal and state laws and may involve the surrogate making a decision based on substituted judgement of what the patient would have wanted (to varying standards of proof thereof), or on the patient's best interests as judged by others. The doctrine of substituted judgement – an American development that is not recognised in the UK – is an attempt to make the decision 'which would be made by the incompetent person, if that person were competent, but taking into account the present and future incompetency of the individual as one of the factors which would necessarily enter into the decision-making process of the competent person.'[13]

Although the doctrine of informed consent has found little formal favour within the British courts, the underlying position as regards consent *per se* is similar. Without consent or other lawful authority, any medical procedure – including touching – however diligently performed, is potentially an assault.[14,15] Other lawful authority may be gained in several ways.

The doctrine of necessity allows emergency medical treatment when consent cannot be obtained, provided that this is limited to what is immediately necessary to save life or avoid significant deterioration in the patient's health.[16] The doctor must then always act in accordance with the patient's best interests – a matter for clinical judgement. The *Mental Health Act 1983* provides for compulsory detention and treatment for mental disorder and any physical disorder arising from that mental disorder, provided it complies with the safeguards contained in the Act. If an adult lacks the capacity to give or refuse consent to treatment – temporarily or permanently – doctors may (arguably must, because of their duty of care towards the patient) act in the patient's best interests.[17] Advice from the General Medical Council (GMC) is that in the case of mentally incapacitated patients, the doctor can carry out any investigation or treatment judged in the patient's best interests provided the patient complies; if the patient does not, he or she can be compulsorily treated for mental disorder only, within the safeguards laid down by the *Mental Health Act 1983*.[18] This leaves an interesting lacuna in the case of uncooperative incompetent patients.

In the UK there is no recognition of substituted judgement and, despite a common belief that the next of kin must be consulted, currently other than under the specific provisions of the *Mental Health Act*, no-one else is entitled to give legal consent for an adult, or to refuse treatment on his or her behalf.[19] Unlike the situation in the US, even the courts cannot declare that a patient *should* have a particular treatment, all they can do is to grant a declaration that doctors would not be acting unlawfully by taking a specific course of action believed to be in the patient's best interests. This situation is expected to change in 2007 when new provisions of the Mental Incapacity bill, going through Parliament in 2005, come into force. This legislation will for the first time allow patients to appoint someone to take medical decisions for them when they are no longer able to do so themselves, as with healthcare proxies in the US.[20]

However even at present, in practice doctors usually take the views and wishes of the patient's family into consideration, and this may have a bearing on what is, ultimately, the doctor's decision. The courts encourage consultation with relatives, provided this does not result in undue delay in giving necessary treatment, as it 'may reveal that the patient has made an anticipatory choice which, if clearly established and applicable in the circumstances – two major "ifs" – would bind the practitioner'.[21] It may also offer information as to the patient's personal circumstances or the choice that the patient might have preferred, although the views of relatives as to these questions do not bind the doctor nor override any clearly established anticipatory refusal of treatment.[22]

In the final analysis, assessment of both competency and best interests usually falls to the medical practitioner;[23] in cases of doubt, doctors are advised to obtain legal advice. A declaratory order may be sought from the courts to protect medical personnel or organisations from subsequent adverse criticisms and claims[24] where there are doubts about capacity or best interests, or where the patient or family object to the treatment proposed.[25]

The Right to Refuse Treatment

The right of competent adults to consent to medical treatment necessarily carries with it a concomitant right to refuse such treatment. In the UK, otherwise than in the limited situations of temporary or permanent incapacity, in English law a competent adult has an absolute right to refuse consent to medical treatment,[26] and this is so even if refusal risks death or permanent injury to health:

> The right to refuse consent to treatment is not abrogated even where the treatment is necessary to preserve life and generally the right will override the public interest in the preservation of life.[27]

It applies irrespective of whether the reasons for the refusal are rational or irrational, understandable or not, or even unknown or non-existent.[28, 29, 30] Similar principles apply in Australia, New Zealand and Canada.[31, 32, 33]

An advance refusal of treatment, provided it is clear and applicable to the situation that presents itself, is just as valid as one made at the time, and an advance directive ('living will') – by which patients, when still capable, can state in advance their refusal of specific treatments under certain situations, typically terminal illness, when they can no longer communicate their wishes – is arguably already binding upon doctors at common law. However, in addition to its provisions allowing patients to give power of attorney for health care decisions to someone else, the Mental Incapacity Bill[34] referred to above will also give clear legal recognition to advance directives, so giving them statutory footing – as is supported by both the British Medical Association and the Law Commission.[35,36]

In the US, the legal position is slightly different. The right to refuse unwanted medical treatment is protected not only under common law but also constitutionally – the Supreme Court in the prolonged *Cruzan* case[37] (which concerned 'right-to-die' issues) ruled bodily integrity a liberty interest protected by the Fourteenth Amendment to the Constitution. However, in marked contrast to the UK position, this right is not absolute – *Cruzan*[38], whilst upholding the right to refuse treatment, cited a previous case stating:

> Whether [an individual's] rights have been violated must be determined by balancing his liberty interests against the relevant state interests.[39]

These state interests (discussed at length in Chapter 2) may impact upon pregnant women's rights to bodily integrity in the US.

Does the Presence of a Foetus Affect the Right to Refuse Treatment?

The legal status of the foetus obviously has a bearing on, *inter alia*, medical treatment of pregnant women, including the extent to which they may refuse treatment supposed to benefit the foetus. In the UK – and, generally, in other common law jurisdictions – the position is, on the face of it, clear-cut. Although the foetus has some protections it has no *locus standi* to assert these rights unless and until it is born alive and has an existence separate from its mother. As expressed by Sir George Baker in *Paton v British Pregnancy Advisory Service Trustees* [1979] – a case concerning a husband's application to stop his wife having an abortion:

> The fetus cannot, in English law ... have a right of its own at least until it is born and has a separate existence from its mother. That permeates the whole of the civil law of this country ... and is, indeed, the basis of the decisions in those countries where law is founded on the common law, that is to say, in America, Canada, Australia and, I have no doubt, in others.[40]

The husband in *Paton*, dissatisfied with this ruling, took his case to the European Commission of Human Rights (ECHR) alleging that it breached Article 2(1) of the European Convention for the Protection of Human Rights and Fundamental Freedoms, which stipulates that the right to life shall be protected by law. The ECHR ruled decisively that Article 2 cannot apply to a foetus, reasoning that:

> The 'life' of the foetus is intimately connected with, and cannot be regarded in isolation from, the life of the pregnant woman. If Article 2 were held to cover the foetus and its protection under this Article were, in the absence of any express limitation, seen as absolute, an abortion would have to be considered as prohibited even where the continuance of the pregnancy would involve a serious risk to the life of the pregnant woman. This would mean that the 'unborn life' of the foetus would be regarded as being of a higher value than the life of the pregnant woman.[41]

As in the US therefore (*vide infra*), UK law concerning abortion has potential influence on the issue of control of pregnant women insofar as, to an extent, it delimits foetal status.

However, although the *Paton* case did stimulate some debate as to whether the court's *parens patriae* (parental) jurisdiction could be extended to allow wardship of a foetus so as to prevent an abortion, the upshot for present purposes is that since, as subsequent cases have confirmed, a foetus *per se* has no legal personality in British law,[42,43] so its interests cannot be set up in preference to the pregnant woman's rights.

The Influence of Foetal Status

In the US the position is both different and substantially more controversial. To the extent that the foetus is accorded 'personhood' or granted legal rights, these may conflict with those of pregnant women and could be used to restrict pregnant women's rights including, as well as the right to refuse unwanted medical treatment, the right to abortion – making the issue highly politically charged.

Traditionally in the US, as in England, the foetus under common law had no legal persona unless and until born alive. This concept gained formal recognition under American law in the landmark decision in *Roe v Wade* (1973),[44] in which the United States Supreme Court, in striking down a Texas law criminalising abortion, ruled that a foetus does not fall within the definition of the word 'person' as an entity entitled to protection under the Fourteenth Amendment of the Federal Constitution. This thereby gave American women the legal right to choose abortion in early pregnancy, before the foetus is viable (capable of surviving outside the womb), although individual states retain the right to impose restrictions on abortion thereafter. Despite numerous challenges, since *Roe v Wade* the Supreme Court has ruled consistently that a woman's right to health and life cannot be subordinated to the state's interest in potential life, even if the potential life is a that of a viable foetus – so, for example any state restrictions on later abortion must make exception for situations in which the woman's life or health is endangered.[45]

However, in terms of other rulings affecting the foetus, which may vary from state to state, the American position is more complex and subject to ongoing political manoeuvring as to foetal status, largely related to the influence of the 'religious right' and the vastly more vociferous US anti-abortion movement. For supporters of abortion, any attempt to grant the foetus legal status or personhood, or to give it rights independent of those of the mother, potentially represents an attempt to undermine the ruling in *Roe v Wade* and may be detrimental to women's rights and health.

The foetus's status has been at issue in a number of contexts. For example, in Kansas, a court held that a physician has a doctor-patient relationship not only with the pregnant woman but also with any foetus that she intends to carry to term.[46] A court in Texas decided that an *in utero* foetus is a patient for the purposes of the Texas *Medical Liability Act*.[47] Such verdicts extend the doctor's duty of care to the foetus while it is *in utero*, and not only once it has been born alive – creating potential conflicts if this duty is at variance with that owed to the pregnant woman, or with her expressed wishes that go against medical advice. It does however dispose of the anomaly that otherwise exists in that, without such a duty, a physician may be sued for damage occurring *in utero* once the child has been born alive, but not for the same damage to a foetus which never achieves an independent existence. So, for example, in New York a foetus injured *in utero* can sue once born[48] but, except for wrongful death laws applying to the foetus, or those providing for specific remedies for pregnancy loss (*vide infra*), neither the foetus nor the woman has a cause of action if the result is miscarriage or stillbirth.[49] Traditionally, the woman cannot recover in the absence of an independent physical injury both distinct from that suffered by the foetus and not a normal incident of childbirth.[50] Such provisions place a limit to medical liability but with the peculiar result that the negligent physician is liable to a malpractice suit if the foetus survives, but not if the negligence causes the foetus to die, which is clearly discrepant.

Foetal Rights

More crucially, there is currently a wide range of specific foetal rights legislation active or under consideration in the US. For example, in a move widely viewed as an attempt to elevate foetal status, under the Bush administration the Department of Health and Human Services (DHHS) in 2002 adopted regulations that allowed the State Children's Health Insurance Program (SCHIP) to redefine the word child to include 'unborn children', so expanding eligibility to include any individual 'between conception and birth up to age 19.'[51] This resulted in classifying the earliest embryo, as well as the foetus, as an 'unborn child'. Since pregnant women themselves (other than minors) are not included, any medical treatments that do not benefit the foetus directly are not covered, nor is post-natal care. Whilst States have some discretion in determining what conditions in the mother may affect the foetus, 'there must be a connection between the benefits provided and the health of the unborn child.'[52] Women may be left without financial cover for post-natal health complications so, for example the scheme could cover a Caesarean to deliver the baby but not its aftercare for the woman – nor treatment for any complications such as haemorrhage or infection.

The change has been criticised as being possibly detrimental to women's health rather than promoting it. There is an obvious potential for conflict should the medical needs of the woman and those of the foetus diverge – which is especially worrying given that the original announcement of the change commended its coverage of pre-natal testing, noting that '[o]nce detected, such conditions can often be surgically or medically treated *in utero*,' and suggesting that the beneficial effects of this included ultimately lower care costs for children. Moreover, the way in which the original language of the legislation was reinterpreted to include the foetus suggests that the DHHS has potential regulatory power to re-write other federal laws to include 'unborn children'. The measure 'reflects a fundamental contempt for pregnant women', according to the New York-based organisation National Advocates for Pregnant Women: it suggests that 'in key circumstances women's lives and health are a secondary consideration to those of the fetus, or are simply non-existent.'[53] Roth concurs: under the expanded coverage, '[w]omen are just the transport vehicle to deliver the fetus for the doctor's appointment'.

Is it Possible to Murder a Foetus?

As a further example, in the wake of numerous well-publicised attacks on pregnant women, an increasing number of states (31 at the time of writing) have enacted foetal homicide laws. Such laws address acknowledged deficits in the penalties available for violent acts that result in harm to a foetus or pregnancy loss, and enable prosecutors to bring charges in addition to those for assault on the woman, including murder charges even where the woman survives. However, even though most (though not all) of them contain an exception for acts of the pregnant woman herself, as well as for abortion and other medical procedures, pro-abortion groups have tended to see any attempt to give the foetus 'personhood' as a slippery slope towards undermining abortion rights. Rather, they have supported alternative proposed measures – such as the failed *Motherhood Protection Act*[54] – that would enhance penalties for attacks on pregnant women that harm the foetus or interrupt the pregnancy, so recognising the loss to the woman that is otherwise limited only to recognition of the physical damage to her, without reclassifying such crimes as involving two distinct victims. A few of these state foetal homicide statutes are carefully crafted to avoid implying personhood to the foetus. The law in California, which dates from 1970, followed public outrage at an attack on a pregnant woman – as do many more recent statutes. In the now-infamous California case of *Keeler v. Superior Court of Amador County* (1970), a man deliberately sought out his ex-wife, who was 35 weeks pregnant, and attacked her – saying 'I'm going to stomp it out of you' – with the express purpose of killing the foetus she was carrying by another man. The foetus sustained a fractured skull and was stillborn at an emergency Caesarean section. The man was charged with murder, but the California Supreme court ruled (by a majority of 5 to 2) that the then-prevailing common law definition of murder as unlawful killing of a 'human being' could not be applied to the foetus until it had been born alive.[55] Foeticide was not then a crime under California law.

In response to the resulting outcry that the man could not be convicted of the killing, the state of California added the foetus to its existing penal code, making murder 'the unlawful killing of a human being, *or a fetus*, with malice aforethought.'[56] The last phrase here, which implies intention to harm the foetus, or knowledge that the action may do so, was more recently much argued upon in *People v Taylor* (2004),[57] an attempt to evade conviction by a man who battered, then shot and killed his former girlfriend when neither of them was aware that she was 11 to 13 weeks pregnant. In that case, the man was originally convicted of two counts of murder; however the foetal homicide conviction was reversed on appeal when he argued that he was not aware of the pregnancy. In overturning the appeal court verdict, the Supreme Court in 2004 reinstated the conviction, ruling that implied malice murder liability would attach provided the state could demonstrate criminal intent towards someone; it was not necessary to prove that the attacker knew of the existence of the foetus (implied malice here operating on a similar basis to the principle of transferred malice in the UK). Therefore California's foetal homicide law may now apply even if the assailant has no knowledge that the woman is pregnant.

Similar attempts to evade foetal homicide laws in other states have met with an equally firm response. For example, Minnesota's Supreme Court in 1990 upheld the double homicide indictment of a man whose victim was found at post-mortem to be around one month pregnant, the judge commenting:

> The possibility that a female homicide victim of childbearing age may be pregnant is a possibility that an assaulter may not safely exclude.[58]

Other examples of states with foetal homicide laws that avoid implying personhood to the foetus are Idaho, where the law provides for murder or manslaughter charges to be brought for killing a 'human embryo or fetus';[59] Virginia, which in July 2004 enacted provisions for killing 'the fetus of another', with increased penalties for deliberate and premeditated killing,[60] and Indiana, where killing 'a fetus that has attained viability' may be murder, voluntary manslaughter, or involuntary manslaughter.[61] The law in Ohio applies to an 'unborn member of the species homo sapiens, who is or was carried in the womb of another'.[62] Notably, the use of the word 'another' in a couple of these provisions neatly excludes the pregnant woman from such charges.

Most such laws however do not discuss embryos and foetuses but utilise the more emotive term 'unborn child' – hence in Arizona, the killing of an 'unborn child' at any stage of pre-natal development is manslaughter;[63] in Arkansas, the killing of an 'unborn child' of twelve weeks or greater gestation may be capital murder, murder in the first degree, murder in the second degree, manslaughter, or negligent homicide;[64] in Illinois the 'unborn child' may be subject to various degrees of homicide[65] or to battery.[66] The latter is illustrative in specifically excluding injury inflicted by a pregnant woman upon her own foetus, as well as legally performed abortion provided that the woman consented, and acts committed pursuant to usual and customary standards of medical practice during diagnostic testing or therapeutic treatment.

The term 'unborn child' is used similarly in Georgia,[67] Louisiana,[68] Minnesota,[69] Missouri,[70] Nebraska,[71] Nevada,[72] North Dakota,[73] Rhode Island,[74] South Dakota,[75] Tennessee,[76] Texas,[77] Wisconsin[78] and Utah.[79] Florida law refers to an 'unborn quick child'[80] for the purposes of manslaughter charges,[81] as does Michigan,[82] Oklahoma[83] and Washington;[84] Florida also refers to an 'unborn child' after viability for the purposes of vehicular homicide.[85]

The term is also used in case law that has held the killing of an 'unborn child' after viability to be, in Massachusetts, first vehicular homicide[86] and then involuntary manslaughter;[87] and in South Carolina homicide.[88] These cases, all in the 1980s, all went as far as the state Supreme Courts which, unlike the California

Supreme Court in *Keeler* (*supra*), held that the (viable) foetus could be subsumed under the wording of more general homicide statutes – so dispensing with the need for specific legislation at all. In Oklahoma the Court of Criminal Appeals has ruled similarly in 1994.[89]

A Kentucky statute[90] enacted in February 2004, contrarily, provides for a crime of 'fetal homicide' to be perpetrated against an 'unborn child,' defined as 'a member of the species homo sapiens in utero from conception onward, without regard to age, health, or condition of dependency.'

In a similar spirit, the state law in Pennsylvania utilises both 'fetus' and 'unborn child', then defines both terms similarly: 'Each term shall mean an individual organism of the species Homo sapiens from fertilization until live birth.'[91] Under state law in Mississippi[92], effective since July 2004, the term 'human being' includes an 'unborn child' at every stage of gestation from conception until live birth and the term 'unborn child' means 'a member of the species homo sapiens, at any stage of development, who is carried in the womb.'

New York has no specific foetal homicide laws, although a measure has been proposed that would create offences of murder, manslaughter, criminally negligent homicide and vehicular manslaughter applying at any stage of gestation.[93] At present however two other – apparently contradictory – statutory provisions apply to the foetus. The state's abortion statute could be interpreted to mean that intentional procurement of a miscarriage against the pregnant woman's will falls under the definition of criminal abortion; moreover, this section of the penal code defines the killing of an 'unborn child' after twenty-four weeks' gestation as homicide.[94] However a separate provision defines the 'person' who is the victim of a homicide as a 'human being who has been born and is alive,'[95] which is more in keeping with the traditional English definition.

Time or Stage Limits

Some state laws apply only to the later part of pregnancy. In California, the addition to the penal code provision to incorporate a foetus was later refined by the California Supreme Court to define the foetus as one 'beyond the embryonic stage of seven to eight weeks,' although it upheld an appellate court ruling that such a foetus did not have to be viable for the law to apply.[96] Arkansas similarly has specific time limits, the law applying only to the killing of an 'unborn child' of twelve weeks or greater gestation. New York's statutory provision (*supra*) applies only after twenty-four weeks of pregnancy.

Other states use the more flexible terms quickening (vitality – movement, generally first detected by the pregnant woman) and viability (ability to survive outside the womb, a matter for medical assessment), sometimes interchangeably, to delimit the beginning of liability. Viability is a matter of opinion and is subject to change, as technology enables survival outside the womb at ever earlier stages (though not necessarily prolonged or handicap-free survival). Georgia's statute defines the killing of an 'unborn child' after quickening; Florida, Nevada and

Washington laws refer to an 'unborn quick child'; Florida also has a provision for vehicular homicide of an 'unborn child' after viability.[97] In Rhode Island, the statute refers to an 'unborn quick child' but states 'quick child' to mean viable; similarly, while the Oklahoma statute refers to the killing of an 'unborn quick child' as manslaughter, case law has held that the killing of an unborn child after 'viability' is homicide.[98] Indiana law applies only to 'a fetus that has attained viability'; Massachusetts, South Carolina and Tennessee also require that the 'unborn child' be viable. The Michigan statute refers to the killing of an 'unborn quick child' as manslaughter; however the Michigan Supreme Court has interpreted this as applying only after viability.[99]

In many other states – Arizona, Idaho, Illinois, Kentucky, Louisiana, Minnesota, Mississippi, Missouri, Nebraska, the Dakotas, Ohio, Pennsylvania, Texas, Virginia, Wisconsin and Utah – foetal homicide laws apply at any stage of pre-natal development.

What Type of Wrong may be Done to a Foetus?

Most state laws simply create a separate offence of foetal homicide and, in some cases, battery of the foetus. Some allow for murder but not manslaughter charges. Others are more comprehensive: Minnesota's statute, for example, provides for varying degrees of murder, manslaughter, and assault.[100] Under the Texas *Prenatal Protection Act*,[101] the protections of the entire criminal code extend to 'an unborn child at every stage of gestation from fertilization until birth,' except for exclusions relating to 'conduct committed by the mother of the unborn child [or] a lawful medical procedure performed by a physician or other licensed health care provider with the requisite consent.' Under some foetal homicide statutes, penalties for killing a foetus are identical to those for murder of a person.[102]

Arkansas and Idaho also recognise the specific wrong done to the pregnant woman. Idaho provides for a separate offence of aggravated battery for acts done to a pregnant female that cause 'great bodily harm, permanent disability or permanent disfigurement to an embryo or fetus;'[103] in Arkansas it is battery if, during the commission of a Class A misdemeanor, someone causes injury to a woman that causes her to undergo a miscarriage or stillbirth, or causes injury under conditions manifesting extreme indifference to human life and that results in a miscarriage or stillbirth.[104] In addition, in 1999, Michigan enacted a law, separate from its much older foetal homicide provisions, that provides felony penalties for actions that intentionally, or in wanton or wilful disregard of the consequences, cause a miscarriage, stillbirth or aggravated physical injury to an embryo or fetus.[105]

Recognition of harm done to a foetus – though not that done to the woman by having her pregnancy interrupted – now has federal backing. The *Unborn Victims of Violence Act (UVVA)* signed into law by President Bush on 1 April 2004 gives the foetus legal rights separate from its mother in the event of an attack on the mother that kills or injures the foetus during a crime committed under federal or US military jurisdiction. Bush is known personally to oppose abortion, except in cases of rape, incest or danger to the woman's life, and has presided over previous several measures, such as denying international aid to foreign groups that promote or publicise abortion, that are supported by anti-abortion campaigners. The *UVVA* resulted from a five-year campaign by the National Right to Life Committee (NRLC), a prominent anti-abortion group, and was hailed by them as a 'landmark right-to-life victory'.[106]

The legislation is also known by its official alternative title as 'Laci and Conner's Law' after a pregnant woman, Laci Peterson, who was murdered by her husband in her eighth month of pregnancy and whose foetus was to have been named Conner. It is limited in scope but predicted by many to have potentially far-reaching consequences. The law amends title 18 of the United States Code, and the Uniform Code of Military Justice, to protect 'unborn children' from assault and murder. It defines a potential victim as any 'child *in utero*' who is killed during the commission of a federal crime of violence. A 'child *in utero*' is further defined as 'a member of the species homo sapiens, at any stage of development, who is carried in the womb.'[107] The perpetrator needs neither to have intended harm to the foetus nor even to have known that the woman was pregnant.

During the bill's stormy passage through the Senate, two amendments – one to incorporate provisions on domestic violence, and the second proposing an alternative 'single-victim substitute' bill, backed by pro-abortion advocacy groups, to create a new federal offence of 'interruption of the normal course of a pregnancy' with equal penalties to the *UVVA* – were narrowly defeated (by 46-53 and 49-50, respectively) The bill was then passed with a majority of 61 to 38 votes.

The law applies only to harm to a 'child *in utero*' that occurs during commission of one of 68 defined existing federal or military crimes, such as a kidnapping, terrorist bombing or drug-related shooting, or crimes committed on federal or military territory such as a military base or airport. It allows charges to be brought for harm to the second, foetal victim, separate to those for harm to the pregnant woman herself. Generally, the punishment is the same as the punishment provided under Federal law for death or injury to the 'unborn child's mother' from the same conduct – except that the death penalty is specifically excluded. The *UVVA* does not affect state crimes nor alter any state laws, but brings federal law into a degree of harmony with state laws on foetal homicide, where these exist.

Ironically, Laci Peterson's husband, Scott, was actually convicted under California's foetal homicide law, not the *UVVA*, despite its alternative title. The ruling in *People v Taylor*[108] means that under California law once criminal intent towards one victim is proven, an attacker will be held responsible for the harm he does to any other victims as well. Peterson was found guilty on two counts of murder – first degree with special circumstances in the case of his wife, and second degree in the case of her foetus – making him eligible for the death penalty, which would not be the case with a single murder conviction.[109] In other states, the effect of such statutes may not be as dramatic – for example, in 2000 an Ohio teenager was sentenced to two consecutive periods of 15 years to life under Ohio foetal homicide laws for killing his pregnant girlfriend and her foetus.[110]

Problems with the UVVA

The broader scope of such laws, and the controversy they engender, is generally beyond the remit of this book. However, the *UVVA* is the first time that federal law has recognised an embryo or foetus as a separate person and, unlike *Roe v Wade*, it makes no distinction as to the stage of pregnancy or the foetus's potential ability to survive outside the womb – so, according to the American Civil Liberties Union (ACLU), it is also the first federal law to recognise a zygote (fertilised egg), blastocyst (pre-implantation embryo), embryo or foetus as a crime 'victim' independent of the pregnant woman who is harmed by a violent criminal act.[111]

This seems likely inevitably to cause the legislation to be dragged further into the abortion debate – according to dissenting democrats as the *UVVA* bill passed through the House of Representatives, '[t]his is a clear and unprecedented challenge to *Roe*' (ie *Roe v Wade*); moreover, its ambiguous terminology leaves open the question of whether the intention is 'to equate the rights of a zygote with those of a fully mature woman whose constitutional rights have vested at birth' – leaving the measure vulnerable to a constitutional challenge.[112]

A further constitutional challenge could come from the *UVVA* provision that the perpetrator need have no knowledge of the pregnancy, nor intention to cause the harm – in other words the mental element required for the crime (*mens rea*) is missing. Indeed, it does not require even recklessness or negligence, making it a strict liability offence – rare if not unique for a crime of violence. A conviction under the *UVVA* does not require a conviction for the underlying offence against the woman – so this cannot be overcome by using the notion of 'implied malice' (even assuming that the foetus constituted a 'person' to whom the intent could be transferred.)

Unsurprisingly perhaps, this provision has come in for particularly resounding criticism from many quarters for contravening the Constitution's guarantee of due process, which requires that under criminal laws the perpetrator must have *mens rea*, that is, *criminal* intent. Without this, the *UVVA* may thus punish conduct engaged in innocently – something for which courts have struck down criminal statutes,[113] and which makes it 'unlikely that these *mens rea* deficiencies would pass constitutional muster.'[114]

Several challenges to equivalent state foetal homicide statutes have been aired already; at the time of writing all had been rejected.[115] Nevertheless the potential remains on a number of grounds.

Any such challenges to the *UVVA* could well involve not the emotive cases of vicious killings of women carrying near-term foetuses that attracted support to the Act (though would not generally be chargeable under it), but charges much harder to sustain – suppose a woman sustains a trivial assault on a military base before she is noticeably pregnant, has no noticeable after-effects but subsequently suffers early pregnancy loss, as occurs in a high proportion of pregnancies in any case – how could she prove it was due to the assault? If her assailant is convicted of murder, the crime and penalty could seem disproportionate. Suppose a woman is killed in the course of a drive-by shooting (one of the specific crimes covered by the Act) and the post-mortem reveals an early pregnancy – with twins. Does this make the perpetrator liable for three homicides? And is it right that the woman's life would be the lesser element in the ensuing charges? It has also been suggested that the *UVVA* 'opens the door to litigation over when life begins and [to] mini-trials on fetal pain embedded within criminal prosecutions'.[116] It is arguable that such prosecutions could readily bring the law into disrepute.

For present purposes, the extent to which elevating foetal status may carry dangers of eroding the liberty of the pregnant woman carrying the foetus is likely to become an increasing concern. However, some commentators believe that the law will be able clearly to distinguish foetal homicide cases from those involving pregnant women's rights, and do not see them as in any way undermining the principle of *Roe v Wade*. According to Dorf, for example, 'there is nothing especially troubling about permitting the law to define the word "person" differently for different purposes. Statutes routinely define various words, including "person," so that they will mean exactly what the legislature intends in a particular context'.[117] Similarly Dellinger has stated: 'I don't think they [foetal homicide laws] undermine *Roe v Wade*... The legislatures can decide that fetuses are deserving of protection without having to make any judgment that the entity being protected has freestanding constitutional rights.'[118]

Foetal Protection in Australia

A similar approach has been followed in other countries. In Australia, for example, Queensland in 1997 introduced legislation that criminalised attacks on pregnant women that harm or destroy the life of 'the child before birth', including incidents that transmit a serious disease to the foetus.[119] In New South Wales (NSW) there was a public outcry following a case in 2001 in which a foetus of seven months' gestation was killed during a 'road rage' incident. Separate charges could not be brought in relation to the death (although it was taken into account when sentencing the perpetrator for the driving offence and resultant harm to the woman) and, in response, the Attorney General commissioned a review of such cases.

In the intervening period however, another case hit the headlines when a man kicked and stomped on the abdomen of a woman 24 weeks pregnant with his foetus. He was charged with maliciously inflicting grievous bodily harm with intent, but the District Court granted a permanent stay on the charge on the ground that the injury to the foetus could not be recognised by the court – its death did not constitute harm to the mother and the 'born alive' rule meant there was no offence of killing a foetus. When the Crown appealed, the Court of Criminal Appeal made the historic finding that 'the close physical bond between the mother and the foetus is of such a character that for the purposes of offences such as this the foetus should be regarded as part of the mother.' Therefore the loss of a foetus could constitute grievous bodily harm in a pregnant woman, even in the absence of other injury. The man duly pleaded guilty to the crime as originally charged and was sentenced accordingly, the case being described as one that 'changed the legal landscape.' Its effect, which accorded with the recommendations of the Attorney-General's review, was subsequently codified by Government, with the definition of grievous bodily harm in the *Crimes Act* amended to include the loss of a foetus.[120,121,122]

The NSW Government took pains to stress that the change in no way interfered with abortion law. However, unfortunately perhaps, the legislation was drawn into the abortion debate even in Australia, when during discussion of the proposed changes in the NSW Legislative Council the deaths of foetuses in violent incidents were compared with those due to abortions.[123] The new law has been duly hailed as a 'bold move' that 'will send a major pro-life message which says that New South Wales recognises the rights of the unborn against acts of violence', according to NSW Christian Democratic Party MP the Rev Dr Gordon Moyes.[124]

Why Foetal Status Matters

To return to the US, in terms of the state interests that may be brought to bear in cases of treatment refusal, these have generally been considered to embrace the preservation of life, the prevention of suicide, the protection of third parties and the ethical integrity of the medical profession[125] (see further Chapter 2).

As an early example, in *Jefferson v Griffin Spalding County Hospital Authority*,[126] the court held that the state's interest in protecting third parties extended to a pregnant woman's foetus. A similar verdict was reached in *In re Madyyun*,[127] in which, as in *Jefferson*, the mother as well as the foetus was alleged to be at risk without the operation. This could not be said of the emotive case of Angela Carder (*Re AC* 1987),[128] discussed in more detail in Chapter 2, in which a woman dying of cancer was forced to have a Caesarean on the basis of the state interest in protecting the potential life of her foetus, despite evidence that the operation would hasten her own death – a verdict overturned on appeal after both mother and foetus died.

The *Carder* case, as later with the case of *R v Louize Collins, ex parte S* (1998)[129] (see Chapter 2) in the UK – notably both extreme situations ultimately resolved only on appeal to the higher courts and too late for the women involved – garnered substantial media coverage and arguably, in the various official responses to the appeal verdicts, prompted more definitive protection for pregnant women's rights.

Many US cases have now applied these interests to the foetus, often, in the process, utilising a variety of local legal mechanisms to ward or appoint guardians for foetuses, so enabling control of the mother. These mechanisms may depend heavily upon tangential definitions of foetal status. For example, in the case of *In re Brown* (1997),[130] discussed more fully in Chapter 2 in terms of the way it illuminates the state interests that may be brought to bear, the court used the definition given in an abortion statute – that an unborn child is a human being from the time of conception and a legal person – to justify appointing a guardian *ad litem* for the foetus. In some cases, a separate lawyer has been appointed for the foetus (see also Chapter 5).

Maternal Liability

Irrespective of rights of refusal of consent, a further issue is whether a mother might be liable in law for damage done to the foetus, either by treatment refusal or by harmful actions such as drug use during pregnancy.

In the UK, again, the position is relatively clear. Firstly, the foetus has no rights until birth. In *Paton v BPAS*, Sir George Baker re-stated that, notwithstanding the 'fictional construction' that allows rights of succession from conception (but only once the child has been subsequently born alive):

> … in England and Wales the fetus has no right of action, no right at all, until birth.[131]

Any claim by a child – such as the right to take, on a will or intestacy, or for damages for injuries suffered before birth:

> … crystallises upon the birth, at which date, but not before, the child attains the status of a legal persona.[132]

Furthermore, by statute, under English law not only may a child sue for prenatal injuries only once born alive, but also the child cannot even then sue its mother,[133] except for injuries sustained in a road traffic accident (the rule is to avoid the undesirable mother-child and intra-family conflict that might arise from such suits; the exception because such cases usually represent insurance settlements); a Scottish child is in a similar position under common law.[134] Moreover, the Law Commission has specifically rejected the idea that a child should be able to claim against its mother for injuries sustained before birth,[135] so ruling out the possibility of a suit by a child whose congenital handicap is apparently linked with refusal of treatment by the mother during pregnancy.

A woman in the UK thus has no potential civil liability to her foetus for actions taken during pregnancy (road accidents excepted). This view similarly is held in many Commonwealth countries, including Canada where, for example, the High Court of Ontario has ruled that an unborn child is not a person and any rights accorded to the foetus are held contingent upon a legal personality being acquired by the foetus upon its subsequent birth alive.[136]

In terms of criminal liability for actions harmful to the foetus, in the UK the *Offences against the Persons Act 1861* made it an offence for any person to procure an abortion, and s1 *Infant Life (Preservation) Act 1929* criminalized the intentional destruction of a child that was capable of being born alive before it had an existence independent of its mother. The *Abortion Act 1967*, as amended by the *Human Fertilisation and Embryology Act 1990*, allowed abortion under specific circumstances – others remaining illegal – distinguishing abortions before 24 weeks, allowed on fairly broad grounds, from those after this point, allowed only on grounds of grave injury to the mental or physical health of the pregnant woman.[137]

However, a British mother's criminal liability for her foetus's death, other than for unlawful abortion or child destruction, remains uncertain. Except under statute, a foetus cannot be the victim of a violent crime, so violence to the foetus causing its death *in utero* is not murder.[138] Where the child is subsequently born alive the possibility of liability for murder or manslaughter was raised in a case of a pregnant woman stabbed by her boyfriend; on reference to the House of Lords it was held that inflicting injury on a pregnant woman causing the death of her child following premature birth amounted to manslaughter.[139] The House of Lords ruled that criminal responsibility for manslaughter may be established by showing causation and an action creating risk (to anyone). In theory this could allow a charge of manslaughter via gross negligence. However this might be difficult to apply to the woman if the foetus is viewed as part of the mother (so she would have to be found guilty of harming (a part of) herself) (see also Chapter 6).

In the UK, then, the potential for either civil or criminal actions is limited – although there have been instances of child abuse proceedings being instituted on the basis of pre-natal conduct (see Chapter 5).

Civil Liability in the US

In the US, the position is, again, in a state of flux and varies between states. As in the UK, it was settled that a child may have a cause of action in tort for injuries sustained in the womb, but only once the child has been born alive.[140] In the British case of *Paton v BPAS*,[141] Sir George Baker noted that the only known possible exception to the rule that in order to have a right the foetus must be born and be a child was an American case, *White v Yup*,[142] in 1969, in which a US court allowed an action for 'wrongful death' of an eight-month-old viable foetus that was stillborn as a consequence of injury. Notwithstanding this exception, 20 years later the Supreme Judicial Court of Maine was still ruling that a viable foetus was not a 'person' under the provisions of the state's wrongful death statute, which stipulated that the deceased must be a minor child at the time of the injury which resulted in death, and so a wrongful death action could not be brought by the parents on behalf of a viable foetus not born alive.[143]

Since then there have been a profusion of such 'wrongful death' cases brought on behalf of foetuses and 37 states have allowed wrongful death claims for stillborn children; however the Texas Supreme Court recently ruled that parents could not claim against a hospital for negligence over a foetus that died *in utero* in 1998, because the foetus is not a person under state laws – notwithstanding the extensive provisions of the Texas *Prenatal Protection Act* (2003) (*vide supra*).[144]

A very few decisions have allowed a live-born child to claim against its mother for pre-natal injuries. One, as with the British situation, allowed a child to claim for injuries received *in utero* in a motor vehicle accident in which the pregnant woman was negligent, but only up to the limit of the mother's insurance cover.[145] In another, *Bonte v Bonte* (1992), a court in New Hampshire allowed a claim by a child for the mother's failure to use reasonable care when crossing the street while pregnant, resulting in premature Caesarean delivery of a child with brain damage and cerebral palsy.[146] Two of the judges dissented on the grounds of unreasonable intrusion into women's privacy and physical autonomy rights and the profound implications of such a ruling for 'all women in this state who are, or may become, pregnant.'[147] Even more disquieting perhaps than this extraordinary verdict was that in *Grodin v Grodin*, in which the Michigan Appeal Court, reversing the lower court decision to dismiss the case, allowed a child to claim against his mother for having ingested a drug, tetracycline (an antibiotic) whilst pregnant, with the alleged result that the child's teeth became discoloured. Although the drug was legally prescribed, the mother had neglected to inform her physician that she was pregnant.[148]

In both of these cases the basis of the decision appeared to be to allow a claim that would be met by the mother's liability insurers. In the New Hampshire case – brought by the baby's father against the mother – the court looked to earlier cases that had abolished parental immunity for similar reasons. It suggested that the existence of insurance reduced the likelihood that a claim would promote family disharmony or deplete the family exchequer and so mitigated the arguments in favour of parental immunity. If there was no such immunity for parental negligence after birth, it was not logical to disallow a claim for negligent conduct that caused the child injury before its birth. Pregnant women were required to act with an appropriate duty of care with respect to the foetus and 'the mother will be held to the same standard of care as that required once her child is born'.[149]

This comment carries a number of problematic implications. Whilst it may not be unreasonable to expect a pregnant woman to exercise due care as a pedestrian, just as would a mother with young children alongside, to adopt a generalised standard of care irrespective of whether the woman owes a duty to a child or to a foetus carried within her own body potentially expands the duties of pregnant women beyond those expected of mothers. For example, to extend the principle to circumstances such as those in *Grodin* would raise troubling questions as to the extent to which a pregnant woman might be required to abstain from needed drug treatment or otherwise act in ways that would subordinate her best interests to those of the foetus.

However, the principle enunciated in *Bonte* and *Grodin* may be regarded as an anomaly. Generally, repeated court rulings have been fairly clear that the mother herself has no civil liability, following the authority of the leading case of *Stallman v Youngquist* (1988).[150] Here, the Illinois Supreme Court held, as in the UK, that the foetus's legal right to begin life with a sound mind and body can only be asserted after it has been born alive, and then cannot be asserted against its mother. Therefore a child may not sue its mother in tort for the unintentional infliction of pre-natal injuries. The court's reasoning included both that the law did not treat the foetus as an entity entirely separate from its mother, and that a foetus cannot have rights superior to those of its mother, therefore a pregnant woman can owe no duty recognisable in law to her developing foetus. Similarly the later case of *In re Baby Boy Doe* (1994) agreed that foetal rights may not be asserted against the unintentional affliction of injuries by the mother,[151] therefore in the context of a pregnant woman's refusal of treatment, the potential impact upon the foetus is not legally relevant – the mother's rights cannot be balanced against the putative rights of the foetus.

The position as regards a woman's criminal liability for acts that may harm the foetus has however recently become more complicated. Although the *UVVA* specifically exempts abortion, medical treatment, and acts of the pregnant woman herself, similar state laws have been used to initiate prosecutions against pregnant women for behaviour judged potentially harmful to the foetus, including drug and alcohol use, smoking, suicide attempts and failure to follow medical advice. In some cases the actions proceeded – and often the child was removed from the mother's custody – notwithstanding that the baby was perfectly healthy and despite the neonate no longer being exposed to the potentially hazardous substance (see further Chapter 5).

In most states the courts have resisted this trend, refusing to grant the foetus personhood for this purpose and recognising that homicide and child abuse statutes were not intended to apply to a pregnant woman's behaviour. The first such decision by a state high court was in 1997, when the Wisconsin Supreme Court ruled that state officials had erred in detaining a drug-using pregnant woman in the attempt to take custody of her 'unborn baby'. The judges, by a narrow 4-3 majority, held that a foetus is not a child under welfare laws, and thus cannot, as the authorities requested, 'be removed from his or her present custody' and placed in state custody. In order to do this, the pregnant woman would have to be detained as well, and the court did not have jurisdiction over an 'unborn child.'[152]

However, several states have instituted 'drug mother' laws enabling pregnant women to be incarcerated until the birth, and in a few cases women have been charged with homicide when adverse pregnancy outcomes were apparently the result of their behaviour. One woman in South Carolina was sentenced to 12 years in prison for homicide after a stillbirth when traces of cocaine were found in the baby's system.[153] In March 2004, a woman in Utah was charged with murder after one of her twins died when her initial refusal to undergo a Caesarean section delayed delivery by two weeks. Although the prosecution subsequently dropped the murder charge, this was stated to be on the basis of revelations about her mental health, not doubt about the validity of the charge[154] (this case is discussed more fully in Chapter 5). Despite the outcry raised by the case, the legal position as to such charges therefore remains uncertain, and further developments in this area seem almost inevitable.

Ethical Viewpoints – The Morality of Maternity

Nevertheless, the theoretical possibilities of maternal liability, both civil and criminal, find favour among many commentators, not least as a means of encouraging 'good' antenatal behaviour and compliance with medical recommendations. Many are also in favour of compulsion where necessary to achieve such behaviour. The argument is superficially compelling – a theoretical respect for patient autonomy cannot be absolute, and must pale in comparison with the prospect of needless harm being done to an innocent foetus (and prospective child). Moreover, such harm, if allowed, is to be perpetrated by a woman wilful (or stupid) enough to disregard professional advice, or actively to threaten her future baby's safety through clearly unhealthy behaviour such as illegal drug-taking. In this view, the human potential of the foetus makes pregnant women a special case and, in postulated conflicts between maternal autonomy and foetal 'rights', the foetus – perhaps after a certain point in gestation – holds the trump card.

Thus Sutherland, for instance, argues that if legal termination of pregnancy is available and a woman chooses not to pursue this option, she then assumes responsibility for protecting the foetus's well-being and, further, that this justifies antenatal regulation and intervention, with potential maternal liability for any harms caused by failures in such duty.[155]

Kluge too concludes that where abortion is available, a woman voluntarily chooses to let the foetus develop to the point of 'personhood', a certain stage of neurological development which she defines as somewhere before the 22nd week of pregnancy. Thereafter the right-to-life of the foetal person must be balanced against the right to autonomy and inviolability of the woman; moreover, she suggests that foetal rights should usually take precedence.[156]

In the US, the *Roe v Wade* ruling means that a woman's right to abortion in the early stages of pregnancy is absolute,[157] so if this view held sway she could perhaps be said voluntarily to assume such a choice – at least in situations where she is adult, competent, aware of the pregnancy and of her right to a termination, has access to and is financially capable of obtaining one. Even with the authority of *Roe v Wade*, getting an early abortion in America is not necessarily straightforward – even where a woman can deal with harassment at clinic entrances, mandatory delays and biased counselling, a majority of counties in the US have no abortion providers, meaning that women must often travel long distances to obtain one.[158] Moreover, the Hyde amendment passed by Congress in 1976, and upheld by two Supreme Court decisions in 1980, banned federal funding, such as Medicaid, for abortions excepting those necessary to save the life of the mother.[159]

Also, an obvious criticism is that there is an ethical discrepancy between a woman's entitlement to dispose of the foetus entirely up to a certain point, yet thereafter be required to accept a degree of supervision, medical intrusion and constraint on daily living that would almost certainly be unacceptable applied to any other class of adult, competent American. The comment of the United States Supreme Court in the seminal abortion case of *Planned Parenthood v Casey* (1992) seems resonant in this context too:

> The liberty of the woman is at stake in a sense unique to the human condition and so unique to the law. The mother who carries a child to full term is subject to anxieties, to physical constraints, to pain that only she must bear. That these sacrifices have from the beginning of the human race been endured by woman with a pride that ennobles her in the eyes of others and gives to the infant a bond of love *cannot alone be grounds for the State to insist she make the sacrifice.* Her suffering is too intimate and personal for the State to insist, without more, upon its own vision of the woman's role, however dominant that vision has been in the course of our history and our culture. The destiny of the woman must be shaped to a large extent on her own conception of her spiritual imperatives and her place in society.[160]

If the State cannot insist that a woman 'makes the sacrifice' of carrying a foetus to term, is it entitled to demand the arguably more onerous sacrifice of submitting to major abdominal surgery should her physicians deem a Caesarean desirable?

Such arguments are also practically flawed in jurisdictions such as the UK where abortion is a discretionary facility not available as of right – a woman is entitled to *ask* for an abortion up to 24 weeks of pregnancy – later if there is evidence of severe foetal handicap or risk to the mother's life or health – but must convince two doctors that she 'deserves' one. Therefore a British woman cannot be said voluntarily to assume such responsibilities to the foetus. However Robertson, whilst agreeing with the broad argument that once a woman chooses to become or remain pregnant, the foetus's interests should take priority,[161] argues contrarily that where abortion is *not* available, duties to the foetus may be owed from conception.[162]

Positions such as these would potentially leave all women of reproductive age hostage to the capricious whims of fertility or the vagaries of abortion law. Furthermore, since behaviour-related damage may occur even in early pregnancy, often before the woman is aware of conception, it would seem illogical on these grounds to reserve State attention for those obviously pregnant. Indeed, as knowledge of the importance of preconceptual health increases, it is arguable that surveillance, and intervention where necessary, might best be initiated even before conception.

To offer preconceptual advice and prenatal care seems an admirable goal; to compel it a dangerous interference with individual liberty. Moreover, such arguments about duties owed to the foetus assume that there is a body of inviolate knowledge capable of imparting some absolute truth about foetal well-being whereas, as will be shown in later chapters, the alleged facts are often capable of different interpretations; there is a lack of even professional consensus and, by analogy, many of the 'convictions' secured against pregnant women have been later deemed 'unsafe'.

Positions that expropriate the moral high ground (as well as the vocabulary) of foetal well-being may pose considerable dangers to the civil liberties of all fertile women. For example, Shaw has suggested that once a woman has abandoned her right to abort she incurs 'conditional prospective liability' for any actions that might harm the foetus, in which she includes withholding prenatal care, improper nutrition and even exposure to a 'defective intrauterine environment' such as in maternal phenylketonuria (PKU)[163] – a woman would then be liable in negligence for a decision to carry a genetically defective foetus to term.[164]

Douglas attacks this stance as 'both anti-woman and eugenically indefensible' and suggests it reveals the ultimate dangers of attempts to control pregnant women's freedom or hold them liable for the birth of a damaged child. 'Advocates of foetal rights would not stop at imposing liability on women who indulge in anti-social or illegal behaviour', she warns; moreover control could be attempted by people with all sorts of motives, such as vengeful fathers.[165]

Such considerations present a strong counterbalance to the apparently reasonable position of those who argue in favour of the supremacy of 'foetal rights' even, for present purposes, restricting consideration to such interests as interpreted by the medical profession.

Pregnant Women's Vulnerability to Legal and Medical Control

Moreover, any such attempts at third party interference in the course of pregnancy – which inevitably involve compromising a woman's physical liberty, autonomy and bodily integrity – place pregnant women in a unique legal position. There is no general duty to rescue in English law and in the US such a duty has been held specifically not to exist even towards a relative.[166] In neither jurisdiction do parental duties of care towards their existing children extend as far as forced medical intervention, and in any case such duties as do exist are not generally taken to encompass the foetus.

Whilst commentators such as Steinbock argue that women owe a moral duty to avoid harming their future children,[167] moral duty does not equate to legal compulsion, nor does it encompass the rescuer putting herself in danger. A woman cannot be compelled to become a live kidney donor (or even a blood donor) for her child after birth, even if the child will otherwise die, so to compel her to submit to a major operation (Caesarean section carries, *inter alia*, between a five- and 16-fold increase in maternal death,[168,169] as well as numerous other potentially hazardous sequelae – see Chapter 3) to enable it to be born imposes a duty on a pregnant woman over and above any normal parental duties:

No mother has ever been legally required to undergo surgery or general anaesthesia (eg. bone marrow aspiration) to save the life of her dying child. It would be ironic and unfair if she could be forced to submit to more invasive surgical procedures for the sake of her fetus than of her child.[170]

As Flagler comments: 'such coercion is far in excess of any nonvoluntary intervention that would be tolerated to save nonfetal lives'.[171]

In the UK, pregnant women are already in a unique position as regards compulsion in medical care. Under the *Nurses, Midwives and Health Visitors Act 1979* it is a criminal offence, other than in an emergency, for anyone other than a doctor or midwife to attend a woman in childbirth, and the mother herself may in theory be charged with aiding and abetting. This followed previous public health legislation designed, in essence, to prevent unsanitary and untrained midwives (the 'Sairey Gamps' of Dickens' era) from *making a living* out of endangering women (the *Midwives Act 1902* confined the offence to those operating 'habitually and for gain'; this clause was removed in the 1926 Act). Yet it has been used to create a medical monopoly on childbirth, even to the extent of prosecuting fathers for delivering their own child,[172] so that a British woman now has only two legal choices: to submit to medical interference (which, even though choice has been Government policy for more than a decade,[173] will usually involve 'encouragement' towards hospital delivery[174] and its attendant risks of intervention) or to give birth alone.[175] (One further other option, expedient, if less than honest, is to claim everything happened too quickly to seek medical attention.)

In the US laws vary from state to state and there are similar laws in a few places, such as Nebraska and Colorado, supposedly to protect women from unlicensed attendants – including fathers. More serious is the very real threat of 'child endangerment' reports (see Chapter 5).

On both sides of the Atlantic, as well as the often intense pressure towards hospitalisation and medicalisation at the time of birth (which at grass roots level may be as much practical as legal – see Chapter 6), there has been a dramatic shift in the emphasis of antenatal care away from screening for the minority of women at physical risk, to attempts to select those few women deemed able to give birth *without* obstetric supervision, based on the assumption that pregnancy is pathological. As Aksoy has commented:

> Pregnancy has come under medical control to such a degree that it is almost treated as a disease, and pregnant women have accepted their role as patients in need of medical help.[176]

Similarly, since the availability of antenatal screening and diagnostic tests for foetal abnormality, the assumption that the foetus is healthy unless shown otherwise has been displaced by the need to prove that the foetus is normal and not defective – fundamentally changing the whole experience of pregnancy.[177] The expectation of universal foetal testing within routine antenatal care carries with it the covert implication that foetuses found to be abnormal or defective will be aborted (see further Chapter 3) – as the British Royal College of Physicians has commented:

> Unless prenatal diagnosis is to be devoid of practical application when it reveals a major defect in the fetus, a responsible doctor must discuss with the parents the option of terminating that pregnancy and must in some circumstances provide information that may deter them from further reproduction.[178]

This position, arguably at odds with society's general current hostility towards 'eugenics', means that pregnancy is often regarded as tentative until such test results are known, and its very existence becomes dependant on medical acceptability. Rothman has argued that the medical profession has created an anxiety that capitalises on women's fear of having a socially unacceptable, 'defective' child, thereby making pregnant women need antenatal diagnosis for reassurance.[179]

As a further factor, tensions may arise between medical care of the mother and detection of problems in the foetus, as with, say, amniocentesis or intrauterine surgery – and technological progress is likely to increase the number of such potential conflicts. Often a pregnant woman's absolute best interests may, with her consent, be treated in a more flexible manner to try to optimise conditions for the foetus, for example in foregoing drugs that might otherwise be recommended. While most mothers actively seek to protect the foetus even at their own expense, it is arguable whether they should be compelled to do so. Moreover, the justifications advanced for procedures and other interventions is often subjective (see Chapter 3), and it may be the case with conflicts arising because of disagreements as to the utilisation or implications of tests and interventions, not that mothers are deliberately choosing to inflict harm, but rather that their interpretation differs from traditional medical assumptions, or that their choices take into account factors that the doctor's recommendations cannot, such as the need to care for other children.

In the UK, most women are dependent on the NHS (National Health Service) and have little choice as to the type of care they receive, which is variable from place to place. In the US non-paying patients may be in a similar position, while many more will be dependent on the facilities offered by their insurance provider. Although a few women with the confidence and financial means may withdraw themselves from the system altogether to give birth in a domiciliary setting with a private midwife, the vast majority have come to believe in the necessity for medical supervision and back-up in case of problems, and so submit themselves, willingly or otherwise, to the system.

On both sides of the Atlantic, and notwithstanding multiple major criticisms of the technological approach, those who fail to attend for antenatal appointments, question procedures involved or fail to 'co-operate' are likely to be labelled 'difficult' or irresponsible.[180] From the perspective of the professionals involved there is, of course, little point in antenatal care if findings cannot be acted upon.[181]

Pregnant women are thus in a position of considerable disadvantage within health care systems that wield substantial power over them, and over their foetuses and neonates. Such vulnerability may be reflected in the legal responses to conflict between a pregnant woman and her medical advisers. In the following chapters, this book explores the power imbalance that has confronted pregnant women in conflict with the medical system, and examines how the legal system in many such cases has been manipulated as a means to enforce compliance with medical recommendations. It describes the considerable incentives that exist to find alternative routes to achieve the desired outcome, in the face of higher court verdicts that the law should not be used thus, and assesses ways in which this trend might be perpetuated in future notwithstanding recent verdicts that appear to guarantee competent pregnant women's autonomy.

Notes

1 Mattingly SS. 'The maternal-fetal dyad. Exploring the two-patient obstetric model'. *Hastings Cent Rep.* 1992 Jan-Feb;22(1):13-8.
2 Alasdair R Maclean. 'Caesarean Sections, Competence and the Illusion of Autonomy'. *Web Journal of Current Legal Issues* (1999) 1 Web JCLI , 1/2/99 [Lawtel].
3 Mill, John Stuart. *On Liberty and Representative Government.* Second edition, chapter 1, 1859.
4 *Union Pacific Railway Co. v Botsford*, 141 U.S. 250, 251 (1891).
5 *Winston v Lee* 470 US 753 (1895) – in which the court refused to allow forcible removal of a bullet from the suspect's arm.
6 *Schloendorff v Society of New York Hospital* 211 N.Y 125, 129-30; 105 N.E. 92, 93 (1914).
7 *Harnish v Children's Hospital Medical Center* 387 Mass. at 154-155, 439 N.E.2d 240 (1982).
8 Richman S. 'Patient, doctor should discuss delivery options. Scenario: Does an obstetrician always have to follow the patient's wishes?' Ethics Forum. 7 April 2003. *American Medical News*:
   www.ama-assn.org/amednews/2003/04/07/prca0407.htm.
9 *Lane v Candura* 6 Mass.App.Ct. 377, 383, 376 N.E.2d 1232 (1978).
10 *Matter of Conroy* 98 N.J. at 352-353, 486 A.2d 1209 (1985).
11 *McFall v Shrimp* 10 Pa D&C 3d 90 (1978).
12 *Medical Patient Rights Act* 410 ILCS 50/0.01 – 50/99.
13 *Superintendent of Belchertown State School v. Saikewicz* 373 Mass. 728 at 752-53. 370 N.E.2d 417 (1977).
14 'assault' here taken to include battery.
15 *Collins v Wilcock* [1984] 3 All ER 374 at 378.
16. *Re F (mental patient: sterilisation)* [1990] 2 AC 1, *sub nom F v West Berkshire Health Authority* [1989] 2 All ER 545.
17 *Re F (mental patient: sterilisation)* [1990] *ibid.*

18 General Medical Council. *Seeking Patients' Consent: The Ethical Considerations.* General Medical Council. London 1999 at p12.
19 *In Re T (adult – refusal of medical treatment)* [1992] 4 All ER 649; 3 WLR 782; [1993] Fam 95.
20 *Mental Capacity Bill.* HL Bill 13 House of Lords Session 2004 – 05.
21 *In Re T (adult – refusal of medical treatment), Op cit.*
22 *In Re T (adult – refusal of medical treatment), Ibid.*
23 *In Re T (adult – refusal of medical treatment)* [1993] Fam 95 at 115.
24 *Re F (mental patient: sterilisation)* [1990] 2 AC 1 at 56.
25 Laurence Oates, official solicitor to Supreme Court. 'The courts' role in decisions about medical treatment'. *BMJ* 2000; 321:1282-1284.
26 *Sidaway v Board of Governors of the Bethlem Royal Hospital* [1985] AC 871 per Lord Templeman at pp 904-905.
27 *In Re J. (A Minor) (Wardship: Medical Treatment)* [1991] Fam 33, at 44.
28 *In Re T (adult – refusal of medical treatment)* [1993] Fam 95 per Lord Donaldson MR at p102; [1992] 4 All ER 649; 3 WLR 782.
29 *Re C (Refusal of Medical Treatment)* [1994] 1 FLR 31.
30 *Re MB* [1997] EWCA Civ 1361.
31 *Secretary, Department of Health and Community Services (NT) v JWB & SMB (Marion's Case)* (1992) 175 CLR 218.
32 *Smith v Auckland Hospital Board* [1965] NZLR 191.
33 *Malette v Shulman* (1990) 67 DLR (4th) 321.
34 *Mental Capacity Bill.* HL Bill 13 House of Lords Session 2004 – 05.
35 Dyer C. 'Mental capacity bill to punish abusers'. *The Guardian*, 19 June 2004.
36 Hall S. 'Under what circumstances can you ask to die?' *The Guardian*, 15 December 2004.
37 *Cruzan v Director, Missouri Department of Health,* 497 U.S. 261 (1990).
38 *Cruzan, Ibid* at 279.
39 *Youngberg v Romeo* 457 U.S. 307, 321 (1982).
40 *Paton v British Pregnancy Advisory Service Trustees* (1979) 1 QB 270 at 276.
41 *Paton v United Kingdom* [1980] 3 EHRR 408.
42 *C v S* (1988) QB 135.
43 *Kelly v Kelly* (1997) 2 FLR 828 [Lawtel].
44 *Roe v Wade,* 410 U.S. 113, 158 (1973).
45 *Stenberg v Carhart* 530 U.S. 914 (2000).
46 *Nold v Binyon* 31 P.3d 274 (Kan. 2001).
47 *Brown v Shwarts* 968 S.W.2d 331 (Tex. 1998).
48 *Woods v Lancet* 303 NY 340 [1951].
49 *Endresz v Friedberg,* 24 NY 2d 478 [1969].
50 *Tebbutt v Virostek* 65 NY 2d 931 [1985].
51 State Children's Health Insurance Program; *Eligibility for Prenatal Care and Other Health Services for Unborn Children* 67 FR 61956-01 (Oct. 2, 2002), codified as 42 C.F.R. pt. 457.
52 SCHIP, *Ibid*, Final Rule, 67 Fed. Reg. 61968.
53 National Advocates for Pregnant Women. *Commentary on 42 C.F.R. Part 457.* http://www.advocatesforpregnantwomen.org/issues/finalcommentonCHIP.htm.
54 A bill proposed by California Democratic representative Zoe Lofgren. The measure – rejected by the Judiciary Committee – would have made pregnant women a

specially protected class and provided additional penalties for violent attacks that resulted in harm to the foetus or loss of the pregnancy.

55 *Keeler v. Superior Court of Amador County* 87 Cal.Rptr. 481, 470 P.2d 617 (1970).

56 California Penal Code § 187(a) (my italics).

57 *People v Taylor* (2004) 32 Cal 4th 863.

58 *State v Merrill* 450 N.W. 2d 318 (Minn 1990) cert denied 496 U.S. 931 (1990).

59 Idaho Sess. Law Chap. 330 (SB1344)(2002).

60 Code of Virginia Section 18.2 – 32.2.

61 Indiana Code 35-42-1-1, 35-42-1-3, 35-42-1-4.

62 Ohio Rev. Code Ann. §§ 2903.01 – 2903.07, 2903.09 (Anderson 1996 & Supp. 1998).

63 Ariz. Rev. Stat. §13-1103 (A)(5) (West 1989 & Supp. 1998). Also to be read with Ariz. Rev. Stat. § 13-702(c)(10).

64 Ark. Stat. Ann. § 5-1-102(13)(b)(i)(a), read with Ark. Stat. Ann. §§ 5-10-101 to 5-10-105.

65 Ill. Comp. Stat. ch. 720, §§ 5/9-1.2 [Intentional Homicide of an Unborn Child], 5/9-2.1 [Voluntary Manslaughter of an Unborn Child], 5/9-3.2 [Involuntary Manslaughter and Reckless Homicide of an Unborn Child] (1993).

66 Ill. Rev. Stat. ch. 720 § 5/12-3.1.

67 Ga. Code Ann. § 16-5-80 (1996), § 40-6-393.1 (1997), § 52-7-12.3 (1997).

68 La. Rev. Stat. Ann. §§14:32.5 – 14.32.8, read with §§14:2(1), (7), (11) (West 1997).

69 Minn. Stat. Ann. §§609.266, 609.2661- 609.2665, 609.268(1) (West 1987).

70 Mo. Ann. Stat. §§1.205, 565.024, 565.020 (Vernon Supp. 1999).

71 Neb. Rev. Stat. § 28-391 to § 28-394. (2002).

72 Nev. Rev. Stat. § 200.210 (1997).

73 N.D. Cent. Code §§12.1-17.1-01 to 12.1-17.1-04 (1997).

74 R.I. Gen. Laws § 11-23-5 (1994).

75 S.D. Codified Laws Ann. §22-16-1, 22-16-1.1, 22-16-15(5), 22-16-20, 22-16-41 read with §§ 22-1-2(31), 22-1-2(50A) (Supp. 1997).

76 Tenn. Code Ann. §39-13-201, 39-13-202, 39-13-210, 39-13-211, 39-13-213, 39-13-214, 39-13-215 (1997 & Supp. 1998).

77 Prenatal Protection Act, SB 319.

78 Wis. Stat. Ann. §§939.75, 939.24, 939.25, 940.01, 940.02, 940.05, 940.06, 940.08, 940.09, 940.10 (West 1998).

79 Utah Code Ann. § 76-5-201 *et seq.* (Supp. 1998), UT SB 178 (2002).

80 Quickening is the point in pregnancy at which the foetus's movements can be felt by the mother-to-be.

81 Fla. Stat. Ann. § 782.09 (West 1999).

82 Mich. Stat. Ann. § 28.555.

83 Okla. Stat. Ann. tit. 21, § 713 (West 1983).

84 Wash. Rev. Code Ann. § 9A.32.060(1)(b) (West Supp. 1999).

85 Fla. Stat. Ann. § 782.071 (West 1999).

86 *Commonwealth v Cass* 467 N.E.2d 1324 (Mass. 1984).

87 *Commonwealth v Lawrence* 536 N.E.2d 571 (Mass. 1989).

88 *State v Horne* 319 S.E.2d 703 (S.C. 1984); *State v Ard* 505 S.E.2d 328 (S.C. 1998).

89 *Hughes v State* 868 P.2d 730 (Okla. Crim. App. 1994).

90 HB 108.

91 18 Pa. Cons. Stat. Ann. §§ 2601 to 2609 (1998).

92 SB 2869.

93 New York Civil Liberties Union. *Legislative Memo: Crimes of Violence Against a Fetus. S. 57-B/A.6681-A – An Act to amend the penal law, in relation to unborn victims of violence.* NYCLU 2003.
94 N.Y. Pen. Law § 125.00 (McKinney 1998).
95 N.Y. Pen. Law § 125.05 (McKinney 1998).
96 *People v Davis* 7 Cal 4th 797, 872 P.2d 591 (Cal 1994).
97 Fla. Stat. Ann. § 782.071 (West 1999).
98 *Hughes v State* 868 P.2d 730 (Okla. Crim. App. 1994).
99 *Larkin v Cahalan* 208 N.W.2d 176 (Mich. 1973).
100 Minnesota Code s609.266-2691.
101 SB 319.
102 Including: Cal Penal Code § 187 (West Suppl 1986) ; Ill. Ann. Stat. Ch 38, §9-1.1(Smith-Hurd Supp. 1985); Iowa Code Ann §707.7 (West 1979); Mich Comp. Laws Ann. §750.322 (West 1968); Miss. Code Ann. §97-3-37 (1973); N.H. Rev. Stat. Ann. §585:13 (1974); Okla. Stat. Ann. Title. 21, § 713 (West 1983); Utah Code Ann. §76-5-201 (Supp. 1983); Wash. Rev. Code Ann. §940-04 (West 1982).
103 Idaho Sess. Law Chap. 330 (SB1344)(2002).
104 Ark. Stat. Ann. § 5-13-201 (a)(5)(a)).
105 M.C.L. 756.90.
106 National Right-to-Life Committee. *President Bush Signs Unborn Victims of Violence Act Into Law, After Dramatic One-vote Win in Senate.* NRLC news release, April 6, 2004: http://www.nrlc.org/Unborn_Victims/BushsignsUVVA.html.
107 H.R. 1997, Unborn Victims of Violence Act of 2004.
108 *People v Taylor* (2004) 32 Cal 4th 863.
109 As of December 2004, the jury had recommended the death penalty; at the time of writing the judge had yet to decide – in formal sentencing in February 2005 – whether to reduce this to life imprisonment. In any event, it is anticipated that appeals will take many years: Dornin, Rusty. 'Jury recommends death for Peterson'. *CNN.com*. 14 December 2004. http://www.cnn.com/2004/LAW/12/13/peterson.case/.
110 Anon. Tristate News Summary. *The Cincinnati Enquirer.* 5 April 2000.
111 American Civil Liberties Union. *ACLU Letter to the Senate Urging Opposition to S. 146/S. 1019, 'The Unborn Victims of Violence Act'.* 24 March 2004: http://www.aclu.org.
112 Conyers J, Jr., Berman HL, Boucher R and nine other Representatives. *Dissenting Views to H.R. 1997, 'Unborn Victims of Violence Act of 2003.'* Washington, 2004: http://www.house.gov/judiciary_democrats/hr1997dissenting108cong.pdf.
113 American Civil Liberties Union. *Legislative Analysis of The Unborn Victims Of Violence Act.* ACLU, 18 February 2000: URL: http://www.aclu.org/ReproductiveRights/ReproductiveRights.cfm?ID=9013&c=144.
114 Conyers J, Jr., Berman HL, Boucher R *et al, op cit.*
115 See, for example, *People v Taylor, op cit*; *People v Davis* 872 P.2d 591 (Cal. 1994), holding that the state's addition of the word 'fetus' to its homicide statute was valid, but restricting the term to mean an embryo of more than seven to eight weeks' gestation; *Brinkley v State* 322 S.E.2d 49 (Ga. 1984), rejecting a challenge on the grounds of vagueness of the statute and lack of due process; *State v Smith* 676 So.2d 1068 (La. 1996), rehearing denied, 679 So.2d 380 (La. 1996), rejecting a challenge on the basis of the double jeopardy rule; *State v Merrill, op cit.*

116 Conyers J, Jr., Berman HL, Boucher R *et al*, *Op cit*.

117 Professor Michael Dorf, Columbia University School of Law, reported along with other commentaries in: National Right to Life Committee. *What supporters of legal abortion say about "fetal homicide" laws*. NRLC 2 February 2004: www.nrlc.org.

118 Professor Walter Dellinger, Duke University School of Law, reported along with other commentaries in: National Right to Life Committee. *What supporters of legal abortion say about "fetal homicide" laws*. NRLC 2 February 2004: www.nrlc.org.

119 This was achieved by adding s313 (2) to the Queensland Criminal Code. The section reads: 'Any person who unlawfully assaults a female pregnant with a child and destroys the life of, or does grievous bodily harm to, or transmits a serious disease to, the child before its birth, commits a crime.'

120 Wallace, Natasha. 'New law to protect unborn as killer father jailed'. *Sydney Morning Herald* 17 June 2004.

121 Debus, Bob. Questions Without Notice. 'Unborn victims of violence legislation'. *NSW Legislative Assembly. Hansard* 7 December 2004, at p13390.

122 The amendment covers a range of situations from maliciously inflicting grievous bodily harm with intent (section 33 Crimes Act), which carries a maximum penalty of 25 years imprisonment, to causing grievous bodily harm by an unlawful or negligent act (s54), which carries a maximum penalty of two years imprisonment.

123 Clarke, The Hon. David. 'Unborn victims of violence'. *New South Wales Legislative Council. Hansard* 17 March 2004, at p7411.

124 Moyes, Gordon. *Victory for unborn child protection*. Christian Democratic Party Media Release, Wednesday, 25 June 2003, on: www.cdp.org.au.

125 *In re Baby Boy Doe*, 260 Ill. App. 3d 392, 632 N.E.2d 326 (1994).

126 *Jefferson v Griffin Spalding County Hospital Authority*, 247 Ga. 86, 274 S.E.2d 457 (1981).

127 *In re Madyyun*, 114 Daily Wash L Rptr 2233 (DC Super Ct July 26, 1986).

128 *Re AC*, 533 A.2d 611 (DC 1987).

129 Full title: *St George's Healthcare National Health Service Trust v S : R v (1) Louize Collins (2) Pathfinder Mental Health Services Trust (3) St George's Healthcare NHS Trust, ex parte S (No.2)* (1998)LTL 7/5/98 : TLR 8/5/98 : ILR 12/5/98 : (1998) 2 FLR 728 [Lawtel].

130 *In re Brown* 689 N.E. 2d 397 (1997).

131 *Paton v BPAS*, op cit, at 279.

132 Per Heilbron J: *C v S* [1988] QB 135, 141A, at 140.

133 s1 *Congenital Disabilities (Civil Liability) Act 1976*.

134 *Hamilton v Fife Health Board* (1992) TLR 28/01/92 [Lawtel]; on appeal [1993] SLT 624.

135 Law Commission Report No 60, Cmnd 5709.

136 per Reid J: *Medhurst v Medhurst* (1984) 46 O.R (2d) 263.

137 Note that this gives precedence to the health of the woman over the life of the foetus.

138 *Attorney-General's Reference* (No.3 of 1994) (1997) LTL 25/7/97 : TLR 25/7/97 : (1997) 3 WLR 421 : (1997) 3 AER 936 : ILR 1/10/97 : (1998) CAR 91 [Lawtel].

139 But not murder, for which the *mens rea* would have to be an intention to kill or cause really serious bodily injury to the mother: *Attorney-General's Reference* (No.3 of 1994) (1997) *op cit*.

140 *Woods v Lancet* 303 NY 340 [1951].

141 *Paton v BPAS*, op cit.

142 *White v Yup* (1969) 458 P.2d 617.
143 Anon. *Milton v Cary Medical Center*, 22 February 1988. United States. Maine. Supreme Judicial Court. *Annu Rev Popul Law*. 1988;15:48-9.
144 Anon. 'Justices: Fetus is Not a Person.' *The Houston Chronicle*, 30 August 2004: http://www.chron.com/cs/CDA/printstory.mpl/front/2767852.
145 *National Cas. Co. v Northern Trust Bank* 807 So. 2d 86, 87 (Fla. Dist. Ct. App. 2002).
146 *Bonte v Bonte*, 136 N.H. 286, 289 (1992).
147 Brock C.J., dissenting, joined by Batchelder J.: *Bonte v Bonte*, 136 N.H. 286, 291 (1992).
148 *Grodin v Grodin*, 102 Mich. App. 396, 400-401, 301 N.W.2d 869 (Mich. Ct. App. 1980).
149 *Bonte v Bonte* 136 N.H. at 289-90.
150 *Stallman v Youngquist*, 125 Ill. 2d 267, 531 N.E.2d 355 (1988).
151 *In re Baby Boy Doe, op cit*, 260 Ill. App. 3d at 398, 632 N.E.2d at 330.
152 *Angela MW v William Kruzicki et al*, 209 Wis 2d 112, 561 NW2nd 729 (1997).
153 Talvi, Silja JA. Criminalizing Motherhood. *The Nation*, 11 Dec 2003: http://www.thenation.com/.
154 Sage, Alexandria. Utah C-Section Mom Gets Probation. *CBS News.com*, April 29, 2004: http://www.cbsnews.com/stories/2004/03/12/national/main605537.shtml.
155 Sutherland E. Regulation of pregnancy. In: Sutherland E, McCall Smith RA. *Family Rights: Family Law and Medical Advance*. Edinburgh University Press 1990, at pp105-114.
156 Kluge EH. 'When caesarean section operations imposed by a court are justified'. *J Med Ethics* 1988;14(4):206-11 [Medline].
157 *Roe v Wade, op cit.*
158 Benshoof J. 'Beyond Roe, after Casey: the present and future of a "fundamental" right'. *Womens Health Issues* 1993;3(3):162-70.
159 Rosenfield A. 'Women's reproductive health'. *Am J Obstet Gynecol* 1993;169(1):128-33.
160 *Planned Parenthood of Southeastern Pa. v Casey* 505 U.S. at 852, 120 L. Ed. 2d at 698-99, 112 S. Ct. at 2807 (my italics).
161 Robertson J. 'Legal issues in prenatal therapy'. *Clin Obstet Gynecol* 1986;29(3):603-11.
162 John A Robertson. *Children of Choice. Freedom and the new reproductive technologies*. Princeton University Press, New Jersey 1994 at pp 191, 180.
163 A genetic disorder in which the enzyme needed to metabolise phenylalanine in the diet is lacking, leading to a build-up of harmful chemicals in the bloodstream; a strict diet is required to avoid progressive brain damage.
164 Shaw M. 'Preconception and parental torts'. In: Milunsky A, Annas G (eds). *Genetics and the Law II*, 1980, at p228.
165 Gillian Douglas. *Law, Fertility and Reproduction*. Sweet & Maxwell 1991, at pp186, 188.
166 *McFall v Shrimp, op cit.*
167 Steinbock B. 'Maternal-fetal conflict and *in utero* fetal therapy' (1994) 57 *Albany Law Rev* 781.
168 American College of Obstetricians and Gynecologists. *Weighing the Pros and Cons of Cesarean Delivery*. ACOG Press release, July 31, 2003.
169 Sultan AH, Stanton SL. 'Preserving the pelvic floor and perineum during childbirth: elective caesarean section?' *Br J Obstet Gynaecol* 1996; 103: 731-734 (Medline).
170 Annas, George G. *Judging Medicine*. Human Press 1988, at p122.

171 Flagler E, Baylis F, Rodgers S. 'Bioethics for clinicians: 12. Ethical dilemmas that arise in the care of pregnant women: rethinking "maternal-fetal conflicts"'. *CMAJ* 1997;156(12):1729-32.
172 Brian Radley was convicted of an offence under the *Midwives Act 1951* at Wolverhampton Stipendiary Magistrates Court on 6.8.82; Rupert Baines was tried in Bristol shortly afterwards.
173 Cumberledge J. *Changing childbirth*. London: HMSO, 1993.
174 See, for example, Nicole Martin. 'Family doctors accused of steering mothers away from home births'. *Daily Telegraph*, 25 June 2001.
175 It was reported that women were having to resort to this option, rather than face their partners being prosecuted, when several health authorities refused to supply midwives to attend home births: Browne A. 'Midwife crisis puts home births at risk.' *Observer*, 7 May 2000.
176 Aksoy S. Antenatal screening and its possible meaning from unborn baby's perspective. *BioMed Central Medical Ethics* 2001 2: 3.
177 Marteau TM. 'Psychological Implications of Prenatal Diagnosis.' In: Drife JO, Donnai D (Eds). *Antenatal Diagnosis of Fetal Abnormalities*. Springer-Verlag, London 1991, at 243-54.
178 Royal College of Physicians: *Prenatal Diagnosis and Genetic Screening: Community and Service Implications*. RCP, London 1989.
179 Rothman B. *The Tentative Pregnancy: Prenatal Diagnosis and the Future of Motherhood*. Viking Penguin, New York 1986, at p 230.
180 Gillian Douglas. *Law, Fertility and Reproduction*. Sweet & Maxwell 1991, at pp 179, 173.
181 A recent exposé of the 'birth industry' in the US has highlighted the pressures on women that this approach presents: Wolf, Naomi. *Misconceptions. Truth, Lies and the Unexpected on the Journey to Motherhood*. Doubleday Books New York 2001.

Chapter 2

Power Imbalance in Court

It is only relatively recently that the law has been drawn into conflicts in which doctors have asked the court to authorise treatment against the wishes of the patient. Such actions are often brought to protect doctors from criticism and claims that they have acted unlawfully.[1] In most such cases there is time for the due process of the law to take its course, even if considerations must be expedited. However, in cases involving pregnant women, decisions have usually been taken in a hurry and there has been minimal, if any, representation for the woman. Medical evidence has been generally accepted without demur, and assessment of the woman's competence has often been perfunctory. In particular, the use of forced Caesareans in the UK has been described as 'an Orwellian scenario' revealing 'the blanket assumption of maternal incompetence and the widespread use of thinly veiled coercion'.[2]

Seeking Compulsion by Law

The traditional principle is that the foetus has no legal personality so, as held in *Paton v BPAS*,[3] its interests cannot be set up in preference to those of the mother. This was applied to an English obstetric case in *In Re F (in utero)* (1988), in which both *Paton* and the subsequent similar case of *C v S*[4] were affirmed. *In Re F* concerned a pregnant woman whose first child had already been taken into care. When she disappeared within two weeks of the expected delivery date of her next child, the local authority – which had already planned wardship of this child too once born – applied to the court to commence proceedings in advance of the birth. The application was dismissed at first instance because the judge held that the court had no jurisdiction, and the local authority appealed and obtained a further emergency hearing. This also failed.

The local authority had accepted that if the application succeeded, it would require an order to detain the mother and further orders for her detention and treatment in a suitable maternity unit. In dismissing the application, May LJ stated that to apply the paramount welfare principle would create undesirable conflicts between the existing legal interests or civil liberties of the mother and the interests and welfare of the unborn child. He also stressed the practical difficulty of enforcing such an order against the mother:

... there could well be medical problems which have to be solved: the mother might wish one course of action to be taken; it might be in the interests of the child that an alternative procedure should be followed. Until the child is actually born there must necessarily be an inherent incompatibility between any projected exercise of wardship jurisdiction and the rights and welfare of the mother. [5]

Notwithstanding that *In Re F* established firm authority for the principle that the court has no jurisdiction over an unborn child, thus precluding attempts to detain a pregnant woman in order to protect her foetus,[6] the presence of a foetus, perhaps inevitably, nevertheless led to some wavering.

In *In Re T*,[7] a woman who was 34 weeks pregnant was admitted to hospital following a road accident. The following day her condition deteriorated and she was visited by her mother, a Jehovah's Witness. T had been brought up in accordance with the tenets of this sect, although she never became a member. T's parents were separated and T had originally moved out of the family home to live with her paternal grandmother; at the time of the accident she was living with her boyfriend and had a close relationship with her father, who was not a Jehovah's Witness. During her mother's visit, T spontaneously stated to a nurse that she had been a Jehovah's Witness and retained some beliefs, and that she did not want a blood transfusion.

When later that evening she went into labour, she was transferred to a maternity unit, and was alone with her mother during the journey. At the maternity unit a Caesarean section was recommended, and T reiterated to both a midwife and a doctor that she did not want a transfusion. The doctor told her that this was not usually necessary with a Caesarean and, when she asked specifically, told her that other procedures were available though these were less effective. She signed a form refusing consent for a blood transfusion, though this was neither read to her nor explained. Her child was delivered stillborn the following morning. Thereafter her condition further deteriorated and, but for her express refusal, she would have been transfused. She was sedated and placed on a ventilator, at which point, her father, supported by her boyfriend, applied to the court for a declaration that the hospital could administer a blood transfusion without her consent.

At first instance the judge concluded that due to her condition and the effect of the narcotics she had been given, T had not been fully rational when she signed the refusal form. He made an interlocutory order allowing the transfusion, which was duly administered. At the subsequent full hearing, it was held that T's capacity to make a rational decision had been unimpaired, and was voluntary despite the influence of her mother. However, she had been lulled into a sense of false security and misinformed as to the availability and effect of alternative procedures, and so her refusal did not extend to the situation as it had developed. The declaration was therefore granted.

The Official Solicitor, as guardian *ad litem* for T, appealed. The Court of Appeal considered that 'in all the circumstances, including T's mental and physical state when she signed the form, the pressure exerted on her by her mother and the misleading response to her inquiry as to alternative treatment, her refusal was not effective'. The order had been properly made and the doctors were justified in treating T on the principle of necessity. Nevertheless, the judgment applied to the instant circumstances only. Lord Donaldson MR was quite clear that a competent adult has an absolute right to refuse treatment or to choose one rather than another of the treatments being offered. However he added:

> The only possible qualification is a case in which the choice may lead to the death of a viable fetus.[8]

This remark, albeit *obiter*, was then cited in the first British forced Caesarean case, *In Re S* (1992),[9] in which the court ordered a Caesarean to deliver a baby six days overdue and in a transverse lie position, despite the mother's refusal on religious grounds. The approach in *Re S*, later discredited,[10] was directly contrary to the principles of English law, both as to the rights of competent adults and as to the fact that a foetus has no legal personality, so its interests should not supersede those of a (legal) person – indeed, the decision has been described as 'logically untenable'.[11]

In the event the baby in *Re S* was delivered dead – exemplifying also Mason and McCall Smith's criticism that Lord Donaldson's use of the term 'viable' must be interpreted in relative rather than absolute terms, since viability results from a combination of gestational age and obstetric expertise[12] (a comment interesting in itself for its total disregard of any maternal input). Although the decision was not appealed, criticism led the Royal College of Obstetricians and Gynaecologists (RCOG) to advise against court-ordered obstetric interventions, stating that it is inappropriate to invoke judicial intervention to overrule 'an informed and competent woman's refusal ... even though her refusal might place her life and that of her foetus at risk'.[13]

Nevertheless, in the wake of the apparent authority of *Re S*, further cases arose. Whilst there had been no suggestion that S was not competent, this became a key issue in each one of the spate of subsequent British cases. They included two in which the stress of labour was held to impair decision-making capacity;[14,15] one where the court justified a forced Caesarean on a woman detained under s3 *Mental Health Act 1983* as being treatment for her mental condition,[16] and two cases where capacity was held impaired due to needle phobia[17,18] (for further discussion of competency issues raised by these cases, see Chapter 4). In the last of these, *Re MB* (1997), the woman had attended for an antenatal appointment at 33 weeks and both initially and at subsequent appointments had refused to have blood samples taken because of her needle phobia. The issue of needles was not explored when she agreed to a Caesarean section after the foetus was discovered to be in a breech position. On admission for the Caesarean, she twice refused consent for venepuncture, as she did again two days later when the anaesthetist visited her after the operation had been scheduled, notwithstanding her earlier problems with needles. The operation was duly cancelled. A consultant anaesthetist visited her and discussed the possibility and risks of anaesthetic by mask only, and she agreed. Two more days elapsed and an anaesthetist again visited, spending an hour with her and explaining the risks in detail. MB now refused consent for the Caesarean, and later that day went into labour.[19]

The hospital now sought a court order, and the High Court duly gave a declaration that it was lawful for a consultant to perform a Caesarean section along with the necessary administration of agents intravenously. On appeal, while upholding the order on the basis that MB's ability to consent had been impaired by the needle phobia, the court re-stated that a competent woman was absolutely entitled to refuse treatment, and the court did not have jurisdiction to take into account the interests of the unborn child put at risk from that refusal. With regard to the issue of a mother withholding treatment, the child [*sic*] did not have rights.[20]

The corollary of this is that in the case of an incompetent woman – where necessary emergency treatment may be given in the best interests of the patient[21] – the best interests to be considered are those of the *woman*, not of the foetus.

In *Re MB*, the court made it clear that had the woman been competent, even foetal death would not be grounds to overrule her decision. Detailed guidance was given on cases of treatment refusal and assessment of competency, which at the time was widely hailed as finally putting an end to forced Caesareans.[22]

Yet a further case arose in which a forced Caesarean was performed on a pregnant woman detained under s2 of the *Mental Health Act 1983 (R v Louize Collins & Ors, ex parte S (No.2)* (1998)).[23] The Court of Appeal later stated unequivocally that the woman concerned had been unlawfully admitted and detained and that the procedures performed on her amounted to trespass (this case is discussed in greater depth *infra* and in Chapter 4).

The *Collins* decision would seem, again, to give competent mothers absolute autonomy to refuse medical advice. However, in practice, as will be discussed in the chapters following, the position may not be as clear-cut as this emphatic judgment appears to state.

Compulsion Stateside

The US has a substantially longer history of court-ordered treatments. One of the earliest reported cases was that of *Raleigh Fitkin-Paul Morgan Memorial Hospital v Morgan* in 1964, in which a New Jersey court ordered a blood transfusion against the wishes of a pregnant woman in the interests of her viable foetus.[24] In *Jefferson v Griffin Spalding County Hospital Authority*,[25] the Georgia Supreme Court affirmed a lower court order compelling a woman to submit to Caesarean section and other medical procedures allegedly necessary to save the foetus's life. The court held that the state's interest in protecting a viable foetus outweighed the woman's rights to religious practice, to refuse medical treatment, and to parental autonomy. The verdict implied that the foetus has rights that attach at viability, and that pregnant women have a corresponding duty to ensure live birth, contemporary commentators presciently noting: 'The decision foreshadows substantial conflict between fetal and maternal rights.'[26]

The subsequent decade indeed produced several similar cases; for example, in *Crouse Irving Memorial Hospital Inc v Paddock* (1985),[27] a New York hospital was granted an order authorising blood transfusions against the wishes of a pregnant woman, and in *In Re Madyyun* (1986),[28] the District of

Columbia Court of Appeals upheld an order that a woman should undergo Caesarean section where there was a substantial risk to the foetus even though the risk to the woman was slight. These cases culminated in 1990 with that of Angela Carder already mentioned.

A survivor of childhood cancer, who had fought back against a second tumour that ultimately involved removal of her left leg and pelvis, Carder had been in remission for several years when she became pregnant, aged 27. Because of her disability, she was referred to a high risk pregnancy clinic, where she stressed to her doctors that she wished to be monitored closely for cancer recurrence, and that she did not want her own health to be compromised by the pregnancy. At 25 weeks of pregnancy, she was found to have a recurrence, with a cancerous tumour in her lung, and was admitted to hospital with a terminal prognosis. Having survived so much already, she requested that everything possible be done to prolong her life, including aggressive chemotherapy and radiation, notwithstanding its risks to the foetus.[29] She did discuss with her obstetricians the possibility of having a Caesarean section at 28 weeks, when the foetus might be capable of survival. However five days after admission her condition rapidly deteriorated and at one stage the foetus was deprived of oxygen for several hours. Notwithstanding that her obstetricians had decided not to intervene, the hospital administration – fearing legal liability for failing to save a potentially viable foetus – sought a declaratory order from the District of Columbia Superior Court as to whether it should intervene, by performing a Caesarean section, to save the life of the foetus.

At this stage, her doctors estimated that Carder had between 24 and 48 hours to live. Without Caesarean, the foetus would otherwise die when she did. In her weakened condition however, Carder's own death would probably be hastened by surgery. Her doctor, when asked by the court as to the likely prognosis if a foetus of this gestation were to be delivered by Caesarean section, stated that although usually it would have a 50 to 60 per cent chance of survival, given Carder's condition and the medications to which it had been exposed the chance would be 'much lower.' Moreover, he testified that Carder understood the risks to the foetus of premature delivery, including cerebral palsy, neurological deficits, deafness and blindness, and she would not want to bring a baby into the world suffering such handicaps, having had so much illness and pain in her own short life. However, the court also heard evidence from a neonatologist – who had neither examined Carder nor had any knowledge of the condition of the foetus or the medications to which it had been exposed – who stated that it would have a 50 to 60 per cent chance of survival, with a less than 20 per cent chance of serious birth defects, if delivered immediately by Caesarean section.[30]

The Superior Court accepted this assessment over that of Carder's own obstetricians, and ordered that the surgery should go ahead, holding that there was a legitimate state interest in protecting the potential life of the foetus, which – unlike Carder's own doctors – it deemed viable.[31] Carder had been heavily sedated and was on a ventilator at the time of the hearing – her mother later stated that the family had been called from her bedside as she lay dying to a 'short meeting', without being told that it was a court hearing (which was considerably more prolonged).[32] Carder was later informed of the decision and, after initially consenting, said she did not want the procedure if it meant she might die as a result. An appeal to the District of Columbia Court of Appeals requesting a stay of the order was turned down (by telephone), and the Caesarean was performed notwithstanding the repeated objections of Carder herself, her family and her own physician – the hospital had to recruit a reluctant staff obstetrician to perform the surgery since Carder's own doctors refused to do so. The foetus died (subsequent medical opinion suggested that it may have been brain-dead already),[33] as did Carder two days later, with the Caesarean recorded as a contributing factor.

The ultimate implications of such a court order are readily apparent. If a choice must be made between the life of the foetus and that of the woman, is any woman to be so sacrificed – or only a dying one? How soon must she be expected to die to make this acceptable – a day, a month, a year? If a court was prepared to see Carder's life foreshortened for the sake of her foetus, what about a severely disabled woman with a low quality of life? How disabled? How low? (for further discussion of the ethical issues raised by this case, see Chapter 6).

In the event, the decision in *Re AC* was vacated on appeal,[34] following submissions by more than 120 civil rights and health care groups including the American Medical Association (AMA) and American College of Obstetricians and Gynecologists (ACOG), arguing against the use of court-ordered intervention. Carder's parents also instituted an unprecedented damages claim against the hospital on behalf of her estate, claiming discriminatory treatment of her cancer and her pregnancy, negligence and medical malpractice on the part of the hospital, and lack of informed consent.[35] This was settled out of court, five days before the trial, and included not only an undisclosed sum of money but also an agreement that the hospital would develop policies to protect the right of pregnant patients to make health care decisions. [36]

In the subsequent case of *In Re Baby Boy Doe* (1994), an attempt to compel Caesarean section against the woman's wishes, the order was denied on the basis that the state's interest in the preservation of life was irrelevant where the procedure, although allegedly necessary for the health of the foetus, was not necessary to preserve the woman's life or health. The Illinois Appellate Court concluded that a woman's right to refuse invasive medical treatment derives from her rights to privacy, bodily integrity, and religious liberty, and is not diminished during pregnancy. The woman retains the same right to refuse invasive treatment, even of lifesaving or other beneficial nature, that she can exercise when she is not pregnant, and the potential impact upon the foetus is not legally relevant. The state's interest in protecting the potential life of the foetus cannot override a competent woman's refusal of invasive treatment whose only purpose is to save the life of her foetus. The court noted that in such circumstances the procedure posed a greater risk to the woman's health, and concluded that since a pregnant woman has no duty to guarantee the mental or physical health of her child at birth, she therefore cannot be compelled to act to safeguard it. The courts should not engage in a balancing of maternal and foetal rights, and ultimately:

... a woman's competent choice in refusing medical treatment as invasive as a cesarean section during her pregnancy must be honored, even in circumstances where the choice may be harmful to her fetus.[37]

In fact, after the appellate court refused to overturn the lower court verdict denying the order for forced surgery, the woman gave birth vaginally to a healthy baby boy.

However, the court in *Baby Boy Doe* specifically left open the question of whether or not relatively non-invasive and risk-free procedures, such as blood transfusions, could be ordered in such circumstances. In the leading case of *Fosmire v Nicoleau*,[38] the New York Court of Appeals held that the previous court ruling erred in ordering a Jehovah's Witness to undergo life-saving transfusions *after* a Caesarean birth. The court rejected the hospital's principal argument that the State had an interest in preserving the mother's life for the benefit of her child; however this did not address the issue of a similar situation arising during pregnancy. Just such a case subsequently arose in Illinois (*In re Brown* 1997[39]) and, unlike the *Baby Boy Doe* case, this time the proposed treatment would benefit both pregnant mother and viable foetus.

In *In re Brown*, 26-year-old Darlene Brown had gone into hospital for a urinary investigation and removal of a urethral mass, unrelated to her 34-week pregnancy. She was fully conscious during the procedure, which was anticipated to produce a small blood loss of about 100cc. In fact, she bled more heavily than expected, and the treating doctor decided to order blood for transfusion. At this point, the patient informed him that she was a Jehovah's Witness, and refused the blood.

Although Brown carried on bleeding, and ultimately lost almost 1,500cc blood during the procedure, the doctors assessed that she was competent to make her own decisions and completed the surgery using other techniques to control bleeding. Post-operatively, her haemoglobin (Hb) level was 4.4g/dl – where between nine and 12g/dl would be normal for a woman at her stage of pregnancy – and continued to fall notwithstanding the efforts of the treating physician to correct it by alternative medical procedures compatible with the beliefs of Jehovah's Witnesses. Brown, with the support of her husband, continued to refuse transfusion despite being told that her low haemoglobin level and its abrupt change posed a significant, life-threatening risk to herself and her foetus.

Eventually, the other measures having failed, the State filed a petition for adjudication of wardship and a motion for temporary custody of Baby Doe, a foetus [*sic*]. On the morning of the hearing, Brown's haemoglobin had sunk to 3.4g/dl and medical opinion was that both the woman and her foetus had, without transfusion, only a five per cent chance of survival.

The Court's first act was to appoint the public guardian of Cook County to represent the foetus, determining that it had the authority to appoint a guardian *ad litem* on the basis that the Illinois *Abortion Law* of 1975 stated that an unborn child is a human being from the time of conception and a legal person[40] – an interesting example of the way that other legislation affecting foetal status may be brought to bear in such cases.

However, the court then found it inappropriate to proceed under the State's initial petition for adjudication of wardship, being uncertain as to its jurisdiction under the *Juvenile Court Act*, which did not include a foetus under its

definition of 'minor'. The State accordingly sought to invoke the court's equitable powers and filed a petition for a hearing to determine whether a temporary Custodian could be appointed to consent to a medical procedure, in this case blood transfusion. The State urged the court that the issue was not one of balancing the mother's interests against those of the foetus, but rather the State's substantial interests in the viable foetus as against the mother's expressed desire to forego the minimal invasion of a blood transfusion. The balance of interests thus being semantically shifted, the trial court decided that it could, and appointed the hospital administrator as temporary custodian of the viable foetus, with the right to consent to one or more blood transfusions for the mother, when advised of the necessity by any attending physician.

The guardian *ad litem*, charged with protecting the interests of the foetus, ordered that Darlene Brown should undergo the transfusions. She subsequently gave birth to a healthy baby boy and was discharged from the hospital. Shortly afterwards the court held a status hearing and, in the light of the apparently successful outcome, vacated the temporary custody order, dismissed the State's petition, and closed the case.

A number of interesting questions arise as to the legal and ethical ramifications of such an order. The very assumption that custody of a foetus gives the guardian *de facto* control of the pregnant woman may be questionable. Clearly it is only possible to make such a guardianship order if the foetus is regarded as a separate entity. Yet if so, on what basis can guardianship of one 'patient' (the foetus) entitle the guardian to consent to invasive treatment of another patient (the woman)? Is the guardian, charged only with protecting the interests of the foetus, thereby obliged to disregard the pregnant woman's interests altogether? Who, in such a case, protects the interests of the woman where these do not converge with those of the foetus (other than considering the presumed foetal interest in having a mother once born)?

It is also worth noting here that phrases such as 'minimally invasive' are matters of opinion that depend very much on the point of view of those who hold them. Jehovah's Witnesses belong to a Christian sect that believes, based on biblical interpretations, that to accept into one's body the blood of another person (including substances derived from blood) precludes an individual resurrection and everlasting life after death, and will result in permanent separation from God and eternal damnation.[41] However incomprehensible or irrational such beliefs may seem to outsiders, they are of greater than life-and-death importance to those who hold them.

In the event, Darlene Brown later appealed, challenging the propriety of the trial court's order appointing a temporary guardian to consent, on her behalf, to blood transfusions for the benefit of her viable foetus, and contending that, as a competent adult, she had an absolute right to refuse medical advice and treatment, a right grounded in both federal and Illinois law. She also argued that description in *Baby Boy Doe* of blood transfusions as 'minimally invasive' was not a valid legal basis for divining when a patient's right to refuse treatment will be followed – to qualify a patient's choice in refusing treatment undermines the patient's authority to make a competent treatment decision.

The public guardian also appealed, seeking guidance as to its role in protecting foetal rights.

Although the case was moot (that is, the factual controversy had by then resolved), the Illinois Appellate Court found the issue to be one of public policy, so justifying a hearing – 'the issue is a public one requiring authoritative determination for the future guidance of public officials, especially given the emergency and expedited nature of such proceedings'.

The resulting hearing produced an interesting and considered analysis that helpfully summarises the underlying legal principles in such cases from the US perspective, especially in terms of the State interests that may be taken into account in decisions as to whether or not to override a patient's autonomy. It also exemplifies the many facets of individual State law that a court may need to examine in reaching its verdict.

The *In re Brown* appeal court noted that, according to the Supreme Court, religious-based objections to medical treatment are protected under the First Amendment to the United States Constitution. Bodily integrity is also, as discussed above, protected under the Fourteenth Amendment.

However the right of refusal is not absolute, and the State may intervene where the State's interests outweigh those of the patient, whether the patient's refusal is based on common law or constitutional principles.[42] The court considered each of the relevant State interests as they applied to Darlene Brown's case.

State Interests

1. The Preservation of Life

The circuit court had determined that the transfusion was necessary to preserve the life of both mother and foetus, and that the State had an interest in both. However the appeal court, citing *Baby Boy Doe*,[43] pointed out that this factor usually only concerns preserving the life of the decision-maker (the individual who refuses to consent to the treatment), and determined that this remained the position in the current case. Although most cases of refusal of medical treatment concerned competent adults who are not pregnant, and public policy in Illinois valued the sanctity of life,[44] the State also had an interest that must be considered in protecting the autonomy of the individual:

> The State rarely acts to protect individuals from themselves. This is consistent with *the primary function of the State* to preserve and promote liberty and the personal autonomy of the individual.[45]

The State of Illinois recognised the right of competent adults to refuse medical treatment both under statute and at common law. Under statute, the *Health Care Surrogate Act* provided that 'all persons have a fundamental right to make decisions relating to their own medical treatment, including the right to forgo life-sustaining treatment', and the aim of the Act was to define the circumstances under which such decisions can be made, either by patients with decisional capacity or by surrogate decision-makers on behalf of patients lacking such capacity, 'without judicial involvement of any kind'.[46]

The court also noted that the right of refusal at common law[47] was based on the doctrine of informed consent,[48] and this right of refusal extended both to life-saving and life-sustaining procedures and included blood transfusion. The appeal court therefore concluded, when considering the State's interest in preserving life in conjunction with its interest in protecting individual autonomy, that the interest in preserving the life of Darlene Brown was not determinative.

However, previous case law in Illinois had held that the State could impose blood transfusions on an infant over the expressed religious objections of parents[49] (and, moreover, that refusal to consent to a blood transfusion for an infant would constitute neglect[50]). After first disposing of the other state interests (*vide infra*), the ultimate issue then arose of whether the State had an interest in protecting a viable foetus – a question not previously addressed by either the Illinois Constitution or the Illinois Supreme Court. Perhaps inevitably, such a question drew in complex issues concerning both foetal status and the interaction of federal and state law.

To summarise briefly, the Appellate Court noted that the United States Supreme Court had held in the landmark abortion ruling of *Roe v Wade* (1973) that the State maintains an 'important and legitimate interest in preserving and protecting the health of the pregnant woman [and] the potentiality of human life';[51] indeed, the state maintains 'a substantial interest in potential life throughout pregnancy'.[52]

Under the Illinois *Abortion Law* of 1975, an unborn child was defined as a human being from the time of conception and was, therefore, a legal person entitled to the right to life from conception under the laws and Constitution of the State (the Act achieved this specifically *without* restricting the right to abortion under *Roe v Wade*).[53] As under *Roe v Wade*, the State's important and legitimate interest becomes compelling at the point of viability – at which point abortion could be restricted (by the State) except when necessary to preserve the life or health of the mother[54] – which, again under Illinois *Abortion Law* of 1975, was defined as 'that stage of fetal development when, in the medical judgement of the attending physician based on the particular facts of the case before him, there is a reasonable likelihood of sustained survival of the fetus outside the womb, with or without artificial support'.[55]

However the appellate court also noted, as had the lower court, that a foetus was not considered a minor for the purposes of the Illinois *Juvenile Court Act*, and that although Illinois courts had held viable foetuses to be persons with regard to wrongs caused by third parties, such instances were distinguished from injuries caused by the mother.[56]

While noting that the case involved neither abortion nor substance or other abuse by a pregnant woman (the implication being that in the case of such abuse, or of an attempt by the mother to procure a late term abortion where her own life was not in danger, there might be grounds for State intervention), the court stated that 'without a determination by the Illinois legislature that a fetus is a minor for purposes of the *Juvenile Court Act*, we cannot separate the mother's valid treatment refusal from the potential adverse consequences to the viable fetus.' In other words, and following the lead of previous cases (*Baby Boy Doe* and *Stallman v. Youngquist* (1988)[57]), in 'balancing the mother's right to refuse medical treatment against the State's substantial interest in the viable fetus, we hold that the State may not override a pregnant woman's competent treatment decision, including refusal of recommended invasive medical procedures, to potentially save the life of the viable fetus.'

The court further commented:

> In reaching this difficult conclusion, *we note the mother's apparent disparate ethical and legal obligations*. Under the law of this State, however, we cannot impose a legal obligation upon a pregnant woman to consent to an invasive medical procedure for the benefit of her viable fetus.[58]

2. The Prevention of Suicide

Both trial and appeal courts accepted that this interest was not at issue here as Darlene Brown had clearly sought and accepted all possible medical treatment, with the exception of blood transfusions. It should be noted that although the State will intervene to prevent suicide, refusal to accept medical treatment, even treatment deemed essential, is *not* considered evidence of suicidal intent or incompetence.[59]

3. The Protection of Third Parties

Most cases of refusal of medical treatment where this interest has been considered by the courts have involved women with minor children (although, in an interesting reversal, *In re EG* noted the impact of a mature minor's decision to refuse a blood transfusion upon parents, guardians, adult siblings, and other relatives).[60]

In *Application of the President & Directors of Georgetown College, Inc* (1964)[61], it was held that that the State's interest in protecting the well-being of the patient's children outweighed the patient's right to refuse life-saving treatment. However, as the *Brown* court noted, in that case the patient was not competent to take her own decisions, so the state intervened on the basis that it had the responsibility of authorising treatment to save her life when she could not consent herself.[62]

Moreover, commentators had noted that in that case the patient's husband had refused to authorise transfusion, implying that he supported her decision even if it might result in leaving her child motherless. It did not seem right that one parent should be deemed to have abandoned her child in a situation where the other parent agreed to her leaving and, presumably therefore, to provide for the child single-handed,[63] a conclusion reached in the later case of *Matter of Farrell* (1987), in which a mother's right to refuse treatment was upheld because the father's capacity to care for the children in her absence was 'unquestioned'.[64]

When the issue of overriding treatment refusals by competent adults with minor children[65] was discussed in *Fosmire v Nicoleau*, the appeal court noted disagreement as to whether the perceived State interest was to preserve the family unit intact – the 'two-parent rule' as proposed by the hospital in the case – or simply to ensure that the child was not left parentless – the 'one-parent rule' adopted by the previous court ruling. In this case, the court determined that the State's interest in the welfare of third parties cannot be determinative of the patient's right to refuse medical treatment;[66] however, other cases have left a window open, holding instead that this interest will not override a competent patient's refusal *if* there is no evidence that the minor children would be abandoned.[67]

In the event, the circuit court in *In re Brown* had held this to be a strong State interest, as Darlene Brown had two existing minor children, aged three and eight, who could be orphaned if she did not receive the transfusion. However the Appellate Court heard that Brown's husband, the father of the three-year-old, was supportive of her decision not to accept blood transfusion and was willing, as were Brown's parents, to care for and support both children. The Appellate Court therefore concluded that there was no evidence of abandonment of minor children, and therefore the State's interest in protecting the existing children was not determinative.

4. Maintaining the Ethical Integrity of the Medical Profession

This interest, as described by the appeal court in *In re Brown*, seeks 'to protect the role of hospitals in fully caring for their patients as well as to promote the prevailing medical ethical standards'. However, the court noted that in this type of situation the American Medical Association (AMA) had stated that generally 'judicial intervention is inappropriate when a woman has made an informed refusal of a medical treatment designed to benefit her fetus.'[68] The court concluded therefore (presumably because the AMA's view could be said to represent 'prevailing medical ethical standards') that the State's interest in maintaining the ethical integrity of the medical profession was also not dispositive in this case.

As an additional factor, the trial court had considered the *dicta* in *Baby Boy Doe*,[69] that blood transfusion constitutes a 'relatively noninvasive and risk-free procedure'. It decided that transfusions would be minimally invasive for Darlene Brown as she already had two intravenous lines set up – therefore they could be administered without additional pain or intrusion. The Appellate Court disagreed, finding rather that 'a blood transfusion is an invasive medical procedure that interrupts a competent adult's bodily integrity'.

Having considered all of these matters, the Appellate Court therefore determined that the circuit court had erred in ordering Brown to undergo the transfusion on behalf of the viable foetus, and held that a competent pregnant woman's right to refuse medical treatment overrides the State's 'substantial interest' in the welfare of a viable foetus.

It further considered the appeal of the public guardian, who argued that in the light of *Baby Boy Doe*, the circuit court had erred in appointing a guardian *ad litem* to represent the alleged interests of the viable foetus in opposition to the express wishes of its mother. The Appellate Court held that although the public guardian was correct to assert that *Baby Boy Doe* (where the alleged risk was to the foetus alone) held that maternal and foetal rights may not be balanced, *In re Brown* did not involve such a balancing but, rather, involved the mother's right to refuse medical treatment as considered against the State's interest in the viable foetus. This therefore did not require representation for the separate putative interests of the foetus, and the trial court had therefore abused its discretion and erred in appointing the public guardian as temporary custodian of the foetus with authority to consent to blood transfusion for Darlene Brown – again, the state's interest in preserving the life of the mother and of the foetus cannot override a pregnant woman's competent refusal of recommended invasive medical procedures.

Accordingly, the trial court's decision was reversed – representing a moral if not a spiritual victory for Darlene Brown.

Cases Continue

As in the *Brown* decision, since the Carder case higher courts have consistently held that forced interventions are inappropriate, and leading medical groups such as the AMA[70] have voiced clear opposition to such actions. In 2000 the ACOG re-stated its opposition to forced procedures, declaring:

> Once a patient has been informed of the material risks and benefits involved with a treatment, test or procedure, that patient has the right to exercise full autonomy in deciding whether to undergo the treatment, test, or procedure or whether to make a choice among a variety of treatments, tests, or procedures. In the exercise of that autonomy, the informed patient also has the right to refuse to undergo any of these treatments, tests or procedures. . . . Performing an operative procedure on a patient without the patient's permission can constitute 'battery' under common law. In most circumstances, this is a criminal act. ... Such a refusal [of consent] may be based on religious beliefs, personal preference or comfort.[71]

Yet cases are still occurring. In 2000, it was reported that a judge had allowed a hospital to take a pregnant woman into custody to 'ensure' that her baby was born safely, after she refused medical treatment because of religious convictions.[72] In an incident reported in January 2004, a woman – referred to in court as Jane Doe and in press reports named as Amber Marlowe – went into a hospital in Pennsylvania to have her seventh baby and was repeatedly pressurised to have a Caesarean section. She refused, despite being told repeatedly by the doctors that not having one could kill her and/or her child, and left the hospital against medical advice, along with her husband. The hospital promptly obtained a court order giving it guardianship of the foetus and the right to take custody of the pregnant woman and perform the surgery by force if she returned to the hospital.[73] She did not, having gone to another hospital and given birth vaginally and without difficulty to a healthy baby girl, without the supposedly necessary surgery – the need for which was never raised at the other hospital – and without, at the time, knowing of the court order.

This demonstrates the difficulty, discussed further in Chapter 6, of expecting local courts to adopt a stance based on higher legal and ethical principles when faced with an urgent decision and a foetus at apparently accelerating risk. Increasing pressure to enact foetal rights legislation is also confusing the issue in many states (see Chapter 5).

Moreover, it may be that even higher court judgments leave some room for manoeuvre. For example, the appeal judgment in *Re AC* still left a possible loophole:

> In virtually all cases the decision of the patient . . . will control. We do not quite foreclose the possibility that a conflicting state interest may be so compelling that the patient's wishes must yield, but we anticipate that such cases will be extremely rare and truly exceptional.[74]

Indeed, in *Pemberton v Tallahassee Memorial Regional Medical Center* (1999), the judge claimed to be hearing just such a case.[75] In this case, Laura Pemberton had delivered one child by Caesarean section and wished to avoid surgery for her next birth. For reasons that are unclear, her first Caesarean had used a vertical incision, and she could not find a doctor prepared to accept her as a patient to attempt vaginal birth thereafter. She therefore decided to give birth at home, with a midwife but without a physician. After 24 hours in labour she decided that she needed an intravenous drip set up to avoid dehydration and attended the emergency department with the intention of having a drip sited and then returning home. Various obstetricians again advised her to have a Caesarean and notified the hospital authorities of the situation; meanwhile she and her husband left the hospital, 'apparently surreptitiously,' according to the court report.[76]

The hospital called its attorney, who called the State Attorney, who deputised the hospital attorney as a Special Assistant State Attorney for the purposes of dealing with the matter. The latter then called a judge, who in turn convened a hearing in the hospital, listened to medical testimony that vaginal birth would pose a substantial risk (four to six per cent, disputed by Pemberton's witness as being nearer two per cent) of uterine rupture resulting in near certain death of the baby (subsequently retracted to being a 50 per cent risk), and duly ordered Pemberton returned to the hospital. The State Attorney, accompanied by a law enforcement officer, then went to Pemberton's home and brought her back to the hospital by ambulance, against her will. The forced Caesarean was performed, and she later filed a claim for damages, alleging violation of her constitutional rights to due process, conspiracy, common law negligence and false imprisonment. The hospital moved for summary judgment.

The judge duly ruled that Pemberton's constitutional rights did not outweigh the state's interest in preserving the life of a viable, full-term foetus whose delivery is imminent.[77] He distinguished *re AC* on the basis that in that case the woman's death was unduly hastened by the Caesarean, and the Illinois *Baby Boy Doe* ruling (*vide supra*) on the basis that, whilst Illinois state law might hold that that a mother has an absolute right to refuse a Caesarean section regardless of her foetus's interests, that does not mean that a state *must* choose that approach, and Florida law was not that 'inflexible'.[78]

Moreover, the hospital argued that since Pemberton did not voluntarily seek care, she was therefore not a 'patient' to whom they owed any duty, and in any case she did not rely on the physicians' advice; therefore she should have no claim against the physicians, or the hospital on their behalf, based on their advice, even if this was rendered negligently. This is a curious argument, not least since the advice was the basis for the hospital's application to recover Pemberton as a patient. The judge disagreed with the hospital's assertions, but on different grounds. Rather, he suggested, the risk was substantial even if it was only one per cent (a two per cent risk of rupture with a 50 per cent risk that in such event the foetus would die), and the hospital and physicians were not negligent in rendering such advice – though they were not in fact required to quantify an 'unacceptable' risk in percentage terms.

Finally, since the action of bringing the woman back to the hospital was undertaken pursuant to a court order, it could not count as false imprisonment. Pemberton's claim was thus dismissed on all counts.

Decisions in Haste

The urgency with which British courts are prepared to deal with this type of case was first demonstrated in *In Re F*,[79] the application to ward a foetus in order to track down and detain the mother for the birth. When the application was dismissed at first instance, the Local Authority obtained an emergency hearing from the Court of Appeal on the following Saturday, seven days before the estimated delivery date.

In the first British forced Caesarean case, *In Re S* (1992),[80] the judge was presented with an emergency application, demanding an instant decision, in the lunch hour. A declaration authorising surgery was made in a 20 minute *ex parte* hearing, with 'little or no legal argument or analysis in the judgment'.[81] The judge did not specify grounds except to cite 'expert evidence' that 'two lives were in danger', and the court's rationale was criticised (and later the judgment declared wrong[82]), in particular for citing the *obiter* remark in *Re T* that the only possible qualification to the absolute right of competent adults to refuse treatment might be where this could lead to the death of a viable foetus.[83] It could also be asked why this *obiter* comment was cited when the judgment in *Re F*[84] – of vital importance to intervention in pregnancy, albeit concerning a different type of order – was not considered at all. The judge also apparently misinterpreted the American case of *Re AC*[85] (the *Carder* case), suggesting that it showed that 'an order would be likely to be made in such circumstances' when, in fact, that case had already been overturned (albeit too late for the woman involved) on appeal.

Similar haste was evident in other British cases. In *In Re T* itself, the application to authorise blood transfusion was made at the judge's lodgings at 11 o'clock at night and the decision taken at 1:30am the following morning.[86] In *Rochdale Healthcare Trust v C*,[87] where the court was told that a Caesarean must be carried out within the hour to avoid foetal death and risk of damage to the woman's health, after a two-minute hearing in the absence of the woman and without psychiatric assessment, the judge overruled the obstetrician's opinion that C was competent and ruled it in her best interests that a Caesarean be performed. In *In Re L* (1996),[88] where a woman with needle phobia refused to consent to having a drip set up in order to proceed with Caesarean section, an emergency application was made just after 6pm and the judge gave the order by 6.24pm, based on telephone conversations with the woman's doctors and the trust's barrister, the court having agreed to proceed without affidavit or oral evidence. In *Re MB*,[89] the original court order was sought at 9.25pm and a declaration was made at 9.55pm. Unusually, MB had been provided with a lawyer and appealed, but at 1am the decision was upheld.

Clearly in such cases, if the courts are to heed medical appeals for an urgent decision, there will be little scope for detailed examination of the evidence, securing representation or ensuring that the woman's competence has been adequately assessed. As was accepted in *Re MB*:

> In this most difficult area of the law, practical decisions ... frequently require urgent resolution without the luxury of time to analyse the complex ethical problems which invariably arise.[90]

However, the considerable dangers in accepting medical evidence at face value are amply highlighted by the most recent British forced Caesarean case, *R v Louize Collins & Ors, ex parte S (No.2)* (1998).[91]

In the *Collins* case – heard during the lunchtime adjournment – S was a pregnant woman detained for assessment under s2 of the *Mental Health Act 1983* with a somewhat imprecise diagnosis of 'moderate depression'. Although initial medical assessment was that her capacity to consent was intact, an *ex parte* application to authorise investigation and treatment, including operating by way of Caesarean section if necessary, was made, with neither summons nor evidence, and without S's knowledge, even though she had refused intervention three times in writing and instructed a solicitor – facts of which the court was not apprised.[92] The scant information that the judge was given included the incorrect fact that S had been in labour for 24 hours and 'might die at any minute',[93] hence the need for an urgent decision without representation. In fact labour had not started, and the judge's further question about length of the labour was not answered. On this basis, the judge granted the declaration authorising continued detention and forced operation. During her detention (later declared illegal), no specific treatment for mental disorder or mental illness was prescribed and, once the Caesarean had been performed, S's detention was terminated and she discharged herself (see also Chapter 4).

The immediate question that arises from these facts is whether such blatant misrepresentation to the legal system (albeit excused at the later appeal as resulting from communication failures) is an isolated event. Even if it was, the fact that it could happen at all seems ample justification for ensuring that such an abuse of medical power cannot be perpetrated again – and indeed the stated aim of the guidelines issued supplementary to the *Collins* case is to avoid recurrence of such 'unsatisfactory events'.[94] The Appeal Court also noted that: 'The affidavits of witnesses prepared for these proceedings include several important conflicts of recollection'[95] and pointed out later deletion and substitution in the records.

In addition, the abuse of mental health legislation (which also occurred in a different context in the case of *Tameside and Glossop Acute Services Trust v CH* (1996),[96,97] discussed further in Chapter 4) is especially worrying in the light of criticisms of the use of psychiatry as a misogynist weapon,[98] and of the apparent trend towards questioning competence or child welfare in the face of non-compliance with medical advice (see further Chapters 4 and 5).

US Decisions – Similar Speed

In the US similarly, the court may order a speedy hearing for such proceedings of an emergency nature.[99] In the first reported court-ordered Caesarean, in Colorado in 1979, the juvenile court hearing took place in the patient's hospital room on the same day as the application.[100] Similarly, in *Mercy Hospital v Jackson* (1986), an application to determine whether a pregnant woman could be transfused against her wishes in the course of a Caesarean section, a bedside hearing was rapidly convened during labour.[101] Unusually, the application was denied. In *Re AC*, as noted above, the court hearing was convened in the hospital and Carder's family was summoned from her bedside without even being told it was to attend a hearing. In *Jefferson v Griffin Spalding County Hospital Authority*, the initial order granting the hospital's petition was given at an emergency hearing later the same day; the woman and her husband had been notified but did not appear.[102] In *In re Brown* (1997),[103] the hearing was convened on the same day as the application and forced transfusions began that night.

In a 1987 US survey of applications to compel Caesareans over the wishes of the mother – of which 86 per cent were granted – the vast majority (88 per cent) reached a verdict within six hours.[104] This survey also revealed several instances in which the medical evidence presented to the court did not match the ultimate clinical outcome (see further Chapter 3).

In the 2004 case of Amber Marlowe (*vide supra*), a court order to perform forced surgery was granted within hours of the woman leaving the hospital.[105] The woman herself learned of this only later, after having given birth elsewhere – and then only because her husband was told of the order by a reporter.[106] Even where there would, in theory, be time to allow at least some measure of due process, and give the woman some time to make her case, this will not necessarily be granted. In *Fosmire v Nicoleau*, the hospital's application (to override refusal of consent for blood transfusion for a woman newly delivered by Caesarean) was made at 9am, and the *ex parte* order signed by noon. The woman was given no advance notice of the application, notwithstanding that she had deliberately and repeatedly stated her opposition to transfusion since signing on for pre-natal care, and had done so specifically and in writing on admission to hospital. When the order was later appealed, the court noted that such applications 'should generally comply with due process requirements of notice and the right to be heard before the order is signed' and that in this case no effort seemed to have been made to communicate the fact of the application to the patient and her family, notwithstanding that her medical file recorded her long-standing unequivocal personal decision to decline transfusions. Moreover, not only had three hours elapsed between the time the application was made and the time the order was signed, but also an additional six hours passed before it was executed – curiously, having obtained the order the hospital did not start the transfusions until about 6pm – thus 'there was ample time to provide notice and an opportunity for a hearing, however informal.'[107]

In Canada, a case raised against a solvent-addicted woman in the early stages of pregnancy sought to order her to be confined until the birth. Her request for a two-week adjournment to prepare for the hearing was denied and the proceedings were handled on an emergency basis. An interim order was granted seven days after the initial motion was filed, without any evidence being called on the woman's behalf.[108] Two days later, the order was stayed, and was ultimately set aside on appeal following considerable publicity and protest by a number of organisations – by the time of the appeal, the case was moot as the respondent had given birth to a healthy child.

Legal Validity

As well as the scope for procedural irregularities and inadequate presentation of evidence in such cases, a further important issue concerns the legal effects of any order given by the court. A declaratory order as granted in the UK has effect (only) between the parties to the proceedings, as a conclusive definition of their legal rights, and therefore should only be made as a final order. It should not be made (*inter alia*) against a party in default of appearance, or otherwise than after a full investigation of the merits of the case.[109] As was stated in the *Collins* case,[110] this means that a declaration should not be made without adequate investigation of the evidence put forward by either side and – especially where the declaration will affect someone's personal autonomy – ought not to be made on an *ex parte* basis. Moreover, it generally operates by estoppel between the parties, which is impossible without notification. If a declaration is granted in haste and without due regard to representation and presentation of evidence, its legal effect may thus be in doubt.

The court in *Collins* discussed these issues at length,[111] and commented that an application for declaratory relief has been (since *Re F*[112]) the usual procedure when a health authority has taken the initiative in seeking a ruling on lawfulness of treatment. In the UK, when it is the patient who is taking the initiative (for example as in *Re C*[113]), the usual procedure is to apply for an injunction.

Despite stating that 'At the initial hearing no evidence was presented: Instead, *in accordance with normal practice* when an application is very urgent, the formalities were temporarily put on one side,'[114] the Collins court did not discuss whether therefore such applications are the appropriate way to proceed in cases such as these where alleged urgency is generally the rule. This would seem to be a question worthy of further consideration, notwithstanding that the guidelines issued with the *Collins* case stress that in future *ex parte* applications will not be binding.[115]

In the US, forced intervention cases have proceeded on the basis of either declaratory relief or injunction. Declaratory judgments are provided for by both federal and state law and are intended to determine rights, duties, obligations or status between parties to a controversy. Under the *Uniform Declaratory Judgement Act* (1922), courts of record within their respective jurisdictions have power to declare rights, status, and other legal relations, whether or not further relief is or could be claimed. While the Act is primarily directed at persons interested under a deed, will or contract, its powers are extended to any proceeding where declaratory relief is sought, in which a judgment or decree will terminate the controversy or remove an uncertainty (s5). The intention is to examine and comment on the rights of the parties before either acts on an erroneous view of its legal status.

The Act specifically states that when declaratory relief is sought, all persons shall be made parties who have or claim any interest that would be affected by the declaration (s11). Again, this raises questions as to the validity of orders obtained without notification of or representation for the woman.

Nor is the use of injunctions in such cases beyond criticism. The court in *In re Brown*[116] had noted the practical difficulties in enforcing court orders compelling forced procedures on pregnant women, 'even assuming their validity'. Such orders, the court noted, would be in the nature of an injunction, issued by the court and requiring the mother to consent.[117] Yet the only enforcement of such injunctive orders is a contempt citation issued against the mother for wilfully violating an order of the court; contempt being punishable by the imposition of a fine, imprisonment, or other sanction.[118]

The court – clearly not envisaging that other 'sanction' could embrace forced intervention – therefore questioned the efficacy of a court order requiring a blood transfusion for someone who is facing death. What, curiously perhaps, it did not question is the legal implications of using such a court order to justify proceeding with a medical procedure in the face of continuing patient refusal (as indeed occurred with Darlene Brown) – an action that in any other circumstances would amount, at least, to battery.

Relief for Whom?

A further factor is that the usual intention of declaratory relief in this type of case is to establish the lawfulness of the proposed actions of medical staff and to protect them from subsequent adverse criticisms and claims,[119] including providing (practical) protection against criminal liability.[120] Its function is not, therefore, primarily focussed on the *patient's* needs (whether in terms of autonomy, best interests, substituted judgement or any other concern) and this subtle difference in focus may tend to encourage *ex parte* applications, inaccurate presentation of facts, minimal examination of evidence and lack of proper competency assessment – just the kinds of injustice which so permeated the *Collins* case.

This potential bias is further exemplified in the UK by the role of the Official Solicitor in such cases, which reveals something of a conflict of interest. The current incumbent has stated, in an article for doctors, that:

> The courts' intervention is justified *in support of the doctors concerned* when a declaration from the court ... will protect them.

and, further:

> Doctors who are likely to face these situations (or their hospital administrators) should have an easy means of contacting their lawyers. I operate an emergency hotline to ensure that I can assist in securing a speedy hearing of these issues by the court whenever they arise.[121]

Yet, as noted in the same paragraphs, 'Conversely, the court is available to safeguard the welfare of a patient' and 'This office cannot, however, advise doctors, as I am likely to be brought in to represent the child or adult patient'.[122] Indeed, if a patient does not have a solicitor, or is deemed (after competence assessment) incapable of instructing one, the hospital, according to the *Collins* guidelines, *must* notify the Official Solicitor, who may act as guardian *ad litem*.[123] Hewson has noted[124] that in cases where the Official Solicitor appears, he tends to support intervention.

Discrimination?

Women subject to legal proceedings may be an unrepresentative selection. The few English cases have suggested that there is a risk of women with unconventional lifestyles and beliefs, or who fail to cooperate with medical routine, being unduly 'set upon'. S in *Collins*[125] had reached 36 weeks of pregnancy without seeking antenatal care and planned a home birth; she was said to have 'a deep-seated aversion to medical intervention'. In *In Re F (in utero)*,[126] the mother was said to be using drugs and had a 'nomadic existence'. The woman in *Norfolk and Norwich Healthcare (NHS) Trust v W* (1996) had a history of psychiatric treatment and 'consistent refusal to co-operate with doctors', but no mental disorder under the *Mental Health Act 1983*.[127] MB had missed three antenatal appointments and refused to have blood samples taken when she did attend.[128]

Clearly this may be simply because women who are less compliant and/or more likely to be irresponsible during pregnancy are more likely to be subject to such actions – although notably in England those who contend for the rights of pregnant women to determine their own treatment have been labelled – by a judge – 'feminists'.[129] However, evidence from North America – where such cases have been far more numerous – also suggests blatant discrimination.

In the national survey published in 1987, 81 per cent of court-ordered obstetric interventions in the US up to that time had been perpetrated on African-American, Asian or Hispanic women; the overwhelming majority of whom were poor (uninsured and attending non-paying clinics), and a high proportion of whom were unmarried and did not speak English as their main language; in all of the cases the court application stemmed from a public hospital or the woman involved was receiving public financial assistance.[130] Similarly, 70 to 80 per cent of women arrested under 'drug mother' laws (which seek to incarcerate drug-using pregnant women for foetal protection; see Chapter 3) are black, even though the majority of pregnant drug users are white.[131] In one study in Florida, similar rates of substance abuse during pregnancy were discovered among black and white women, but black women were ten times more likely than white women to be reported to the authorities after delivery for pre-natal exposure of the infant to illegal drugs.[132]

In Canada, although there have been few such cases, 'state intervention is disproportionately oppressive of poor women, aboriginal women and women who are members of other racial and ethnic minorities'.[133] Notably, in the case referred to above, in which attempts were made to confine a solvent-addicted woman from early pregnancy, the woman concerned was 'aboriginal'.

Given the huge power wielded by health professionals in such circumstances, and the willingness of the courts to take crucial decisions in great haste based almost exclusively on the evidence of those same professionals, an apparent tendency to single out vulnerable groups is worrying.

It may be also that simply being female *per se* is an important factor in the courts' willingness to override treatment refusals. At the time of the *Cruzan* case,[134] a study of similar court cases in which either family or physicians believed that an incompetent patient would prefer to die rather than continue on life support, revealed that the courts respected the patient's wishes in 75 per cent of cases involving men, but only 14.3 per cent of those involving women. Statistically, gender was a more significant factor in the decision than the patient's age, medical condition or treatment. The authors suggested that the language of the judges' opinions revealed that they viewed life support as an assault for men, and saw men's preference for death as rational. When the patient was a woman, they perceived her rather as protected from neglect when on life support, and viewed her decision as unreflective, emotional, and immature.[135] (See also Chapter 4 for discussion of statutes excluding pregnant women from advance directive or health care proxy provisions).

Certainly it is clear that pregnant women are being treated differently from other adults. Aside from the cases of purely obstetric intervention discussed, for which there is no comparator, it is notable that in blood transfusion cases, authorisation to override the wishes of, usually, Jehovah's Witnesses, is more likely to be given if the patient is a woman pregnant with a viable foetus.[136]

Thus respect for autonomy seems to be compromised where the adult concerned is pregnant, female, has an 'unconventional' lifestyle or, in the USA at least, is poor, unmarried or of non-white origin. Thus far, it has been demonstrated that pregnant women are both disempowered by the medical profession and at a significant disadvantage in the legal system should their medical advisers resort to this ultimate solution to resolving conflicts. It might be assumed that when such cases do go to court, professional opinion is highly likely to be, as a minimum, accurate, unbiased, evidence-based and wielded responsibly. However, as will be discussed further in the next chapter, the courts' willingness to take medical opinion at face value in these cases may have been somewhat credulous.

Notes

1 Laurence Oates, official solicitor to Supreme Court. 'The courts' role in decisions about medical treatment.' *BMJ* 2000; 321:1282-1284.
2 Cahill H. 'An Orwellian scenario: court ordered caesarean section and women's autonomy.' *Nurs Ethics* 1999;6(6):494-505 [Medline].
3 *Paton v British Pregnancy Advisory Service Trustees* (1979) 1 QB 270 at 276.
4 *C v S* (1988) QB 135.
5 *In Re F (in utero)* (1988) TLR 5.2.88 : (1988) 2 AER 193 : (1988) 2 WLR 1288 : ILR 10.2.88 : (1988) FCR 529: (1988) 132 SJ 820 : (1988) 18 FAM LAW 337 : (1988) 138 NLJ 37 : (1988) 152 JPN 538 [Lawtel].
6 For further discussion of the contra position frequently adopted in the USA, see Chapter 3.
7 *In Re T (adult - refusal of medical treatment)* [1992] 4 All ER 649; 3 WLR 782.
8 *In Re T (adult - refusal of medical treatment)* [1992] 3 WLR 782 at 786.
9 *In Re S* (1992) ILR 14.10.92:TLR 16.10.92 3 WLR 806:4 AER 671; (1993) 4 Med LR 28 [Lawtel].
10 *Re MB* [1997] EWCA Civ 1361 (26th March, 1997).
11 Mason JK, McCall Smith RA. *Law and Medical Ethics.* Butterworths London 1999, at p266.
12 Mason JK, McCall Smith RA. *ibid,* at p265.
13 Royal College of Obstetricians and Gynaecologists. *A consideration of the law and ethics in relation to court-authorised obstetric intervention.* Ethics No. 1. RCOG. April 1994.
14 *Norfolk and Norwich Healthcare (NHS) Trust v W* (1996) 2 FLR 613 [Lawtel].
15 *Rochdale Healthcare (NHS) Trust v C* (1996) LTL 12/7/96 [Lawtel].
16 *Tameside and Glossop Acute Services Trust v CH (a patient)* (1996) ILR 26/2/96 : (1996) 1 FLR 762 [Lawtel].
17 *In Re L* (1996) LTL 18/12/96 : TLR 1/1/97 : ILR 10/2/97 : (1997) 2 FLR 837 [Lawtel].
18 *Re MB (Caesarian section)* [1997] 8 Med LR 217.
19 *Re MB* [1997] EWCA Civ 1361.
20 *Re MB, Ibid.*

21 *Re F (Mental Patient: Sterilisation)* [1990] 2 AC 1.
22 Michalowski, Sabine, 'Court-authorised Caesarean Sections - The end of a trend?' 1999 *Modern Law Review* 62 (1), at pp 115-127 [Lawtel].
23 Full title: *St George's Healthcare National Health Service Trust v S : R v (1) Louize Collins (2) Pathfinder Mental Health Services Trust (3) St George's Healthcare NHS Trust, ex parte S (No.2)* (1998)LTL 7/5/98 : TLR 8/5/98 : ILR 12/5/98 : (1998) 2 FLR 728 [Lawtel].
24 *Raleigh Fitkin-Paul Morgan Memorial Hospital v Morgan* (1964) 201 A 2d 537.
25 *Jefferson v Griffin Spalding County Hospital Authority,* 247 Ga. 86, 274 S.E.2d 457 (1981).
26 Finamore EP. 'Jefferson v Griffin Spalding County Hospital Authority: court-ordered surgery to protect the life of an unborn child.' *Am J Law Med* 1983;9(1):83-101.
27 *Crouse Irving Memorial Hospital Inc v Paddock* (1985) 485 NYS.
28 *In Re Madyyun* (1986) 573 A 2d 1259.
29 Thornton, TE, Paltrow L. 'The Rights of Pregnant Patients. Carder Case Brings Bold Policy Initiatives'. *HealthSpan* 1991; 8(5).
30 Steinbock, Bonnie. *Life Before Birth: The moral and legal status of embryos and fetuses.* Oxford University Press, Oxford 1996 (paperback edition), at p156.
31 *In re AC*, 533 A.2d 611 (DC 1987).
32 Steinbock, Bonnie. *Life Before Birth: The moral and legal status of embryos and fetuses. Op cit,* at p155.
33 Thornton, TE, Paltrow L. 'The Rights of Pregnant Patients. Carder Case Brings Bold Policy Initiatives'. *HealthSpan* 1991; 8(5).
34 *In re AC* 573 A.2d 1235 (DC Ct App 1990).
35 *Stoners v George Washington University Hospital et al*, Civil Action No. 88-0M33 (Sup. Ct. D.C. 1990).
36 Thornton, TE, Paltrow L. 'The Rights of Pregnant Patients. Carder Case Brings Bold Policy Initiatives'. *HealthSpan* 1991, Volume 8, Number 5.
37 *In re Baby Boy Doe,* 260 Ill. App. 3d at 404, 632 N.E.2d 326 - 335 at 334.
38 *Fosmire v Nicoleau* 551 N.Y.S.2d 876 (NY 1990).
39 *In re Brown* 689 N.E. 2d 397 (Illinois 1997).
40 720 ILCS 510/1 (West 1996).
41 *Norwood Hosp v Munoz* 564 N.E. 2d 1017 (Mass. 1991); *In re Brown* 478 So 2d 1033 (Miss. 1985) (Note this is a different *In re Brown* from the case under discussion).
42 *Cruzan v Director, Missouri Department of Health* 497 U.S. 261 (1990), at 279.
43 *In re Baby Boy Doe, op cit.*
44 *In re EG* 133 Ill. 2d at 110, 549 N.E. 2d at 327.
45 *Fosmire v Nicoleau* 75 N.Y.2d 218, 227, 551, N.E.2d 77, 81-82, 551, N.Y.S.2d 876, 880-81 (1990) (my italics).
46 *Health Care Surrogate Act* 755 ILCS 40/5 (West 1996) (as amended by Pub Act 90-246, § 5, eff January 1, 1998), as cited in *In re Brown.*
47 *In re EG, op cit.*
48 *In re Estate of Longeway* 133 Ill.2d 33, 45, 139 Ill.Dec. 780, 785, 549 N.E.2d 292, 297 (1989).
49 *People ex rel Wallace v Labrenz* 411 Ill. 618, 620, 104 N.E.2d 769, 771 (1952).
50 *People ex rel Wallace v Labrenz, Ibid,* 411 Ill. at 624, 104 N.E.2d at 773.
51 *Roe v Wade* 410 U.S. 113, 162, 35 L. Ed. 2d 147, 182, 93 S. Ct. 705, 731 (1973), as cited in *In re Brown.*

52 *Planned Parenthood of Southeastern Pennsylvania v Casey* 505 U.S. 833, 876, 120 L. Ed. 2d 674, 714, 112 S. Ct. 2791, 2820 (1992), as cited in *In re Brown*.

53 720 ILCS 510/1 (West 1996), as cited in *In re Brown*.

54 *Roe v Wade*, 410 U.S. at 163-64, 35 L. Ed. 2d at 182-83, 93 S. Ct. at 732.

55 720 ILCS 510/2(1) (West 1996).

56 *Cullotta v Cullotta* 287 Ill. App. 3d 967, 969-70, 678 N.E.2d 717, 718 (1997), as cited in *In re Brown*.

57 *Stallman v Youngquist* 125 Ill. 2d 267, 531 N.E.2d 355 (1988).

58 *In re Brown, Op cit* (my italics).

59 *Matter of Storar* 52 N.Y.2d at 377-378, n. 6, 438 N.Y.S.2d 266, 420 N.E.2d 64 (1981).

60 *In re EG* 133 Ill. 2d at 111-12, 139 Ill. Dec. at 816, 549 N.E.2d at 328.

61 *Application of the President & Directors of Georgetown College Inc.* 331 F.2d 1000, 1006-07 (DC Cir), cert. denied, 377 U.S. 978, 84 S.Ct. 1883, 12 L.Ed.2d 746 (1964).

62 *Application of the President & Directors of Georgetown College Inc.* 331 F.2d, *Ibid*, at 1008.

63 Anon. Case Comment, Constitutional Law. 'Transfusions Ordered for Dying Woman over Religious Objections'. 113 *U Pa L Rev* 290, 294 (1964).

64 *Matter of Farrell* 108 N.J. 335, 352-353, 529 A.2d 404 (1987).

65 As noted elsewhere, the overwhelming majority of such cases that have come before the courts have involved the female parent.

66 *Fosmire v Nicoleau*, 75 N.Y.2d 218, 230, 551 N.E.2d 77, 83-84, 551 N.Y.S.2d 876, 882-83 (1990).

67 *Norwood Hospital v Munoz*, 409 Mass. at 129, 564 N.E.2d at 1024 (1991).

68 American Medical Association Board of Trustees. 'Legal Interventions During Pregnancy. Court-ordered medical treatments and legal penalties for potentially harmful behaviour by pregnant women'. *J Am Med Assoc* 1990; 264: 2663-70.

69 *Baby Boy Doe, op cit*, 260 Ill. App. 3d at 402, 632 N.E. 2d at 333.

70 American Medical Association Board of Trustees. 'Legal Interventions During Pregnancy', *Op cit*.

71 American College of Obstetricians and Gynecologists. *Informed refusal. Committee Opinion No 237*, June 2000.

72 Anon. *Pregnant Woman Being Forced Into Custody at a State Medical Facility in Massachusetts to Ensure That Her Baby is Born Safely*. National Public Radio 14 September 2000.

73 Weiss D. 'Court Delivers Controversy'. *Times Leader Northeastern Pennsylvania*, January 16, 2004.

74 *In re AC,* 573 A.2d 1235 at 1252 (DC Ct App 1990).

75 *Pemberton v Tallahassee Memorial Regional Medical Center Inc* (1999) 66 F.Supp.2d 1247 (N.D.Fla. 1999), at 1254 n18.

76 *Pemberton v Tallahassee. Ibid*, at 1249, 1253 n16.

77 *Pemberton v Tallahassee. Ibid*, at 1252 n10.

78 *Pemberton v Tallahassee. Ibid*, at 1252 n12.

79 *In Re F (in utero)* (1988) TLR 5.2.88 : (1988) 2 AER 193 : (1988) 2 WLR 1288 : ILR 10.2.88 : (1988) FCR 529: (1988) 132 SJ 820 : (1988) 18 FAM LAW 337 : (1988) 138 NLJ 37 : (1988) 152 JPN 538 [Lawtel].

80 *In Re S* (1992) ILR 14.10.92:TLR 16.10.92 3 WLR 806:4 AER 671; (1993) 4 Med LR 28 [Lawtel].

81 Mason JK, McCall Smith RA. *Law and Medical Ethics.* Butterworths London 1999, at p265.

82 *Re MB* [1997] EWCA Civ 1361 (26th March, 1997).

83 *In Re T (adult - refusal of medical treatment)* [1992] 3 WLR 782 at 786.

84 *In Re F (in utero)* (1988) TLR 5.2.88 : (1988) 2 AER 193 : (1988) 2 WLR 1288 : ILR 10.2.88 : (1988) FCR 529 : (1988) 132 SJ 820 : (1988) 18 FAM LAW 337 : (1988) 138 NLJ 37 : (1988) 152 JPN 538.

85 *Re AC* (1990) 573 A 2d 1235 at pp 1240,1246-1248, 1252 (as cited in *Re S*).

86 *In Re T (Adult: Refusal of Medical Treatment)* [1993] Fam 95 at 106.

87 *Rochdale Healthcare (NHS) Trust v C* (1996) LTL 12/7/96 [Lawtel].

88 *In Re L* (1996) LTL 18/12/96 : TLR 1/1/97 : ILR 10/2/97 : (1997) 2 FLR 837 [Lawtel].

89 *Re MB (an Adult: Medical Treatment)* [1997] 2 FCR 541.

90 *Re MB (an Adult: Medical Treatment)* [1997] 2 FCR 541.

91 Full title: *St George's Healthcare National Health Service Trust v S (No. 2)* (1998): *R v (1) Louize Collins (2) Pathfinder Mental Health Services Trust (3) St George's Healthcare NHS Trust, ex parte S (No.2)* (1998) LTL 7/5/98 : TLR 8/5/98 : ILR 12/5/98 : (1998) 2 FLR 728 [Lawtel].

92 *In the matter of an application for judicial review: Queen v Louize Collins ; Pathfinder Mental Health Services Trust and St George's Healthcare NHS Trust, ex parte 'S'* [1998] EWHC Admin 490 (7th May, 1998).

93 Anon. 'Mother fails in challenge on caesarean.' *Telegraph* 15 March 1997.

94 *In the matter of an application for judicial review: Queen v Louize Collins & Ors, op cit,* at 122.

95 *In the matter of an application for judicial review: Queen v Louize Collins & Ors, op cit,* at 7.

96 *Tameside & Glossop Acute Services Unit v CH (a patient)* [1996] 1 FLR 762.

97 Dolan B, Parker C. 'Caesarean section: a treatment for mental disorder?' *BMJ* 1997; 314: 1183.

98 See, for example: Jane Ussher. *Women's Madness: Misogyny or mental illness?* Harvester Wheatsheaf, Hemel Hempstead, 1991.

99 Under Rules 57 and 65(a) of the *Federal Rules of Civil Procedure.*

100 *Memorandum in Support of Petition and Order. Unborn Baby Kenner,* #79JN83, Juvenile Court, City and County of Denver and State of Colorado, 6 March 1979, reported by: Irwin S, Jordan B. 'Knowledge, Practice, and Power: Court-Ordered Cesarean Sections'. *Medical Anthropology Quarterly* 1987; 1(3):319-334.

101 *Mercy Hospital v Jackson,* 510 A.2d 562 (Md. 1986).

102 *Jefferson v Griffin Spalding County Hospital Authority,* 247 Ga. 86, 274 S.E.2d 457 (1981).

103 *In re Brown* 689 N.E. 2d 397 (1997).

104 Kolder VEB, Gallagher J, Parsons MT. 'Court-ordered obstetrical interventions.' *New Engl J Med* 1987; 316: 1192-6.

105 Weiss D. 'Court Delivers Controversy'. *Times Leader Northeastern Pennsylvania* January 16, 2004.

106 Caruso, David B. 'Court cases revive debate about rights of mothers during childbirth'. *Boston Globe* 19 May 2005.

107 *Fosmire v Nicoleau* 551 N.Y.S.2d 876 at 879 (NY 1990).

108 *Winnipeg Child and Family Services (Northwest Area) v G (D.F.)* [1997] 3 S.C.R. 925.

109 *Wallersteiner v Moir* [1974] 1 WLR 991.

110 *In the matter of an application for judicial review, Queen v Louize Collins& Ors, op cit,* at 111.

111 *In the matter of an application for judicial review, Queen v Louize Collins & Ors, op cit,* at 106-113.

112 Where the limited effect of a declaratory order was acknowledged: *Re F (Mental Patient: Sterilisation)* [1990] 2 AC 1, at 20, 42.

113 *Re C (Adult: Refusal of Treatment)* [1994] 1 WLR 290.

114 *In the matter of an application for judicial review, Queen v Louize Collins & Ors, op cit,* at 26 [my italics].

115 *In the matter of an application for judicial review: Queen v Louize Collins & Ors, op cit,* at 122.

116 *In re Brown* 689 N.E. 2d 397 (1997).

117 *In re Minor* 127 Ill. 2d 247, 261, 537 N.E.2d 292, 298 (1989).

118 *Fidelity Financial Services Inc. v Hicks* 267 Ill. App. 3d 887, 890, 642 N.E.2d 759, 761 (1994).

119 Per Lord Brandon: *In Re F (Mental Patient: Sterilisation)* [1990] 2 AC 1, at 56.

120 Although this is ineffective in real terms as civil courts cannot bind criminal ones: per Lord Goff in *Airedale NHS Trust v Bland* [1993] AC 789 at 862-3.

121 Laurence Oates, official solicitor to Supreme Court. 'The courts' role in decisions about medical treatment.' *BMJ* 2000; 321:1282-1284 (my italics).

122 Laurence Oates, *ibid.*

123 *In the matter of an application for judicial review: Queen v Louize Collins & Ors, op cit,* at 122 (ii) and (viii).

124 Hewson B. 'How to escape the surgeon's knife.' *New Law Journal* 23 May 1997, at p 752.

125 *Queen v Louise Collins; Pathfinder Mental Health Services Trust and St George's Healthcare NHS Trust, ex parte M.S. [1997]* EWCA Civ 2020 (3rd July, 1997).

126 *In Re F (in utero)* (1988) TLR 5.2.88 : (1988) 2 AER 193 : (1988) 2 WLR 1288 : ILR 10.2.88 : (1988) FCR 529 : (1988) 132 SJ 820 : (1988) 18 FAM LAW 337 : (1988) 138 NLJ 37 : (1988) 152 JPN 538.

127 *Norfolk and Norwich Healthcare (NHS) Trust v W* (1996) 2 FLR 613 [Lawtel].

128 *Re MB* [1997] EWCA Civ 1361 at para 4.

129 Thorpe LJ. 'The Caesarean Section Debate'. 1997 *Family Law* 663.

130 Kolder VEB, Gallagher J, Parsons MT. 'Court-ordered obstetrical interventions.' *New Engl J Med* 1987; 316: 1192-6.

131 Maia Szalavitz. 'War On Drugs, War On Women.' *On The Issues*, New York, Winter 1998.

132 Chasnoff IJ, Landress HJ, Barrett ME. 'The Prevalence of Illicit-Drug or Alcohol Use During Pregnancy and Discrepancies in Mandatory Reporting in Pinellas County, Florida'. *New Eng. L Med.* 1990; 322: 1202-6.

133 *Proceed with care: final report of the Royal Commission on New Reproductive Technologies.* vol 2. Ottawa: Minister of Government Services1993, at p953, cited in Flagler E, Baylis F, Rodgers S. 'Bioethics for clinicians: 12. Ethical dilemmas that arise in the care of pregnant women: rethinking "maternal-fetal conflicts"'. *CMAJ* 1997 Jun 15;156(12):1729-32.

134 *Cruzan v Director*, Missouri Department of Health, 497 U.S. 261 (1990).

135 Miles SH, August A. 'Courts, Gender and "The Right to Die."' *Law, Medicine and Health Care* 1990; 18: 85-95.

136 Williams L. 'Religious restrictions and the trauma patient.'*Certified Registered Nurse Anaesthetist* 1997; 8(1): 40-4.

Chapter 3

Is the Law Being Used to Enforce Compliance with Medical Advice?

As discussed in the last chapter, applications for declaratory relief or injunction to override refusals of recommended treatment may leave pregnant woman at a significant disadvantage and, in particular, the urgency of these decisions usually leaves little time for examination of the evidence. Such evidence as has been presented has tended to be taken at face value by the courts, yet there are worrying indications that, as well as at times abusing the power imbalance in such hearings, obstetric recommendations are often subjective, fluid and divergent.

Accuracy of Medical Evidence

As Caesarean section is one of the most common procedures subject to legal intervention as well as, currently, the most invasive, the evidence supporting its use will be considered in detail.

There is no doubt that appropriate use of Caesarean section can be life-saving. Equally, there is substantial evidence (*vide infra*) that Caesarean sections are much over-used in developed countries. No-one can know what would have happened in individual cases of completed court-ordered Caesarean, had such compulsion not succeeded, and there have been no systematic attempts to assess outcome after refusal of medical advice in pregnancy (or, for that matter, after compliance with it). However, there have been several reports of healthy infants born naturally after the woman refused consent for a Caesarean section deemed necessary, calling into question the assumption that such a course was of vital benefit to the foetus.[1]

Notably, in a substantial proportion of US cases seeking court orders for Caesarean, the mother in the end successfully gave birth without intervention[2,3,4] in some cases evading court officials in order to do so.[5] Whilst in individual cases this may be regarded as merely anecdotal evidence, in the 1987 series of US cases assessed by Kolder *et al*, the prediction of harm to the foetus was incorrect in six of 15 cases.[6] This is a remarkably high proportion, particularly when one considers that in those cases where the Caesarean actually went ahead, it may never have been possible to assess whether the proposed harm would in fact have materialised. It is also alarming, given the gravity of the situation, in terms of both the supposed risk and the major nature of the intervention being proposed – one might have expected the evidence in such cases to be even more precise, and accurate, than usual.

There have been insufficient cases in the UK for a series like this to be evaluated. However, in *In re F (in utero)* (1988),[7] one of the local authority's purposes in attempting to make an unborn child a ward of court was to compel the mother to attend hospital for the birth – yet in the event the child had already been born safely by the time wardship was granted after birth.

In one early US case, *Jefferson v Griffin Spalding Memorial Hospital* (1981),[8] medical evidence stated that, without Caesarean, the child had a 99per cent chance of dying and the mother a 50per cent risk. An order compelling Caesarean should the woman present to the hospital for delivery was duly given – yet she went on to give birth successfully without assistance, her doctors reportedly 'surprised' that her alleged complete placenta praevia had 'righted itself spontaneously', and contrary to their evidence that it would be 'virtually impossible' for this to happen.[9] In fact, the clinical outcomes of placenta praevia are now known to be highly variable and, moreover, cannot be predicted confidently from antenatal events – in one recent series rapid emergency delivery for bleeding was required for only three of 58 women (five per cent), in none of whom could the bleeding have been predicted.[10]

In *In re Madyyun* (1986),[11] doctors in Washington D.C. succeeded in obtaining a court order forcing a woman to have a Caesarean against her will, based on their evidence that she had been in labour too long and that her baby was at risk of dying from infection. Medical testimony stating that the foetus had a 50 to 75 per cent chance of infection if the operation was not performed was given more weight by the court than the woman's request to wait and attempt natural delivery if possible before resorting to surgery. When the forced Caesarean was duly performed, it was found that there was, in fact, no infection present.

In the same year, in the case of *Mercy Hospital v Jackson*, a hospital in Maryland petitioned the court for guardianship of a foetus, in order to be enabled to transfuse against her will a pregnant Jehovah's Witness in premature labour who required a Caesarean section. Medical evidence was that without a transfusion the operation posed a risk to the mother's life, but virtually no risk to the foetus. Unusually, after a bedside hearing, the application was refused. The hospital appealed, although by that time the operation had taken place without the transfusion, with both mother and child surviving. Nevertheless the appeal was heard as the issue was likely to arise again and resolution was felt to be in the public interest. The appeal court reached the same conclusion – there was no danger to the foetus and women's right to informed consent carried the corollary right to refuse treatment.[12]

In the 1994 Illinois case of *In Re Baby Boy Doe*,[13] the Public Guardian appealed against the juvenile court's refusal to grant an order overriding refusal of Caesarean section, offering the court a portrayal of the foetus as: 'a real life being kept prisoner in its mother's womb and tied to an oxygen source that is not working'. After the order was denied again, the woman gave birth vaginally to a healthy baby boy.[14] Similarly, in a Michigan case where a court order permitting forced Caesarean allowed the woman to be brought forcibly to hospital by police, she fled into hiding and two weeks later gave birth without complications.[15]

In the Marlowe case in Pennsylvania in 2004 (see Chapter 2), Amber Marlowe had given birth to a healthy daughter – her seventh child – vaginally and without incident at another hospital (where Caesarean was never mentioned) before learning that the first hospital had obtained a court order giving it guardianship of the foetus and authorising forced Caesarean should she return there, based on evidence submitted by the hospital's attorney that the foetus was under 'imminent threat of irreparable harm … in the absence of an immediate order.'[16] The rationale appeared to be solely the size of the foetus as predicted from ultrasound, the hospital's complaint stating that:

> Even in the absence of present fetal distress and even with ongoing fetal monitoring, a vaginal delivery of this size fetus could result in complications occurring during the delivery ... and result in unavoidable death or serious impairment to the baby.[17]

However the couple – distressed subsequently to learn of the hospital's actions and the court judgment – publicly disputed the hospital's account and claimed rather that a doctor insisted that Marlowe undergo a Caesarean section operation, even though there were no problems with the foetus, because it was over 11lbs and 'the doctor didn't want a lawsuit'.[18] The Marlowes said that it was not true, as the hospital claimed, that they had cited religious reasons for not wanting to have the operation – in fact Amber Marlowe had a friend who had died during a Caesarean; she had given birth normally to all her previous babies, weighing up to 12lbs, and was confident that this birth too would be normal. In addition the hospital stated that a previous baby had suffered shoulder impairment because of the size of the foetus at birth, which the couple said was also untrue.[19]

Risks to the Mother

Such discrepancies call into question both the accuracy of medical evidence in such cases and the underlying motives. As Tauer has commented, predictions of harm from refusal of Caesarean delivery are highly uncertain, yet the woman is being asked to accept risk and harm for the sake of another.[20]

This potential harm is not insignificant: the figures vary widely according to background maternal mortality rate, place of delivery (itself worrying), indication for the operation and numerous other individual factors, but overall the mortality risk attached to Caesarean section ranges from double[21] through four to seven times[22,23,24] up to 16 times[25] that of vaginal birth. Caesarean section risks multiple potentially fatal short-term consequences including haemorrhage requiring hysterectomy[26] (ten times as common as after vaginal birth[27]); pulmonary embolism, deep vein thrombosis, Mendelson's syndrome (aspiration pneumonitis) and anaesthetic mishaps; as well as surgical injury to the uterus, urinary tract or blood vessels.[28,29,30]

There is little evidence that elective Caesarean section can prevent damage to the pelvic floor or incontinence,[31,32] although this has been regularly offered as a reason for choosing elective Caesarean section in the absence of other indications (*vide infra*). Indeed, the rate of later incontinence is very similar among women who have only experienced Caesarean delivery compared with those who have given birth vaginally – unnoticed by previous studies, which had not made the direct comparison, it seemed to be pregnancy that was the risk factor, not birth.[33]

However 1.4 per cent of mothers undergoing Caesarean operation incur damage to the bladder or ureter. Blood loss is doubled and between one and six per cent of women having a Caesarean require a transfusion. Even with the use of prophylactic antibiotics, there is a 20 per cent incidence of endomyometritis (uterine infection); up to 50 times the risk of infection as after vaginal birth and, as with any major abdominal surgery, a risk of ileus (paralysed bowel) and later pelvic adhesions with potential complications of infertility, intestinal obstruction and chronic pelvic pain.[34, 35, 36,37] Twice as many mothers require re-hospitalisation after a Caesarean birth compared with women having normal vaginal birth.[38]

Recovery after Caesarean is prolonged, necessitating a longer hospital stay, and the operation may cause ongoing pain for months – 25 per cent of women report pain at the incision site as a major problem and seven per cent still have pain six months later.[39] Ten per cent report difficulties with normal activities two months after the birth,[40] and this may include pain on intercourse and problems looking after other children, interfering with normal family relationships.

Between a quarter and one-third of all mothers report emotionally traumatic symptoms associated with childbirth, and these are often associated with obstetric interventions.[41] Many mothers report feelings of inadequacy, guilt, low self-esteem, loss of control, disappointment and a sense of failure after a Caesarean; post-partum depression or post-traumatic stress disorder (PTSD) are not uncommon,[42,43,44,45,46,47,48] and some women express dominant feelings of fear and anxiety even five years later.[49] Negative emotions are more frequent with unplanned Caesareans – and it is not difficult to envisage must be even more so with surgery performed by compulsion overriding the mother's wishes.

There is evidence that Caesareans reduce the likelihood of breast-feeding;[50, 51] may impair mother-child bonding,[52,53,54] especially if the operation was conducted under general anaesthetic,[55] and discourage future births.[56] In terms of court-ordered surgery, a 'wrong' decision could affect mother and child for a lifetime.

Risks to the Foetus

Caesarean also poses significant risks to the foetus and neonate – compared with vaginal birth, babies born by elective Caesarean section, or Caesarean for reasons unrelated to the foetus, are 50 per cent more likely to have low Apgar scores, five times as likely to need assistance with breathing, and five times more likely to be admitted to intermediate or intensive care.[57] Respiratory complications are common, often leading to intensive care admission and ventilation for the neonate.[58] Caesarean babies are up to seven times more likely to suffer from respiratory distress syndrome, partly because with planned (elective) Caesarean, some babies will inadvertently be delivered prematurely before 39 weeks' gestation (due to factors such as uncertain dates or irregular cycles in the mother, or for 'scheduling convenience') – this complication can be avoided by awaiting spontaneous onset of labour, which is probably initiated by an endocrine signal from foetus to mother timed to ensure that the newborn can successfully make the adaptation to breathing air.[59,60] Even in term infants, Caesarean can lead to transient tachypnoea of the newborn, which also necessitates intensive care unit (ICU) admission and invasive interventions.[61] The incidence of persistent pulmonary hypertension – which is also life-threatening – is nearly five times higher in newborns delivered by Caesarean section than among babies delivered vaginally.[62]

There is also a risk of pure physical damage – one to three per cent will sustain some form of laceration, especially during emergency Caesarean[63,64] and Erb's palsy and skull fractures have occurred in infants during Caesarean delivery.[65] As one obstetrician puts it:

> Although cesarean delivery appears to the public as a gentler, more controlled manner of coming into the world, nothing could be further from the truth.[66]

Given the vast range of influences in early pregnancy that have been postulated to have potentially detrimental long-term effects, it seems at least possible that such a traumatic entry into the world might also have consequences beyond the immediate physical sequelae. The long-term effects of Caesarean birth remain largely unexplored. However Caesarean delivery may be a risk factor for diarrhoea and allergic sensitisation in infants with family history of allergy.[67] Preliminary evidence is emerging that suggests a 30 per cent increased risk of gastroenteritis and of asthma severe enough to require hospitalisation in seven-year-olds,[68] and a tripled rate of asthma by adulthood.[69] Asthma is a disease currently undergoing an alarming increase in both incidence and severity in most developed countries, and the association with Caesarean is not explained by common maternal or foetal influences.[70]

It has also been postulated that there may be long-term social consequences to current obstetric trends. For example, high rates of Caesarean section in the US – which could be regarded as 'a general indicator for the presence of other highly traumatic and invasive procedures … [that] damage the maternal-infant bond' – have even been linked, along with numerous other factors, with increasing violence among young males, compared with other cultures where births are less medicalised.[71]

If a large proportion of Caesareans are medically unnecessary (*vide infra*), the short-term consequences for the foetus potentially dire and the long-term results little explored, a woman who questions whether the operation is really necessary is not necessarily acting either selfishly or foolishly. Moreover, there are considerable risks for her future chances of having more children, which could impact on the whole family.

Risks to Future Pregnancies

Future reproductive consequences can also be substantial. Women who have had a Caesarean section are less likely to decide to become pregnant again; more likely, if they do, to experience difficulty conceiving, and have a higher incidence of infertility compared with those having a vaginal birth.[72,73,74,75] In one study of mothers who underwent Caesarean section in the second stage of labour three years earlier, 32 percent wished to avoid a further pregnancy and 42 per cent reported fear of childbirth (as did 51 per cent after instrumental vaginal delivery).[76]

Women who do achieve another pregnancy have an increased risk of complications including uterine rupture, ectopic pregnancy (implantation outside the womb, usually in the Fallopian tubes), placenta praevia (where the placenta lies over the cervix), abruptio placentae (placental detachment before birth) and premature birth.[77,78,79,80] They also have higher rates of miscarriage[81] and stillbirth – aside from those due to uterine rupture, the rates of unexplained stillbirth are doubled compared with vaginal birth, possibly due to altered uterine blood flow or abnormal placentation following surgery.[82]

Uterine rupture occurs in one in 500 women who have previously had a Caesarean, even if they plan for a repeat Caesarean, compared with one in 10,000 in women with no uterine scar.[83] Rupture may occur before recognition of labour, and can range from benign separations of the incisions to catastrophic rupture with expulsion of the pregnancy into the abdomen.[84]

Moreover, having had one Caesarean increases the likelihood of repeat Caesareans in future pregnancies, and even women planning vaginal birth after Caesarean section (VBAC) will be strongly advised to give birth in an institution equipped to deal with emergencies that may arise.[85] In addition to the 'ordinary' risks of Caesarean, repeat sections increase the risk of complications, and the presence of scar tissue increases the risk of surgical injury. Women having elective repeat Caesareans are more likely to have hemorrhage requiring transfusion, blood clots, and infection.[86,87,88] The risks are cumulative, with each Caesarean increasing the risks of placenta praevia, abruptio placentae and placenta accretio (where the placenta grows into and sometimes through the uterus).

The risk of placenta praevia is raised more than four-fold with one previous Caesarean and seven-fold with two or three Caesareans. Four or more Caesareans imparts 45 times the risk, compared with women with no uterine scar.[89,90] Placenta praevia, in turn, more than doubles the risk that the baby will die, and increases the risk of premature birth more than six-fold.[91] It also increases the risk of placenta accreta, 75 per cent of which is associated with placenta praevia; the incidence of placenta praevia increased over a hundred-fold between 1950 and 1985.[92]

The risk of abruptio placentae is increased up to three-fold in women who have had one or more Caesareans, compared with women who have given birth without Caesarean;[93] 30 per cent of affected babies will be born prematurely and six per cent will die.[94]

The risk of placenta accretio increases sharply with increasing number of Caesareans, from around one in one thousand after one previous section to about one in one hundred with two or more.[95] It has the potential to invade the bowel or bladder, often leading to massive haemorrhage that may require multiple transfusions and/or Caesarean hysterectomy or uterine artery embolisation to prevent death from exsanguination.[96] Nearly half of affected women have massive haemorrhage, with an average four litre blood loss; 80 per cent need a hysterectomy, sometimes with resection of at least part of the bladder, and two to three per cent sustain injuries to the ureter; up to one in 14 will die, as will up to one in 11 affected babies.[97,98] The incidence of placenta accreta has increased ten-fold in the past fifty years, and it now occurs in 1 in 2,500 births overall.[99]

A recent study in London found that women with previous Caesareans are up to 27 times more likely than those with only vaginal births to need obstetric hysterectomy in subsequent births, and most cases are now due to abnormal placentation following previous Caesarean section.[100]

Multiple Caesareans also increase the risk of ectopic pregnancy by one per cent.[101] Haemorrhage associated with ectopic pregnancy is one of the leading causes of maternal death in the US.[102]

It would seem therefore that even where a Caesarean section might yield an overall lower risk for either mother or baby in the current birth, at least some of this reduction may be offset by the increased risks posed to future pregnancies. Furthermore, performing a Caesarean may shift any current risk from one attaching to medical responsibility (if the clinician fails to intervene, or delays 'too long' – notions readily arguable in court) to one attaching to the procedure for which, if it is properly performed, no liability is incurred even if the outcome is negative. The temptation to 'err on the safe side' may be as much to do with safety for the clinician as for the woman and her foetus.

Basis of Recommendations

Clearly the hazards of Caesarean, although substantial, constitute an acceptable risk as far as most mothers are concerned if the alternative poses greater dangers. For the most serious complications of Caesarean, the absolute danger is small – few women will suffer major morbidity or life-threatening events – even if the risk is significantly increased relative to vaginal birth. Medical evidence presented to the court in applications to override pregnant women's refusals of consent to Caesarean have clearly implied that in these cases vaginal birth poses major hazards and Caesarean is much the safer option. However the many cases where women successfully gave birth notwithstanding these predictions raise some serious questions as to the accuracy and objectivity of the evidence presented.

In the US particularly, there has been a strong movement towards regarding Caesarean as an alternative option in normal pregnancy, with a past president of the American College of Obstetricians and Gynecologists stating only in 2003 that:

> Currently there is no evidence to refute the statement that 'the safest mode of delivery for a baby is by elective cesarean at 39 to 40 weeks gestation.'[103]

This view is challenged by the American College of Nurse-Midwives, which suggests that women 'are being enticed to consider c-sections on demand based upon questionable promises'.[104] Women are also often urged to have a Caesarean because they have had one before – repeat Caesarean represents a major indication and one that inevitably increases the overall Caesarean rate. The International Cesarean Awareness Network comments:

> In many cases, women are being lied to and manipulated into 'choosing' repeat Caesareans. Some simply give up and submit. What happened to informed consent? [105]

In the face of its obvious risks, it is surprising also to find that indications for Caesarean section are not necessarily based on objective criteria. In particular, although there are figures for the increased risk of specific complications, no proper data exist as to the risks and benefits of elective Caesarean section versus labour in uncomplicated pregnancy, looking at multiple medical outcomes as well as psychological, social, and economic implications[106] – although the limited data available on both short- and long-term maternal and perinatal morbidity and mortality generally favour vaginal delivery.[107]

In itself, this is a startling lack of knowledge given that around one in four American births[108] (perhaps as high as one in three for first-time mothers[109]) and over one in five British ones[110] are currently via Caesarean and that this is generally acknowledged to be too many – the World Health Organisation recommends no more than a 15 per cent Caesarean rate.[111] In the UK, the Coalition for Improving Maternity Services (CIMS) is concerned about the dramatic increase and ongoing over-use of Caesarean section and points out:

> No evidence supports the idea that cesareans are as safe as vaginal birth for mother or baby. In fact, the increase in cesarean births risks the health and well being of childbearing women and their babies.[112]

Many experts believe that 'a large proportion of cesareans confers a broad array of risks without providing any medical benefit' and may have hazardous effects on women, infants and families and, indeed, that 'a largely uncontrolled international pandemic of medically unnecessary cesarean births is occurring.'

In the UK, rates have increased from four per cent in 1970 to 21.5 per cent in the latest national audit,[113,114] with wide (and unexplained) regional variations. According to the Royal College of Obstetricians and Gynaecologists:

[O]bstetricians are rightly concerned that the caesarean rate in the U.K. may be too high. What we need to do is make sure that when caesarean sections are carried out they are done in appropriate circumstances.[115]

In the US similarly, the rate was about 5.5 per cent in 1970, but had reached nearly 15 per cent by 1978 and was already 24.4 per cent by 1987. By 1995, when both overall and primary Caesarean rates had remained relatively stable for a decade, concern was sufficient that a reduction to 15 per cent or less was declared a national health objective for the year 2000.[116] In 1998 however a survey showed that only 48 per cent of 'opinion leaders' in obstetrics supported a reduction to this level,[117] which may be one reason why by 2001 figures from the National Center for Healthcare Statistics still showed a national Caesarean section rate of 24.4 per cent[118] (billed as 'an all-time high' notwithstanding the 1987 figure). This represents 'a rate that cannot be justified', according to the American College of Nurse-Midwives, which describes current US practice as 'an assembly line model of childbirth'.[119] Notably, when low risk women are cared for by nurse-midwives rather than physicians, they have a lower Caesarean section rate, and fewer other interventions including lower rates of operative delivery, epidural anaesthesia and induction – yet maternal and infant outcomes are equally good.[120]

The variations between hospitals may be considerable. In one British analysis of all births at 64 hospitals in the London area over two years, the Caesarean section rate ranged from eight per cent to 33.4 per cent. Similar variations were seen in rates of other interventions – instrumental vaginal deliveries (forceps and vacuum-assisted) varied from five per cent to 19 per cent, inductions of labour from 12 per cent to 40 per cent, and the number of women having an epidural from 9.7 to a staggering 74.7 per cent. Further analysis showed that the Caesarean section rate rose, as expected, with the epidural rate, as did the number of instrumental deliveries. Because women in higher social classes were more likely to have an epidural, they were also more likely to have an operative delivery. Yet even allowing for this, the Caesarean section rate varied with the number of maternity beds available: more beds yielded more interventions, perhaps because women could be admitted earlier in labour and monitored for longer; and with the number of junior doctors, who may use more invasive monitoring and be more likely to intervene than more experienced obstetricians.[121]

There is certainly no evidence that the increase in Caesareans is driven by an increase in patient risk factors – indeed, one survey of North Carolina births over five years showed that the rate of primary Caesarean delivery rose significantly, from 16.6 to 18.4 per cent, even though the proportion of low risk women also increased over the same period – and the Caesarean rate even increased even among women in the lowest risk group.[122]

There is however evidence that obstetrician characteristics have an influence. In one UK study a major influence on the type of birth a woman had was which doctor was on duty at the time, with the rate of straight forceps delivery varying from 11 to 63 per cent between different doctors, that of ventouse extraction from 6 to 48 per cent, and that of Caesarean in the second stage of labour from 24 to 33 per cent. While one doctor performed ten Caesareans after failed attempted vaginal delivery in a total of 74 births, another managed 206 births without any failed forceps or vacuum deliveries.[123] Another study in America revealed that in 13 per cent of Caesareans performed during labour, operative delivery was offered by the obstetrician before there was any clear medical indication for it. Older obstetricians, maternal-foetal medicine specialists, and full-time faculty members were significantly more likely to offer Caesarean delivery. The researchers noted:

> Physician characteristics, as opposed to patient characteristics or intrapartum factors, are a major determinant of whether laboring patients are being offered cesarean delivery.[124,125]

This may be true even of women perceived to be at higher obstetric risk. Older women have significantly higher rates of Caesarean delivery than younger ones, yet in fact this may not be due to objective need – evidence suggests that the increase is independent of complications of labour and delivery, as well as of other confounding factors such as race and level of education.[126,127,128] The perception of risk, rather than actual risk, may be the problem.

Rates of Caesarean delivery in the US are also higher for mothers with private health insurance.[129]

Various scheduling and other system pressures may also influence the rate of Caesareans and other pregnancy interventions (*vide infra*). Moreover, the indications for Caesarean section are often not evidence-based, and the usual indications are rarely catastrophic events where there is no doubt as to the need and life-saving value of major surgery – although in the case of one potentially catastrophic event, umbilical cord prolapse, almost half of the cases may be due to obstetric intervention itself.[130] However, most Caesareans are performed for 'softer' indications, in which the threshold for intervention varies widely and may often be a matter of opinion. The UK National Caesarean Audit,[131] using figures from 2000 and including information on 158,299 births of which there were 33,492 Caesarean sections, showed the main indications for Caesarean to be:

Foetal distress	22%
Failure to progress	20%
Previous Caesarean section	14%
Breech baby	11%
Maternal request (no medical reason)	7%

There is evidence that the threshold of intervention has dropped across the board: at one hospital in Scotland, Caesarean rates rose three-fold over 30 years, from between six and eight per cent in 1962 to 18.1 per cent in 1992; however the main indications were similar, although there had been larger relative increases in Caesareans performed for malpresentation and for previous Caesarean. Investigators concluded 'there has been a lowering in the overall threshold concerning the decision to carry out a caesarean section, rather than changes in obstetric management'.[132]

As an aside, it is interesting to note that, in response to increasing criticism of the rising tide of Caesareans, there has been a concerted rebuttal in recent years alleging that a significant part of the problem is due to maternal choice – some obstetricians complaining in the British Medical Journal that:

> ... obstetricians have been largely blamed for the rising trend without consideration that women's preference may play a part (caesarean section on maternal request).[133]

The British press eagerly seized upon the notion that maternal request for Caesarean by women who are 'too posh to push' is an important influence. Yet the National Audit figure (*supra*) showing that only seven per cent of Caesareans (representing only about 1.5 per cent of all births) are performed for reasons of maternal choice[134] somewhat undermines this argument, and an assessment of all births in NHS hospitals for 2000–2002 found no evidence in support of the alleged trend.[135] The corresponding figure for primary elective Caesareans in the US is only two per cent. [136] In reported series in the US, between four per cent and 18 per cent of all primary elective Caesareans are performed at the patient's request (and 14 to 22 per cent of elective Caesareans overall, including repeat Caesareans); the most common reason for patients requesting Caesarean is tocophobia, or fear of childbirth[137] (a factor often linked, ironically, with previous negative obstetric experiences, including previous Caesarean).[138]

Other Interventions

Justification for other interventions may be similarly subjective. It is arguable that obstetrics has a less than noble record in terms of intrusions and invasions claimed to be vital yet proven either useless, counterproductive or positively harmful, including routine ultrasound scanning,[139,140] post-term induction[141,142] and electronic foetal heart monitoring,[143,144] one lawyer arguing cogently that the latter – which has a very high false positive rate and considerably increases Caesarean rates[145,146,147] – is both medically and legally unsound.[148]

Evidence suggests that use of induction, foetal heart monitoring and Caesarean section in low risk women increases with the level of available perinatal technology rather than with clinical need, implying that technology may cause excess interventions.[149] Indeed, it has been claimed that hospital-based birth may exacerbate maternal risk, particularly because of the widespread increase in rates of 'emergency' Caesarean section and associated (at least) quadrupled risk of severe morbidity.[150] Tew has suggested that, statistically, modern obstetrics has made childbirth *more* not less hazardous,[151] and that the reduction in maternal and perinatal mortality seen in developed countries over the last 50 years owes more to better maternal health due to improved nutrition, better living standards and sanitation facilities than it does to obstetric management of childbirth.[152]

In this light, it would seem that the courts would do well to scrutinise medical evidence presented in cases of treatment refusal by pregnant women rather more closely:

> Obstetricians do not always know best; no doctor can say whether a mother or fetus will be damaged in labour; and current surveillance tests are not always reliable indicators of poor outcome.[153]

Stein queries the evidence on which polices of forced intervention in pregnancy are based:

> Professionals are allowed the freedom perhaps to make mistakes in judgement in overusing technology under the protective umbrella of court orders, but patients are denied the opportunity to make the opposite choice.[154]

Moreover, although in the UK court cases are rare, the very possibility of legally overruling a woman's autonomy carries dangers for social and medical control of women generally which are not merely theoretical – the Association for Improvement in Maternity Services (AIMS) reported[155] that with the advent of coerced Caesareans, some obstetricians were threatening women reasonably questioning proposed interventions that 'if you do not consent we will simply get a court order'.

Since obstetricians do not agree on what constitutes professional standards,[156] greatly differ in their utilisation of various procedures, and lack consensus about the absolute utility of many of these measures, it is debatable whether medical evidence as presented to the courts should be accepted so unquestioningly. As Flagler comments, one of the justifications for state intervention in pregnancy is the belief that it benefits the foetus, yet the harm to women that such coercion represents often occurs without any countervailing benefit to the foetus.[157]

System Pressures Promoting Intervention

Cahill has pointed out that even though UK policy is now that pregnant women should be 'at the centre of maternity care',[158] obstetricians' concerns appear to lie more with the unborn foetus: 'medical discretion in such problematic cases seems to err on the side of safety'.[159] With the modern focus on pregnancy as pathological, this safety is often assumed to lie in intervention. The rise of 'defensive medicine', although less prominent in the UK than the US, may also tend to promote an interventionist stance,[160] including amongst hospital administrators.

This trend may be boosted by system pressures, such as staffing constraints, operating theatre hours and 'convenient' time schedules, that favour particular options. For example, UK studies showed that after the advent of inductions, births were more likely to take place on weekdays[161] – and so were 'emergency' Caesarean sections.[162] The weekday trend continues to the present day across America,[163] and although its significance is now blurred by the large number of scheduled Caesareans, there is still a weekend deficit of vaginal births.[164] In addition, many younger obstetric staff now lack experience with 'old-fashioned', less-interventionist alternatives – it has been said, for example, that 'Vaginal delivery of a fetus in breech presentation is becoming a rare obstetric art'.[165]All these factors also contribute towards a trend to manage particular 'pathology' according to current policy or 'rules' pertaining to the institution. For example, in *Re MB*, it was stated that there was little physical danger to the mother but the risk to the unborn child was assessed as 50 per cent and, because of this, '*it was the practice* to recommend that a breech presentation by the foot should always be delivered via a Caesarean section'.[166,167]

Yet, as discussed, prevailing obstetric thinking may not be evidence-based. For example, inducing labour in post-term pregnancy is common practice, and a further candidate for legal intervention. In a recent US discussion of an example case of a woman with a 41-week intra-uterine pregnancy who was refusing induction, medical opinion was that 'without the labor induction, the fetus may die'.[168] Some evidence suggests an increase in the intrauterine death rate as gestation progresses beyond the due date.[169] Yet a recent direct comparison among women giving birth in Liverpool[170] revealed no difference in significant neonatal pathology between term and post-term pregnancies in uncomplicated cases – there were, however, increased rates of Caesarean section and neonatal interventions in the post-term group. Researchers commented that this increased intervention rate 'does not appear to be a result of underlying pathology associated with post-term pregnancy' – rather, 'a lower threshold for clinical intervention in pregnancies perceived to be "at-risk" may be a significant contributing factor'.

Singly or in combination, such pressures may create substantial incentive to achieve compliance. Anecdotal reports suggest that it is not uncommon for medical staff to pressurise women in highly emotive language ('... the baby could die').[171] The International Cesarean Awareness Network (ICAN) has stated that it is:

> ... contacted daily by women who are told by doctors that they will kill their babies by not complying with their advice to have an immediate cesarean. Many times they find their physician's advice is not based upon evidence. Sometimes conditions are misdiagnosed or doctors are simply wrong. Many women go on to safely birth healthy babies when their physicians had advocated cesareans, even to the point of obtaining court orders against the woman's will.[172]

Amber Marlowe reported that throughout the night while medical staff were attempting to persuade her to have a Caesarean, they told her 'horror stories' about how her baby was going to be handicapped if she didn't have the operation.[173] In one instance reported by ICAN president Tonya Jamois (herself a licensed attorney), a woman in Florida was terrified she could be put in jail after being told by a nurse that having a natural birth after a Caesarean was illegal.[174] ICAN vice-president Pam Udy was herself told by a doctor in the middle of her labour that her baby's skull could collapse and her brain bleed out. Having spent much of her pregnancy resisting what she felt were unnecessary recommendations for Caesarean (and presumably being relatively knowledgeable and confident in her assessment), she resisted this too – and her daughter was born safely without any problem, despite such dire warnings.[175]

The evidence presented suggests that should such scare tactics fail, medical representatives are sometimes not averse to presenting arguments to the court in similarly dramatic terms. From the perspective of a clinician sufficiently concerned to initiate legal action this is perhaps hardly surprising – but it provides a strong argument that the court (and of course the woman) should be entitled at least to an independent professional assessment in such actions.

Using the Law to Provide Sanctions for Non-Compliance

A further, compelling illustration of the potential for inappropriate use of legal measures to ensure medical compliance is provided by so-called 'drug mother' laws in the US. The US is a different jurisdiction – notably, one more prone to recognise both foetal rights and maternal liability – and its legal position on interference during pregnancy stands in marked contrast to that in the UK, as does the scope of its drug problem and proactive responses to it. Nevertheless, attempts by many states to intervene to prevent foetal harm from drug use reveal many of the features discussed in UK forced Caesarean cases, namely the use of emotive terminology ('crack babies'), the manipulation of legal measures to force medical compliance, and the less-than-objective basis of evidence used to justify intervention. It also shows the potential for medical pronouncements to engage those in authority in supporting measures to achieve compliance, and to sway both public opinion and public policy.

A programme of surreptitious drug testing of pregnant women and new mothers was instituted in 1989 in South Carolina, at a public hospital serving a largely poor and minority community, and later spread to a state-wide initiative. Women testing positive were arrested on charges of distributing drugs to a minor; later the policy was modified so they were given the choice of incarceration or a drug treatment programme.

Use of child abuse and neglect statutes in such cases – discussed more fully in Chapter 5 – led to suggestions that mothers could be prosecuted for *any* activity that might harm the foetus;[176] one official brochure issued by the Department of Alcohol and Other Drug Abuse Services and withdrawn only in 2000 stated that it was a crime in South Carolina for pregnant women to 'smoke, drink, use other drugs or engage in other activities that risk harming their babies'.[177] The South Carolina Supreme Court in 1996 upheld a conviction for pre-natal abuse, according separate legal status to the foetus,[178] and the following year confirmed that such prosecutions of women suspected of using drugs were allowed, again holding that a foetus was a person under the state's child-abuse laws.

The South Carolina approach had a wide impact – attempts to prosecute women for using drugs or, in some cases, alcohol, during pregnancy ensued in more than 30 states,[179] although most actions outside South Carolina failed. In addition, pregnant women were sometimes given sentences tailored to incarcerate them until the birth, where 'ordinary' offenders would escape jail[180] – demonstrating that to subject pregnant women to different treatment from that of other adults, it is not necessarily crucial to enact positive laws in favour of foetal rights; simply interpreting other legislation or adapting penalties to suit the purpose may suffice. Some states have passed specific 'drug mother' laws enabling endangered foetuses to be 'taken into custody' or ordering drug-using pregnant women into treatment programmes. In 1998, South Dakota became the first state to allow judges to order pregnant women who drink to attend an alcoholism treatment programme;[181,182] Wisconsin shortly followed suit[183] and also enabled the state to take charge of a pregnant women who habitually used alcohol[184] (see also Chapter 5). This approach also spread to Canada – a ruling that allowed a solvent-addicted mother to be confined until the birth was overturned by the Canadian Supreme Court in 1997.[185]

Meanwhile in South Carolina, in 1993 ten women had sued the original hospital, arguing that drug testing without warrants violated their constitutional rights – specifically, the Fourth Amendment right to be free of unreasonable searches – and that the policy was racially discriminatory (only one of the women was white and she, unlike the others, had not been arrested). Both District and Appeals courts ruled against them, the latter holding[186] that the (urine) tests were minimally intrusive and reasonable[187] due to the risk to foetuses and public cost of crack use.[188] The policy had by then been discontinued at the index hospital,[189] but continuing protests led the US Supreme Court to agree to assess the legality of non-consensual drug testing and release of results to the police[190] (it did not, however, address the validity of the arrests or prosecutions *per se*). A final ruling in the case[191] held (but only by a 6:3 majority) that women cannot be subject to warrantless, suspicionless searches simply because they are pregnant.

It should be noted also that, when it is known that test results must be given to governmental authorities or other third parties, obstetricians have an ethical obligation to inform patients of this fact during the consent process.[192] Aside from the issues of drug-testing without consent, and the expansion of the scope of such laws to include smoking and alcohol consumption, the notable feature of the South Carolina case for present purposes is that whilst officially only women suspected of drug use were tested, suspicions were aroused, *inter alia*, by seeking little, late or no pre-natal care – frequently missed antenatal appointments are regarded in the US as a 'major indicator' of crack cocaine use[193] – and by certain adverse pregnancy outcomes, features which, it has been argued, are as much an indicator of poverty as of cocaine use.[194] The hospital notified the local prosecutor's office if the woman failed a second drug test *or declined to attend pre-natal appointments.*[195]

Although the appeal court in *Charleston* exonerated the motives of those responsible for the testing and prosecution policy, claiming their purpose was not vindictive, it noted: 'the very real possibility of arrest was employed as an incentive for women to comply with treatment obligations'.[196] This is a clear instance of legal sanctions being used as a 'penalty' not for illegal acts but for non-compliance with routine medical care.

Flawed Evidence

Moreover, whilst the appeal court found that those responsible were primarily motivated by a desire to protect the health of children born at the hospital,[197] such justification for the brutalising actions which ensued (some women were taken to prison in chains and shackles still bleeding after giving birth, and one woman was shackled to the hospital bed during two days' labour[198]) is dubious. Although 'popular attitudes and public policies still reflect the belief that cocaine is a uniquely dangerous teratogen',[199] no specific effects of pre-natal cocaine exposure on physical growth, language or developmental parameters in young children were found in a recent review of 34 major studies;[200] recent cocaine use has not been found adversely to affect the foetus during birth[201] nor, despite strenuous efforts to uncover them, has any increase in congenital abnormalities after foetal cocaine exposure been found.[202]

Indeed, according to many researchers, the notion of 'crack babies' is purely a media creation. It is impossible to single out the effects of drug use from other, often interrelated, factors that may cause harm during pregnancy, such as poverty, inadequate nutrition, stress and violence. Cocaine does not produce physical dependence, and exposed foetuses do not show symptoms of drug dependency or withdrawal after birth. Indeed, without an admission of drug use by the pregnant woman, or medical tests to reveal the drug in the bloodstream, doctors would be unable to distinguish so-called crack babies from infants born to mothers from comparable backgrounds who had never used cocaine.[203] In *Charleston*, submissions by the American Public Health Association and other professionals argued that testing was not necessary to prevent a public health risk:

> Medical research is increasingly finding that the sense of impending 'crack baby' crisis that impelled the prosecutors, doctors, and nurses here to discard ethical and legal responsibilities ... [was] without solid foundation.[204]

Indeed, one view is that: 'At that time the gravest risks related to perinatal substance exposure seemed to be excessively punitive treatment of mothers by over-zealous criminal justice prosecutors'.[205]

Similarly, some US researchers suggest that concern about foetal alcohol syndrome (FAS) has 'escalated beyond the level warranted by the existing evidence', taking on the status of a 'moral panic' and prompting a 'vapid public policy response'.[206] This stance has also led to policies – which Robertson regards as desirable[207] – to 'inform' pregnant women of the dangers of alcohol, such as by notices in bars and on bottles. Yet their effects may be less to promote informed choice than to exert moral pressure by public condemnation, as in an infamous case where restaurant staff refused to serve alcohol to a pregnant woman.[208,209]

Indeed, FAS has been described as an invented diagnosis:

> FAS is ... an example of the social construction of clinical diagnosis ... the medical literature on FAS is infused with moral rhetoric, including passages from classical mythology, philosophy, and the Bible.[210]

With supreme irony however, there *is* evidence that *obstetric* drugs create a risk of adult drug addiction among offspring.[211,212] In one recent such study that followed 4,000 children in Rhode Island born between 1959 and 1966, 23 per cent of those who had developed drug addiction problems were found to have been exposed to three or more doses of opiates or barbiturates given to their mother around the time of birth, compared with only six per cent of their non-addicted siblings.[213] Furthermore, these 'foetal abuse' cases are occurring in a nation where the recent trend has been for courts to grant orders *compelling* parents to put their children on Ritalin or other prescribed stimulant drugs for attention deficit hyperactivity disorder (ADHD), often following allegations of 'medical abuse' by divorcing parents or public schools against parents who refuse to medicate their children.[214]

Yet the dangers of a similar 'offensive' with new street drugs remain: the effects of methamphetamine hydrochloride, popularly known as 'crank', and billed as 'cheaper and more powerful than cocaine', have stirred similar sentiment in the 'American heartlands', including talk of 'crank babies'.[215]

Hijacking the Language of Debate

Without in-depth analysis of such issues, it is understandable that emotional entreaties to safeguard the welfare of 'unborn babies' against the actions of mothers presented as feckless and self-seeking find instinctive appeal, with both the courts and the public. The concept of 'foetal rights', which has both arisen from and perpetuated attempts to find legal solutions to problematic medical encounters, has contributed to a prevailing notion of pregnant women and foetuses as potential adversaries.[216] In the wake of the *Carder* forced Caesarean case in the US (*Re AC*),[217] it was recommended that all hospitals should have a 'maternal-fetal conflict' policy.[218] Yet it has been argued that the very use of such language sets the woman up as a selfish, irresponsible being unwilling to do what is best for her baby.[219]

This notion that there is an opposition between the interests of the woman and those of the foetus overlooks the fact that these interests are inextricably linked, and that the few women who do risk harming their foetuses are not usually seeking actively to cause such harm.[220] It carries the implication not only that doctors possess superior knowledge but also that they have a greater claim to having the foetus's best interests at heart, and obscures the vital point that the conflict is actually between the mother and others who believe that they know best how to protect the foetus.[221]

Yet women too may be acting according to their view of their baby's best interests in avoiding unnecessary interventions and the hazards and sequelae thereof – and, in some instances at least, they may be right. In practice, the mother's autonomy is not actually to be subordinated to her baby, but to the medical profession – the issue might be more accurately termed 'obstetric conflict'. It is interesting that in the UK, as Douglas points out, such issues of judicial compulsion surfaced just when women had begun to reassert some control over pregnancy and childbirth.[222] Obstetric conflict may have reached the courts in the attempt to maintain medical paternalism in the face of patients increasingly questioning doctors' natural authority; such tactics also serve to discount women's experiences of their own bodies and previous birth experiences, instead elevating medical knowledge and technological interpretation to a superior position, to demonstrate the need for 'professional' intervention and control.

A further criticism of the notion of 'maternal-foetal conflict' is that such language obscures the fact that it is not only maternal actions which may harm the developing foetus – the father (*vide infra*), doctors (thalidomide) and the wider society (chemical contamination) may also be 'hostile' agents. In one study that demonstrated 'substantial exposure of neonates to xenobiotic agents' (foreign substances), 82.7 per cent had positive tests, of which only 11 per cent were accounted for by illicit drugs, compared with 30 per cent for local anaesthetics, 25 per cent for food additives and 10 per cent for medical analgesics.[223] Moreover, state intervention that primarily attacks women's behaviour and choices is arguably hypocritical given widespread tolerance for the unacceptable and sometimes dangerous living conditions of many mothers and children.[224,225] Court cases utilise disproportionate resources in terms of both time and cost; arguably attention would be more productively directed to measures that improve the status and well-being of all women and children.

It could also be argued that much of the language of everyday obstetrics is designed, consciously or otherwise, to reinforce medical control of the birthing process and to negate or deny women's collective experiences – for example, most women (or 'standard nullipara',[226] etcetera) now are generally passively 'delivered' of their babies rather than actively giving birth to them, yet even then the medical profession judges the *woman's* 'obstetric performance,' as well as her 'reproductive success'.

Many of those women at greatest risk of forced interventions have been described (often scathingly) by medical staff as having had little or no pre-natal care – yet there is evidence, at least in the West, that input by obstetricians (as against midwives) into the antenatal care of women with normal pregnancies offers little or no clinical or social benefit.[227] Moreover, the word 'care' in this context 'masks domination as well as self-deception among medical workers', according to anthropologists Irwin and Jordan.[228] There has been little attention paid to medicine's role as an agent of social control and the arbiter of reproductive behaviour, according to Stephenson and Wagner. They suggest that the medical profession makes arbitrary decisions in individual cases and attempts to intervene in problems that are essentially social in nature. In cases of forced intervention, criminal sanctions for foetal abuse and attempts to limit the practice of midwifery, home birth, or the operation of alternative birth centres, 'medicine has been complicit or proactive in attempts to control the behavior or health care options of pregnant women'.[229]

Care or Cost Control?

Screening the foetus for unwanted defects is now a major focus of 'prenatal care' programmes on both sides of the Atlantic, and indeed in most Westernised nations. On the face of it, the whole panoply of screening and diagnostic tests now applied to the average foetus was devised to reduce prenatal mortality and morbidity; to allow early treatment (including *in utero* treatment) where possible, or preparation for the birth of an affected child or selective termination of severely affected pregnancies, and to allow informed choice for parents in deciding between these options. In practice, abortion is the most likely outcome if a severely abnormal foetus is detected, and often parents are likely to be pressurised – implicitly or explicitly – to 'choose' this option (*vide infra*). Almost from the outset, questions have been raised as to the underlying aim of these techniques and whether they actually serve women's interests.[230]

Aksoy has highlighted the numerous economic analyses applied to the introduction of pre-natal screening and diagnosis – for example an early UK Department of Health and Social Services (as it then was) assessment that the costs of alpha-fetoprotein (AFP) screening and amniocentesis would be 'more than offset by the economic benefits in terms of savings on expenditure on [avoiding the life of] children and adults with Down's Syndrome and spina bifida.'[231] Although not discussed with prospective parents, these analyses undoubtedly play a large role in government decisions as to health care expenditure on such technology. Aksoy comments:

> This kind of rational-economic thinking may degrade society's willingness to accept and care for abnormal children, while at the same time enlarging the category of unacceptable abnormality and narrowing the range of acceptable normality. If Down's syndrome and spina bifida are 'too' expensive today, what will become 'too' expensive if the economic climate becomes gloomy?[232]

He points also to the costs to both mother and foetus of the risks of antenatal diagnosis, especially if the cost-benefit balance becomes less favourable, for example in populations at low risk of the relevant defect, when 'it is possible that more unaffected pregnancies may be harmed than handicapped children avoided.'[233] Moreover, there is a conflict of interests between providers and users of antenatal screening services:

> At all stages of screening, counselling is systematically biased towards encouraging women to take up the tests and have an abortion if an abnormality is detected, rather than providing women with the information and support they require to make an informed choice and to avoid unnecessary distress.[234]

Moreover, there is evidence that women are shockingly badly informed about the tests they undergo – in an early study, 24 per cent of women who had undergone amniocentesis were unaware that it carried a risk of miscarriage, and 86 per cent were unaware of any other possible hazards. Of the few women who were aware of possible risks, three-quarters had obtained this information from sources other than the medical staff members who had counselled them about amniocentesis.[235] In one study, 39 per cent of women having serum AFP screening were unaware that they had even had the test.[236]

Furthermore, the tests used are not perfect – both false-negative and false-positive results may occur, and the implication of many smaller abnormalities detected remains uncertain. While for many the results are reassuring, other parents may suffer anxiety while awaiting the results, and perhaps for most of the pregnancy, even where the foetus is perfectly healthy – and antenatal anxiety may have long-term detrimental effects in promoting children's behavioural and emotional problems – apparently a direct effect of maternal mood on foetal brain development.[237]

If the foetus seems affected, there may be difficulties with social acceptance of the decision, whichever choice is made about termination. Parents who choose termination when there is less than 100 per cent certainty that the foetus is affected may experience lingering doubt on top of guilt and distress at losing a wanted pregnancy. The process may also have unanticipated consequences for a couple's relationship – in one study, in 38 per cent of couples the partners had a different attitude towards antenatal diagnosis.[238]

Overall, 'it is possible that some [antenatal] screening programmes currently do more harm than good.'[239] Certainly, screening comes to seem more concerned with society's largely economic priorities than with the interests of the individual pregnant woman, potential father or family – much less those of the foetus. Would women be as inclined to cooperate with the antenatal care system if their appointments were described, more accurately perhaps, as foetal surveillance, or quality control checks?

Mothers are Not the Only Danger

The focus on 'maternal' conflict may be the easy option but is not necessarily the most realistic. It has been suggested that *paternal*-foetal conflict is worthy of examination,[240] and that current policies reveal unacceptable gender bias. Paternal violence, drug and alcohol abuse, excessive caffeine or nicotine intake and certain occupations are also potentially hazardous to the foetus.[241,242,243,244] In an infamous early US case, Pamela Rae Stewart gave birth in San Diego, California, in 1985 to a brain damaged baby who died shortly afterwards. Traces of amphetamines were found in the baby's system, arousing suspicion that drug use may have contributed; however further medical examinations revealed that the cause was massive haemorrhaging from placenta praevia that had occurred before Stewart went to hospital for the birth. She was charged with failing to provide medical attention to a minor child, the list of accusations including disregarding medical advice to attend hospital immediately if she started to bleed, to stay off her feet and to avoid sex with her husband and 'street drugs' – an interesting example of the range of activities which could be controlled under 'foetal rights' laws. The charges were eventually dismissed as the court found that the statute used was aimed only at financial child support obligations. [245,246,247] However, as Robertson points out, her husband, who was aware of all this advice, and gave her drugs, was not prosecuted. [248]

Stewart's husband also beat her. In the US, domestic violence is the most common cause of injury to women[249] and 24 to 31 per cent of all women report being raped and/or physically assaulted by a husband or partner at some point in their life.[250,251] Worldwide between one in five and half of all women experience domestic violence during marriage.[252] As Pollitt points out, we do not know how many miscarriages, stillbirths or damaged newborns are due, or partly due, to male violence.[253] However what evidence there is suggests that health care providers might more productively direct their attentions to physical abuse of pregnant women rather than drug abuse by them (especially since the latter is linked with the former).

Violence in Pregnancy and its Relation to Outcome

Interpersonal violence generally is associated with increased mortality, injury and disability; worse general health; chronic pain; substance abuse; reproductive disorders and poorer pregnancy outcomes, as well as over-use of health services and strained relationships with providers.[254] Male violence against women often increases in frequency or intensity during pregnancy, a time when many previously non-violent men may turn on their partner.[255] In one London study, 15 per cent of pregnant women reported experiencing violence during their pregnancy, and nearly 40 per cent of them experienced the first attack during pregnancy.[256] In another study of 500 consecutive pregnant women attending an antenatal clinic in Hull, in the north of England, 17 per cent had experienced violence at the hands of their partner and ten per cent of those reported forced sexual activity.[257] Pregnant women are 60.6 per cent more likely to be beaten than women who are not pregnant, and violence is cited as a pregnancy complication more often than diabetes, hypertension or any other serious complication.[258]

Violence against women is typically redirected from the face to the abdomen (or sometimes the breasts or genitals[259]) when they are pregnant.[260] Although the conventional reason given for the increased risk of violence during pregnancy is that the father/male partner is suffering stress over the impending birth,[261] new mothers are also subject to attack. In a Canadian study of women presenting to an accident and emergency department, the lifetime prevalence of domestic violence was 51 per cent, with a one-year prevalence of 26 per cent (unusually high); nine per cent reported violence during their most recent pregnancy and nine per cent of previously pregnant women reported attacks during the six months after the birth.[262] According to another study, at least two per cent of Swedish women giving birth in 2000 were hit by their partner during the year after childbirth. The risk was increased by being aged under 24, unmarried, born or with a partner born outside Europe, low educational level and unemployment, and by various physical factors in *early* pregnancy – back pain, chronic illness, coital pain, depression-related symptoms, stomach pain and urinary tract problems.[263] A man who attacks his pregnant partner is likely also to abuse his children.[264]

Although it has been formally studied only relatively recently, evidence is emerging that physical violence during pregnancy is associated with significant adverse maternal and foetal outcomes. Among other risk factors, women with pre-term labour experience significantly more partner violence than others, both throughout their lives and while pregnant.[265] Among women living in a refuge in Northern Ireland, 60 per cent had experienced violence during pregnancy and 13 per cent lost the baby as a result.[266] In one London study, 30 per cent of women who reported violence during pregnancy also reported that they had at sometime suffered a miscarriage as a result.[267]

One study showed that pregnant women subject to physical violence are more likely to be hospitalised ante-natally for maternal complications such as trauma due to blows or kicks on the pregnant abdomen, abruptio placentae, pre-term labour and kidney infections, and found a positive association between physical violence during pregnancy and Caesarean section, abruptio placentae, foetal distress and prematurity.[268] Higher rates of miscarriage, low birth weight, foetal injury and foetal death have also been reported.[269] According to the World Health Organization,[270] physical effects of violence during pregnancy include: insufficient weight gain; vaginal, cervical and kidney infections; vaginal bleeding; abdominal trauma; haemorrhage; exacerbations of chronic illnesses; complications during labour; delayed pre-natal care; miscarriage; low birth weight; ruptured membranes; abruptio placentae; uterine infection; foetal bruising, fractures and haematomas – and death.

In the US at least, assault causes more pregnancy complications than motor vehicle accidents or falls, the other two major causes of trauma during pregnancy.[271,272] According to one extensive recent review, adverse pregnancy outcomes are significantly more likely among abused than non-abused mothers and both maternal and infant mortality are increased. Abused pregnant women have more kidney infections, gain less weight during pregnancy, and are more likely to undergo operative delivery. Maternal mortality is increased three-fold. Their foetuses too have higher morbidity, and are more often of low birth weight, premature and small for gestational age, and are more likely to die – the increased foetal death rate in pregnancies affected by so-called 'intimate partner violence' is about 16.0 per 1000. Researchers conclude:

> Intimate partner violence is often a life-threatening event to both the mother and the fetus. This, in addition to the heightened level of feto-maternal morbidity and mortality, represents clear-cut justification for routine systematic screening for the presence of abuse during pregnancy.[273]

In addition to deaths due to obstetric complications, studies in both Maryland[274] and Massachusetts[275] have shown that, in these states at least, homicide is the leading cause of pregnancy-associated death (death from any cause during pregnancy or within one year of delivery or pregnancy termination). A significant proportion of all female homicide victims are killed by their intimate partners,[276] and abuse during pregnancy is a significant risk factor for homicide in abusive relationships.[277] Homicide is responsible for more deaths of pregnant and recently-pregnant women than cancer, respiratory disease or motor vehicle accidents.[278] In the UK, the Confidential Enquiries into Maternal Death – a document prepared every three years by the Department of Health – recently acknowledged domestic violence as a cause of maternal death for the first time. It found that 14 per cent of the women whose deaths were reported were either murdered by their male partners or were known to have been subject to domestic violence before their deaths, either through revealing it during antenatal care or because abuse was already known to health and social services. As none of the women had been routinely asked about violence, this figure is probably an underestimate. As a result, medical staff members are now recommended to make sensitive, routine enquiries about domestic violence when taking a social history during pregnancy, ideally seeking this information in a private consultation in the absence of the woman's partner.[279]

This may pose problems of its own however – the recent introduction in the UK of an extensive information sharing scheme around child databases[280] (discussed further in Chapter 5) allows a variety of 'concerns' about children – including possible household domestic violence – to be logged by involved professionals. There are proposals to allow such concerns to be recorded before birth. The question could arise as to what action the state could or should take to protect a foetus thought to be at risk in such a situation and, given existing trends, to what extent it could be regarded as the woman's duty to avoid any such risk.

In the US, the focus has often remained on the woman even in the presence of known male violence, as in the Stewart case discussed above. In one reported instance in Wyoming, a pregnant woman fled to a police station and attempted to file a complaint against her husband for beating her, concerned that continued abuse could endanger her pregnancy. The police instead arrested her after she admitted that she had consumed alcohol.[281]

In a further ironic twist, notwithstanding that in many cases women have had their foetus or neonate placed into state custody on sometimes tenuous grounds (see Chapter 5), family courts awarding child custody and visitation rights are reported often to ignore the risks to children posed by abusive men – to an extent that public health officials have described as: 'A recurring pattern of potential human rights violations'.[282] In the UK, the Women's Aid Federation of England, a national domestic violence charity, describes a clear overlap between domestic violence and child abuse. It has compiled details of a series of 29 children from 13 families killed by their fathers between 1994 and 2004 as a result of contact arrangements after parental separation. In five families, such contact was ordered by the court, and in three of these cases the court not only granted orders for unsupervised contact or residence to fathers known to be very violent, but also made such decisions either in the absence of or against professional advice. In five cases the father killed the children in order to take revenge on his ex-partner for leaving him.[283]

Law Enforcement

In such light it would seem especially poignant for a woman to feel violated by the health professionals she should be able to trust. Yet there is evidence of an association between emotional, physical and/or sexual abuse, both in childhood and lifetime experiences, and perceived abuse in the health care system.[284] The potential pitfalls discussed also make it all the more pertinent to heed the note of caution sounded by the court in many appeal cases, as to just how orders for compulsory treatment are actually to be carried out.

In the UK, it is lawful to use reasonable force when needed to give compulsory treatment to a patient under s63 *Mental Health Act*; however the position with compulsory treatment on the grounds of incapacity is less clear, and other than the declaration in *In Re S*, [285] there is no precedent for the use of force to compel treatment for a competent, unconsenting patient. As discussed in Chapter 1, the General Medical Council (GMC) advises that doctors may treat mentally incapacitated patients in their own best interests, *provided* the patient complies; if the patient does not, compulsory treatment can be given only for a mental disorder falling within the terms of the *Mental Health Act 1983*.[286] There is therefore a legal and professional vacuum in terms of guidance about forced treatment for uncooperative patients, even where deemed incompetent – much less for competent ones. (It is especially interesting therefore that, as will be discussed in Chapter 4, most UK cases of obstetric conflict have found the woman incompetent, compared with those in the US where court judgments may indeed authorise the use of force and the issue of competency is rarely raised.)

The courts in cases of obstetric conflict have clearly envisaged that force may indeed be necessary; for example, the court in *Tameside and Glossop Acute Services Trust v CH* (1996)[287] ruled that in the circumstances it had power at common law to authorise the use of reasonable force, and the order duly allowed the doctor to use restraint to the extent reasonably required to achieve the birth of a healthy baby. Similarly, the order in *Re MB* allowed the treating doctors to carry out such treatment as was necessary, including both the desired Caesarean section and the feared insertion of needles for the purposes of intravenous infusions and anaesthesia, and to use reasonable force in the course of such treatment. There was however a caveat that staff were 'to furnish such treatment and nursing care as may be appropriate to ensure that the proposed defendant suffers the least distress and retains the greatest dignity.' The court also noted that the issue of force was especially problematic should the patient resist:

> The extent of force or compulsion which may be necessary can only be judged in each individual case and by the health professionals. It may become for them a balance between continuing treatment which is forcibly opposed and deciding not

to continue with it. This is a difficult issue which may have to be considered in greater depth on another occasion.[288]

In the US, the court in *Baby Boy Doe* also noted the practical difficulties of enforcing such orders.[289] The appeal court in *Carder* had already recognised the potential consequences for the physician-patient relationship of court-ordered Caesarean sections:

> Enforcement could be accomplished only through physical force or its equivalent. [The patient] would have to be fastened with restraints to the operating table, or perhaps rendered unconscious by forcibly injecting her with an anesthetic, and then subjected to unwanted major surgery. Such actions would surely give one pause in a civilized society, especially when [the patient] had done no wrong.[290]

This bleak word picture of what compulsion actually means harks back to much older judicial recognition of the hazards of attempts to compel one individual to submit to medical treatment for the sake of another. In the case of *McFall v Shrimp* (1978), discussed above, the court stated that forcibly restraining someone to compel them to submit to such surgery would 'raise the specter of the swastika and the Inquisition, reminiscent of the horrors this portends.'[291]

It is curious that in the case of pregnant women (who are in addition being asked to submit for the alleged benefit of a foetus that is not even a legal person in many states), this caution seems to have been so readily forgotten. The practical details are rarely mentioned in court reports (or, indeed, in medical notes), but make disturbing reading when they do come to light. For example, in one early case for which anecdotal details are available, a Nigerian woman in Chicago in 1984 refused a recommended Caesarean section on the grounds that she planned to return to Nigeria, where Caesarean sections would be unavailable for future births (one of the hazards of Caesarean delivery being that it may necessitate future such deliveries, and pose potentially fatal consequences if surgical assistance is not available). Having obtained a court order authorising forced operation, the hospital staff, according to contemporary reports, 'tied her down with leather wrist and ankle cuffs while she screamed for help'.[292]

Angela Carder was in no condition to scream or struggle, but reportedly whispered 'I don't want it' as she was being taken against her will to theatre for the operation that hastened her death.[293]

In the wake of the *Carder* case, which generated unprecedented publicity, the American Medical Association had positioned itself firmly on the side of pregnant women's autonomy.[294] Yet in the subsequent case of *In re Brown* (discussed above), Darlene Brown later told the Appellate Court that she was transfused with six units of packed red cells, beginning on the evening of the court order and continuing until approximately noon the next day, and that when she resisted, the doctors 'yelled at and forcibly restrained, overpowered and sedated' her.[295]

It could be asked whether a court order enabling doctors to behave thus can be said in any way to be upholding the ethical integrity of the medical profession – in the US one of the potential state interests that may be considered when making such an order. Is it right that the medical profession, perhaps uniquely, should be called upon to exercise physical enforcement of a legal declaration that they have been granted? Further, is it acceptable for medical personnel physically to enforce an order that they themselves applied for, especially when in all probability they were the sole witnesses in court as to the need for the procedure in question? While such actions arguably debase those involved even where they are convinced of the righteousness of what they are doing, what is the effect upon other staff – usually lower ranking – who may be drawn in to witness or even assist with enforcement? While Carder's own obstetrician refused to participate in the forced treatment – the hospital, in danger of being in contravention of the order it had sought, had to persuade a (reluctant) staff obstetrician to perform the Caesarean – it is doubtful whether, say, the porter or anaesthetic technician would have had such a choice.

The Consequences of Legal Conflict in Maternity Care

It would hardly be surprising if women subjected to forced obstetric interventions were traumatised by such invasions of their liberty and bodily integrity. When she recovered from the forced Caesarean, S in the *Collins* case developed strong feelings of revulsion and at first rejected her baby; she was said to be very angry and resentful at what had happened and complained of physical assault;[296] it took several months to 'resolve the future of the child'.[297] Again, 'foetal benefit' in individual cases may be more complex than the picture presented to the court. In the case of US 'drug mothers', there is ample evidence of deficient pre-natal care and outcomes in prison; as Siefert and Pimlott comment:

> Reproductive health and drug treatment services for women in prison are inadequate, if they are available at all, and although illicit drugs are readily available in prison, drug-involved pregnant women often are incarcerated to protect fetal health. Studies of pregnancy outcome among women prisoners have demonstrated high rates of perinatal mortality and morbidity.[298]

Whilst the number of court cases in the UK has been small, the victories achieved in terms of forced Caesareans have, as noted, had a wider impact on the attitude of obstetricians. The fallout has also had the contrary influence on pregnant women – AIMS describes inquiries from women worried about having *any* contact with obstetricians since court-ordered Caesarean sections were reported, and believes that such 'draconian methods' deter women from taking up care, putting far more women and babies at risk.[299] In the US it is reported that drug-related actions against pregnant women not only deter women from seeking pre-natal care or drug addiction treatment but may also prompt some abortions to avoid prosecution.[300]

Furthermore, in the wake of UK decisions suggesting that the effects of labour and drugs rendered parturient women incapable of giving a valid refusal to surgery, it was reported that 'lawyers are advising pregnant women who want to resist Caesarean sections to state this in an advance directive long before they go into labour'.[301] Such a defensive stance suggests that the court cases may well have contributed to a view at 'grass roots' level (on the part of both lawyers and pregnant women) that obstetric advice must be regarded with a degree of scepticism. Whilst this may be congruent with the evidence presented above, it is hardly a tendency likely overall to enhance pregnant women's well-being. Nor is the US attitude likely to assist paediatricians attempting to follow recommendations that they should ask specifically about tobacco, alcohol, and other drug use during the pre-natal visit, with a view to instituting preventive measures.[302] Women are hardly likely to be honest if they fear that they may be incarcerated, or that their child(ren) may be taken away in such situations (see Chapter 5), and women who genuinely want help may be thereby penalised by such policies.

Overall, the evidence suggests that in cases of forced Caesarean in both the UK and US, and instances of punitive measures during pregnancy in the US, the harm of legal intervention outweighs the alleged benefits. As was stated whilst the evolution of court intervention was in its infancy: 'Coercive legal actions damage patient-doctor relationships and may thereby create greater harm for children'.[303]

Moreover, the usual rigour of the courts in examination of evidence to arrive at a just decision appears too often to have been left in abeyance in cases of obstetric conflict. Yet, as has been demonstrated, the assumption that medical evidence is necessarily accurate and unbiased may well be flawed, and the interests being fought for in such cases are not exclusively those of the foetus. This – along with the system pressures discussed above – implies a continuing impetus to achieve compliance. Although it may meet with increasing resistance, in the US both the interventionist approach and the ascendancy of obstetric supremacy over maternal autonomy remain strong. In the UK, despite theoretical support for a different approach, mother-centred care has yet to arrive in the health service.[304] Now that English law has stated categorically on numerous occasions that a competent pregnant woman may refuse intervention without qualification, this impetus to achieve compliance with medical recommendations may need to find alternative outlets, as will be discussed in the chapters following.

Notes

1 Flagler E, Baylis F, Rodgers S. 'Bioethics for clinicians: 12. Ethical dilemmas that arise in the care of pregnant women: rethinking "maternal-fetal conflicts"'. *Canadian Med Assoc J* 1997;156:1729-32 [Medline].

2 Annas G.J. 'Forced cesareans: the most unkindest cut of all'. *Hastings Cent Rep* 1982; 12(3):16-7, 45.

3 Annas G. 'Protecting the liberty of pregnant patients'. *New Engl J Med* 1987; 316: 1213-4.

4 Kolder VEB, Gallagher J, Parsons M.T. 'Court-ordered obstetrical interventions'. *N Engl J Med* 1987;316:1192-6.

5 Margaret Brazier. *Medicine, Patients and the Law.* Penguin London 1992 at pp 257-8.

6 Kolder VEB, Gallagher J, Parsons MT. *Op cit.*

7 *In Re F (in utero)* (1988) TLR 5.2.88 : (1988) 2 AER 193 : (1988) 2 WLR 1288 : ILR 10.2.88 : (1988) FCR 529: (1988) 132 SJ 820 : (1988) 18 FAM LAW 337 : (1988) 138 NLJ 37 : (1988) 152 JPN 538 [Lawtel].

8 *Jefferson v Griffin Spalding Memorial Hospital* (1981) 247 Ga 86; 274 SE 2d 457 (Georgia Supreme Ct).

9 John A Robertson. *Children of Choice. Freedom and the new reproductive technologies.* Princeton University Press, New Jersey 1994, at p187.

10 Love CD, Wallace EM. 'Pregnancies complicated by placenta praevia: what is appropriate management?' *Br J Obstet Gynaecol* 1996;103(9):864-7.

11 *In re Madyyun,* 114 Daily Wash L Rptr 2233 (DC Super Ct July 26, 1986).

12 *Mercy Hospital v Jackson,* 510 A.2d 562 (Md. 1986).

13 *In re Baby Doe* 632 N.E.2d 326, 327 (Ill. App Ct 1994).

14 American Civil Liberties Union. *Coercive and Punitive Governmental Responses to Women's Conduct During Pregnancy.* American Civil Liberties Union, September 1997: www.aclu.org/issues/reproduct/coercive.html.

15 Cited in: *Amicus* brief to the Supreme Court in: *Ferguson v City of Charleston* [2001] 99-936 (Supreme Court of the United States), 1 June 2000.

16 Weiss D. 'Court Delivers Controversy.' *Times Leader Northeastern Pennsylvania* 16 January 2004.

17 Napersky, Lisa. 'Woman hits hospitals' stance that she agree to C-section.' *The Citizens' Voice,* Pennsylvania 17 January 2004.

18 Napersky, Lisa, *Ibid.*

19 Weiss D, *cit.*

20 Tauer CA. 'When pregnant patients refuse interventions.' *AWHONNS Clin Issues Perinat Womens Health Nurs* 1993;4(4):596-605.

21 Richman S. 'Patient, doctor should discuss delivery options. Scenario: Does an obstetrician always have to follow the patient's wishes?' Ethics Forum. 7 April 2003. *American Medical News:*
www.ama-assn.org/amednews/2003/04/07/prca0407.htm.

22 Hall MH. 'Commentary: confidential enquiry into maternal death.' *Br J Obstet Gynaecol* 1990;97:752-3.

23 American College of Obstetricians and Gynecologists. *Weighing the Pros and Cons of Cesarean Delivery.* ACOG Press release, 31 July 2003.

24 Schuitemaker N et al. 'Maternal mortality after cesarean in The Netherlands.' *Acta Obstet Gynecol Scand* 1997;76(4):332-4.

25 Amu O, Rajendran S, Bolaji II. 'Controversies in management. Should doctors perform an elective caesarean section on request? Maternal choice alone should not determine method of delivery'. *BMJ* 1998;317:462-465.

26 Sultan AH, Stanton SL. 'Preserving the pelvic floor and perineum during childbirth: elective caesarean section?' *Br J Obstet Gynaecol* 1996; 103: 731-734[Medline].

27 Amu O, Rajendran S, Bolaji II, *op cit.*

28 Shearer EL. 'Cesarean section: medical benefits and costs.' *Soc Sci Med* 1993; 37(10):1223-31.

29 Richman S, *op cit.*

30 Amu O, Rajendran S, Bolaji II, *op cit.*

31 Richman S, *op cit.*

32 Per Deanne Williams, Executive Director and Mary Ann Shah, former President, American College of Nurse-Midwives. *Soaring Cesarean Section Rates Cause for Alarm.* ACNM statement, 13 January 2003.

33 Faundes A. 'The risk of urinary incontinence of parous women who delivered only by cesarean section'. *Int J Gyn Ob* 2001; 72: 41-46.

34 Amu O, Rajendran S, Bolaji II, *op cit.*

35 Richman S, *op cit.*

36 Shearer EL, *op cit.*

37 American College of Obstetricians and Gynecologists. *Evaluation of Cesarean Delivery.* ACOG. Washington, DC, 2000.

38 Lydon-Rochelle MT, Holt VL, Martin DP. 'Association between method of delivery and maternal rehospitalization.' *JAMA* 2000; 283:2411-6.

39 Declercq ER, Sakala C, Corry MP. *Listening to Mothers: Report of the First National U.S. Survey of Women's Childbearing Experiences.* Maternity Center Association. New York, October 2002.

40 Miovich SM et al. 'Major concerns of women after cesarean delivery.' *J Obstet Gynecol Neonatal Nurs* 1994;23(1):53-9.

41 Murphy DJ, Pope C, Frost J, Liebling RE. 'Women's views on the impact of operative delivery in the second stage of labour: qualitative interview study.' *BMJ* 2003; 327:1132-35.

42 Amu O, Rajendran S, Bolaji II, *op cit.*

43 Declercq ER, Sakala C, Corry MP. *Op cit.*

44 Lydon-Rochelle MT, Holt VL, Martin DP. 'Association between method of delivery and maternal rehospitalization.' *Op cit.*

45 Mutryn C. 'Psychosocial impact of cesarean section on the family: a literature review.' *Soc Sci Med* 1993;37(10):1271-81.

46 Soet JE, Brack GA, Dilorio C. 'Prevalence and predictors of women's experience of psychological trauma during childbirth.' *Birth* 2003;30(1):36-46.

47 Robinson J. 'Post-traumatic disorder - a consumer view.' In: MacLean A, Neilson J. *Maternal Morbidity and Mortality.* RCOG Press 2002, at pp 313-22.

48 Ryding EL, Wiren E, Johansson G et al. 'Group counseling for mothers after emergency cesarean section: a randomized controlled trial of intervention.' *Birth.* 2004 Dec;31(4):247-53.

49 Jolly J, Walker J, Bhabra K. 'Subsequent obstetric performance related to primary mode of delivery.' *Br J Obstet Gynaecol* 1999;106(3):227-32.

50 Tamminen T, Verronen P, Saarikoski S et al. 'The influence of perinatal factors on breast feeding.' *Acta Paediatr Scand* 1983;72(1):9-12 [Medline].

51 Declercq ER, Sakala C, Corry MP. *Op cit.*

52 Ciolli P, Caserta D, Giordanelli E, Russo R. 'Cesarean section and spontaneous birth: clinical aspects and maternal psychodynamic impact.' *Minerva Ginecol* 1995;47(6):263-7 [Abstract - Article in Italian] [Medline].

53 DiMatteo MR, Morton SC, Lepper HS *et al.* 'Cesarean childbirth and psychosocial outcomes: a meta-analysis.' *Health Psychol* 1996;15(4):303-14 [Medline].

54 Lydon-Rochelle MT, Holt VL, Martin DP. 'Delivery method and self-reported postpartum general health status among primiparous women.' *Paediatric Perinatal Epidemiology* 2001;15:232-40.

55 Amu O, Rajendran S, Bolaji II, *op cit.*

56 Zdeb MS, Therriault GD, Logrillo VM. 'Frequency, spacing, and outcome of pregnancies subsequent to primary cesarean childbirth.' *Am J Obstet Gynecol* 1984;150(2):205-12 [Medline].

57 Annibale DJ et al. 'Comparative neonatal morbidity of abdominal and vaginal deliveries after uncomplicated pregnancies.' *Arch Pediatr Adolesc Med* 1995;149(8):862-7.

58 Sabrine N. 'Elective caesarean can increase the risk to the foetus.' *BMJ* 2000; 320: 1072 (letter).

59 Richman S. *Op cit.*

60 American College of Obstetricians and Gynecologists. *Evaluation of Cesarean Delivery. Op cit.*

61 Richman S. *Op cit.*

62 Levine EM, Ghai V, Barton JJ, Strom CM. 'Mode of delivery and risk of respiratory diseases in newborns.' *Obstet Gynecol* 2001;97(3):439-42.

63 van Ham MA, van Dongen PW, Mulder J. 'Maternal consequences of caesarean section. A retrospective study of intraoperative and postoperative maternal complications of cesarean section during a 10-year period.' *Eur J Obstet Gynecol Reprod Biol* 1997;74(1):1-6.

64 Dessole S, Cosmi E, Balata A *et al.* 'Accidental fetal lacerations during cesarean delivery: experience in an Italian level III university hospital.' *Am J Obstet Gynecol* 2004;191:1673-7.

65 Richman S. *Op cit.*

66 Richman S. *Ibid.*

67 Laubereau B, Filipiak-Pittroff B, von Berg A *et al.* 'Caesarean section and gastrointestinal symptoms, atopic dermatitis, and sensitisation during the first year of life.' *Arch Dis Child* 2004;89:993-7.

68 Hakansson S, Kallen K. 'Caesarean section increases the risk of hospital care in childhood for asthma and gastroenteritis.' *Clin Exp Allergy.* 2003;33:757-64.

69 Anon. 'Cesarean Birth Associated with Adult Asthma.' *Ob Gyn News* Vol 36, No. 12, 15 June 2001.

70 Bager P, Melbye M, Rostgaard K *et al* 'Mode of delivery and risk of allergic rhinitis and asthma.' *J Allergy Clin Immunol* 2003;111:51-6.

71 DeMeo, James PhD. 'Why are American boys so aggressive?' *Ashville magazine*: www.newfrontier.com/asheville/American-boys.htm.

72 Bahl R, Strachan B, Murphy DJ. 'Outcome of subsequent pregnancy three years after previous operative delivery in the second stage of labour: cohort study.' *BMJ* 2004;328:311.

73 Jolly J, Walker J, Bhabra K. *Op cit.*

74 Amu O, Rajendran S, Bolaji II, *op cit.*

75 Zdeb MS, Therriault GD, Logrillo VM. 'Frequency, spacing, and outcome of pregnancies subsequent to primary cesarean childbirth.' *Am J Obstet Gynecol* 1984;150(2):205-12 [Medline].

76 Bahl R, Strachan B, Murphy DJ. *Op cit.*

77 Lydon-Rochelle M *et al.* 'First-birth cesarean and placental abruption or previa at second birth.' *Obstet Gynecol* 2001;97(5 Pt 1):765-9.
78 Crane JM, van den Hof MC, Dodds L *et al.* 'Neonatal outcomes with placenta previa.' *Obstet Gynecol* 1999;93(4):541-4.
79 Hemminki E, Merilainen J. 'Long-term effects of caesarean section: ectopic pregnancies and placental problems.' *Am J Obstet Gynaecol* 1996; 174: 1569-1574 [Medline].
80 Amu O, Rajendran S, Bolaji II. *op cit.*
81 Hemminki E, Merilainen J. *Op cit.*
82 Smith GC, Pell JP, Dobbie R. 'Caesarean section and risk of unexplained stillbirth in subsequent pregnancy.' *Lancet.* 2003;362:1779-84.
83 Rageth JC, Juzi C, Grossenbacher H. 'Delivery after previous cesarean: a risk evaluation.' Swiss Working Group of Obstetric and Gynecologic Institutions. *Obstet Gynecol* 1999;93(3):332-7.
84 Richman S. *Op cit.*
85 Lieberman E, Ernst EK, Rooks JP *et al.* 'Results of the national study of vaginal birth after cesarean in birth centers.' *Obstet Gynecol* 2004;104(5 Pt 1):933-42.
86 Mozurkewich EL, Hutton EK. 'Elective repeat cesarean delivery versus trial of labor: a meta-analysis of the literature from 1989 to 1999.' *Am J Obstet Gynecol* 2000:183:1187-97.
87 Rageth JC, Juzi C, Grossenbacher H. *Op cit.*
88 Roberts RG, Bell HS, Wall EM *et al.* 'Trial of labor or repeated cesarean section: The woman's choice.'*Arch Fam Med* 1997;6:120-125.
89 Ananth CV, Smulian JC Vintzileos AM. 'The association of placenta previa with history of cesarean delivery and abortion: a metaanalysis.' *Am J Obstet Gynecol* 1997;177(5):1071-8.
90 Tuzovic L, Djelmis J, Ilijic M. 'Obstetric risk factors associated with placenta previa development: case-control study. *Croat Med J* 2003;44:728-33.
91 Crane JM, van den Hof MC, Dodds L *et al. Op cit.*
92 Anon. 'Diagnosis and Management of Placental Percreta.' *Continuing Medical Education* 1998; 53 (8) (Review Article).
93 Hemminki E, Merilainen J. *Op cit.*
94 Lydon-Rochelle M *et al.* First-birth cesarean and placental abruption or previa at second birth. *Op cit.*
95 Asakura H and Myers SA. 'More than one previous cesarean delivery: a 5-year experience with 435 patients.' *Obstet Gynecol* 1995;85(6):924-9.
96 Richman S. *Op cit.*
97 O'Brien JM, Barton JR, Donaldson ES. 'The management of placenta percreta: conservative and operative strategies.' *Am J Obstet Gynecol* 1996;175(6):1632-8.
98 Anon. 'Placenta Previa, C-section History Ups Accreta Risk.' *Ob.Gyn. News* 15 Sept 2001, Vol 36, No 18.
99 American College of Obstetricians and Gynecologists. *Placenta accreta.* Committee Opinion No. 266, ACOG, Jan 2002.
100 Gould DA, Butler-Manuel AS, Turner MJ, Carter PG. 'Emergency obstetric hysterectomy - an increasing incidence.' *J Obstet Gynaecol* 1999; 19:580-583.
101 Hemminki E, Merilainen J. *Op cit.*
102 Centers for Disease Control. *National Hospital Discharge Survey of the National Center for Health Statistics*, Table 1, 1990.

103 Harer WB. 'Patient, doctor should discuss delivery options. Scenario: Does an obstetrician always have to follow the patient's wishes?' Ethics Forum. *American Medical News* April 7, 2003:
www.ama-assn.org/amednews/2003/04/07/prca0407.htm.

104 Per Deanne Williams, Executive Director and Mary Ann Shah, former President, American College of Nurse-Midwives. Soaring Cesarean Section Rates Cause for Alarm. ACNM statement, January 13, 2003.

105 Jamois, Tonya. Women have right to refuse Caesarean. *The North County Times* (California). 13 April 13 2004 (Tonya Jamois is President of the International Cesarean Awareness Network).

106 Amu O, Rajendran S, Bolaji II, *op cit.*

107 Wax JR, Cartin A, Pinette MG, Blackstone J. 'Patient choice cesarean: an evidence-based review.' *Obstet Gynecol Surv* 2004;59(8):601-16.

108 Martin JA, Hamilton BE, Ventura SJ *et al.* 'Births: final data for 2001.' *Natl Vital Stat Rep* 2002;51(2):1-102.

109 Declercq ER, Sakala C, Corry MP. *Op cit.*

110 Dobson R. 'Caesarean section rate in England and Wales hits 21.' *BMJ* 2001; 323: 951.

111 World Health Organization. 'Appropriate technology for birth.' *Lancet* 1985;2(8452):436-437.

112 Coalition for Improving Maternity Services: www.motherfriendly.org.

113 Dobson R. 'Caesarean section rate in England and Wales hits 21.' *BMJ* 2001; 323: 951.

114 Thomas J, Paranjothy S. 'Royal College of Obstetricians and Gynaecologists Clinical Effectiveness Support Unit. National Sentinel Caesarean Section Audit Report.' *RCOG Press*, 2001.

115 Per Professor Bill Dunlop, President of the Royal College of Obstetricians and Gynaecologists. *National Sentinel Caesarean Section Audit Published.* RCOG press release, 26 October 2001.

116 Centers for Disease Control and Prevention. 'Rates of Cesarean Delivery - United States, 1993.' *Morbidity and Mortality Weekly Report* 1995;44(15):303-307.

117 Kravitz RL, Krackhardt D, Melnikow J *et al.* 'Networked for change? Identifying obstetric opinion leaders and assessing their opinions on caesarean delivery.' *Soc Sci Med* 2003;57(12):2423-34.

118 Martin JA, Hamilton BE, Ventura SJ *et al.* 'Births: final data for 2001.' *Natl Vital Stat Rep* 2002;51(2):1-102.

119 Per Deanne Williams, Executive Director and Mary Ann Shah, former President, American College of Nurse-Midwives. Soaring Cesarean Section Rates Cause for Alarm. ACNM statement, January 13, 2003.

120 Davis LG, Riedmann GL, Sapiro M *et al.* 'Cesarean section rates in low-risk private patients managed by certified nurse-midwives and obstetricians.' *J Nurse Midwifery* 1994;39(2):91-7.

121 Joyce R, Webb R, Peacock J. 'Predictors of obstetric intervention rates: case mix, staffing levels and organizational factors of hospital of birth.' *J Obstet Gynecol* 2002; 22: 618-25.

122 Bailit JL, Love TE, Mercer B. 'Rising cesarean rates: are patients sicker?' *Am J Obstet Gynecol* 2004;191:800-3.

123 Varawalla N, Settatree R. 'Does the attending obstetrician influence the mode of delivery in the standard nullipara?' *J Ob Gyn* 1988; 18: 520-3.

124 Kalish RB, McCullough L, Gupta M *et al.* 'Intrapartum elective cesarean delivery: a previously unrecognized clinical entity.' *Obstet Gynecol* 2004;103:1137-41.

125 The same is true of other obstetric interventions – for example, male obstetricians are more likely to use forceps than their female colleagues, even though their rates of vacuum-assisted births do not differ, and the difference is highly statistically significant: Bonar K *et al*. 'The effect of obstetric resident gender on forceps delivery rate'. *Am J Ob Gyn* 2000; 182: 1050-1.

126 Peipert JF, Bracken M. 'Maternal age: an independent risk factor for cesarean delivery.' *Obstet Gynecol* 1993;81:200-5.

127 Lin HC, Sheen TC, Tang CH, Kao S. 'Association between maternal age and the likelihood of a cesarean section: a population-based multivariate logistic regression analysis.' *Acta Obstet Gynecol Scand* 2004;83(12):1178-83.

128 Bell JS, Campbell DM, Graham WJ *et al*. 'Do obstetric complications explain high caesarean section rates among women over 30? A retrospective analysis'. *BMJ* 2001;322:894-895.

129 Centers for Disease Control and Prevention. 'Rates of Cesarean Delivery - United States, 1993.' *Op cit.*

130 Usta IM, Mercer BM, Sibai BM. 'Current obstetrical practice and umbilical cord prolapse.' *Am J Perinatol* 1999;16(9):479-84.

131 Thomas J, Paranjothy S. RCOG Clinical Effectiveness Support Unit. National Sentinel Caesarean Section Audit Report. *Op cit.*

132 Leitch CR, Walker JJ. 'The rise in caesarean section rate: the same indications but a lower threshold'.*Br J Obstet Gynaecol* 1998;105(6):621-6.

133 Amu O, Rajendran S, Bolaji II, *op cit.*

134 Thomas J, Paranjothy S. RCOG Clinical Effectiveness Support Unit. National Sentinel Caesarean Section Audit Report. *Op cit.*

135 Dr Foster's Case Notes. 'Social class and elective caesareans in the English NHS.' *BMJ* 2004; 328:1399.

136 *Health Grades Report for 2003*, cited in: International Cesarean Awareness Network. ICAN press kit: background information, on: www.ican-online.org.

137 Wax JR, Cartin A, Pinette MG, Blackstone J. *Op cit.*

138 Ryding EL, Persson A, Onell C, Kvist L. 'An evaluation of midwives' counselling of pregnant women in fear of childbirth.' *Acta Obstet Gynecol Scand* 2003; 82:10-7.

139 Bricker L, Neilson JP. 'Routine doppler ultrasound in pregnancy.' *Cochrane Database Syst Rev* 2000; 2: CD001450.

140 Amelia Hill. 'Scans "may damage babies"'. *Observer* 9 December 2001.

141 Hannah ME, Hannah WJ, Hellman J *et al*. 'Induction of labor as compared with serial antenatal monitoring in post-term pregnancy.' *N Engl J Med* 1992; 326: 1587-92.

142 Luckas M, Buckett W, Alfirevic Z. 'Comparison of outcomes in uncomplicated term and post-term pregnancy following spontaneous labor.' *J Perinat Med* 1998;26(6):475-9 [Medline].

143 Kaiser G. 'Do electronic fetal heart rate monitors improve delivery outcomes?' *J Fla Med Assoc* 1991; 78: 303-7.

144 Vintzileos AM, Nochimson DJ, Guzman ER *et al*. 'Intrapartum electronic fetal heart rate monitoring versus intermittent auscultation: a meta-analysis.' *Obstet Gynecol* 1995; 85:149-55.

145 Prentice A, Lind T. 'Fetal heart rate monitoring during labour - too frequent intervention, too little benefit?' *Lancet* 1987; 8572: 1375-7.

146 Vintzileos AM, Nochimson DJ, Guzman ER *et al*. *Op cit.*

147 Nelson KB, Dambrosia JM, Ting TY, Grether JK. 'Uncertain Value of Electronic Fetal Monitoring in Predicting Cerebral Palsy.' *New Engl J Med* 1996; 334: 613-8.

148 Lent M. 'The medical and legal risks of the electronic fetal monitor.' *Stanford Law Rev* 1999;51(4):807-37.

149 Albers LL, Savitz DA. 'Hospital setting for birth and use of medical procedures in low-risk women.' *J Nurse-Midwifery* 1991; 36: 327-33.

150 Murphy DJ. 'Commentary: Obstetric morbidity data and the need to evaluate thromboembolic disease.' *BMJ* 2001; 322: 1093-4.

151 Tew, Marjorie. 'Do obstetric intranatal interventions make birth safer?' *Br J Obstet Gynaecol* 1986; 93: 659-74, at p671.

152 Tew, Marjorie. *Safer Childbirth? A Critical History of Maternity Care.* First edition. Chapman & Hall 1990. The 1998 (third) edition also notes that despite an extensive Government enquiry, Parliamentary recommendations and the 1993 Government report *Changing Childbirth*, the promised revolution in maternity care in the UK, which was to offer an evidence-based, mother-centred service, never materialised: Marjorie Tew. *Safer Childbirth? A Critical History of Maternity Care.* Free Association Books, London 1998.

153 Amu O, Rajendran S, Bolaji II, *op cit.*

154 Stein Ellen J. 'Maternal-Fetal conflict: Reformulating the equation.' In: Grubb, Andrew (Ed). *Challenges in Medical Care.* John Wiley & Sons. Chichester 1992, 91-108, at p103.

155 Beech BAL. 'Court ordered caesarean sections are discouraging women from seeking obstetric care.' *BMJ* 1997;314:1908 (Letter) [Medline].

156 Margaret Brazier. *Medicine, Patients and the Law.* Penguin London 1992 at p253.

157 Flagler E, Baylis F, Rodgers S. 'Bioethics for clinicians: 12. Ethical dilemmas that arise in the care of pregnant women: rethinking "maternal-fetal conflicts"'. *Canadian Med Assoc J* 1997;156:1729-32 [Medline].

158 Cumberledge J. *Changing childbirth.* London: HMSO, 1993.

159 Cahill H. 'An Orwellian scenario: court-ordered Caesarean section and women's autonomy.' *Nurs Ethics* 1999 Nov;6(6):494-505 [Medline].

160 Wagner, Marsden. 'Bad Habits.' *AIMS Journal*, Winter 1999/2000 Vol 11, No.4.

161 Macfarlane AI. 'Day of birth.' *Lancet* 1984; Sept 27: 695 .

162 Evans M, Richardson D, Sholl J, Johnson B. 'Caesarean section: Assessment of the convenience factor.' *J Reprod Med* 1984; 29: 670-3.

163 Ventura SJ, Martin JA, Curtin SC, Mathews TJ. 'Births: Final Data for 1997.' *National Vital Statistics Reports* 1999, Volume 47, Number 18.

164 Gould JB, Qin C, Marks AR, Chavez G. 'Neonatal Mortality in Weekend vs Weekday Births.' *J Am Med Assoc* 2003;289:2958-2962.

165 Paterson-Brown S. 'Should doctors perform an elective caesarean section on request? Yes, as long as the woman is fully informed' *BMJ* 1998;317:462-465 (letter).

166 *Re MB* [1997] EWCA Civ 1361 at para 4 (my italics).

167 In evidence the obstetrician did mention that an alternative procedure which he had carried out as a Senior Registrar was vaginal delivery with epidural anaesthesia to minimise the risk of pushing prematurely, but since this also required the use of a needle it did not, on the face of it, help in MB's case.

168 Mohaupt SM, Sharma KK. 'Forensic implications and medical-legal dilemmas of maternal versus fetal rights.' *J Forensic Sci* 1998 Sep;43(5):985-92.

169 Hilder L, Costeloe K, Thilaganathan B. 'Prolonged pregnancy: evaluating gestation specific risks of fetal and infant mortality.' *Br J Obstet Gynaecol* 1998; 105: 169-173.

170 Luckas M, Buckett W, Alfirevic Z. 'Comparison of outcomes in uncomplicated term and post-term pregnancy following spontaneous labor.' *J Perinat Med* 1998;26(6):475-9.

171 Reported response of a GP to a woman choosing home birth: Wick, Alison. 'Choosing to have your baby at home is set to become less of a battle.' *Daily Telegraph* 18 January 1997. Other examples include: '... if you want to leave your children without a mother ... try for a normal labour', cited on: www.sheilakitzinger.com/BadBirthHaunts.htm#Post Traumatic Stress Disorder.

172 International Cesarean Awareness Network. *Statement on Melissa Rowland.* ICAN E-News Line, Volume 17, 22 March 2004.

173 Napersky, Lisa. *Op cit.*

174 Jamois, Tonya. *Op cit.*

175 Udy P. 'Legal system organizing against rights of pregnant women.' *Standard Examiner* (Utah), May 20, 2004.

176 Kowalski S.L. 'Looking for a Solution: Determining Fetal Status for Prenatal Drug Abuse Prosecutions.' *Santa Clara Law Review* 1998;38(4):1255-1292.

177 'Editorial: Limits During Pregnancy Should Be Defined In Law.' *The State.* 23 May 2000.

178 Kowalski SL. *op cit.*

179 Wendy Chavkin, professor of clinical public health at Columbia University, reported in: Cooper, Cynthia L. *Pregnant and Punished.* Ford Foundation Report, Winter 2003, on:
http://www.fordfound.org/publications/ff_report/view_ff_report_detail.cfm?report_index=382.

180 John A Robertson. *Children of Choice. Freedom and the new reproductive technologies.* Princeton University Press, New Jersey 1994, at p183.

181 Anon. 'S. Dakota to enforce treatment of pregnant moms who drink.' *CNN*, 24 May 1998: http://www.cnn.com/HEALTH/9805/24/fetal.syndrome/.

182 Anon. 'Pregnant drinkers face a crackdown.' *New York Times*, 24 May 1998.

183 Anon. 'In America: Hidden Agendas.' *The New York Times*, 14 June 1998.

184 Wisconsin statute 48.133.

185 Karen Capen. 'Mother's rights can't be infringed to protect fetus, Supreme Court's landmark ruling states'. *Canadian Med Assoc J* 1997;157 (11):1586-7 [Medline].

186 *Ferguson v City of Charleston* [1998] CA-93-2624-2-12. (U.S. 4th Circuit Court of Appeals).

187 Under a 'special needs' exception to the Fourth Amendment.

188 David Stout. 'Supreme Court to Discuss Legality of Drug Tests of Pregnant Women.' *New York Times* 28 Feb 2000.

189 Paltrow LM. 'Punishing Women for Their Behavior During Pregnancy: An Approach That Undermines the Health of Women and Children.' In: Wetherington CL and Roman AB (Editors). *Drug Addiction Research and the Health of Women.* National Institute on Drug Abuse (DHHS), Bethesda, MD 1998, at pp. 467-501.

190 The Supreme Court had previously declined to review such prosecutions: David Stout, *op cit.*

191 *Ferguson v City of Charleston* [2001] 99-936 (Supreme Court of the United States).

192 American College of Obstetricians and Gynecologists. Patient Testing. In: *Ethics in Obstetrics and Gynecology.* 2nd Ed. ACOG, Washington DC 2004, pp26-28.

193 Pursley-Crotteau S., Kemp V.H. 'Intervening With Prenatal Crack Cocaine Users.' *Nurs Clin N America* 1998; 33(1):15-27.

194 *Amicus* brief to the Supreme Court in: *Ferguson v City of Charleston* [2001] 99-936 (Supreme Court of the United States), 1 June 2000.

195 Steve Lash. 'High Court To Hear Case Of Pregnant Drug Abusers.' *Houston Chronicle*, 29 Feb 2000 (my italics).

196 *Ferguson v City of Charleston* [1998] CA-93-2624-2-12 (U.S. 4th Circuit Court of Appeals).

197 *Ferguson v City of Charleston, ibid.*

198 Center for Reproductive Law and Policy. Press release. *Women Mistreated by Hospital, Police Ask Supreme Court for a Hearing.* Washington DC, 1 December 1999.

199 Frank DA, Augustyn M, Knight WG, Pell T, Zuckerman B. 'Growth, development, and behavior in early childhood following prenatal cocaine exposure: a systematic review.' *JAMA* 2001; 285(12): 1613-25.

200 Frank DA *et al. ibid.*

201 Andres RL, Day MC, Larrabee K. 'Recent cocaine use is not associated with fetal acidemia or other manifestations of intrapartum fetal distress.' *Am J Perinatol* 2000; 17(2): 63-7.

202 Behnke M, Eyler FD, Garvan CW, Wobie K. 'The search for congenital malformations in newborns with fetal cocaine exposure.' *Pediatrics* 2001 May;107(5):E74.

203 Gumbel, Andrew. 'America's New Family Values'. *The Independent* 25 November 2003.

204 Joan Biskupic. '"Crack Babies" And Rights'. *Washington Post.* 29 Feb 2000.

205 Barth R.P. 'Research outcomes of prenatal substance exposure and the need to review policies and procedures regarding child abuse reporting.' *Child Welfare* 2001 Mar-Apr;80(2):275-96.

206 Armstrong E.M., Abel E.L. 'Fetal alcohol syndrome: the origins of a moral panic.' *Alcohol* 2000 May-Jun;35(3):276-82 [Medline].

207 John A Robertson. *Children of Choice. op cit*, at p181).

208 Hiscock, John. 'Waiters sacked over drink and babies warning.' *Daily Telegraph* 1 April 1991, at p5.

209 Notably, Italy's recent ban on smoking in all indoor public places (except in a separate designated, specially ventilated room) imposes higher penalties for both owners of restaurants, cafés and so on, and the smokers themselves, should they expose a child or a pregnant woman to illegal smoke: Johnston, Bruce. 'Smoking ban forced on Italy's cafes'. *Daily Telegraph* 10 January 2005.

210 Armstrong E.M. 'Diagnosing moral disorder: the discovery and evolution of fetal alcohol syndrome.' *Soc Sci Med* 1998 Dec;47(12):2025-42.

211 Nyberg K, Allebeck P, Eklund G, Jacobson B. 'Socio-economic versus obstetric risk factors for drug addiction in offspring.' *Br J Addict* 1992;87(12):1669-76 [Medline].

212 Jacobson B, Nyberg K, Gršnbladh L *et al.* 'Opiate addiction in adult offspring through possible imprinting after obstetric treatment.' *Br Med J* 1990; 301: 1067-70.

213 Nyberg K *et al.* 'Perintal medication as a potential risk factor for adult drug abuse in a North American cohort'. *Epidemiology* 2000: 11: 715-6.

214 Thomas, Karen. 'Parents pressured to put kids on Ritalin. N.Y. court orders use of medicine.' *USA Today.* 8 August 2000.

215 Kershaw, Alex. 'Fighting for the unborn.' *Guardian Unlimited.* 7 March 1999.

216 Flagler E, Baylis F, Rodgers S. 'Bioethics for clinicians: 12. Ethical dilemmas that arise in the care of pregnant women: rethinking "maternal-fetal conflicts"'. *Canadian Med Assoc J* 1997;156(12):1729-32.

217 *Re AC* (1990) 573 A 2d 1235 (DC Ct Appeals).

218 Neumann PG, Valladares L. 'The emergence of maternal-fetal conflict policies.' *Health Care Law News* 1991;6(12):3-7 [Medline].

219 For the contra argument, that the use of the term 'foetus' (a part of the mother which may be aborted) deflects attention from the child that it will become, see: John A Robertson. *Children of Choice. op cit*, at p176-7.

220 Flagler E, Baylis F, Rodgers S. 'Bioethics for clinicians: 12. Ethical dilemmas that arise in the care of pregnant women: rethinking "maternal-fetal conflicts"'. *Canadian Med Assoc J* 1997;156:1729-32.

221 Milliken N. 'Maternal-fetal relationship'. In: Reich WT (Ed). *Encyclopedia of Bioethics*. Vol 3. Simon & Schuster MacMillan, New York 1995, at p 1406.

222 Gillian Douglas. *Law, Fertility and Reproduction*. Sweet & Maxwell 1991, at p198.

223 Ostrea EM Jr, Matias O, Keane C *et al*. 'Spectrum of gestational exposure to illicit drugs and other xenobiotic agents in newborn infants by meconium analysis.' *J Pediatr* 1998; 133(4): 513-5.

224 Flagler E, Baylis F, Rodgers S. 'Bioethics for clinicians: 12. Ethical dilemmas that arise in the care of pregnant women: rethinking "maternal-fetal conflicts"'. *Canadian Med Assoc J* 1997;156:1729-32.

225 Pollitt K. 'Fetal rights: a new assault on feminism.' *Nation* Mar 26, 1990, at p411.

226 Varawalla N, Settatree R. 'Does the attending obstetrician influence the mode of delivery in the standard nullipara?' *J Ob Gyn* 1988; 18: 520-3.

227 Tucker JS, Hall MH, Howie PW *et al*. Should obstetricians see women with normal pregnancies? A multicentre randomised controlled trial of routine antenatal care by general practitioners and midwives compared with shared care led by obstetricians. *BMJ* 1996;312:554-9.

228 Irwin S, Jordan B. 'Knowledge, Practice, and Power: Court-Ordered Cesarean Sections.' *Medical Anthropology Quarterly*; 1987: 1(3):319-334.

229 Stephenson PA, Wagner MG. 'Reproductive rights and the medical care system: a plea for rational health policy.' *J Public Health Policy* 1993;14(2):174-82.

230 See, for example, Farrant W. 'Who's for Amniocentesis?: The Politics of Prenatal Screening.' In: Homans H (Ed). *The Sexual Politics of Reproduction*. Gower Publishing Hampshire 1985, at 96-122.

231 Department of Health and Social Services. *Reducing the Risk: Safer Pregnancy and Childbirth*. HMSO London, 1977, at 48 (my addition in brackets).

232 Aksoy, Sahin. 'Antenatal screening and its possible meaning from unborn baby's perspective.' *BioMed Central Medical Ethics* 2001 2: 3.

233 Aksoy, Sahin. *Ibid*.

234 Aksoy, Sahin. *Ibid*.

235 Medical Research Council. *Report by the Working Group on Screening for Neural Tube Defects*. DHSS, London 1979, at p28.

236 Marteau TM, Johnston M, Plenicar M *et al*. 'Development of A Self-administered Questionnaire To Measure Women's Knowledge of Prenatal Screening and Diagnostic Tests.' *J Psychosomatic Research* 1988; 32: 403-8.

237 O'Connor TG, Heron J, Beveridge M, Glover V. 'Maternal antenatal anxiety and children's behavioural/emotional problems at 4 years. Report from the Avon Longitudinal Study of Parents and Children.' *Br J Psychiatry* 2002;180: 502-508.

238 Sjogren B, Uddenberg N. 'Decision Making During the Prenatal Diagnostic Procedure. A Questionnaire and Interview Study of 211 Women Participating in Prenatal Diagnosis.' *Prenatal Diagnosis* 1988; 8: 263-73.

239 Atkins AFC, Hey EN. 'The Northern Regional Fetal Abnormality Survey.' In: Drife JO, Donnai D (Eds). *Antenatal Diagnosis of Fetal Abnormalities.* Springer-Verlag, London 1991, at pp13-34.

240 Losco J, Shublack M. 'Paternal-fetal conflict: an examination of paternal responsibilities to the fetus.' *Polit Life Sci* 1994;13(1):63-75.

241 Domestic violence not uncommonly leads to pregnancy complications, and men often initiate or intensify their abuse when they learn their partner is pregnant: Fazzone PA, Holton JK, Reed BG. *Substance Abuse Treatment and Domestic Violence.* Treatment Improvement Protocol (TIP) Series 25. US Department of Health and Human Services, MD 1997 (DHHS Publication No. (SMA) 97-3163).

242 Sperm abnormalities are prevalent among men who use recreational drugs, and birth defects are more often linked with paternal than with maternal DNA damage: Pollard I. 'Substance abuse and parenthood: biological mechanisms - bioethical challenges.' *Women Health* 2000; 30(3): 1-24.

243 Flagler E *et al, op cit.*

244 Olshan AF, Teschke K, Baird PA. 'Paternal occupation and congenital anomalies in offspring.' *Am J Ind Med* 1991;20:447-75.

245 Johnsen D. 'A new threat to pregnant women's autonomy.' *Hastings Cent Rep* 1987;17(4):33-40.

246 Chamber E. 'Dead Baby's Mother Faces Criminal Charge on Acts in Pregnancy'. *New York Times*, 9 October 1986, p A22.

247 DeBettencourt, Kathleen B. 'The wisdom of Solomon: cutting the cord that harms - children and crack exposure.' *Children Today*, July-August 1990.

248 John A Robertson. *Children of Choice. op cit*, at p191.

249 Chambliss LR, Bay RC, Jones RF 3rd. 'Domestic violence: an educational imperative?' *Am J Obstet Gynecol* 1995;172(3):1035-8.

250 The Centers for Disease Control and Prevention and The National Institute of Justice. *Extent, Nature, and Consequences of Intimate Partner Violence*, July 2000. (National Violence Against Women Survey).

251 Commonwealth Fund. *Health Concerns Across a Woman's Lifespan: 1998 Survey of Women's Health*, May 1999.

252 Feminist Women's Health Center statistics: www.fwhc.org/stats.htm.

253 Pollitt, Katha. *Reasonable Creatures: Essays on Women and Feminism.* Vintage 1995, at p182.

254 Plichta SB. 'Intimate partner violence and physical health consequences: policy and practice implications.' *J Interpers Violence* 2004;19(11):1296-323.

255 Mezey GC. 'Domestic violence in pregnancy.' In: Bewley S *et al. Violence Against Women.* RCOG, London 1997, Ch 21.

256 Coid, J. *Domestic Violence. A Health Response.* Working in a Wider Partnership Conference Report, Department of Health, London 2000, at p41.

257 Johnson JK, Haider F, Ellis K *et al.* 'The prevalence of domestic violence in pregnant women.' *Br J Obstet Gynecol* 2003;110(3):272-5.

258 Pan American Health Organization (regional office of the World Health Organization), Washington DC. Program on Women, Health and Development. Factsheet: *Domestic violence during pregnancy.*

259 Pan American Health Organization, *Ibid.*

260 Reardon David C. 'Report misses association of violence with pregnancy.' *BMJ* 2003; 326: 104 (letter).

261 Pan American Health Organization *op cit.*

262 Cox J, Bota GW, Carter M *et al*. 'Domestic Violence, Incidence and prevalence in a northern emergency department.' *Canadian Family Physician* 2004; 50: 90 – 97.

263 Radestad I, Rubertsson C, Ebeling M, Hildingsson I. 'What factors in early pregnancy indicate that the mother will be hit by her partner during the year after childbirth? A nationwide Swedish survey.' *Birth*. 2004;31(2):84-92.

264 Pan American Health Organization, *op cit*.

265 Schoeman J, Grove DV, Odendaal HJ. 'Are Domestic Violence and the Excessive Use of Alcohol Risk Factors for Preterm Birth?' *J Trop Pediatr* 2004; 15 December.

266 McWilliams M, McKiernan J. 'Bringing It All Out Into The Open: Domestic Violence in Northern Ireland.' HMSO, Belfast 1993.

267 Coid J, *op cit*.

268 Rachana C, Suraiya K, Hisham AS *et al*. 'Prevalence and complications of physical violence during pregnancy.' *Eur J Obstet Gynecol Reprod Biol* 2002;103(1):26-9.

269 Mezey GC, *op cit*, at p121.

270 Pan American Health Organization, *op cit*.

271 Goodwin T, Breen M. 'Pregnancy outcome and fetomaternal haemorrhage after noncatastrophic trauma.' *Am J Obstet Gynecol* 1990; 162: 665-71.

272 Grossman NB. 'Blunt trauma in pregnancy.' *Am Fam Physician* 2004;70(7):1303-10.

273 Boy A, Salihu HM. 'Intimate partner violence and birth outcomes: a systematic review.' *Int J Fertil Women's Med* 2004;49(4):159-64.

274 Horon IL, Cheng D. 'Enhanced Surveillance for Pregnancy-Associated Mortality - Maryland, 1993 – 1998.' *JAMA* 2001; 285(11): 1455-9.

275 Nannini A, Weiss J, Goldstein R, Fogerty S. 'Pregnancy-Associated Mortality at the End of the Twentieth Century: Massachusetts, 1990 – 1999.' *J Am Med Women's Assoc* 2002; 57(23): 140-3.

276 Frye V. 'Examining Homicide's Contribution to Pregnancy-Associated Deaths.' *JAMA* 2001; 285: 1510-1.

277 Campbell JC, Webster D, Koziol-McLain J *et al*. 'Risk factors for femicide in abusive relationships: results from a multisite case control study.' *Am J Public Health* 2003; 93: 1089-97.

278 Nannini A, Weiss J, Goldstein R, Fogerty S. *Op cit*.

279 Lewis G. Chapter 14: 'Coincidental (Fortuitous) deaths.' In: Lewis G, Drife J, editors. *Why Mothers Die 1997–1999. Fifth Report of the Confidential Enquiries into Maternal Deaths*. London: RCOG Press; 2001, at pp 225– 30; 241–51.

280 House of Lords. Children Bill. HL Bill 35, 2004.

281 Paltrow, Lynn M. Perspective of a Reproductive Rights Attorney. The Future of Children; 1991 (Spring); 1(1), article 9 at p 85.

282 Silverman JG, Mesh CM, Cuthbert CV *et al*. 'Child custody determinations in cases involving intimate partner violence: a human rights analysis.' *Am J Public Health* 2004;94(6):951-7.

283 Saunders, Hilary. *Twenty-nine child homicides: Lessons still to be learnt on domestic violence and child protection*. Women's Aid, London 2004: www.womensaid.org.uk.

284 Swahnberg K, Wijma B, Wingren G *et al*. 'Women's perceived experiences of abuse in the health care system: their relationship to childhood abuse'. *Br J Obstet Gynaecol* 2004;111(12):1429-36.

285 *In Re S* (1992) ILR 14.10.92:TLR 16.10.92 3 WLR 806:4 AER.671; (1993) 4 Med LR 28 [Lawtel].

286 General Medical Council. *Seeking Patients' Consent: The Ethical Considerations.* General Medical Council. London 1999 at p12.

287 *Tameside & Glossop Acute Services Unit v CH (a patient)* [1996] 1 FLR 762.

288 *Re MB* [1997] EWCA Civ 1361.

289 *Baby Boy Doe, op cit,* 260 Ill. App. 3d at 405-06, 632 N.E.2d at 335.

290 *Re AC,* 573 A.2d at 1244 n.8. (DC Ct App 1990).

291 *McFall v Shrimp* 10 Pa D&C 3d 90 (1978).

292 Case reported by Lynn Paltrow, Executive Director of National Advocates for Pregnant Women in the US: Paltrow LM. 'Do Pregnant Women Have Rights?' *Alternet,* 22 April 2004. http://www.alternet.org/story/18493.

293 *Re AC* 573 A.2d 1235 (DC Ct App 1990).

294 American Medical Association Board of Trustees. 'Legal Interventions During Pregnancy: Court Ordered Medical Treatments and Legal Penalties for Potentially Harmful Behavior by Pregnant Women.' *J Am Med Assoc* 1990;264:2663, 2679.

295 *In re Brown, op cit.*

296 *In the matter of an application for judicial review: Queen v Louize Collins ; Pathfinder Mental Health Services Trust and St George's Healthcare NHS Trust, ex parte 'S'* [1998] EWHC Admin 490 (7th May, 1998) at para 40.

297 *Queen v Louize Collins ; Pathfinder Mental Health Services Trust and St George's Healthcare NHS Trust, ex parte* M. S. [1997] EWCA Civ 2020 (3rd July, 1997).

298 Siefert K, Pimlott S. 'Improving pregnancy outcome during imprisonment: a model residential care program.' *Soc Work* 2001; 46(2): 125-34.

299 Beech BAL. 'Court ordered caesarean sections are discouraging women from seeking obstetric care.' *BMJ* 1997;314:1908 (Letter) [Medline].

300 Maia Szalavitz. 'War On Drugs, War On Women.' *On The Issues.* New York, Winter 1998.

301 Dyer C. 'Court case may clarify law on caesarean sections.' *BMJ* 1997;314:623 (News).

302 American Academy of Pediatrics. Committee on Substance Abuse. 'Tobacco, alcohol, and other drugs: the role of the pediatrician in prevention and management of substance abuse'. *Pediatrics* 1998 Jan;101(1 Pt 1):125-8.

303 Greenlaw JL. 'Treatment refusal, noncompliance, and substance abuse in pregnancy: legal and ethical issues.' *Birth* 1990;17(3):152-6 [Medline].

304 Marjorie Tew. *Safer Childbirth? A Critical History of Maternity Care.* Free Association Books, London 1998.

Chapter 4

Undermining Capacity to Consent – Another Route to Compliance

As noted previously, incentives to pressurise pregnant women to comply with medical advice may be substantial. Since in law a competent woman, pregnant or not, has been repeatedly stated to have an unqualified right to refuse treatment in the UK, questioning the capacity to give valid refusal has become a major feature of obstetric conflict in this jurisdiction. The way in which this issue has been handled in past court cases has been less than exemplary, and legal loopholes retain the potential for this to be used as an alternative route to achieving compliance.

In the US, the theoretical position as stated in *Fosmire v Nicoleau*[1] is that when there is a *bona fide* question of the patient's competence, the doctor or health care facility may seek a court ruling. In such proceedings, the court should consider whether the patient has made a decision to decline treatment, is fully aware of the consequences and alternatives, and is competent to make the choice. If the patient is not presently competent, the court must determine whether there is clear and convincing evidence that the patient, when competent, made a firm resolve to decline treatment.

However, greater flexibility in balancing individual autonomy with state interests has generally allowed cases attempting to override treatment refusal by pregnant women to proceed along this route, and competency has rarely featured as an issue – in marked contrast to its prominence in UK cases. This may be because of differences in approach to patients deemed incompetent – for example, treatment may proceed without resorting to the courts at all, or cases where the woman was deemed not competent to make her own decision were judged not worthy of reporting, so most such instances are perhaps simply resolved at local level. However, if fewer women, proportionately, have actually been deemed incompetent in the US, the implication is that such cases generally follow the path of least legal resistance.

The US: Disallowing Women's Choices

In the discussion of competency following, this chapter necessarily therefore concentrates largely on the UK position. Nevertheless, it is worth noting that hospitals, courts and legislatures in the US may all treat pregnant women *as if* they were incompetent, solely by virtue of the fact of pregnancy. Such policies in a medical care setting may be institutionalised. In *Norwood Hospital v Munoz* (1991), for example, the hospital had a formal policy that appeared directly related to the potential for overriding autonomy in court. In this case, in which at first instance the judge overruled a woman's refusal of transfusion, despite recognising her as competent, on the basis that she had a minor child who would be abandoned if she died – a judgment reversed on appeal – it was noted that:

> Norwood Hospital has a written policy regarding patients who refuse to consent to the administration of blood or blood products.... If the patient, in a nonemergency situation, refuses to consent to a blood transfusion, and the patient is a competent adult, not pregnant, and does not have minor children, the hospital will accede to the patient's refusal. If the patient, in a non-emergency situation, refuses to consent to a blood transfusion, and the patient is a minor, an incompetent adult, *pregnant*, or a competent adult with minor children, the hospital's policy is to seek judicial determination of the rights and responsibilities of the parties.[2]

The same attitude can be observed in many states that now have specific statutes recognising applicable advance directives and duly appointed health care proxies. While the exact provisions vary from state to state, many explicitly refuse to recognise decisions taken by pregnant women, or qualify their right to refuse treatment. For example, Pennsylvania's *Advance Directive for Health Care Act* allows competent adults to record their instructions as to life-sustaining treatments or the appointment of a proxy health care decision-maker in formal declaration. The Act stipulates:

> However, a declaration by a pregnant woman will not become effective unless a physician has determined that the life-sustaining treatments either (a) will not permit the live birth of the unborn child, (b) will be physically harmful to the pregnant woman, or (c) would cause pain to the pregnant woman.[3]

Similarly, the law in Illinois states that an advanced refusal of life-support cannot take effect for a woman who is pregnant if treating doctors believe that a live birth could be possible. In Rhode Island too, such a declaration is not honoured for pregnant women if the foetus could develop sufficiently for a live birth. In fact, most states will not allow a pregnant woman to make an advance refusal of life-support – of the 47 states plus the District of Columbia (DC) that had living will statutes in force in 2001, the withdrawal or withholding of life-support from a pregnant woman is explicitly forbidden in 32 of them, and explicitly allowed in only four (the relevant statutes in 11 states and DC being silent on the point). The situation is similar with health care proxies – although 49 states plus DC have statutes enforcing the appointment of a durable power of attorney for health care and allowing the proxy to make decisions about life support, 16 states explicitly exclude decisions relating to pregnant women, 28 and DC are silent on the issue, and only five explicitly allow the woman to decide whether or not a proxy can refuse life-support on her behalf during pregnancy.[4]

Removing the Right to Refuse Treatment in Advance

Given the evidence that women's decisions on end-of-life issues are in any case less likely than men's to be honoured even where available,[5] it seems probable overall that few pregnant women will be granted autonomy in this situation. According to Partnership For Caring (formerly Choice In Dying), an organization that works to achieve 'a good death' for all and is involved in professional education about care of the dying and bioethical issues involved in end-of-life decision-making:

> ...the right to refuse medical treatment at the end of life is not the same for women as it is for men. Advance directive laws in individual states often explicitly limit the applicability of living wills or durable powers of attorney for health care during the course of a woman's pregnancy. Even when the law is the same for men and women, there is evidence to suggest that the courts apply that law differently for the two sexes.[6]

This may seem eminently reasonable on the surface, given that women may have made their declaration before becoming pregnant and that circumstances are clearly altered by the pregnancy. However, pregnancy is the time when many women first think about making an ordinary will (which is perfectly capable of covering the situation for a possible child *en ventre sa mere*), and represents a relatively uncommon prompt for a young person to make a 'living will', a lost opportunity if it is disallowed. The position with advance directives is especially ironic, given that under the federal *Patient Self-Determination Act* (1990)[7], US hospitals must now advise patients on admission of their rights under state law to make an advance declaration or to appoint a proxy, and that that pregnancy is one of the most common reasons for hospital admission of women of fertile age. Moreover, given the various higher court decisions upholding a pregnant woman's right to refuse treatment (albeit usually only on appeal) irrespective of the effect on her foetus, and the settled principle that an advance refusal of treatment, where applicable to the situation, is as binding as a contemporaneous one, it seems especially discrepant as a point of law to exclude pregnant women from statutory provisions on advance directives and health care proxies. Where the foetus involved is not yet viable it is also, of course, discrepant with the woman's right under *Roe v Wade*[8] to terminate the pregnancy.

Whose Decision?

Those few women in this age group for whom the circumstances envisaged in such declarations may be predicted as a possibility are perhaps most likely to wish to make such a declaration in anticipation, and it seems curious to disallow them from doing so when there are few other settled medical, legal or ethical principles to guide physicians as to how to manage such a scenario. Indeed, this extreme situation illustrates the tangled web that may ensue when the law attempts to relegate pregnant women's decisions.

One reported case illustrates the type of moral dilemma that might have arisen. A pregnant woman was admitted at 27 weeks' gestation with respiratory distress from fulminant AIDS. After discussion with both the woman and her family, a peri/post-mortem Caesarean section was performed – with survival of the infant – when she suffered a fatal cardiorespiratory arrest.[9] How much more complicated would management have been had the clinicians involved not been able to ascertain her wishes? Yet this is just the type of patient who might have made an advance declaration, or appointed a proxy, were it not for the pregnancy bar in the statute. Such general discouragement for pregnant women to state their wishes in advance is a clear handicap in cases such as this where there may be a balancing to be performed between the needs of the woman and those of the foetus.

In the more common situation of an accident or an assault, the general medical view is that when a pregnant woman sustains trauma, foetal survival is dependent on maternal survival – therefore stabilising the woman's condition takes precedence over concerns about the foetus; however the possible exception is third-trimester trauma in which the prognosis for the woman is poor. In this situation, immediate Caesarean section may be necessary to save the foetus.[10]

This – or similar circumstances arising due to catastrophic events in late pregnancy or during birth itself – is clearly the general type of situation envisaged by such statutes: if the woman has decided that in certain dire circumstances, she would not wish for life-sustaining treatment to be continued, it is not right that her foetus should die with her. The implication is that doctors should be given the chance to intervene to rescue the near-term foetus before withdrawing life-support.

But how are they to effect such a rescue? The woman may be unable to communicate her wishes – possibly because of the life-support itself – but she is not necessarily brain-dead, and the normal considerations of consent still apply. Angela Carder, after all, was sedated and on a ventilator at the time of the initial application to perform a Caesarean to rescue her foetus.

Suppose, as with Carder, that doctors are faced with a woman in a critical condition for whom the Caesarean may hasten her death, even by hours or minutes? In the Carder case, the court clearly ruled that a pregnant woman – even in a terminal situation – is entitled to refuse a Caesarean section.[11] Yet awaiting the onset of a natural labour in such a situation, even if the woman survives that long, may vastly increase the complexity of medical management as well as the risk to the foetus. Are clinicians bound to respect an advance refusal of Caesarean but not a refusal of life-support?

Ironically in this context, the Appeal Court in the Carder case upheld her right to refuse Caesarean section on the basis that it was not possible to find a state interest in protecting foetal life which outweighed her own because the lower court had not first determined her wishes, as expressed either by herself or via substituted judgment.[12]

Even if there is no indication that the woman would have refused a Caesarean, the question arises as to how poor her prognosis must be to justify operation to rescue the foetus, and balanced against what degree of risk to her – and to the foetus itself? As Tuohey has pointed out in just this context, unless there is a threat to her without it, a Caesarean section is not of any clear benefit to the woman: 'it is wrong to insist that a dying woman must always endure burdensome treatment for the sake of a viable fetus.'[13] In which case, should the doctors await brain death – in which case the foetus may die first – before they intervene? Are the doctors to decide this, or must they refer to the courts?

Such questions make it obvious that there may be some, perhaps many, situations likely to arise in this area that are not as clear-cut as simply continuing or withdrawing life-support and where, in fact, the woman's opinions, general values and feelings about this pregnancy – as ideally expressed via her chosen proxy if she cannot communicate them herself – would be, at least morally, a factor of immense value in considering such complex decisions. Generally they are also legally welcome where a substituted judgement standard applies in the case of a woman unable to take her own decisions yet who does not have a validly nominated proxy. Such statutory provisions may exclude a pregnant woman's refusal of life-support but they do not bind doctors to continue it should they assess the situation as futile. Without the woman's own input, or that of her designated proxy, such issues place a heavy burden on clinical judgement.

Women as Incubators

Even more problematic is the rare situation in which the woman's prognosis is deemed hopeless yet the foetus is pre-viable and not yet salvageable by Caesarean section, or would have a substantially better chance if allowed a while longer to mature in the womb. The media has given prominent publicity to a few remarkable cases in which mortally injured pregnant women were sustained on life-support for some time, specifically to allow the foetus to mature to the point of viability to allow birth or, more usually, delivery by Caesarean section. Such situations have inevitably attracted considerable – often colourful – comment, even from professionals. For example, Loewy discusses 'the moral problem of using brain-dead persons as incubators for potential or actual others,'[14] while Lyon has referred to 'extraordinary support measures for the sole purpose of providing a fetal incubator' and to such situations as involving 'a ventilator-dependent, brain-dead patient being kept alive solely as a nursery.'[15]

Unsurprisingly perhaps, this situation is one that not all women would wish to have imposed, especially given that usually the foetus will be delivered prematurely and its survival may in any case be compromised (*vide infra*), with a substantial risk of accompanying handicap if the infant does survive. Again, a multitude of hypothetical questions may be posed to illustrate the complexity of the situation. What if the woman was on her way to have an abortion when she was involved in the accident that rendered her incapable? What if the abortion was recommended because of severe foetal handicap?

Medical experience of cases involving a pregnant woman maintained on life-support awaiting a timely moment to deliver is extremely limited; foetal outcome is difficult to predict; the legal situation is uncertain and probably varies with the status accorded to the foetus in different jurisdictions, and the 'central question' of 'whether continuing maternal organ supportive measures in an attempt to prolong gestation to attain foetal viability is appropriate, or whether it constitutes futile care'[16] remains unanswered.

Viability

Much may hinge on the stage in pregnancy at which the decision arises and, particularly, on the ever-present issue of viability. Loewy regards it as a 'moral necessity' to deliver viable infants from brain-dead mothers – however, he suggests that the further from viability brain death occurs, the more maintaining the mother as an incubator resembles experimental therapy, and as such requires careful, informed consent.[17] Yet such consent (or refusal thereof), even where it might be available, is now barred by statute in many US states, leaving doctors with little guidance as to how to proceed in such cases.

Arguably too, on the basis of *Roe v Wade* and many subsequent cases, the state has no interest in the potential life of the foetus prior to viability – so should not insist on maintaining life-support for the woman carrying the foetus before this point. Except that in one case in which a pregnant woman was deemed to be brain-dead (the *Piazzi* case, *vide infra*), the court ruled that she had no interests at all and therefore her rights – including the constitutional privacy right on which *Roe* is founded – were extinguished by her death. In such a case, no-one has any legal interests – yet there remains a medical possibility, albeit at present a small one, that the foetus might, indeed, survive, and in many cases this may accord with what the pregnant woman would have wanted.

Continuing life-support is most likely to make a difference – and to be viewed as an acceptable option – in the period when the woman is around 24 to 27 weeks pregnant,[18] and a few extra intra-uterine days may make a large difference to the outcome for the foetus. However, the issue is important not just in cases where a woman sustains some kind of brain insult whilst carrying a viable or nearly viable foetus. It has proved possible for foetal development to continue and to result in the birth of a healthy child even in a woman who is comatose from as early as six weeks' gestation.[19] Several cases have been reported in which women remained comatose or were maintained on life-support for prolonged periods after brain death, and several ultimately gave birth to healthy infants.[20,21,22]

When such situations pose extraordinary legal, medical and moral dilemmas, it seems particularly perverse to negate the judgement of the person most involved if it should be available.

Another case reported in Ireland in 2001 concerned a woman who was a British citizen (Ireland, unlike Great Britain, gives constitutional protection to the foetus) and who was fourteen weeks pregnant when she collapsed with a brain haemorrhage. She was taken to hospital, placed on life-support and declared brain-dead. The hospital, uncertain as to its obligations to the foetus, maintained life-support while further opinion was sought; however it was discontinued when the foetus died after two weeks. Treating physicians commented that in Ireland there are neither medical guidelines nor legislation to regulate such areas of medical practice, which have never come before the courts – 'there exists widespread concern as to how healthcare providers will act if such [a] situation were to occur again in the future.'[23]

The complications that may otherwise ensue in the absence of any guidance are further illustrated by an early case that arose in Georgia in 1987, *University Health Services Inc. v Piazzi*, in which a hospital petitioned the court to allow them to continue life-support for a woman declared brain-dead, in order to preserve the life of her quickened but non-viable foetus until it could be delivered with a reasonable chance of survival. The woman's husband had requested that life support be terminated, but both the guardian *ad litem* appointed for the foetus and the putative father of the foetus requested that life-support be continued. The Division of Family and Children Services argued on a point of law that the court lacked jurisdiction. The Court, placed in a somewhat unenviable position, concluded that only the pregnant woman had the right to terminate a non-viable foetus, and that public policy required that life-support be maintained as long as there was a reasonable chance for the foetus to develop and survive.[24]

Uncertain Benefit

If only the pregnant woman may make such a decision, but she is not permitted an advance refusal of life-sustaining treatment in most states, does this mean that the clinician in such states has an obligation to maintain life-support for the woman at any stage of pregnancy, as long as the foetus remains alive? Loewy's 'moral necessity' in the case of a viable foetus (*vide supra*) does not necessarily translate into a legal imperative and certainly not into a medical one. At the borderline of viability, and with aggressive neonatal resuscitation, survival rates increase with increasing gestation from 24 per cent at 23 weeks to 51 per cent at 24 weeks; 68 per cent at 25 weeks and 85 per cent at 26 weeks; however survivors are more or less equally affected with complications such necrotising enterocolitis, retinopathy of prematurity, intraventricular haemorrhage, respiratory distress syndrome, sepsis, and bronchopulmonary dysplasia.[25]

Even in the substantially less complicated situation of a 'normal' premature delivery with a healthy mother, treatment of a premature neonate may be judged futile, and at the threshold of viability, there is considerable variation in clinical management – at 25-plus weeks' gestation, 84 per cent of neonatologists consider treatment clearly beneficial, but this falls to 41 per cent at 24-plus weeks, and at or below 23 weeks' gestation, 93 per cent of neonatologists consider treatment futile. When they consider treatment futile, 76 per cent report that they would follow parental requests to withhold treatment; conversely 33 per cent would provide what they consider futile treatment at parental request.[26] This produces the somewhat inconsistent situation that a pregnant woman is not permitted in advance to refuse life-supportive measures should she be incapacitated, even if the foetus has a poor chance of survival and a high chance of severe handicap (as well as being motherless) if it is delivered alive, but either parent is likely to be able to veto treatment for a neonate – a person in being – after the birth in a case that the doctor judges to be futile.

Thus the benefit in terms of outcome for the foetus of maintaining life support for a brain-dead woman, or one for whom treatment on her own account would otherwise be judged futile, is by no means certain enough to make such a course mandatory for clinicians, who have little in the way of medical experience of such cases to assist their decision. As Tuohey remarks, again: a Caesarean section is not necessarily in the foetus's best interest just because the foetus is viable. 'Given the ambiguity of the prognosis for survival and the risks of significant handicaps for the preterm or low birth weight fetus, it may be ethically appropriate to omit an act on behalf of the fetus.'[27]

Without knowing what the woman would have wanted, her doctors may be left floundering in a soup of clinical judgement, attempting to make decisions on the basis of possible viability versus unknown considerations of futility, best interests and risk prediction – in this area a very uncertain quagmire indeed.

What about the Next of Kin?

The burden on families in situations where a pregnant woman is comatose or in a possibly irreversibly traumatised or moribund condition is hard. Fully informed consent from the next of kin is mandatory in such situations, according to Loewy;[28] Lyon too stresses the importance of next-of-kin decisions,[29] and Lane *et al* the importance of involving the family.[30] It seems odd therefore for states by statute to refuse to recognise, in the case of withdrawal of life-support, not only any decision that the pregnant woman herself may have made, but also any involvement of her appointed proxy – who will quite often be a close relative.

The situation is all the more bizarre given that it has been specifically advocated that obstetrician/gynaecologists assist women patients to develop advanced directives targeted, *inter alia*, to 'the unique risks of the pregnant woman': 'End-of-life decisions are much more stressful when surrogate decision makers do not know in advance what decisions a patient would want made if the patient becomes incapacitated'.[31] Yet in the case of pregnant women, such statutes do not allow an effective end-of-life decision that involves withdrawal of life-support – again, a woman's choices are discounted unless they are the 'right' choices.

The Pennsylvania declaration and others like it would seem to exclude pregnant women from such decisions merely because of the fact of pregnancy – notwithstanding that other than in the tragic circumstances in which such declarations are applicable a competent woman would be just as entitled to refuse life-sustaining treatment as she is to refuse Caesarean section. Such statutes would better respect autonomy, as well as the needs of doctors and relatives, were they to allow women to state the extent to which their wishes would be altered if they happened to be pregnant at the time the declaration was needed. This seems a relatively simple provision, and much to be preferred to the alternative of refusing to respect the otherwise legally valid choices of pregnant women as a class.

Disallowing Refusals in an Emergency

On the other hand, provisions that allow refusals of consent to be overridden for any patient in specific circumstances seem likely, as with end-of-life decisions, to be applied differentially to pregnant women. Several states have laws that allow emergency medical staff to treat patients and transport them to hospital in an emergency, notwithstanding express refusals. Specific provisions may allow exceptions where the patient has an advance directive in force (less likely therefore to be the case with a pregnant woman), or where there is a religious objection, and some statutes bar the use of unreasonable force.

Whilst understandable from the point of view of emergency personnel who, in the field, may be unable to undertake complex assessments of the patient's capacity to consent, such statutes raise a number of ethical problems outside the scope of the present work – though anecdotally the measure has so worried a few patients that they have taken drastic action, such as having 'do not hospitalize' tattooed on their chest.[32] For present purposes, the likelihood is that, faced with a woman in labour and incipient (or even completed) childbirth, even if there is no actual health risk, ambulance personnel immune from civil liability are quite likely to transport first and let the hospital resolve any ensuing problems.

The UK: Competency in Court

As has been discussed, competence assessment in UK forced Caesarean cases has often been perfunctory. In the first case, *In Re S* (1992),[33] the issue of S's competence was simply not addressed; thereafter it formed the major grounds for overriding maternal refusals drawing in, variously, the effects of labour itself, needle phobias and mental health legislation.

Lord Justice Thorpe, a judge in the High Court Family Division at the time of *Re S*, has commented on forced Caesareans:

> Manifestly an issue of such significance should have been presented to the court for decision on the foundation of thorough preparation, extensive research and skilful argument. In the event, the President was presented with an emergency application during the lunch hour. ... The President chose to override patient autonomy in order to maximise the chance of survival for mother and unborn baby. I was then a Family Division judge and I would have reached the same decision. More speculatively I say that the majority, if not all, the judges of the Family Division would have so decided.[34]

Despite the widespread criticism that the decision in *In Re S* provoked, all the subsequent first instance decisions also overrode the woman's refusal, often on the basis that her capacity was transiently impaired during labour. Lord Justice Thorpe has this to say:

> There emerged a sense that the judges strained to find incapacity in order to achieve the outcome that their judicial instinct required, namely the promotion of the well being of the child on the threshold.[35]

The Effect of Labour

Of particular concern were the decisions that seemed to imply that being in labour, in itself, might impair competence. In *Norfolk and Norwich Healthcare Trust v W* (1996),[36] authority to end labour by forceps delivery or Caesarean if necessary was granted in respect of a woman who arrived at the hospital in a state of arrested labour, fully dilated and ready to deliver, but denying she was even pregnant. She had a history of psychiatric treatment with consistent refusal to co-operate with doctors, but no mental disorder under the *Mental Health Act 1983* [*MHA*]. Nevertheless, the court deemed her incapable of making a decision at a time of stress and pain 'in the ordinary course of labour', and held that termination of labour would be in her best interests and would avoid the likelihood of damage to her physical and mental health or of guilt if she were to cause the death of the foetus.

Similarly, in *Rochdale Healthcare (NHS) Trust v C* (1996),[37] a woman who had had a previous Caesarean stated that she would rather die than have another. The judge suggested that a woman 'in the throes of labour with all that is involved in terms of pain and emotional stress ' was not able to weigh-up the considerations that arose so as to make any valid decision. Notwithstanding that no psychiatric opinion was available, and that the woman's obstetrician considered her to be fully competent, the judge ruled it in her best interests that a Caesarean be performed.

Although fears that the stress of labour *per se* might be sufficient to impair decision-making capacity were apparently allayed in *Re MB*[38] (*vide infra*), the later *Collins* case still discussed S's detention under the *MHA* in these terms:

> Her detention under the Act did not undermine or restrict her right to self determination unless she was deprived "either by long term mental capacity ... or by temporary factors such as unconsciousness or confusion or *the effects of fatigue, shock, pain or drugs*"[39] of her capacity to decide for herself.[40]

Clearly assessment of the effects of fatigue, pain or drugs in a labouring woman – especially one being pressured to accept an intervention she does not want – may be somewhat swayed by the perceptions and attitudes of the medical staff involved. As Maclean has pointed out, whilst all these effects may indeed affect competence at the extremes:

A subjective consideration of these factors may tip the balance so that rejection of medical advice will be equated with a woman whose capacity has been temporarily reduced below the acceptable level – a level that in most cases will be determined by a doctor.[41]

Needle Phobias

Two cases dealt with women refusing Caesarean section because of needle phobia. In *In Re L* (1996),[42] operation was approved after emergency proceedings without court papers or affidavits, on the basis of information relayed by telephone from the hospital. The court – in a 22-minute hearing – held that anaesthetising L by injection followed by emergency Caesarean section was in her best interest. At the time, the chairman of the British Medical Association's Medical Ethics Committee commented that:

> I am ... puzzled about the decision which cast doubt on the mother's mental competence, as this could take us back to a time when patients who disagreed with their doctors were deemed to be incompetent.[43]

A similar result was reached in *Re MB*,[44] where the court held MB temporarily incompetent, based on psychiatric opinion that she was 'unable to see beyond' her immediate fear of needles. However, whilst holding that fear and panic may destroy the capacity to make a decision, the Court of Appeal stressed that this must be to the extent that the ability to decide is clearly absent (apparently assuaging fears that labour *per se* could be said to impair capacity). The decision was appealed unsuccessfully[45] but the court made it clear that had MB been competent, even foetal death would not be grounds to overrule her decision. Detailed guidance was given on cases of treatment refusal and competency assessment, which at the time was heralded as putting an end to forced Caesareans.[46]

The stipulations given for instances when the medical profession might feel it necessary to seek declarations from the courts are worth noting in the light of subsequent events in the *Collins* case (discussed below). Specifically, the court stated that it would be unlikely to entertain an application for a declaration unless the patient's capacity to consent or refuse was at issue; if it was, for the time being the doctors should seek a ruling from High Court on the issue of competence. Any such hearings should be *inter partes* and the woman should be represented in all cases, unless she did not wish to be – a circumstance the court regarded as likely to be exceptional.[47]

However, the finding of incompetence in *Re MB* itself was characterised by a significant lack of 'due process' and its basis was not addressed by the Court of Appeal even though MB had challenged it. As Hewson commented at the time: 'If MB had complied with her doctors throughout, her competence would not have been questioned. ... The case makes competence look like a floating charge: it crystallises on compliance'.[48]

Similarly, Mason and McCall Smith note that the actual outcome of *Re MB*, notwithstanding judicial statements as to the paramountcy of autonomy, reveals 'the continued ambivalence of the courts towards such cases', and predict 'a divergence of theory and practice in this controversial area for some time to come'.[49]

Mental Health Legislation

Meanwhile in *Tameside and Glossop Acute Services Trust v CH* (1996),[50] the court justified a forced Caesarean (and the necessary 'reasonable restraint') on a woman detained under s.3 of the *MHA 1983* (which provides for admission for treatment of a precisely diagnosed mental disorder) as being treatment for her mental condition. It managed to rationalise this as being within the broad interpretation of s.63 *MHA*, on the basis that the woman's mental condition could otherwise deteriorate and her schizophrenia could be better medicated once she was no longer pregnant; medical evidence showed that it was in her best interests to give birth to a live child, and achievement of a successful pregnancy was a necessary part of treatment of her psychiatric condition – reasoning that was widely condemned.[51]

Finally, and notwithstanding the *Re MB* guidelines, came the *Collins* case,[52] an even more extreme example of manipulation of mental health legislation to override a patient's wishes, and one of such importance – as well as extraordinary in its unfolding sequence of events – that it will be discussed at length.

The *Collins* Case

Here, S ('MS' in some reports), a veterinary nurse, had reached 36 weeks of pregnancy without antenatal care and planned a home birth. On attendance at a GP's surgery she refused medical advice to have labour induced for pre-eclampsia and a social worker was called in.

The social worker, Louize Collins, having failed to persuade S to go with her to an obstetric facility to have the baby induced, decided to detain her under s.2 of the *MHA 1983*, although it was clear that S fully understood the potential risks. Medical evidence that S had 'moderate depression' was used to justify detention, yet at the later appeal Louize Collins commented:

> I do not think that a psychiatric ward was the best place for this patient but I felt the gravity of the situation was such that she needed some sort of safety containment, assessment and immediate treatment when necessary.[53]

Since it was immediately apparent that treatment for depression was not required – and indeed S was transferred rapidly from the psychiatric hospital to an obstetric facility – the 'treatment' referred to in this statement could only have been for pre-eclampsia, as the Appeal Court later recognised:

> [Louize Collins] believed, rightly, that MS's condition was threatened by her very severe pre-eclampsia. At the time when she reached her conclusion she did not suggest that detention was required for the purpose of assessing MS's mental condition or treating her depression. Put another way, if MS had not been suffering from severe pre-eclampsia there is nothing in the contemporaneous documents to suggest that an application for her detention would have been considered, let alone justified.[54]

The provisions of section 2 allow a patient to be admitted and detained in hospital for assessment on the grounds that:

(a)   he is suffering from mental disorder of a nature or degree which warrants detention ... for assessment...; *and*
(b)   he ought to be so detained in the interests of his own health or safety or with a view to the protection of other persons.

Both of the doctors recommending admission (as required in support of the application) expressed the opinion that detention was necessary in the interests of S's own health and safety and with a view to the protection of other persons. The 'other persons' can only have referred to the foetus she carried[55] yet, since the foetus has no legal persona, the s.2(b) stipulation should not be taken to include a foetus. In accordance with the requirements, both doctors then gave their reasons – and both specifically referred to the risk to her unborn child.

Again, this reasoning was strongly criticised by the Court of Appeal:

> ... those involved ... failed to maintain the distinction between the urgent need of MS for treatment arising from her pregnancy, and the separate question whether her mental disorder (in the form of depression) warranted her detention in hospital. From the reasoning to be found in [the contemporaneous documents], the conclusion that the detention was believed to be warranted in order that adequate provision could be made to deal with MS's pregnancy and the safety of her unborn child is unavoidable.[56]

On admission to a psychiatric hospital, S made it clear both orally and in writing – in a letter later described by the court as 'articulate' – that she declined treatment ('it is against my wishes and I shall consider it an assault on my person'), was aware of the dangers and wished nature to take its course. She also explained her intention to seek legal advice at the earliest possible opportunity next day,[57] which she did, spending an hour discussing her situation with a solicitor by telephone. By this time she had been (unlawfully, as it transpired) transferred to another hospital with obstetric facilities.

Here, notified of S's continuing refusal to consent to treatment, the hospital general manager took legal advice. S was again examined by the same duty psychiatrist who recorded

She appears to fully understand the interventions being proposed; the reasons for them and the serious, life threatening consequences of refusal ... her capacity to consent to treatment appears to be intact... her mental state is not affecting her capacity to consent.

S again explained her views in writing, in terms later described in court as 'unequivocal and again highly articulate'.[58] Nevertheless, an *ex parte* application was made without S's knowledge, with neither summons nor evidence. At this stage S's capacity to consent was still deemed intact, although at the later hearing it was revealed that the hospital notes contained a deletion and substitution at the end of the previous entry, 'late entry – revised opinion', initialled by the same doctor. This amended note reads:

> In my opinion her mental disorder cannot be excluded even though diagnosis may not be clear. Her capacity to consent however may be affected by her current mental state. The MHA allows for assessment and treatment of mental illness. She does not need emergency treatment for her depression.[59]

In the event, S's capacity to consent was not addressed – it was later suggested that this was because it was assumed throughout the hearing that she was competent,[60] and indeed the Court of Appeal concluded that there was 'no sufficient evidence ... that her competence ... was in question' and, moreover, commented that: 'in this particular case we cannot avoid reflecting whether the omission [to address the issue of consent] underlines that the urgent concern of the social worker and doctors was the need somehow to save the mother and her unborn child'.[61]

Nevertheless, the declaration was obtained (as noted, on the basis of an incorrect statement to the court that S had been in labour for 24 hours) giving authority for all necessary investigations and such treatment as might be deemed necessary. These proceedings were later stated by the Court of Appeal to have been 'extraordinary and unfortunate'.[62] In the hospital, S was sedated, a foetal heart monitor was attached and shortly thereafter an emergency Caesarean section deemed necessary. Rather curiously, at this stage S was asked to sign a consent form, and yet again she refused. Of course, if S was incompetent, she lacked the capacity to consent; conversely, if she was competent, her refusal should have been respected.

In the event, the forced Caesarean was performed. Four days later she was transferred back to the psychiatric hospital, and asked her solicitor to appeal to a Mental Health Review Tribunal. However the next day she was seen by a consultant psychiatrist who recorded: 'no clear evidence of mental illness today'. Her detention was terminated the following day, the medical record noting: 'she does not meet criteria for detention under MHA 1983'. S then discharged herself. During her detention no specific treatment for mental disorder or mental illness had been prescribed.

S appealed and applied for judicial review of the decision. On a renewed application, leave to move for judicial review was granted despite being out of time,[63] the judge stating that the case raised issues of public importance both in the interpretation of s2 *MHA* and in connection with the detention of and operating upon a pregnant woman.[64]

The Court of Appeal ruled[65] that S had been unlawfully admitted and detained under the *MHA* and unlawfully forced to have a Caesarean section by the order of a court. It re-iterated that every adult of sound mind is entitled to refuse medical treatment even when his or her life depends on it, and pregnancy did not diminish a woman's entitlement to decide. An unborn child was not a separate person and its need for medical assistance did not prevail over the mother's rights. The 1983 Act could not be deployed to detain an individual merely because her thinking process is unusual. Accordingly, the application for admission and S's detention in hospital were unlawful – indeed, she would have been entitled to apply for *habeas corpus* – and she had been unlawfully forced to have a Caesarean which, together with the accompanying medical procedures, amounted to trespass.

Furthermore, the Court not only allowed the appeal against the original declaration but further stated that 'in the extraordinary circumstances of this case' it provided no defence to a claim of damages for trespass against the hospital performing the surgery. Additional relief by way of judicial review was deemed inappropriate.[66] Supplementary guidelines[67] for future cases stated categorically that any application to dispense with consent for a person of sound mind was 'pointless', and that in future *ex parte* applications would not be binding.

Effects of the *Collins* Case

Several important implications of the *Collins* case may be noted. Firstly, the court overwhelmingly endorsed the supremacy of autonomy in cases of conflict between competent patients and medical staff. Secondly, this autonomy was definitively stated, as part of the *ratio decidendi* (whereas in *Re MB* it had been *obiter*), to apply to the right of a competent pregnant woman to refuse treatment, irrespective of the effects on her foetus. Thirdly, the potential use of mental health legislation to effect compliance in such cases was decisively ruled out:

> In the final analysis a woman detained under the [*MHA*] for mental disorder cannot be forced into medical procedures unconnected with her mental condition unless her capacity to consent to such treatment is diminished.[68]

Hence in future declaratory relief should only be available where it has been conclusively demonstrated that an adult patient (pregnant or otherwise) is incompetent. Lastly, these principles are supported by the guidelines given, which also offer safeguards for patients whose capacity may be in doubt, and were stated to apply to any surgical or invasive treatment needed by any patient.[69]

This, then, would appear to settle the issue. However, it had appeared to be settled after *Re MB* and, as has been argued, the impetus to achieve compliance remains strong. The question has arisen as to whether the current legal position still enables flexible interpretation that gives too much discretion to treating doctors, perhaps allowing coercion to creep in by the 'back door'. The Director of Patient Concern in the UK, responding to an article by the Official Solicitor describing, for doctors, legal principles which might protect patients from treatment against their wishes or specific instructions, recently commented: 'Unfortunately medical practitioners' attitudes and priorities may conflict with the law's laudable intentions'.[70]

Doctors' Discretion

Mason and McCall Smith warn that the decision in *Re MB* 'does little to remove from the medical profession the discretion and power to decide on the patient's capacity to act autonomously – and ultimately, in cases of incapacity, to decide on the patient's best interests', and that this discretion is not removed by the *Collins* case.[71] Moreover, they suggest that, whilst these best interests were relatively unambiguous in MB's case (MB did not object to the Caesarean *per se* and her desired outcome was merely being blocked by her needle phobia), it is less obvious how they should be assessed where the mother's feelings about the birth are 'unclear'.[72] Clearly, in addition, any assessment of best interests is highly likely to be coloured by the views of the assessor, particularly as regards the benefit of obstetric interventions, the desirability of natural childbirth or the importance of 'proper' maternal instinct.

They add further that although the *Collins* guidelines are important and detailed, they notably concern, primarily, procedural matters: 'the court was clearly disinclined to interfere in clinical matters'.[73] Moreover, they are only guidelines, and the court advised that rigid compliance would be inappropriate if this would put the patient's life or health at risk: 'The ball thus remains firmly in the health carers' court – subject, of course, to its being played according to the rules'.[74]

This is profoundly worrying. Haste has been an almost universal feature of the cases discussed, and the sense of urgency prompting disregard of the normal 'rules' of, *inter alia*, evidence and representation was incited by medical pronouncements as to both the need to expedite matters and the suggested outcome should this not occur. Such pronouncements, as noted, have not always been accurate, yet the courts have been notably reluctant to evaluate the accuracy or quality of medical evidence, much less to question the treatment proposed. Arguably most such cases will contain some element of 'emergency' and there would be no point seeking a declaration if there were not some (alleged) risk to the patient's life or health.

Evaluating Competence – More Scope for 'Clinical Judgement'

Evaluation of competence is not an exact science and current practice is acknowledged to be deficient, with assessment of capacity to consent 'often poorly understood and inadequately practiced'.[75]

In the UK, the standard test was laid down in *Re C*, which required that the patient:

(a)   can comprehend and retain relevant information,
(b)   believes the information, and
(c)   can weigh the information in the balance and arrive at a choice.[76]

Beauchamp and Childress have put forward four, slightly more elaborate criteria. The patient must:

(a)   understand the material information (the need to give consent, the nature of the proposed treatment, the risks and benefits, and the consequences of the options),
(b)   be able to judge in the light of his or her own values,
(c)   intend the outcome, and
(d)   be able freely to communicate his or her decision.[77]

Similarly, case law in the US has determined that competency requires that the patient:

(1)   has sufficient mind to reasonably understand the condition they have,
(2)   is capable of understanding the nature and effect of the treatment choices,
(3)   is aware of the consequences associated with those choices, and
(4)   is able to make an informed choice that is voluntary and not coerced.[78]

In Manitoba, Canada, a similar test has been adopted by legislation:

A person has capacity to make health care decisions if he or she is able to understand the information that is relevant to making a decision and able to appreciate the reasonable and foreseeable consequences of a decision or lack of decision.[79]

Assessment of the degree to which a patient's decision matches these criteria is thus both dependent on the information imparted and inevitably subjective.

Although adults are generally presumed to have the capacity to choose whether to consent to or refuse medical treatment, this presumption may be rebutted.[80] In practice, other than with the permanently incapacitated, this becomes an issue only when patients obviously require treatment for a condition generating temporary lack of competency, or for those who refuse to consent to whatever treatment has been recommended – doctors do not question a patient's competence to *agree* to treatment.

In terms of the understanding required to demonstrate capacity to consent or, perhaps more importantly, to refuse treatment, this in turn will depend to an extent on the nature and extent of the information imparted, and on the quality of its communication. Both the patient's ability both to acquire information independently, and the intelligence required to understand it may play a role in complex medical decisions – even though in *In Re T*[81] it was specifically stated that the patient's intelligence *per se* should not play a role in the assessment. In any emergency situation, unless the patient possesses or can call upon specific medical knowledge, this also makes the decision essentially reliant on the information imparted by medical professionals.

In refusing treatment, the important consideration for assessment of capacity in law is that the patient clearly understands the nature and purpose of the treatment and the consequences of refusal.[82] Yet numerous studies have revealed serious flaws in the consent process that question whether such understanding is generally achieved.

'In obstetric practice informed consent is especially important as young, fit patients may request and receive non-essential but potentially life-threatening interventions', one team of anaesthetic researchers comment – yet their study showed that while women generally wish to know about both common, less severe side effects and rarer but more severe complications (such as permanent neurological deficit, meningitis and high spinal block), there remains little consensus amongst anaesthetists about what information to provide, and frequently some complications that patients consider important are not discussed.[83] Others have concluded that patients frequently are not given sufficient information about the risks of obstetric anaesthesia.[84]

Moreover patients may not understand such information as they are given – even though for valid consent clinicians are supposed to ensure that they do. In one British study of obstetric and gynaecology patients, only 80 per cent of those undergoing elective surgery reported satisfaction with the consent process, and the proportion fell to 63 per cent of those having emergency surgery. In the latter group, patients were significantly less likely to have read (odds ratio, OR 0.22) or understood (OR 0.40) the consent form, and more likely to report feeling frightened by signing it (OR 2.52), that they felt they had no choice about signing it (OR 2.11), and that they would have signed regardless of its content (OR 3.14). As the authors of the study comment, 'the implications on the ethical and legal standing of consent are considerable.'[85]

Furthermore, many women have difficulty understanding the need for operative delivery even after the event and despite having been reviewed by medical and midwifery staff before discharge – indeed, few remember a clear discussion of the indication for or method of intervention, or of the implications of such intervention for the future, although most express a desire for an in-depth explanation.[86]

This too raises issues for consent – how can patients be assessed for competency on the basis of their understanding of information that they may never have been given, or failed to retain, or failed to comprehend? The possible potential consequences are considerable.

As an example, in the US, in *In the Matter of Alice Hughes*, a patient's failure to appreciate the possible consequences of a decision resulted in the court rejecting her advance refusal of blood transfusion, made after her doctor had led her to believe that this would not be necessary during a hysterectomy. The court held that while a competent, adult patient is entitled to refuse life-sustaining treatment, the right operates only if the patient has a clear understanding of the illness, its prognosis and the consequences of refusing treatment. Since in this case the doctor had not discussed what she would want should an emergency arise, in which she might die without a transfusion, her refusal did not cover the circumstances, and a surrogate was appointed to consent to transfusion.[87] Although this was not an obstetric case, it is not hard to imagine similar circumstances arising during pregnancy.

The complexity and imprecision surrounding competence assessment has important potential consequences for doctors as well as patients. Assessment of competency in cases of treatment refusal is vital not just to ensure that the patient is offered every opportunity to exercise autonomy, if this is appropriate or, if not, to receive treatment according to their advance directive, proxy decision, substituted judgement or best interests, whichever applies. It is also vital for the health care professionals involved – to treat a competent patient in the face of express refusal violates autonomy and constitutes battery; however not to treat an incompetent patient according to one of the above criteria could cause harm to the patient and may represent negligence. Not only the patient but also, if she dies, her husband and offspring may have a right to sue.

In the US the legal requirement for informed consent arguably imposes a higher standard. In giving informed consent, the patient is assuming responsibility for accepting the risks involved, and therefore, in the absence of negligence, cannot sue should an accepted risk transpire.

Risk-Related Standard

A further area of concern is the citation in *Collins*[88] of an analysis by Lord Donaldson MR in *Re T*:

> It may not be a case of capacity or no capacity. It may be a case of reduced capacity. What matters is whether at that time the patient's capacity was reduced below the level needed in the case of a refusal of that importance, for refusals can vary in importance. Some may involve a risk to life or of irreparable damage to health. Others may not.[89]

In this much-quoted paragraph, Lord Donaldson was referring to evaluation of patients detained under the *MHA 1983*, but elsewhere made clear that the principle applied generally: 'the more serious the decision, the greater the capacity required'. This statement appears in formal guidelines for doctors and lawyers on assessment of mental capacity,[90] and has used in the context of Caesarean cases by Lord Justice Thorpe.[91] The principle was approved in *Re MB*: 'The graver the consequences of the decision, the commensurately greater the level of competence is required to take the decision'.[92]

However Maclean describes this as an error in thinking that confuses the importance of getting a decision right with the competence required to do so – it is the complexity of a decision, and not the risk *per se*, that is correlated with the understanding needed to make a decision and that should determine the level of competence required.[93] Wicclair has said, similarly: '... a stronger reason for making sure that a patient is decisionally capable should not be confused with a stronger standard of decision-making capacity'.[94]

It is not hard to see how flexibility could creep into competency assessment in practice, even with the best intentions. When a patient disagrees, the physician may experience conflict – assuming that the recommendation for treatment was made with the intention of serving the patient's best interests – between respect for the patient's autonomy and the desire to promote his or her well-being. Inevitably, the predicted consequences of the decision will feature in this conflict, and this is likely to be especially so if the physician involved is an obstetrician and the decision also affects the well-being of a foetus that is regarded as a 'second patient'. Whether or not the patient is competent to refuse is the logical next question and, again inevitably, this will be coloured by the nature of the decision and the perceived consequences of treatment refusal: if the standard of competency is flexible, it may well be the apparent quality of the decision that is weighed in the balance, rather than the patient's competency to make it.

The issue has considerable importance. Maclean goes on to point out that the risk-related standard necessarily means that refusal of treatment requires a greater level of competence than does consent (presumably on the assumption that medical opinion is likely to be that refusal is much the riskier course, and that this is more likely to be correct than alternative views). Again, the risk-related standard would seem to make it easier to infer that competence is specific to the type of decision – and to the degree to which the patient's understanding of it accords with that of the professionals involved. As expressed by Mason and McCall Smith: '[t]he implications of refusal may ... be more serious and ... refusal of treatment may require greater understanding than does acceptance.' As Maclean points out, where there is a high risk, consent is the only real option, since if a woman refuses she may be deemed incompetent and her decision overruled:

> Since the foetus may be considered a second patient, the risk involved in refusing a caesarean section is, arguably, the most risky medical treatment decision possible. A risk-related standard allows the doctors – and the courts – who are under moral and emotional pressure, to shift the goal posts and demand an unreachable level of competence in order to find the woman incompetent and so protect the foetus.[95]

Flexibility of Competence Standards

Maclean also suggests that the ability of influences such as fatigue, pain and drugs to tip the balance in assessment of competence in a labouring woman will be especially true where a risk-related standard is applied. Moreover if, as predicted, the *Collins* ruling proves hard for judges in the Family Division to apply in practice (see Chapter 6), 'the competence issue allows room for manoeuvre'.[96]

Maclean suggests that the potential for subjectivity allowed by the test in *Re C* (of which the third part – weighing information in the balance to arrive at a choice – allows greatest scope) also leaves pregnant women vulnerable to being deemed incompetent should they disagree with medical recommendations.[97]

Similarly, Mason and McCall Smith, criticising the judgment for vagueness, describe the tests in *Re C* as 'hurdles ... placed in the path of those seeking to exercise autonomy', and note that 'it remains uncertain how high they must jump in order to clear these hurdles'.[98]

Another hurdle that might be weighed in this equation is mental health in a broad sense. Depressive symptoms 'that do not meet the full diagnostic criteria for a diagnosis of depression' have been described as having the potential 'chronically and variably [to] affect a woman patient's decisions about the management of pregnancy'.[99] Whilst a repetition of the use of diagnoses such as S's 'moderate depression' in *Collins* to justify detention under the MHA is unlikely to occur again, such features could, perhaps, contribute to 'tipping the balance' of competence assessment. Doctors are advised that 'mood may be very important in determining capacity'; that anxiety may have an effect although '*by itself*, it will rarely lead to incapacity' and that a depressed patient 'may make decisions ... on an entirely erroneous and depressive basis'.[100]

This too is worrying, in the light of findings that women are vulnerable to depression during pregnancy as well as post-natally. Using standard screening instruments, 7.7 per cent of pregnant women may be classified as having prenatal depression,[101] and women with antenatal depression have been claimed to be at risk of poor nutrition, substance abuse, and 'prenatal noncompliance'.[102] In the US, one study in California recorded that 38 per cent of pregnant women met screening criteria for psychiatric disorders or substance use; the investigating psychiatrists recommended that 'given the potential impact of antenatal mental disturbances on maternal and infant outcomes, further investigations into the psychiatric evaluation and treatment of pregnant women in the obstetrical sector are required'.[103]

Since the test of competence is a legal one,[104] the courts are the final arbiters in cases of doubt. However, in practice 'doctors frequently give opinions about capacity which are accepted without further legal intervention'.[105] Although the law encourages doctors to refer 'boundary line' decisions to the courts, the medical profession is uncertain both about the circumstances and the mechanism for doing so – the machinery is under-used.[106] Moreover, as has been shown, even where decisions are submitted to the court, 'established legal principle is sometimes circumvented to override a woman's right to autonomy', and both lawyers and health professionals may play a part in 'denying a woman's competence to consent in order to achieve an outcome of which they approve.'[107]

All this makes Maclean's conclusions particularly alarming: despite overtly supporting patient autonomy, he suggests, the Court of Appeal in *Collins* 'has left the concept of capacity to consent so flexible as to allow paternalism to creep in through the back door'; it has failed to confront the issue of competence 'being used as a sword by doctors and the courts instead of a shield by the pregnant woman'. Since the *Collins* guidelines 'effectively allow doctors to decide on the issue of competence and only approach the court if there is doubt, they are given almost a *carte blanche* to treat a labouring woman in the way that they feel would be in her best interests'.[108]

Hewson describes this as a catch-22 situation:[109] women may only refuse consent if they are competent, but refusal signifies lack of competence and may therefore be overridden. Furthermore, assessing capacity to consent to medical treatment differs from other capacity assessments since the assessor may also be the person proposing the treatment.[110] With all this flexibility, and power, doctors would do well to heed the advice of Flagler and colleagues[111] that 'care must be taken not to question the competence of the woman merely because she does not concur with one's recommendations'. They point out that the most common reason for rejecting medical advice is not incompetence but fear of the unknown. Other possible reasons include past experience and a lack of trust in the medical profession,[112] factors whose influence has hardly been reduced by the climate of suspicion following those cases that have come to court.

Lastly, judicial rationale in most forced Caesarean cases fails directly to address relevant policy issues (see Chapter 6). As Maclean comments:

> '[I]t is clear that the issue of competence is so flexible as to allow the Courts, or indeed the doctors who, in effect, will generally be responsible for deciding the issue, to determine it in the way that they feel is easiest on their conscience'.[113]

And further:

> 'Whether or not you believe that women's rights should take precedence over foetal rights, salving the doctor's and judge's conscience by using a conveniently flexible standard of competence cannot be right'.[114]

Notes

1 *Fosmire v Nicoleau* 551 N.Y.S.2d 879 (NY 1990).
2 *Norwood Hosp v Munoz* 564 N.E.2d 1017 Mass.,1991, at 1018-19 (my italics).
3 *Pennsylvania Act No. 24* of 1992.
4 Information from Partnership For Caring: ww.partnershipforcaring.org.
5 Miles SH, August A. 'Courts, Gender and "The Right to Die."' *Law, Medicine and Health Care* 1990; 18: 85-95.

6 Partnership For Caring. *Women and End-of-Life Decisions*. February 2001. ww.partnershipforcaring.org.

7 *Patient Self-Determination Act* [1990] 42 U.S.C. 1395 cc(a) (1990).

8 *Roe v Wade*, 410 U.S. 113, 158 (1973).

9 Esposito MA, DeLony R, Goldstein PJ. 'Postmortem cesarean section with infant survival: a case report of an HIV-infected patient.' *Md Med J* 1997;46(9):467-70.

10 Goldman SM, Wagner LK. 'Radiologic ABCs of Maternal and Fetal Survival after Trauma: When Minutes May Count.' *Radiographics* 1999;19:1349-1357.

11 *In re AC* 573 A.2d 1235 (DC Ct App 1990).

12 *In re AC* 573 A.2d 1235 (DC Ct App 1990).

13 Tuohey JF. 'Terminal care and the pregnant woman: ethical reflections on In Re: A.C.' *Pediatrics* 1991;88(6):1268-73.

14 Loewy EH. 'The pregnant brain dead and the fetus: must we always try to wrest life from death?' *Am J Obstet Gynecol* 1987; 157: 1097-101.

15 Lyon, Deborah MD. 'Perimortem Cesarean Delivery.' *E-medicine*, last updated October 6, 2004. http://www.emedicine.com/med/topic3398.htm.

16 Lane A, Westbrook A, Grady D *et al.* 'Maternal brain death: medical, ethical and legal issues.' *Intensive Care Med* 2004;30(7):1484-6.

17 Loewy EH, *op cit.*

18 Dillon WP, Lee RV, Tronolone MJ, *et al*: 'Life support and maternal death during pregnancy.' *JAMA* 1982; 248: 1089-91.

19 Sampson MB, Petersen LP. 'Post-traumatic coma during pregnancy.' *Obstet Gynecol* 1979 Mar;53(3 Suppl):2S-3S.

20 Heikkinen JE, Rinne RI, Alahuhta SM *et al.* 'Life support for 10 weeks with successful fetal outcome after fatal maternal brain damage.' *Br Med J* 1985;290:1237-8.

21 Powner DJ, Bernstein IM. 'Extended somatic support for pregnant women after brain death.' *Crit Care Med* 2003;31(4):1241-9.

22 Hnat MD, Sibai BM, Kovilam O. 'An initial Glasgow score of 4 and Apgar scores of 9 and 9: a case report of a pregnant comatose woman.' *Am J Obstet Gynecol* 2003;189(3):877-9.

23 Sheikh AA, Cusack DA. 'Maternal brain death, pregnancy and the foetus: the medico-legal implications for Ireland.' *Med Law* 2004;23(2):237-50.

24 Anon. 'Order in the Piazzi case. Georgia. Superior Court, Richmond County.' *Issues Law Med* 1987;2(5):415-8.

25 Louis JM, Ehrenberg HM, Collin MF, Mercer BM. 'Perinatal intervention and neonatal outcomes near the limit of viability.' *Am J Obstet Gynecol* 2004;191(4):1398-402.

26 Peerzada JM, Richardson DK, Burns JP. 'Delivery room decision-making at the threshold of viability.' *J Pediatr* 2004;145(4):492-8.

27 Tuohey JF, *op cit.*

28 Loewy EH, *op cit.*

29 Deborah Lyon, MD, *op cit.*

30 Lane A, Westbrook A, Grady D *et al*, *op cit.*

31 Finnerty JF, Fuerst CW, Karns LB, Pinkerton JV. 'End-of-life discussions for the primary care obstetrician/gynecologist.' *Am J Obstet Gynecol* 2002;187(2):296-301.

32 Gessert CE, Forbes S, Bern-Klug M. 'Planning end-of-life care for patients with dementia: Roles of families and health professionals.' *J Death Dying* 2000-2001;42(4):273-291.

33 *In re S* (1992) ILR 14.10.92:TLR 16.10.92 3 WLR 806:4 AER 671; (1993) 4 Med LR 28 [Lawtel].

34 Thorpe MA. 'Consent for Caesarean Section: Part 1 – development of the law.' *Clinical Risk* 2000;5:173-176.

35 Thorpe MA, *ibid*.

36 *Norfolk and Norwich Healthcare (NHS) Trust v W* (1996) 2 FLR 613 [Lawtel].

37 *Rochdale Healthcare (NHS) Trust v C* (1996) LTL 12/7/96 [Lawtel].

38 *Re MB (Caesarean section)* [1997] 8 Med LR 217.

39 A reference to: *Re JT (Adult: Refusal of Medical Treatment)* [1998] 1 FLR 48.

40 *In the matter of an application for judicial review: Queen v Louize Collins ; Pathfinder Mental Health Services Trust and St George's Healthcare NHS Trust, ex parte 'S'* [1998] EWHC Admin 490 (7th May, 1998), at 75 (my italics).

41 Maclean, Alasdair R. 'Caesarean Sections, Competence and the Illusion of Autonomy.' *Web Journal of Current Legal Issues* (1999) 1 Web JCLI , 1/2/99 [Lawtel].

42 *In Re L* (1996) LTL 18/12/96 : TLR 1/1/97 : ILR 10/2/97 : (1997) 2 FLR 837 [Lawtel].

43 Horner, Prof Stuart, quoted in: Hall, Celia. 'Judge forces mother to be injected to save baby.' *Daily Telegraph,* 14 December 1996.

44 *Re MB (Caesarean section)* [1997] 8 Med LR 217.

45 *Re MB (Caesarean section)* [1997] LTL 26/3/97 : ILR 8/4/97 : TLR 18/4/97 : (1997) 2 FLR 426 : (1997) FCR 541 : (1998) 38 BMLR 175.

46 Sabine Michalowski. 'Court-authorised Caesarean Sections – The end of a trend?' 1999 *MLR* 62 (No.1), pp 115-127 [Lawtel].

47 *Re MB* [1997] EWCA Civ 1361.

48 Hewson B. 'How to escape the surgeon's knife'. *New Law Journal* 23 May 1997, at p 752.

49 Mason JK, McCall Smith RA. *Law and Medical Ethics*. Butterworths London 1999 at p139.

50 *Tameside and Glossop Acute Services Trust v CH (a patient)* (1996) ILR 26/2/96 : (1996) 1 FLR 762 [Lawtel].

51 Goldbeck-Wood S. 'Women's autonomy in childbirth: We may advise and persuade, but never coerce', *BMJ* 1997; 314: 1143 (Editorial).

52 Full title: *St George's Healthcare National Health Service Trust v S (No. 2)* (1998): *R v (1) Louize Collins (2) Pathfinder Mental Health Services Trust (3) St George's Healthcare NHS Trust, ex parte S (No.2)* (1998) LTL 7/5/98 : TLR 8/5/98 : ILR 12/5/98 : (1998) 2 FLR 728 [Lawtel].

53 *Queen v Louize Collins ; Pathfinder Mental Health Services Trust and St George's Healthcare NHS Trust, ex parte MS* [1997] EWCA Civ 2020 (3rd July, 1997).

54 *In the matter of an application for judicial review: Queen v Louize Collins ; Pathfinder Mental Health Services Trust and St George's Healthcare NHS Trust, ex parte 'S'* [1998] EWHC Admin 490 (7th May, 1998), at 92.

55 *Ibid*, at 12.

56 *Ibid*, at 92.

57 *Ibid*, at 18.

58 *Ibid*, at 22.

59 *Queen v Louize Collins & Ors, op cit*, at 10.

60 *In the matter of an application for judicial review: Queen v Louize Collins & Ors, op cit*, at 26.

61 *Ibid*, at 89.

62 *Ibid*, at 103.

63 The original solicitor had taken almost two months to request the medical records and the hospital trust responsible for the psychiatric hospital – having refused to comply until payment had been received – had taken nearly a further two months to produce an incomplete set, omitting the vital section 2 admission documents. Two further months elapsed before a complete set of records was eventually obtained: *Queen v Louize Collins & Ors, op cit,* at 14.

64 *Queen v Louize Collins & Ors, op cit,* at 25.

65 *In the matter of an application for judicial review: Queen v Louize Collins & Ors, op cit.*

66 *Ibid,* at 117.

67 *Ibid,* at 122.

68 *Ibid,* at 76.

69 *Ibid,* at 122.

70 Goss, Roger M. 'In whose best interests is it anyway?' *BMJ* Electronic responses to: Oates L. 'The courts' role in decisions about medical treatment.' BMJ 2000; 321: 1282-1284. www.bmj.com 26 November 2000 (letter).

71 Mason JK, McCall Smith RA. *Law and Medical Ethics.* Butterworths London 1999, at p267.

72 Mason JK, McCall Smith RA. *Ibid,* at p266-7.

73 Mason JK, McCall Smith RA. *Ibid,* at p269.

74 Mason JK, McCall Smith RA. *Ibid,* at p269.

75 Mukherjee S, Shah A. 'Capacity to consent: issues and controversies.' *Hosp Med* 2001; 62(6): 351-4.

76 *Re C* [1994] 1 FLR 31.

77 Beauchamp TL, Childress JF. *Principles of Biomedical Ethics.* Oxford University Press, New York 1994, 4th edition, at 135.

78 *Re Martin* (1993) 504 NW 2d 917 at 924.

79 *Health Care Directive Act* 1992, s2.

80 Per Lord Donaldson: *In Re T (Adult: Refusal of Treatment)* [1993], *op cit.*

81 *In Re T (adult – refusal of medical treatment)* [1992] 3 WLR 782.

82 *In Re F (Sterilisation: Mental Patient)* [1989] 2 Fam 376.

83 Kelly GD, Blunt C, Moore PA, Lewis M. 'Consent for regional anaesthesia in the United Kingdom: what is material risk?' *Int J Obstet Anesth* 2004;13:71-4.

84 Plaat F, McGlennan A. 'Women in the 21st century deserve more information: disclosure of material risk in obstetric anaesthesia.' *Int J Obstet Anesth* 2004;13:69-70.

85 Akkad A, Jackson C, Kenyon S *et al.* 'Informed consent for elective and emergency surgery: questionnaire study.' *Br J Obstet Gynaecol* 2004 Oct;111(10):1133-8.

86 Murphy DJ, Pope C, Frost J, Liebling RE. 'Women's views on the impact of operative delivery in the second stage of labour: qualitative interview study.' *BMJ* 2003; 327:1132-35.

87 *In the Matter of Alice Hughes* (1992) 611 A 2d 1148 (NJ SC App Div).

88 *In the matter of an application for judicial review: Queen v Louize Collins & Ors, op cit,* at 75.

89 *In Re T (Adult: Refusal of Treatment)* [1993] Fam 95 at 116.

90 *Guidance for Doctors and Lawyers on the Assessment of Mental Capacity.* London: Law Society and BMJ Publishing, 1995 at p68.

91 Thorpe MA. 'Consent for Caesarean Section: Part 2 – autonomy, capacity, best interests, reasonable force and procedural guidelines.' *Clinical Risk* 2000;5:209-212.

92 *Re MB* [1997] EWCA Civ 1361 (26th March, 1997).

93 Alasdair R Maclean. 'Caesarean Sections, Competence and the Illusion of Autonomy.' *Web Journal of Current Legal Issues* (1999) 1 Web JCLI , 1/2/99 [Lawtel].

94 Wicclair, MR (1991). 'Patient Decision-Making Capacity and Risk.' 5 Bioethics 91, cited in: Alasdair R Maclean, *op cit.*

95 Alasdair R Maclean. *op cit.*

96 Alasdair R Maclean. *Ibid.*

97 Alasdair R Maclean *Ibid.*

98 Mason JK, McCall Smith RA. *Ibid,* at p264.

99 Coverdale JH, McCullough LB, Chervenak FA et al. 'Clinical implications of respect for autonomy in the psychiatric treatment of pregnant patients with depression.' *Psychiatr Serv* 1997; 48(2): 209-12.

100 *Guidance for Doctors and Lawyers on the Assessment of Mental Capacity.* London: Law Society and BMJ Publishing, 1995, at p93 (my italics).

101 Pajulo M, Savonlahti E, Sourander A, Helenius H, Piha J. 'Antenatal depression, substance dependency and social support.' *J Affect Disord* 2001 Jun; 65(1):9-17.

102 Spinelli MG. 'Antepartum and postpartum depression'. *J Gend Specif Med* 1998; 1(2):33-6.

103 Kelly R, Zatzick D, Anders T. 'The detection and treatment of psychiatric disorders and substance use among pregnant women cared for in obstetrics.' *Am J Psychiat* 2001; 158(2): 213-9.

104 As laid down in *Re C (Adult: Refusal of treatment)* [1994] 1 WLR 290.

105 *Guidance for Doctors and Lawyers on the Assessment of Mental Capacity.* London: Law Society and BMJ Publishing, 1995, at p86.

106 Smith S. 'The role of the court in ethical decision making'. *Clin Med* 2001; 1(5): 371-3.

107 Burrows J. 'The parturient woman: can there be room for more than "one person with full and equal rights inside a single human skin"'? *J Adv Nurs* 2001;33(5):689-95.

108 Maclean, Alasdair R. *op cit.*

109 Hewson B. 'Could the High Court order you to have an operation?' (1998) 115 *Living Marxism* 24.

110 *Guidance for Doctors and Lawyers on the Assessment of Mental Capacity.* London: Law Society and BMJ Publishing, 1995, at p65-6.

111 Flagler E, Baylis F, Rodgers S. 'Bioethics for clinicians: 12. Ethical dilemmas that arise in the care of pregnant women: rethinking "maternal-fetal conflicts"'. *Canadian Med Assoc J* 1997;156:1729-32.

112 Brock DW, Wartman SA. 'When competent patients make irrational choices.' *N Engl J Med* 1990;322:1595-9.

113 Maclean, Alasdair R. *op cit.*

114 Maclean, Alasdair R. *Ibid.*

Chapter 5

Questioning Child Welfare – Protection or Punishment?

The previous chapter assessed the possibility that undermining capacity and flexibility in competency assessments could allow an alternative route for overriding refusals of consent to treatment by pregnant women. A further potential avenue for promoting compliance and 'good behaviour' in pregnancy – either directly or via a policy of 'pour encourager les autres'[1] – is that of questioning child welfare.

Ever since the first reported forced Caesarean, in Colorado in 1979, was justified on the basis of saving the life of a foetus found to be 'dependent and neglected',[2] the American courts have frequently used foetal welfare concerns as a mechanism to deal with obstetric conflict.

Often, the court has gone so far as to appoint a guardian for the foetus, enabling officials also to take custody of the mother – thereby demonstrating the absolute efficiency of such an order in achieving obstetric compliance (see also Chapter 2). For example, in *In re Brown*, the trial court had appointed the public guardian of Cook County to represent the foetus, an action that the appeal court later held in error. Meanwhile however the guardian, whose office was charged solely with protecting the foetus, had little choice but to abide by medical recommendations as to what was best for the foetus and had used this authority to consent to forcible blood transfusions for the (resisting) pregnant woman.[3]

A similar approach spread to Canada. *Re Baby R* concerned a pregnant woman in British Columbia who had refused to undergo a Caesarean section recommended by her doctor because of possible birth complications, whereupon the Superintendent of Family and Child Services ordered the apprehension of the foetus. Meanwhile, the woman consented to operation. Nevertheless, the child was apprehended after birth, and the woman – who had never until then been told of the order – petitioned the British Columbia Supreme Court to cancel the order for apprehension and permanent guardianship over the neonate. The court ruled that the foetus was not a child within the meaning of the relevant *Family and Child Service Act* and therefore could not be apprehended as a child apparently in need of protection. It did, however, note that the Superintendent was free to re-apprehend the child if there was sufficient evidence to warrant doing so.[4]

As such applications must usually utilise existing legal mechanisms, they are generally presented not only in terms of concern for the foetus's well-being but also by way of deeming the pregnant woman guilty of abuse or neglect. So in *Jefferson v Griffin Spalding Memorial Hospital*, the State of Georgia Department of Human Resources petitioned the juvenile court for temporary custody of the 'unborn child', alleging it to be 'a deprived child without proper parental care necessary for his or her physical health.' The court concurred with and repeated this opinion, granting the temporary custody order and giving the Department 'full authority to make all decisions, including consent to the surgical delivery...'[5]

The ultimate implications of such orders, as well as their potential for political manipulation in the service of other causes, are amply illustrated by the somewhat different Florida case of *In re Guardianship of J.D.S.* (2003).[6] Here, JDS was a severely disabled adult with multiple developmental and physical difficulties who was at least six months pregnant as a result of being raped in a state-licensed home – the pregnancy not having been discovered until five months' gestation. She had been declared incompetent (in some reports she was estimated to have the mental capacity of a one-year-old[7]) and a guardian duly appointed, charged with determining what medical care JDS would choose for herself if she were not incapacitated (substituted judgement).

However, supported by the state, one Jennifer Wixtrom – initially apparently with the aim of preventing an abortion – had petitioned to be appointed guardian of JDS's foetus. The circuit court had denied the motion, finding no precedent for the appointment of a guardian for a foetus and citing case law that a foetus was not a person within the meaning of Florida statutes, concluding therefore that appointment of a guardian for a foetus would be a 'clear error'.[8]

Wixtrom appealed, notwithstanding that by this stage JDS's guardian had decided on her behalf, in a plan approved by the court, that she would carry the pregnancy to term. The issue now took on blatant political overtones: Jeb Bush, state governor and Presidential sibling, backed her appeal, submitting an *amicus* brief to the court in support of Wixtrom's guardianship application, as did the State of Florida and Florida Department of Children and Families (DCF). Reproductive rights and disability groups filed briefs opposing.[9]

Wixtron's submission is illuminating. She argued that JDS's psychotropic medications 'may be jeopardizing the welfare of the unborn child;' that future medical procedures, tests and medications could do likewise, and that 'matters such as whether to obtain a sonogram, use of anesthesia for any medical procedure, the type of vitamins, choice of delivery, medications, and other pre-natal "dilemmas" will have a profound impact on the well-being of the unborn child.' These issues, Wixtrom asserted, created a conflict of interest that JDS's court-appointed guardian could not resolve as 'the guardian owes a fiduciary duty to J.D.S., not to the unborn child. . . . To resolve this "dilemma," the Court must appoint a guardian for the unborn child.'[10]

This argument is breathtaking in its implication that a third party – and a non-medically qualified one at that – should be placed in the position, as foetal guardian, of being able to deny the pregnant woman needed medications, or anaesthesia, as well as dictating the type of delivery and other matters. It highlights the profound conflict of interests that the appointment of a foetal guardian may pose, as well as the extreme potential threat to the pregnant woman's well-being. It seems inconceivable that such impositions would even be suggested for any other class of person, adult or not, competent or not; moreover their enforcement would subordinate the rights, status and interests of the woman – a person in being – to those of an entity that is not, under common law, a person at all.

An *amicus* brief opposing the appeal was filed by the Advocacy Center for Persons with Disabilities and the American Association of People with Disabilities. Another brief filed by the American Civil Liberties Union (ACLU), National Organization of Women (NOW) and Center for Reproductive Rights duly pointed out that any such guardian would seek to promote only the interests of the foetus and not those of JDS – a possibility that, they urged 'unquestionably constitutes an unwarranted and unconstitutional intrusion into J.D.S.'s ability to make these decisions'. Although unable to take such decisions on her own, the fact that she needed a guardian to do so did not justify any lesser protection of her constitutional rights – via the guardian, JDS should be entitled to 'the same constitutionally protected choices as a competent woman.'[11]

Fortunately perhaps, while the issue was still awaiting further court determination, JDS successfully gave birth, without the aid or intervention of a foetal guardian. As she was unable to care for a child, the baby girl was placed in foster care with a view to adoption. Although the issue was moot, the court agreed to hear the appeal as an issue of 'great public importance and capable of recurring.' It agreed with the lower court that a guardian could not be appointed for a foetus, one of the judges commenting:

> … taking control of a woman's body and supervising her conduct or lifestyle during pregnancy or forcing her to undergo medical treatment in order to protect the health of the fetus creates its own universe of troubling questions.[12]

The notion of JDS's guardian attempting to safeguard her health and her rights against a foetal guardian is clearly bizarre – which guardian would have precedence? Would the foetus's needs automatically take priority, as seems to have occurred in other cases where guardians have been appointed for the foetuses of competent women, or would there need to be some kind of balancing of rights and interests? Would all differences of opinion unresolved between the guardians need to be presented to a court to resolve? Would the court to be called upon to adjudicate every pre-natal vitamin? If Wixtrom also wished, as she did, to control the exercise that JDS took, how was this to be effected? The application highlights that such claims may be adversarial not necessarily because of inherent conflict between the pregnant woman and her foetus but, again, because of conflict with those who think they know best, and who have scant regard, in comparison, for the woman's well-being, much less her autonomy. The issue is one of power.

Pitting Mother against Foetus

As well as appointing foetal guardians, the American courts have even in some cases, including that of Angela Carder,[13] allowed a separate lawyer to represent the foetus – in the case of JDS's foetus, reports claimed that lawyers were sent personally by Governor Jeb Bush.[14] Such acts not only further imply a degree of personhood to the foetus, but also serve a similar purpose in underlining the messages that the woman and her foetus are adversaries, and that the potential mother is someone against whose choices and actions the potential child needs representation. Nowhere is this clearer than in the case of Amber Marlowe, discussed in Chapter 2, who successfully gave birth without knowledge that a hospital she had left against medical advice had, in her absence, obtained a court order giving it guardianship of her foetus and authority to perform a forced Caesarean. The hospital made its complaint in its own name and that of her foetus (as 'Baby Doe'),[15] thereby making the foetus party to a groundless suit against its parents before it was even born.

Such a view of mother and foetus as adversaries of course finds especial appeal in the case of women who use drugs during pregnancy – and it is sometimes hard to avoid the conclusion that those women likely to be viewed by the public as least deserving of sympathy are most likely to be singled out for such actions when media attention is likely. As discussed in Chapter 3, positive drug tests during pregnancy or at birth have frequently been used in the US to remove children from substance-using mothers,[16] or sometimes to subject such women to prenatal seizure or even to impose criminal penalties. These actions often relied upon stretching the wording of existing child abuse and neglect statutes to include foetuses; in other cases, existing statutes have been amended or specific statutes created to enable interventions based on the notion of foetal abuse, mostly, but not always, related to drug intake. The range of statutes used in this way have included those concerning criminal child support, child abuse or neglect, contributing to the delinquency of a minor, causing the dependency of a child, child endangerment, delivery of drugs to a minor, drug possession, assault with a deadly weapon, manslaughter, homicide, and vehicular homicide.[17] As discussed, there is evidence that such policies are based on less-than-firm evidence; may not be even in the best interests of the mother or child in individual cases, and have profoundly detrimental effects on health care for women and children overall. As with forced Caesareans, penalties applied to women who use drugs in pregnancy have been used disproportionately against African-American women.[18] Conflict based on behavioural choices begins to sound very similar to that based on disagreement with medical recommendations.

Drug-related actions, too, have tended to be initiated by local medical staff – here working in tandem with local child welfare officials or, in the case of criminal charges, with police and local prosecutors – notwithstanding all the major professional associations urging moderation. Criminal sanctions are opposed by all professional bodies that have commented on the issue (*vide infra*) – even the National Right to Life Committee, the main anti-abortion group in the US, is against criminalizing pregnant women[19] (though not necessarily against their detention in the interests of 'foetal well-being').

The actions may also be seen to have a political hue as part of America's hugely expensive and, many would argue, largely ineffective 'war on drugs'. South Carolina has been a prime mover in the application of this 'war' to pregnant women, due in large part to a determined effort on the part of then Charleston solicitor Charlie Condon, who initiated a series of prosecutions against cocaine-using pregnant women in Charleston in the late 1980s, when crack cocaine was hitting the headlines and the media filled with stories of 'crack babies' and cries for sanctions against drug-using pregnant women. The initiative in Charleston saw numerous pregnant women drug-tested without consent, with the results reported to the police, until the policy was eventually ruled unconstitutional (see Chapter 3). However Condon – a 'right-to-life Republican' who at the time of writing is now running for the US Senate[20] – continued the drive state-wide when he became South Carolina Attorney General in 1995.[21] It represented an expansion of legal action from supposedly protective measures for foetuses to outwardly punitive measures for mothers, a move that many states have tried to copy. Surreptitious drug-testing may have been ruled out, but the possibility of arrest remains: South Carolina has prosecuted more women for behaviour that may harm the foetus than any other state, and in the last 15 years more than 100 women in South Carolina have been charged with criminal offences for using cocaine while pregnant.[22,23]

In one of the earliest cases, in 1991, Malissa Ann Crawley, who had given birth earlier that month, was charged under a South Carolina statute with 'unlawful neglect of a child,' on the grounds that she had taken cocaine or crack cocaine while pregnant, thereby endangering her foetus. Even though her son had been born perfectly healthy, she was sentenced to five years in prison. Initially Crawley's sentence was suspended, placing her on probation for five years, and she did not appeal. However in 1994 she was charged with criminal domestic violence; her probation was revoked and her sentence reinstated. She then petitioned for a writ of *habeas corpus*, supported by a wide range of *amici curiae* including the American College of Obstetricians and Gynecologists, American Public Health Association, National Association of Social Workers and several other prominent organisations. After a prolonged course through various state and federal courts up to the United States Supreme Court,[24] during which argument largely concerned procedural grounds as to whether Crawley was time-barred under a recent anti-terrorism measure, ultimately reinstatement of her sentence was upheld and the judgment dismissing her appeal affirmed.[25]

As to the merits of her argument that child endangerment does not extend to a foetus, the South Carolina Supreme Court had held the state's appeal in abeyance until it resolved the appeal of another case raising the same issues as to whether a viable foetus is a 'child' within the meaning of the relevant child abuse and endangerment statute.

Expanding the Range of Unlawful Prenatal Conduct

This case was that of Cornelia Whitner, who in 1992 had been charged with unlawful child neglect and sentenced to eight years in prison for using crack cocaine while pregnant – based on a positive drug-screen while she was pregnant and a single positive test of her neonate for a cocaine byproduct. Whitner pleaded guilty and did not appeal, but later petitioned the court arguing that the plea should not have been accepted on a non-existent charge, and that her court-appointed lawyer had failed to advise her that the charges might not apply to pre-natal drug use. Her lawyers argued that if the word 'child' was interpreted to include the viable foetus, then 'every action by a pregnant woman that endangers ... a fetus ... legal or illegal would constitute unlawful neglect. ... A woman might be prosecuted for smoking or drinking'.[26] Nevertheless, in 1997, the Supreme Court of South Carolina upheld her sentence, ruling that the state had a compelling interest in ensuring the life and health of a viable foetus, and that a viable foetus is a child within the meaning of the state's child endangerment statute. Two judges dissented, one on the grounds that the term 'child' in the endangerment statute did not apply to a foetus, and one on the basis that the statute did not regulate the conduct of a pregnant woman towards her foetus.[27]

The verdict in *Whitner v State* was the first time that a state supreme court had determined that pregnant women could be prosecuted under child abuse laws for actions that may endanger the foetus. It left a potentially broad scope for such actions in noting that although the precise effects of maternal crack use during pregnancy are somewhat unclear, it is well documented and *within the realm of public knowledge* that such use can cause serious harm to the viable unborn child. This implies that if she ingests any substance known to cause possible harm – which could include smoking, alcohol or even aspirin – the woman could be held liable for any damage ensuing. Several such cases have indeed been reported. In New Jersey one woman was charged with neglect for using codeine for pain relief during labour, while another was threatened with losing custody of her baby for following a drug treatment programme using medically prescribed methadone; in Kentucky, a woman was charged with criminal child abuse after taking OxyContin, a painkiller, during pregnancy – the judge dismissed the charges, but expressed regret that the law did not cover her situation.[28]

The Whitner case was appealed to the United States Supreme Court, again supported by an *amicus* brief filed by leading medical and public health organisations, including the American College of Obstetricians and Gynecologists, the American Nurses Association, and the American Medical Women's Association, stating that the verdict posed a real threat to the health and well-being of women and their families by serving to drive pregnant women away from medical, substance abuse, counselling, pre-natal, and other necessary care. Nevertheless, the US Supreme Court refused to overturn the decision.[29]

According to the Drug Policy Alliance, the impact on the health and well-being of women and children in South Carolina has been 'devastating,' enabling further such arrests and prosecutions of pregnant women suffering from drug or alcohol dependence.[30] It has been reported that at least three drug treatment programs in South Carolina (which spends less on drug and alcohol treatment programs than any other state in the nation, according to the Drug Policy Alliance)[31] have seen a drop in the number of pregnant women admitted, and substance abuse experts expressed fears that drug-using women were avoiding pre-natal care, electing to have their babies at home or travelling to North Carolina to avoid punitive actions in South Carolina.[32]

The latter at least may not avail them much. In one case reported from North Carolina, a former 'crack' addict who had been 'clean' since before she became pregnant had a single relapse just before her baby was due, after quitting anti-depressant medication two months earlier because she did not want the drugs to affect the foetus. She made the mistake of confessing this lapse to her midwife, explaining that she needed help. Instead, when she went into labour, the midwife told hospital staff who promptly tested the newborn baby girl and called the police when the test was positive. Even though the baby was totally healthy, the new mother was charged with felonious child abuse, carrying a possible three-year prison sentence.[33]

The Whitner decision also paved the way for South Carolina to become the setting for the first murder charge against an American woman for using cocaine in pregnancy. Regina McKnight gave birth to a five-pound, stillborn baby in South Carolina in 1999. An autopsy revealed evidence of cocaine in the baby's system, and McKnight was charged with homicide by child abuse, based on the *Whitner* ruling that allowed the state's child abuse laws to embrace a viable foetus. Even though the state could not prove that her cocaine use actually caused the stillbirth – indeed, despite the lack of evidence linking cocaine use to stillbirth in general – in 2001 she was convicted and sentenced to 12 to 20 years imprisonment.

Following this extraordinary verdict, McKnight's appeal to the South Carolina Supreme Court was, again, supported by an *amicus* brief submitted by an impressive range of medical and drug policy groups, including the South Carolina Medical Association. This brief offered extensive medical and scientific evidence that McKnight's cocaine use did not cause her stillbirth, and that the prosecution of such cases jeopardizes maternal and foetal health by deterring women from seeking pre-natal care. However, in 2003 the South Carolina Supreme Court affirmed the lower court's decision.

McKnight then petitioned the United States Supreme Court, and was supported by a further *amicus* brief on behalf of 27 organisations including the American Public Health Association, the National Stillbirth Society, American Nurses Association, the American Psychiatric Association and the American Society of Addiction Medicine. This argued that the prosecution makes thousands of women suffering a stillbirth in South Carolina vulnerable to homicide charges if they engage in any conduct during their pregnancy believed to be harmful to the foetus – whether or not that conduct is illegal – and that conviction will deter women from accessing necessary health care services. Moreover, the brief again pointed out that there was no causal link between McKnight's cocaine use and the stillbirth, concluding rather that:

> ...this was an irrational prosecution based largely on the drug hysteria that has historically driven South Carolina's policies towards pregnant women who use drugs.[34]

Notwithstanding this resounding condemnation, the United States Supreme Court declined to review the case, allowing the conviction to stand by default. At the time of writing, McKnight remains in prison.[35,36]

The 'success' of the McKnight prosecution has, inevitably, encouraged others. It was reported that in January 2004 South Carolina prosecutors were to attempt a second murder prosecution against an African-American woman who allegedly smoked cocaine during pregnancy. The woman had a stillbirth five years previously,[37] raising an awesome prospect of retroactive suits against women in South Carolina who have suffered adverse pregnancy outcomes in recent times, should there have been any cause for concern about their behaviour during pregnancy.

Stillbirth affects nearly one per cent of all births in the US.[38]

Equally inevitably perhaps, like-minded public health officials and prosecutors in other states have attempted to follow South Carolina's lead. Again, much may hinge on whether the word 'child' can be expanded to incorporate the concept of a foetus. *State v. Kruzicki*, which reached the Wisconsin Supreme Court in 1997, concerned a pregnant woman dubbed 'Angela' by the media, whose blood tests at 36 weeks of pregnancy had shown drug use. The county took protective custody of the foetus on the grounds that continued use of drugs would cause it serious harm, and sought and obtained a court order requiring the woman to be confined to an inpatient drug treatment facility. She was not, however, charged with any offence. She appealed, seeking release from detention and protective custody, but the appellate court denied the appeal. After the birth, the Wisconsin Supreme Court considered the issue – again, although now moot, on the grounds of its importance – and reversed the appellate court's decision concluding, by a majority, that Wisconsin state law defined a 'child' as one born alive, and that this did not cover a foetus (the dissenting judge argued that both 'child' and 'person' could include a foetus).[39] However, 'Angela' lost custody of her baby after birth and he was subsequently adopted.[40]

This and the subsequent case of Deborah Zimmerman, in which the Wisconsin Supreme Court similarly rejected attempts by prosecutors to charge a pregnant woman with homicide for allegedly trying to drink her foetus to death in 1996, garnered a great deal of publicity. Shortly afterwards, the Wisconsin State Legislature drafted a new law allowing the foetus to be taken into protective custody – effectively detaining the pregnant woman – in the later states of pregnancy, where needed to protect the health of the foetus because of the woman's 'habitual lack of self control' in her use of alcohol or other drugs.[41] The law, which was prominently supported by pro-life members, does not allow for criminal child abuse charges related to behaviour in pregnancy, as the intention is to ensure that the pregnant woman gets treatment. However, in cases where the law has been used, the baby has often been removed from the mother's custody after birth.[42]

An inventive attempt to transform legal pre-natal conduct into a post-natal offence occurred with the arrest of Stacey Gilligan in New York State in September 2003. Gilligan had given birth to a baby boy who allegedly tested positive for blood alcohol. A few days later, she was arrested and charged with two counts of endangering the welfare of a child on the grounds that, at the time of the birth, she 'knowingly fed her blood', containing alcohol, to the baby via the umbilical cord. The baby was removed from her custody.

New York has an established history of refusing to recognise new crimes of endangerment during pregnancy. As early as 1988, in *Matter of Fletcher*, a New York family court held that a pregnant woman's drug use could not alone serve as the basis for finding child neglect – such facts had to be alleged with respect to the mother's neglect *after* the birth of the child.[43] This conclusion was re-iterated in a similar case in 1995.[44] In *People v Morabito* (1992), the court refused to interpret an existing child endangerment statute as applying to allegations of drug use during pregnancy.[45]

In response to Gilligan's arrest, more than fifty leading medical, public health, child welfare and family justice experts and organisations sent an open letter to the District Attorney's office, opposing the prosecution and stating that the arrest sent a dangerous message that seeking pre- and post-natal care can lead to criminal sanctions. The American Public Health Association, National Council on Alcoholism and Drug Dependence and the National Coalition for Child Protection Reform also filed an *amicus* brief asking that the prosecution be dismissed because it violated both New York law and well-established consensus in the medical community that such prosecutions are irrational, ineffective and counterproductive.

Following previous case law, in April 2004 the city court judge dismissed the charges against Gilligan, ruling them to be 'without legal basis.' Agreeing with the decision in *People v Morabito*, the court stated that the state's child endangerment law was not intended to apply to foetuses and furthermore:

> … public policy and due process considerations militate against the prosecutions of mothers for transfer of drugs through the umbilical cord for that brief instant before the mother and the newborn are separated.[46]

In other states, a brief breastfeed may however be sufficient. After the McKnight conviction was allowed to stand, prosecutors in Hawaii in 2001 charged Tayshea Aiwohi with manslaughter, based on her alleged use of crystal methamphetamine ('ice') during pregnancy and after the birth of her son, who died at two days. A reckless manslaughter charge based on pre-natal behaviour was possible under the law in Hawaii because the child was born alive, and there is no immunity for actions of the mother: the state conceded that no manslaughter charge would otherwise have existed.[47] However, here there was the additional twist that the medical examiner's evidence suggested that the drug could have been introduced either before or after birth, such as via breast milk. Aiwohi had five other, healthy children, and had been allowed to nurse her baby and take it home, following evaluation by Child Protective Services, even though the infant had tested positive for methamphetamine after the birth.[48] Aiwohi had taken 'ice' in the days before birth and after returning home with the baby. The morning after the child went home, he was found dead. Aiwohi stated that she had breastfed twice during the night.

After participating in 'intensive drug treatment and parenting education',

Aiwohi – who otherwise had a stable family situation – was given 10 years' probation and put on notice that the sentence would revert to 20 years' jail if she did not comply with the probation terms. The judge, while noting that it was rare for a homicide case not to involve additional jail time, gave clear notice of future prosecutions:

> ... unless the appellate courts rule otherwise, every person in the State of Hawaii should be on clear notice that the use of crystal methamphetamine while pregnant can result in death or serious injury to children born alive... drug usage, including the use of crystal methamphetamine is a matter of choice and not an illness. Certainly it is a conscious choice to obtain and use the drug initially and worse yet, while pregnant... Why anyone would use the drug knowing they are carrying a child is baffling to most people... In this regard the State, with good reason, has served clear notice that such conduct can and will result in serious felony charges brought where the child is born alive and later dies or suffers injury due to knowing, intentional or reckless drug use.[49]

It is also worth noting that in considering whether to allow manslaughter charges against the mother based on pre-natal conduct – the first time such charges had been brought in Hawaii – the court commented:

> What is particularly convincing to this Court is that in other states, third parties have been charged criminally and found culpable for conduct resulting in the injury or death of a born alive infant, even though the conduct was prenatal. The State persuasively contends that the law should treat a mother's acts the same as [those of] a third party...[50]

Thus, as many commentators warned could happen, foetal homicide laws had an impact, even if only persuasive, on foetal abuse charges being brought against a pregnant woman.

The other obvious impact of the Aiwohi case is the possibility of setting a precedent for actions against breastfeeding mothers as well as pregnant women – suppose, for example, an HIV-positive woman breastfed her child against medical advice? When the original charges were made against Aiwohi, prosecutors were also reported as saying that they will now consider prosecutions of women in Hawaii who abuse alcohol, as well as of so-called 'meth moms' (meth is another abbreviation for methamphetamine), whether or not their foetuses survive.[51] This further demonstrates the possibility of charges for actions that, outside the state of pregnancy, are perfectly legal.

The case of Julie Starks in Oklahoma dramatically illustrates the potential for punitive action based almost exclusively on the mere fact of pregnancy. At seven months pregnant, Starks was found guilty of endangering her foetus and was sent to prison when a court allowed the state to take custody of her foetus based on their allegation that it was a 'deprived child'. Her offence was merely to have been present in a trailer when police raided it as an illegal drug laboratory making methamphetamine. The prosecutor alleged that she was present in an environment that 'contained vapors and chemicals and other toxic substances that could not have been healthy for her unborn child or herself' – even though tests revealed her to be drug-free. Starks' bail was set at $200,000, whereas the standard sum was usually $25,000. She was in prison for 36 days, supposedly to protect her foetus, and later commented that the cell was overcrowded with limited bathroom facilities and that she was given no milk or pre-natal vitamins for two weeks; she suffered weight loss, dehydration, bladder and urinary tract infections in prison and was eventually rushed to hospital with premature contractions. Notwithstanding, she gave birth to a healthy baby boy weighing over eight pounds, who also tested negative for drugs.

Starks' case went to trial two months later, by which time she was out on bail after the sum had been reduced to a more reasonable amount. At first instance, she was found guilty, the court agreeing with the state's allegation that she had 'deprived' her child by being present in the trailer. It took over a year for the charges against her finally to be dismissed on appeal to the Oklahoma Supreme Court, which commented that it was 'nonsensical' to consider a foetus as a child under the state's child deprivation statute.[52]

Is Refusing Medical Advice Grounds for a Murder Charge?

Perhaps inevitably came a case in which a woman was charged with homicide for going against medical advice. In March 2004, Utah prosecutors made headlines around the world when they charged Melissa Ann Rowland with murder after one of the twins she was carrying was stillborn. Prosecutors alleged she was responsible for the death by refusing Caesarean section. Rowland, an acknowledged cocaine addict with mental health problems, made an unsympathetic figure in media reports, especially when her alleged comments on wanting to avoid a Caesarean because she did not want the scar were reported.

In fact, it emerged in later reports – although much less prominently – she had already had two previous Caesareans, and did not refuse one this time – she merely delayed the operation, and both twins, one of whom survived, were delivered by Caesarean. Nevertheless, prosecutors argued that her resistance to earlier surgery had caused the stillbirth and that the dead twin, a boy, could have been saved had the Caesarean been performed sooner. She was sent to prison the day after her Caesarean was carried out.

As evidence emerged of her long-standing mental health problems, prosecutors decided to drop the murder charge and instead substituted two counts of child endangerment, based on her drug use while pregnant, to which Rowland pleaded guilty.

In court the district judge, placing her on probation for 18 months and ordering that she attend a drug treatment programme, aptly commented that it was a travesty that the system has no better way of dealing with people like Rowland, and that she had repeatedly 'fallen through the cracks'. He denied the prosecution's request that she be barred from contacting the surviving twin, a girl, who had been adopted shortly after birth.[53]

Rowland was indeed failed by both medical and legal systems, on many counts. Details of her medical history were well-publicised, making a mockery of medical confidentiality. She was pilloried in the world's press for allegedly refusing the operation for reasons of vanity – making her appear shallow, selfish and irresponsible as well as 'mad' (mental health problems) and 'bad' (drug-taking) – although, for those who took the trouble to listen, she was reported as saying from her prison cell: 'I've never refused a C-section. I've already had two prior C-sections.'[54]

The prosecutors did not suggest that they were dropping the murder charge because it was wrong to criminalise a perfectly legal choice to demur in the face of medical advice; nor because such recommendations can never be founded on certainty and predictions can be wrong; nor even because there was no possibility of proving, to criminal standards, that delaying the Caesarean was indeed the cause of the stillbirth. Rather, they reduced the charge to child endangerment because of Rowland's mental health history, which – even aside from the civil liberties aspect – ought to have precluded the murder charge in the first place. Even the substituted endangerment charges were arguably inappropriate, given that in Utah, as most states, the law on drug use in pregnancy provides for public health and child welfare interventions but not criminal sanctions.

Clearly, Rowland needed help, as should have been apparent to the prosecutors and especially, and ideally at a much earlier stage, to the doctors treating her. If there was any possibility that her capacity to consent to, or refuse, medical treatment was impaired, physicians should have proceeded along appropriate routes to determine her competency and best interests. In any event, awaiting the sanctimony of hindsight and then resorting to calling in state prosecutors must rank as the least constructive and least appropriate option for dealing with obstetric conflict.

Given the inaccuracy of predictions of foetal harm, the incidence of handicap among premature babies and the dramatic difference that a few extra days in the womb may make, it is even possible that Rowland's delaying tactic had potential benefits – as it was, the surviving girl was born with complications. Johnson has argued that the medical establishment cannot predict the best course of action for a foetus in distress, that the risk of disability after premature delivery is high and that many babies who survive birth do not make it through their first year: Rowland 'may have made the right decision. At least one of her children survived.'[55]

The implications for autonomy of the murder charge against Rowland naturally also raised multiple protests. National Advocates for Pregnant Women (NAPW) said it represented 'a shocking abuse of state authority and a dangerous disregard for medical ethics. Women do not lose their constitutional and human rights as a result of pregnancy.'[56]

Minkoff and Paltrow commented:

> ... if Ms. Rowland is to be judged legally culpable for the death of her fetus, then the courts must first create a new and significant exception to the doctrine of informed consent and the common law and constitutional principles upon which it is based. Such a precedent could introduce a substantial disparity between the rights of pregnant women and those of all other persons.[57]

According to ICAN (International Caesarean Awareness Network) Vice-President Pam Udy, the Rowland case:

> ...ought to scare all of us. It sets a legal precedent that makes doctors into all-knowing authorities or, worse, fortunetellers; and it reduces mothers to uninformed, blind followers or, worse, criminals. Pregnant women already face manipulation by their doctors. Are we also to face coercion by our legal system?[58]

The UK: No Jurisdiction – until Birth

In contrast to the contentious and fluid state of such actions in the US, the position in the UK seems markedly settled and sedate. Under English law, as repeatedly stated, child protection mechanisms cannot be invoked for a foetus *in utero*, effectively ruling out the kind of 'pre-natal seizures' of pregnant women that have occurred in the US. Judicial reluctance to interfere in pregnancy was established in *In Re F (in utero)* (1988),[59] in which the local authority, in an *ex parte* application, attempted to make the foetus a ward of court on the grounds of concern that the pregnant woman, who was stated to be mentally disturbed and leading a 'nomadic existence', would neither take sufficient care nor seek medical attention for the well-being of the child at the time of birth and thereafter. The authority sought orders to authorise finding the woman, restraining her nomadic tendency and ensuring that she attended hospital for the birth of the child.

The Court of Appeal refused, holding (as later did *Re MB*[60]) that it had no jurisdiction over a foetus – until the child was born and had an existence independent of its mother, there was an inherent incompatibility between the exercise of wardship jurisdiction and the rights and welfare of the child: 'The only purpose of extending jurisdiction to include the foetus is to enable the mother's actions to be controlled'.[61]

The only orders a court could make to protect an unborn child would be with regard to the mother, and such a course was deemed incompatible with the woman's liberty, Staighton LJ stating:

> The court can not care for a child or order that others should do so, until the child is born, only the mother can. The orders sought by the local authority are not by their nature such as the court can make in caring for the child, they are orders which seek directly to control the life of both the mother and child.[62]

Nevertheless, at least one of the judges regretted the court's lack of power to exercise such control for the benefit of the foetus,[63] and two suggested that this was a question for Parliament[64] (see Chapter 6). Moreover, wardship was granted upon birth (which had occurred successfully, notwithstanding the local authority's prior concerns). One of the arguments cited in court was that 'notwithstanding *Paton*[65] [*Paton v British Pregnancy Advisory Service Trustees* – the case discussed in Chapter 1 that is authority for there being no legal right invested in an unborn child], there might be no legal obstacle to commencing proceedings and obtaining an order that the child becomes a ward on birth. *This might provide a good method for authorising local authorities to remove a child at birth.*'[66]

Retrospective Assessment

Clearly the threat of removing a child at birth, or of criminal charges, or both, also has considerable potential for ensuring compliance during pregnancy. In the UK criminal action seems unlikely (see Chapter 1); however, there is authority for such post-natal sanction in *In Re D (a minor)* (1987),[67] in which the baby of a woman who had used heroin during pregnancy was taken from her at birth. The mother was stated to have endangered the child's health and development by failing to co-operate with medical advice during pregnancy, and the local authority applied for an order under s1(2) *Children and Young Persons Act 1969*. This provided for a juvenile court to make a care order if (*inter alia*) the child's proper development was being avoidably prevented or neglected, or its health avoidably impaired or neglected *and* the child was in need of care or control.[68] It was not disputed that the latter condition was satisfied; it was the meaning and effect of 'is being avoidably impaired...' that was at issue.

The child had been kept in hospital after birth and placed on the abuse register; she was thereafter discharged to the care of foster parents. Submissions made to the Divisional Court of the Family Division, which it accepted and upheld, included the facts that the only evidence as to the cause of the condition of the child related to events which had taken place before its birth; there had been no opportunity for the mother to care for the baby at all and, accordingly, no conduct on her part which could be said to have avoidably impaired the child's health or prevented her proper development. Therefore, applying a strict construction to the present tense wording of section 1(2)(a), the primary condition to enable the court to proceed to make a care order was not satisfied.

However, on appeal the House of Lords stated that the statute had to be given a broad and liberal construction to give full effect to its purpose; there were compelling reasons for concluding that what was being referred to was a continuing rather than an instant situation, and the Court was justified in looking back to the time before the child was born, when those situations had been caused and the possibility of their avoidance had existed. The court was therefore justified in considering pre-natal circumstances in determining that the child's development was being avoidably impaired or neglected.

Stein has commented that this represents an extension of the concept of maternal-foetal conflict *in retrospect*, evidence for child neglect being back-applied to the time the child was *in utero*, yet: 'there was no cause to believe that the mother would neglect the child in the same way, in the future, by administering drugs to it', making it an example of 'fetal abuse' as applied in the US.[69]

Post-Birth Sanctions as an Alternative to Pre-Birth Seizures?

Indeed, Stein (herself an obstetrician) suggests that there is a continuum from the concept of maternal-foetal conflict – which dangers have already been discussed – to that of foetal abuse; a conceptual slope which 'has proved slippery indeed' and has grave implications both for appropriate health policy and for the proper practice of everyday obstetric medicine. She notes:

> Our legal and medical policies should be formulated more on the basis of sound empirical data and less on the basis of intellectually compelling but unscientifically grounded moral philosophies.[70]

There are no national figures on the number of children taken into care at birth or shortly afterwards,[71] although in the UK a high proportion of care orders relate to children under one year of age[72] (the peak age for physical abuse). Nor is there any specific policy document for local authorities on taking children into care at birth,[73] and most such cases are not reported.[74] However, in discussing the Court's view in *Re F* of situations in which there may be conflict between the child's welfare and the mother's liberty during pregnancy, Mason and McCall Smith note that removing the child at birth is 'the preferred course of action in such cases'.[75]

There is both professional and academic support for a policy of applying post-natal sanctions to compel pre-natal compliance. It has been suggested that in assessing the appropriate response to pre-natal drug exposure:

> ... the postnatal effects of parental substance abuse (e.g., in terms of abuse/neglect, attachment, and development) are the more appropriate focus of child protection efforts.[76]

Robertson too has argued that 'post-birth sanctions' are a sounder health policy than pre-natal seizures.[77] Eekelaar argues that it is justifiable, when a pregnant woman's actions are not thought to be in her foetus's interests, for orders to be made supervising or monitoring her behaviour after the birth, to attempt to ensure (via the threat of later sanctions) that mothers meet their duties to their unborn children.[78]

There are increasing possibilities for these kinds of action. For example, there have been petitions for mandatory dietary adherence during pregnancy in women with phenylketonuria (PKU).[79] In 2001 the Irish Supreme Court rejected a Health Board application to countermand the refusal of parents to have their newborn baby tested for phenylketonuria (PKU).[80,81] The court suggested that the health board was effectively seeking to have the test made compulsory, and that to acquiesce would have 'far reaching effects' and would establish 'a very low threshold for court intervention in future cases involving children'.

However, such stalwart support for parental autonomy may depend on the perceived likelihood of threat to the baby. Already there has been one English case in which a local authority obtained an order for an HIV test to be performed, against the wishes of the parents (who did not accept the accuracy of conventional theories concerning HIV and AIDS), to establish whether or not a neonate had contracted HIV from her mother.[82] The Court held that the presumption that parental views regarding the best interests of the child were correct had been rebutted by the 'overwhelming case' put forward by the local authority. It stated that a positive test could lead to the provision of sound medical advice, whilst a negative test 'must result in an urgent reconsideration by the mother of her decision to breastfeed'. This comment would seem to imply the likelihood of post-natal supervision and, ultimately, the possibility of child removal should the mother not comply. As breastfeeding must generally be established soon after birth, it is also worrying in terms of its potential for retrograde effects, for example, regarding the desired location and supervision for the birth and perinatal period in an HIV-positive pregnant woman. Moreover, all UK women are now heavily recommended to take an HIV test in pregnancy and, as well as avoiding breastfeeding, Caesarean delivery is recommended for women who test positive, to reduce the risk of transmission to the foetus.[83]

In this regard it is noteworthy that in some US states, HIV testing of pregnant women has been made mandatory[84] – although this is now contrary to the policy of the American College of Obstetricians and Gynecologists[85] – and in New York mandatory testing of all newborns is already policy and women 'lose all right to dissent' as soon as the child is delivered.[86] There have already been several instances in the US of pregnant women's decisions on anti-HIV treatment being overruled, as well as cases where parents have been forced to medicate neonates with anti-retroviral drugs. This notwithstanding, anti-retroviral drugs have known risks during pregnancy, and postulated further unknown risks – less than half of all hospitals treating HIV-positive pregnant women report adverse effects to the Antiretroviral Pregnancy Registry – and that it is acknowledged that there is 'limited experience with these agents in the setting of pregnancy'.[87]

In one instance reported from New Jersey, a pregnant woman who had been prescribed the anti-retroviral drug AZT stopped taking it when she experienced extreme side-effects. She wanted to remain lucid during delivery, so took only Tylenol with codeine for pain relief. Police were called to the hospital to remove the baby when it was born, and the state government charged her with child neglect because of her actions, including ingestion of codeine.[88]

Is it Less Contentious to Take the Child After Birth?

Such actions, or the threat of them, clearly have the potential to be effective in achieving pre-natal compliance without the need to resort to formal legal attempts to override a pregnant woman's decision. They may also be less ethically contentious and, invoking as they do emotive areas of child abuse and neglect, may both allow professional judgement more leeway to err on the side of safety and be less likely to be challenged than direct interference with pregnant women's autonomy and liberty.

Moreover, the potential for assessing parental competency (in a child care sense) is wide. As Douglas has pointed out, antenatal care now embraces a degree of 'lifestyle supervision' that implies vetting for social and emotional fitness to parent.[89] As awareness and reporting of child abuse has increased, maternal ability to care for newborns is more often called into question, and it has been recommended that 'future directions should include more involvement by psychiatrists in preventive efforts and interventions that focus on pregnant women at risk in prenatal clinics and in the community'.[90]

This may be representative of a wider trend: as courts maintain the primacy of competent patients' autonomy, questioning competence or child welfare seems to be increasingly common amongst doctors faced with 'recalcitrant' parents. For example, in a recent article for general practitioners on management of a mother refusing immunisations (a perfectly legal option) for her child – the child having presented with an unrelated minor medical problem and being otherwise very healthy, the lack of immunisations being discovered incidentally – two of the three British GPs asked to advise queried the mother's mental health and the third suggested she would assess whether the child was 'at risk.'[91]

Paediatricians have recently compared parental non-compliance with medical advice with physical and sexual abuse (notwithstanding non-compliance being assumed to reflect 'ignorance or misunderstanding of the clinical situation'), and it was suggested that such parents 'may be vulnerable to psychological reactions which inhibit rational thinking'; moreover 'extreme parental non-compliance may represent a special form of child abuse where, due to parental psychopathology, parents are unable to consider the child's best interest'.[92]

As with pregnancy conflicts, the implication of such statements is both that the doctor has a higher claim to knowing, and safeguarding, the child's best interests, and that parental non-compliance with medical advice is symptomatic of some mental or moral disorder. Yet the pejorative tone of some such comments suggests defensiveness as well as hostility and, often, utilises the emotive effect of phrases such as 'child abuse' to attempt to justify actions that may be more concerned with medical control than with child protection. In the 1970s and 1980s, women who wanted to give birth at home were likely to be regarded in both the UK and US as irresponsible, and one President of the American College of Obstetricians and Gynecologists described home birth as 'the earliest form of child abuse'.[93] Most alarmingly, some US couples who achieved home births were indeed so charged, after paediatricians reported them to state authorities.[94] Yet the lack of supporting evidence for the almost universal policy of hospitalised birth at the time[95] finally provoked a change of UK policy.[96]

Nevertheless, in the US the ACLU is still warning that foetal protection statutes could encourage more criminal prosecutions or child abuse or neglect proceedings against women who make childbirth choices of which doctors or judges disapprove, and report that even in 1997, a Wisconsin judge ordered the detention of a woman who had disclosed her intention of giving birth at home over a doctor's objection.[97]

Are Such Measures Largely Punitive?

In the wake of the South Carolina initiative, the number of states in which attempted prosecutions of pregnant women for drug use occurred increased almost threefold, from 12 to 34, between 1992 and 1995.[98] Since the mid-1970s, around 300 women in the US have been arrested on foetal abuse charges,[99] the majority – but by no means all – relating to drug or alcohol use in pregnancy. In most states, prosecutions and attempts to legislate for criminal penalties for behaviour in pregnancy have failed – South Carolina remaining the notable exception.[100] However at least 17 states now have laws to enable child removal from women who test positive for drugs during pregnancy, and estimates suggest hundreds and perhaps thousands of children have been removed like this[101] – often on the basis of a single positive test, and even if the child (and often its siblings) is otherwise healthy.

Various public health groups and professional societies have argued against removing children on the grounds of positive drug tests of the mother, asserting that one drug test is not a determinant of parenting ability and, indeed, that such sanctions may operate more as a punishment than a child protection mechanism.[102] Moreover, the statutory approach has been heavily criticised. For example, De Ville and Kopelman, commenting on Wisconsin's revision of its child abuse and protection laws to address substance abuse by pregnant women, with a new statute enabling the state to take the foetus into protective custody, argue that:

> ... approaching fetal protection using a child abuse model creates a series of symbolic, conceptual, and practical problems of such severity as to undermine its justifiability as a public health measure.[103]

Charo has suggested that when the American courts entertain prosecutions of pregnant drug abusers under the guise of child protection strategies, they are engaging in eugenic manipulation as surely as with forced sterilisation laws in the past.[104]

In one US case (*Johnson v State* 1989[105]), which ultimately failed thanks to the support of the ACLU, a woman voluntarily confided to her obstetrician that she had used cocaine whilst pregnant. She and the neonate were subjected to toxicology testing at birth and she was convicted under a drug trafficking statute for delivering drugs to an infant through the umbilical cord. Notwithstanding that both the baby and the woman's older child were found to be non-addicted and perfectly healthy, civil proceedings were instituted to remove the children from her custody, and a criminal prosecution begun for alleged drug-related harms to both children. Although the trial court dismissed the charge of child abuse for lack of any evidence of harm or injury, the woman was initially convicted on two counts of delivery of a controlled substance to a minor and sentenced to various punishments including 14 years' probation. She was also ordered to submit to physical examinations and random searches, to remain employed and to undergo court-supervised pre-natal care in the event of becoming pregnant again, as well as being forbidden to use drugs or alcohol, go to bars, or associate with people who use drugs or alcohol.[106,107]

Such responses are hardly likely to enhance doctor-patient obstetric relationships and, again, seem both draconian and out of proportion to the crime when, as discussed, once the child is born any drugs are no longer being delivered, and in many cases there is a lack of concrete evidence of harms to the foetus. Similarly, in the *Charleston* case, although most of the women had tested positive for cocaine multiple times during the pre-natal period when, according to the purported purpose of the policy, intervention was crucial, seven of the ten women were not arrested until after giving birth – several were taken into custody at the hospital wearing only their hospital gowns. As the District Judge (in a partially dissenting opinion) pointed out during the appeal hearing:

> By that time [after birth], any adverse effect of maternal cocaine use on the developing fetus had already occurred, and the arrest could only have had a punitive rather than a preventive purpose.[108]

Overall, such actions may hinder rather than aid the majority of children of drug-using women. In the US, publicity about the possible introduction of 'drug mother' laws is reported to dramatically reduce the number of addicted women seeking help, one director of a drug treatment centre commenting: 'The primary reason pregnant women with alcohol and drug problems do not seek pre-natal care or treatment for their addiction is fear of being turned in to the authorities and ultimately losing their children'.[109]

The ACLU reported in 1997 that although most prosecutions of women for conduct during pregnancy had failed, 'studies indicate that the prosecutions did have the unfortunate effect of scaring some women away from pre-natal care' and, moreover, that the American Public Health Association has warned: 'Flight from the health care system has a dramatic and detrimental impact on the health of women and their children'.[110]

When, three years after the original penalties were imposed, the Supreme Court of Florida overturned the conviction in *Johnson v State*, it issued a warning that:

> Prosecuting women for using drugs and 'delivering' them to their newborns appears to be the least effective response to this crisis. Rather than face the possibility of prosecution, pregnant women who are substance abusers may simply avoid prenatal or medical care for fear of being detected.[111]

The reasons for this trend have been much pondered upon. Prosecutions such as that of Regina McKnight have been described as 'an extreme manifestation of an increasingly successful antichoice agenda wrapped in the cloak of the War on Drugs.'[112] Paltrow warns that the tactics used in foetal abuse cases may be paving the way for abortion – the ultimate violation of 'foetal rights' – to be declared legally murder: 'These cases represent the intersection of the war on drugs and the war on abortion.'[113]

Other experts contend that an emotional undercurrent to do with anger at enhanced female status drives the prosecutions of pregnant women. Chavkin points out:

> There's a lot of anger about changes in gender roles and family relationships, and it's reflected in efforts to constrain the behavior of women and require them to accord priority to the fetus.[114]

Parents at a Disadvantage

Although the situation in the UK is different, at least as regards major public concern over drug use in pregnant women, and there has been little publicity attached to cases of child removal on such grounds, there is evidence that parents likely to come to the attention of social workers have an overwhelming fear that their child may be taken from them.[115] In a pre-natal situation, such fears would provide strong pressure to acquiesce to whatever demands were being made. It has been noted in the context of actions under the *Children Act 1989* that the power differential between parents and workers is such that parents generally feel they have no choice but to comply or their children will be removed.[116]

Such concerns are also likely to hinder open communication and appropriate trust between women and their doctors, or other agencies designated to 'help', which, as in the US, may drive 'high risk' women underground and so endanger far more children in the process. It may create additional dangers — in the UK, the Association for Improvement in Maternity Services (AIMS) has received reports of women refusing to seek help for post-natal depression, for fear their children may be taken away.[117] This is not an idle concern – reportedly one baby of a mother with post-natal depression was 'placed on the adoption track' even though her older children were healthy, happy and doing well at school.[118]

As suicide is the leading cause of death for women in the year after childbirth, this is potentially very dangerous. Worse, in 2004 AIMS demanded an enquiry by the Department of Health into a series of cases of false allegations about possible child abuse made to social services after mothers had made legitimate complaints about health care. AIMS claimed that pregnant women and new mothers are particularly vulnerable to such accusations, since their babies are seen as prime candidates for adoption.[119]

Children – and -Parents – Under Surveillance

Clearly, engendering a climate in which women fear their health care providers as agents of a state with designs on their children would be an immensely damaging step. However the balance with child protection concerns is delicate. In the wake of the well-publicised Victoria Climbié child abuse scandal in the UK,[120] the British Government proposed a new system to track all children with a unique identifying number from birth, enabling records of all agencies that may come into contact with a child to be linked – including health, education, social services, the probation service and the police. Any representative of these organisations will be enabled to note any concerns about the child, or anyone in contact with the child, as well as to see what has been logged by others; certain indicators, or combinations thereof, may result in the record being 'flagged' to show concerns for the child.[121] As well as identifying suspected child abuse, the scheme would support initiatives to intervene in youth offending.

Superficially, this sounded sensible, until it emerged that 'concerns' might include such factors as low birth weight, missed medical appointments, not being registered with a health care professional, failure to immunise, single parenthood, depression in the mother, missing school, poor school performance, financial or housing difficulties, frequent house moves, parental or sibling criminality, living in a high crime area and even a relative's health problems, alleged drug use or alcohol intake. Any professional with access to the database may record such concerns, which do not need to be justified by any evidence. Parents are not to be asked for consent nor permitted to see the files, much less correct any errors. [122,123,124,125,126,127,128] In a similar 'information sharing' scheme already running for teenage children, ostensibly to supply careers and personal advice to schools, young people have, reportedly, been asked to disclose details of parental problems such as drink or drug abuse, eating disorders and frequent domestic rows. The Government department responsible has been quoted as stating that parental profiles could help advisers (who may have as little as 17 days' training) to identify the need for intervention from other agencies.[129]

Such measures clearly hold immense potential for false and malicious allegations, injustice and breaches of confidentiality as well as for abuse by the known paedophiles haunting the childcare system. Concerns were expressed that the database would simply lead to professionals being overwhelmed by trivial information, resulting in serious concerns being overlooked. The National Society for the Prevention of Cruelty to Children (NSPCC) commented on the proposals:

> Local authorities could end up with complex databases [that] contain too much highly-sensitive information that would be difficult to interpret out of context. The cost of this, both in human and financial terms, could be very high.... databases of this kind will only succeed if the information on them is factual and objective.[130]

The question has also been raised as to whether such records will be destroyed at age 18 – if not, the Government would be well on its way to having a highly personal database on all citizens. The surveillance programme, once adopted, is designed to play a central role in the Government's planned future identity card scheme.

Notwithstanding such concerns, the Children Bill containing these measures was enacted by Parliament in November 2004, and empowers the Government (s8(1)) to require local authorities to establish and to operate such databases and to allow the Secretary of State to do the same – potentially establishing a national database of every child in the UK. The initial model, officially called the Information Sharing Index, will create 150 indices, one for each major local authority, and a further one coordinating the system. Although the information to be held electronically will include name, address, date of birth, person with parental responsibility, unique identifying number, educational setting and NHS general practice details, it will not – as yet – include full case records.

However the Government has retained enormous flexibility as to the type of databases it may operate or require to be set up, the specific information they may contain, and the provisions as to its disclosure. These are to be defined by Regulations (s8(4)) – therefore no longer to be debated by Parliament and a potentially unlimited authority to hold all records, including medical and social services records, in one central database. Moreover, anything done under the Regulations may done 'notwithstanding any rule of common law which prohibits or restricts the disclosure of information' (s8(7)), thereby abolishing any restrictions on the basis of confidentiality. Although professionals have long been permitted to breach confidentiality in the case of serious concerns about child abuse, this now permits confidentiality to be overridden in the case of a range of more trivial information, and for possibly trivial reasons, including professional prejudice against parents of whose lifestyles and belief systems they disapprove.

The records will run from birth, or even before – neonates were already being allocated numbers before discharge from hospital at the end of 2004, and there are proposals to issue numbers to foetuses still in the womb. The number is in use already within national initiatives such as screening programmes for neonatal deafness. The potential to 'flag' in advance a child-to-be whose mother-to-be fails to cooperate in pregnancy is clear – home birth, refusal of antenatal tests, a flawed lifestyle or delivering a less than perfect 'product' could become child welfare concerns before the child is even born. Already, failure to attend paediatric outpatient appointments is regarded as a possible indicator of child welfare concerns, for which medical staff members are recommended to 'make contact with social services'.[131] The spectre of 'foetal abuse' interventions looms large – without even any need for specific legislation overtly recognising the foetus, or for recourse to the courts.

As AIMS has pointed out, such interventions can cause immense stress to a pregnant woman – itself harmful to the foetus. Moreover, separations in the neonatal period can interfere with breastfeeding and, as later in childhood, even brief interventions not formally pursued may cause immense harm to children and families, as well as damaging parents' relationships with health care providers and putting a permanent stain on their child's health and medical records. Even under the old system, intended to cover only those about whom there were existing concerns, notes were often of poor quality and contained many inaccuracies and, while damaging assertions and misconceptions were recorded, there was often no appropriate correction or addition made to the file when they were disproved. Moreover:

> Many of the personnel involved in sharing information – midwives, health visitors, doctors, nurses, nursery school teachers, teachers and social workers – seem more concerned about covering their own backs than in genuinely listening to, caring about and caring for worried mothers.[132]

The possibility for coercive action if child welfare is questioned is immense, and its potential scope broad: child abuse has been defined as: 'anything which individuals, institutions or processes do or fail to do which directly or indirectly harms children or damages their prospects of a safe and healthy development into adulthood'.[133]

Lest concerns on this score be seen as mere speculation, and to demonstrate the potential scope of child 'welfare concerns', it should be noted that authorities in the US have ordered children to be removed from the custody of their parents because of head lice infestation;[134] arrested the mother of children seen at a fairground with sunburn;[135] imposed civil liability on women for actions such as taking a prescribed antibiotic while pregnant[136] or failure of care in crossing the street when pregnant[137] (these two cases were discussed in Chapter 1); ruled that exposure to second-hand smoke was *determinative* of the best interests of the child in a custody dispute,[138] and allowed a long-running case to be taken against parents by social workers demanding their right to inspect the family home, on the grounds that their two-year-old child was seen playing naked in their garden.[139]

Misleading Medical Evidence in UK Child Death Cases

The potential for injustice is further revealed by a series of infant death scandals that hit the UK at the turn of the Millennium. These cases will be briefly discussed even though most concern children beyond the neonatal period, because the acceptance of medical evidence in court has certain parallels with some cases of obstetric conflict, and because babies have sometimes been removed at birth based on the ensuing concerns.

In rapid sequence, several women who had had more than one 'cot death' (sudden infant death syndrome or SIDS) and had been accused of killing their infants were exonerated after serious doubts were cast on expert medical evidence given at their trials. Sally Clark, a solicitor, convicted and imprisoned for two life sentences for murdering her two baby sons, had her conviction quashed on appeal in February 2003, having served three years in prison, when new evidence was presented to show that the infants died of natural causes. In June that year, Trupti Patel was found not guilty of killing her three sons after the jury heard evidence that her family may have suffered from a rare inherited predisposition to SIDS, and in December Angela Cannings, who had served three years for the murder of two sons, had her conviction was quashed and was freed from prison when expert evidence from her trial was 'demonstrably undermined' at the appeal hearing.

In all these cases, the prosecution relied on expert testimony from Professor Sir Roy Meadow, a respected paediatrician who formulated what became known as 'Meadow's Law'. This stated that unless proven otherwise, 'one sudden infant death is a tragedy, two is suspicious and three is murder'. In court, he had said that there was a 73 million to one chance of two children in the same family dying of cot death – a statistic that made a clear impression on both jury and public, but was later shown to be erroneous. More recent research has suggested that previous estimates of the incidence of abuse in SIDS cases, at between 20 and 40 per cent, may have been too high – thorough investigation and monitoring of the well-being of subsequent siblings in a sample of such families revealed a risk of abuse of the order of three to ten per cent, and the investigator concluded that the need to place a sibling on the Child Protection Register as a result of a previous case of SIDS in the family is rare.[140] A further study published in 2005 showed that even with a second sudden unexpected death in infancy in the same family, the vast majority – 87 per cent – occurred naturally.[141] Although child abuse is not uncommon, and all sudden infant deaths require intensive investigation, these figures further undermine Meadow's evidence. In fact, 50 families in the UK suffer a second infant death each year,[142] and international experts have heavily criticised the UK approach of trying cases on the basis of mere statistical evidence.[143]

In the Clark case, Professor Meadow's evidence was later condemned by the Court of Appeal as 'manifestly wrong' and 'grossly misleading'; in the Cannings case it was found unreliable and 'simply wrong', and the Appeal Court stated that in future, if there was disagreement between experts, prosecutions should not be brought without physical evidence, and criminal convictions should not be made based on the testimony of expert witnesses alone.[144,145] At the time of writing, both Meadow and the pathologist involved in the Clark case, Dr Alan Williams, were under investigation by the General Medical Council (GMC). However, after Sally Clark's acquittal, one paediatrician warned that the acknowledged problems in the field of suspected child abuse were not solely, or even mainly, due to individuals giving flawed advice but also to 'systems failure'.[146]

Following the Cannings verdict, an investigation by the Royal College of Pathologists and the Royal College of Paediatrics and Child Health, chaired by Baroness Helena Kennedy QC, recommended inquests for all SIDS cases, along with standardised post-mortem examinations, and urged greater rigour in assessing the evidence given by expert witnesses in such cases. While pointing out that the ultimate responsibility lies with judges and barristers, who should make sure that self-styled experts have the required knowledge and are not pushed into turning belief into fact, the working group said that the experts themselves should remember that they represented justice, owed a duty of impartiality, and must disclose any evidence that they knew disputed their opinion. 'It is also important that the courtroom is not used by doctors to fly their personal kites or push a theory from the far end of the medical spectrum', the group warned. Families who have suffered a sudden infant death should be treated with 'sensitivity, discretion and respect', and all those involved, including police, doctors and social workers, should work on the presumption of innocence.[147,148]

Also in the wake of the Cannings verdict, a review was ordered in January 2004 of all cases in England and Wales in the previous decade which a parent or carer had been convicted of killing a child under age two. The cases of thousands of other parents who had a child removed on the basis of similar evidence were also to be re-examined. In December 2004 the Attorney General, Lord Goldsmith, stated that there was 'cause for concern' in at least 28 further cases of the 297 investigated (9.4 per cent), and that appeals could be made against the verdicts in these cases; he had notified the defence solicitors, the Criminal Cases Review Commission (CCRC) and the Court of Appeal accordingly. The defendants in each case – nine of whom remained in custody at the time – are therefore entitled to decide whether to appeal their conviction directly or via the CRCC, which has the power to investigate the cases as suspected miscarriages of justice. Three of the cases involved SIDS, like the Cannings case, and eight were instances of 'shaken baby syndrome'. Three further cases in which prosecutions were pending were abandoned on the grounds that it was not safe to proceed. Although Lord Goldsmith proposed to take no further action in 180 of the cases, the remaining 89 cases, identified as 'shaken baby syndrome', he had decided not to refer 'at this stage', though further action – including a major test case — is expected in 2005.[149,150,151] Commenting on the cases, one MP told Parliament that they highlighted the problems that could arise 'when the opinion of consultants, doctors however eminent, substitutes itself for the scrutiny of the evidence before a court. It is greatly to be hoped that in future this sort of problem won't arise again because of a greater awareness of the potential fallibility of expert witnesses.'[152]

Doubts Cast on Other 'Abuse' Cases

As the review noted, some cases in which parents were accused of so-called 'shaken baby syndrome' (SBS) also deserve re-examination. The term is used to describe injury from forceful shaking of infants, leading to brain damage and sometimes death. Parents have been accused when the severity of their children's injuries seemed inconsistent with the explanation given, or when a seemingly trivial injury resulted in serious consequences. SBS is specific to infancy, when children have unique anatomic features, and is widely held to be 'the most common cause of death or serious neurological injury resulting from child abuse',[153] with some studies suggesting that shaking alone can cause fatal brain injury.[154]

The syndrome is also recognised in North America. In one case reported from North Carolina, a 14-month-old baby boy was admitted with a severe head injury that shortly proved fatal, and meanwhile was found to have, *inter alia*, intraretinal and preretinal haemorrhages, and perimacular retinal folds. Since these signs were considered diagnostic of abusive head trauma from shaking, Child Protective Services removed the baby's three-year-old brother from the home, notwithstanding what the case report later described as the father's 'repeated detailed, consistent account provided to emergency staff, the paediatric child abuse specialist, paediatric intensive care doctors, and law enforcement authorities' of a television stand collapsing and falling on the baby while he and his brother were in a different room as the father prepared dinner.

At post-mortem, bilateral and extensive retinal haemorrhages and perimacular retinal folds were observed without direct trauma to eyes or orbits, along with skull fractures, subarachnoid haemorrhage and severe brain injury. Investigators who went to the house before the family returned home found the television set and stand as described, still on the floor, with marks corresponding to the impact site on the child's head. A re-enactment found that the television stand could indeed have collapsed as described. The next day, the baby's brother – by now in foster care – corroborated the father's account. However the paediatric opthalmologist repeated the assertion that perimacular retinal folds coincident with retinal haemorrhages were considered specific for SBS.

A comprehensive review of the medical literature was then undertaken and demonstrated that 'statements in the medical literature that perimacular retinal folds are diagnostic of SBS are not supported by objective scientific evidence'. Moreover, 'an evidence based analysis of indexed medical publications on shaken baby syndrome from 1966-1998 uncovered a weak scientific evidence base'. The authors urged caution in interpreting eye findings in such cases out of context.[155] In an accompanying editorial, experts stress the need to reconsider the diagnostic criteria, if not the existence, of shaken baby syndrome.[156] In the case described, the older brother was returned to the family five days later following review by the magistrate; however, he was not allowed to attend his brother's funeral, which was further upsetting to the parents.[157]

The significance of the features often used by doctors to make a diagnosis of SBS, especially in the absence of external trauma, are now the subject of considerable debate.[158] Other recent research has suggested that both subdural and retinal haemorrhage in infants may result from excessive intraluminal pressure including during mechanical ventilation for respiratory distress syndrome; in prolonged expiratory apnoea and in intense airway irritation such as laryngeal infection, inhalation of regurgitated feed, fluff or smoke – these could induce similar bleeding, dubbed 'paroxysmal cough injury (PCI)'.[159]

Another series of cases in the UK has called into question verdicts based on Munchausen Syndrome by Proxy (MSBP),[160] a diagnostic entity coined by Professor Meadow, the paediatrician whose evidence was discredited by the Court of Appeal in the Cannings murder trial. Mothers were typically accused of MSBP when they repeatedly presented to hospital with children for whose symptoms medical science struggled to find a conventional diagnosis: the assumption was made that they were fabricating their children's illnesses in order to gain medical attention. MSBP has been proposed in over 100 patterns of illness, including epilepsy, abdominal pain, bleeding disorders, diarrhoea, fevers and lethargy.[161] As with cases of obstetric conflict, the 'evidence' used to underpin such accusations frequently emerged as seriously flawed – and the consequences were often dire. In one reported case, a mother was accused of MSBP after taking her little girl to hospital saying that she was suffering from epileptic fits. The doctors, having failed to observe a fit over a two-week observation period in hospital, accused the mother of repeatedly suffocating her, and the child was removed from her custody. Only when the girl was observed having fits while in foster care was the mistake acknowledged.[162]

The existence of MSBP is now being questioned, and numerous other families are fighting such accusations. The episode has been compared with the Cleveland child abuse scandal of the 1980s,[163] when dozens of children were removed from their families based on false accusations of sexual assault, again as a result of controversial medical theories. Many of the cases of MSBP were brought based on the evidence of a single medical witness – either Professor Meadow or another doctor, David Southall.

In June 2004, Southall was barred from child protection work for three years by the Professional Conduct Committee of the GMC, not for his MSBP work (although that, and other research into a controversial treatment for neonatal breathing problems, were also under investigation), but because of his repeated accusations that Stephen, rather than Sally Clark, killed their two baby sons. These allegations were made solely on the basis of watching a television interview with Stephen Clark at the time that Sally Clark was in prison, and stemmed from Southall's theory that nosebleeds in a baby were a sign of smothering. Southall – who at the time was suspended from his job as a consultant paediatrician and barred from undertaking any new outside child protection work – contacted the Child Protection Unit of the Staffordshire Police to state that Stephen Clark had deliberately suffocated one son, thus implicating him in the deaths of both boys; he also raised concerns about Stephen Clark's access to, and the safety of, the Clarks' third child. He later met with a Detective Inspector from the force to reiterate these opinions, submitted a report on the same lines declaring that its contents were true and could be used in a court of law, and later stated in writing that it was 'beyond reasonable doubt' that Mr Clark was responsible for the deaths of his two sons – all without any knowledge of the case papers or meeting with either of the Clarks. He did, however, later acknowledge that Professor Meadow had helped to confirm his theory on the case. The Committee found Southall's actions to be 'inappropriate, irresponsible, misleading and an abuse of [his] professional position'. It expressed concern that at no time during its proceedings had Southall seen fit to withdraw his allegations or to offer any apology, and found him guilty of serious professional misconduct.[164, 165]

Consequences for Children and Families

In addition to miscarriages of justice when parents were charged on the basis of diagnoses such as MSBP, 'shaken baby syndrome', or were accused of smothering or killing babies who had suffered from SIDS, in many more cases children or new babies were taken into care based on similarly flawed evidence, without any charges being made against the parents. Such cases are heard in the family court and, even though they involve potentially drastic actions up to and including adoption of the children removed, are not subject to the same standards of proof – they are decided on the civil basis of 'balance of probabilities' rather than the criminal standard of 'beyond reasonable doubt.' This means that verdicts may be discrepant, with a parent exonerated in the criminal courts but still found 'guilty' in the family court and subject to having the child, or other children, removed.[166] In two post-Cannings cases in which mothers brought their own appeals, the Court of Appeal upheld the civil standard as applied to cases of child removal.[167]

Clearly in some cases this may be the right approach to protect children at serious risk of harm, even if the evidence is not sufficient to convict a parent of a crime. However for an innocent parent – and for their child or children – the potential results are appalling. Yet many cases in which children were removed based on what is now known to be flawed evidence, particularly those in which the child was subsequently adopted, may never even be reviewed and, because of the secrecy surrounding family court proceedings,[168] the parents are not allowed to talk about their cases publicly. The volume of such cases remains hidden, and the details rarely come to light.

Such cases have included one family, suspected of a cot death killing on the basis of Meadow's evidence, whose next baby, a daughter, was taken into care just 25 minutes after being born.[169] Even after being cleared in court, Trupti Patel remained barred from seeing her remaining child unless supervised by someone approved by social services, under a court order imposed soon after one baby died suddenly in 2001.[170] In another case reminiscent of the treatment of 'drug mothers' in South Carolina (see Chapter 3), a woman whose baby had died suddenly aged 14 days was found guilty of murder and sentenced to life imprisonment, by which time she was three months pregnant. When the time came for the birth, she was taken to hospital in handcuffs and chains by prison guards, and the baby, born by Caesarean, removed immediately. Meanwhile her lawyers had appealed her conviction, producing new medical evidence that her first baby's injuries were due not to her hitting or shaking him, but to birth injuries during her prolonged labour with a ventouse extraction — as was argued at her original trial. She was acquitted on appeal. Notwithstanding the verdict, social services ordered a family court hearing where, on the civil 'balance of probabilities' standard, she was found guilty, despite the same medical evidence, on the basis of a child psychologist's report that she had a 'momentary loss of temper' and had shaken her baby to death. Social services banned her from returning to the family home, allowing her just four hours of supervised access to her surviving son each month, and reportedly warning the child's father that the boy would be taken into care should his relationship with the mother continue.[171]

In February 2004, the Government promised that once the review of criminal cases was complete, cases decided in the family courts in which a final care order was made based on similarly disputed medical evidence would also be re-examined. Initially it was predicted that this would involve several thousand families – as many as five thousand children are estimated to have been taken into care based on theories about MSBP alone[172] – then the estimate was revised to 'low hundreds'. Social services departments of local councils were to be asked to examine their files to find instances of such cases and to consider whether to apply for care orders to be discharged or to support an application by parents. Children's Minister Margaret Hodge gave councils responsibility for reviewing their own cases, and discretion not to reopen them even if the evidence was disputed, if this was judged against the child's best interests, for example, if they were settled and happy in a new home.[173] Despite the hopes of many families, a survey in June 2004 failed to show any parents who had been reunited with their children on this basis. Most local councils had opted not to reopen cases, and less than one in ten had brought in an independent agency to help review disputed care orders – leading to criticisms of the decision to allow local authorities to act as 'judge and jury' in their own cases.[174]

Nor do cases even have to come before the family court to produce severe consequences for the family. One mother who filed a complaint with the GMC was accused by Southall of creating her child's symptoms – later shown to be due to the severe allergies for which the child was referred by the GP for paediatric consultation on breathing problems. Her son was placed on the 'at risk' register after Southall wrote to the local authority stating that the boy was at risk of 'significant harm'. The mother also attempted to sue the NHS trust for the resulting severe anxiety and depression she suffered.[175] In common with other such cases, her application was denied: courts have ruled that whilst children may sue if there is negligence over investigation of abuse or in care proceedings, parents cannot recover for the psychological stress of false allegations of abuse[176] even if there is negligence – the paediatrician in such a case owes no duty of care to the parent.[177] Yet young children removed from their families, especially if wrongly adopted will, of course, not often be in a position to initiate court action.

A year after being freed, Angela Cannings was denied compensation for the time she spent in prison – although fighting her case cost the family their home as well as all their savings and life-insurance policies, and meant that her husband had to give up his job in order to care for their surviving child.[178] The Clark family reported that they were in a precarious financial position following the Government's refusal to reimburse £130,000 of their legal costs, which were awarded by the Court of Appeal.[179]

The controversies over such cases may also have detrimental effects on children in real need of protection. After the Clark, Patel and Cannings verdicts, and the Attorney General's announcement of a review of such cases, it was reported that, increasingly, doctors were avoiding testifying as expert witnesses in child injury cases, in case they too faced intensive media scrutiny and GMC investigation. Notably the media gave much more limited coverage to Dr Ruby Schwartz, the paediatrician who failed to diagnose that Victoria Climbié (*vide supra*) was being brutally abused, and the GMC dropped the misconduct charges against her – giving the impression that failing to spot child abuse is less risky professionally than raising concerns that may be later challenged.[180] A survey of members of the Royal College of Paediatrics and Child Health revealed that between 1995 and 2003 there was a five-fold increase in complaints made against paediatricians, many of which received coverage in the media – doctors are not allowed to 'answer back' in such cases because of their duty of confidentiality, even if a patient has already spoken to the press – yet only three per cent were eventually upheld.[181]

Is the Child Care System Dysfunctional?

Finally, one expert defence witness and child protection advocate, in the flurry of correspondence in the British Medical Journal following the Southall hearing, recommended a complete reform of a 'dysfunctional child protection system' that, he alleged, 'is causing serious harm to children and is destroying families under the perverse pretext of protecting those children'. He described the system as 'punitive and uncaring and engaged in a crude form of social engineering aimed at stealing children from families "thought to have" caused harm to their children', and predicted a similar pending crisis in child protection services in America and Australia. Some of his comments seem relevant to similar concerns about obstetric conflict:

> [T]here are increasing concerns of professionals in medicine, social work, the law, researchers, academics, and parents falsely accused of child abuse, that the child protection system is deeply flawed, erratic, and dysfunctional and the child protection system is 'per se', causing severe and long-lasting harm to many thousands of children every year. On the other hand, many children are suffering harm and death because of failures to intervene appropriately and responsibly.
>
> A major contribution to this dysfunctionalism ... is the unscientific theories espoused by a small number of paediatricians and the dogmatic, inappropriate, irresponsible, misleading presentation of their opinions and suppositions to Courts and the abuse of their professional positions.[182]

This strongly suggests that the courts need to take a more proactive position in assessing professional opinions in child welfare cases. It is not an isolated opinion. One solicitor specialising in public Children Act work has commented that under the British child protection system, the local authority 'will consider rehabilitation [of the family unit] only if forced to by the courts or the guardian.' Since local authorities vary in approach, sometimes the best advice that can be offered if a child has already been removed is 'to relocate to a neighbouring jurisdiction, prior to the birth of a further child'. This seems an outrageous position in which to put parents when, according to this opinion, most truly incapable parents accept child removal at an early stage, so generally it is those who believe in their innocence who continue to struggle. Moreover, most social workers apparently view the minority of parents who are well-educated and from stable backgrounds as 'dangerous' and see all efforts by such parents to exonerate themselves or work with the local authority as attempts to manipulate 'the system'. In the solicitor's opinion, 'the power of the guardian and the local authority combined is almost without limit'.[183]

These concerns are echoed on a more general level by the British Association of Social Workers, commenting on the relationship between state and family in children's upbringing:

> We are increasingly concerned that services to children and their families are being driven by a more punitive and coercive agenda based on social control which would indicate a low level of trust between the state, its agencies and its citizens.[184]

Court Proceedings in Cases of Concern

The extent to which such concerns may impinge upon those who may be called upon to assess cases of obstetric conflict in future remains unknown. In the UK, the philosophy of the *Children Act 1989* is that children are best cared for within their family of origin, and court proceedings should be 'a last resort'. Although the threshold for court involvement has increased, the changes introduced by the Act have 'placed a heavy burden of risk assessment and management on practitioners'.[185] For a social worker (like Louize Collins, perhaps) faced with a medical professional expecting some action and a parturient woman apparently endangering her neonate, questioning the medical evidence is not likely to play a large role in immediate decision-making.

Furthermore, despite a far more formalised and extensive assessment procedure,[186] there is evidence that parents in care proceedings still suffer some of the disadvantages faced by pregnant women in legal conflict with their medical advisers. Proceedings of the family courts are held in secret, guardians are invariably seen as being on the side of Social Services;[187] many parents receive poor-quality legal representation and often do not have access to the same experts as the professional parties, and there are no measures for clinicians' accountability or feedback.[188]

Although the extent of such actions is unknown, instances of child removal at birth clearly do occur already, and in at least some of these cases, grounds for removal will be concerns raised about the mother's behaviour during pregnancy.[189] Indeed, following numerous anecdotal reports, AIMS reported in 2002 that it was compiling a dossier of cases in which expectant or new mothers were exposed to social-work intervention after allegations of child abuse or neglect.[190] In the UK, where interference in pregnancy (at least on wardship grounds) has apparently been conclusively ruled out since the judgment in *In Re*

F^{191}, the possibilities for post-birth sanctions could offer an attractive alternative in cases where the mother's behaviour or compliance during pregnancy or in the neonatal period is regarded as obstetrically sub-standard.

Society treads a thin line in dealing with child welfare concerns. Both the public and the media are unforgiving should a child slip through the net and a tragedy occur – yet recent events on both side of the Atlantic suggest that the 'cause' of child abuse may be readily hijacked for special interest purposes and political gains, creating gross injustice for some families and leaving children who truly need protection vulnerable. The net costs in terms of maternal and child welfare may be substantial. The need for high standards of evidence in individual cases must be continually borne in mind by those who may be charged with making decisions crucial to the future well-being of women, children and families. Moreover, in this area legislators concerned with child protection, as well as those who would re-interpret existing legislation to embrace foetuses, would do well to remember Lyndon Johnson's admonition:

> You do not examine legislation in the light of the benefits it will convey if properly administered, but in the light of the wrongs it would do and the harms it would cause if improperly administered.

Notes

1 The phrase is from Voltaire's Candide. Translated: 'In this country [England] we find it pays to shoot an admiral from time to time *to encourage the others.*' (my italics): Voltaire, Francois M. *Candide or Optimism*. Penguin Classics, London 1990 re-issue of 1947 edition, translation by John Butt, at p111.

2 Memorandum in Support of Petition and Order. Unborn Baby Kenner, #79JN83, Juvenile Court, City and County of Denver and State of Colorado, 6 March 1979, reported by Irwin S, Jordan B. Knowledge, Practice, and Power: Court-Ordered Cesarean Sections. *Medical Anthropology Quarterly* 1987; 1(3):319-334.

3 *In re Brown* 689 N.E. 2d 397 (1997).

4 *Re Baby R*. 15 Annu Rev Popul Law 29, 53 Dom Law Rep 69-81 (British Columbia Supreme Court 1988).

5 *Jefferson v Griffin Spalding Memorial Hospital* (1981) 247 Ga 86; 274 SE 2d 457 at 459 (Georgia Supreme Ct).

6 *In re guardianship of J.D.S., an adult*. In the Circuit Court for the Ninth Judicial Circuit, in and for Orange County, Florida. Case No. 48-2003-CP001188-O (Fla 2003).

7 Colb, Sherry F. 'Governor Jeb Bush Sends Lawyers to Represent a Fetus: Targeting A Mentally Retarded Pregnant Woman for Pro-Life Intervention'. *FindLaw* 27 August 2003: www.findlaw.com.

8 Order denying verified petition for appointment of guardian over unborn child, Nos. 48-2003-CP001188-O, 48-2003-MH-000414-O, at 3 (May 30, 2003) (citing *In re TW*, 551 So. 2d 1186, 1190 (Fla 1989)).

9 For example, see: Women's Law Project. 'In re guardianship of JDS'. *Women's Law Project Newsletter*. Fall 2003. Philadelphia Pa: www.womenslawproject.org.

10 *In re Guardianship of J.D.S.*, Jennifer Wixtrom, Appellant, Case No. 5D03-1921: J Wixtrom's brief, at pp 28-29.
11 American Civil Liberties Union. *ACLU, Center for Reproductive Rights, and Florida NOW Fight Efforts to Interfere With Care of Severely Disabled Rape Victim.* ACLU Press Release June 17, 2003: www.aclu.org.
12 Center for Reproductive Law and Policy. *Florida Court Refuses to Appoint Guardian for a Fetus.* CRLP Press Release 9 January 2004: http://www.crlp.org/pr_04_0109JDS.html.
13 *Re AC* (1990) 573 A 2d 1235 (DC Ct Appeals).
14 Colb, Sherry F. Governor Jeb Bush Sends Lawyers to Represent a Fetus, *op cit.*
15 Napersky, Lisa. 'Woman hits hospitals' stance that she agree to C-section'. *The Citizens' Voice* (Pennsylvania) 17 January 2004.
16 American Civil Liberties Union. *Coercive and Punitive Governmental Responses to Women's Conduct During Pregnancy.* American Civil Liberties Union, September 1997, www.aclu.org/issues/reproduct/coercive.html.
17 Paltrow Lynn M. *Criminal Prosections Against Pregnant Women. National Update and Overview.* Reproductive Freedom Project, American Civil Liberties Union Foundation. April 1992.
18 Paltrow LM. 'Punishing Women for Their Behavior During Pregnancy: An Approach That Undermines the Health of Women and Children.' In: Wetherington CL and Roman AB (Editors). *Drug Addiction Research and the Health of Women.* National Institute on Drug Abuse (DHHS), Bethesda, MD, 1998.
19 Taylor, Diane. Does a foetus have more rights than its mother? *The Guardian*, Friday April 23, 2004.
20 see: www.condonforsenate.com.
21 Stevens, Kathy. Fetal-drug prosecution ignites debate in S.C. State stands alone in arresting women who engage in risky behavior during pregnancy. *The Post and Courier* (South Carolina), February 23, 2003.
22 Stevens, Kathy. *Ibid.*
23 Smith, Elmer. 'Regina McKnight: The Baby Drug War'. *Philadelphia Daily News* 8 October 2003.
24 *Crawley v South Carolina*, 523 U.S. 1145 (1998).
25 *Crawley v Catoe*, U.S. 4th Circuit Court of Appeals, decided 16 July 2001.
26 Stevens, Kathy. Fetal-drug prosecution ignites debate in S.C., *op cit.*
27 *Whitner v State*, 492 S.E.2d 777–88 (S.C. 1997).
28 Cooper, Cynthia L. *Pregnant and Punished.* Ford Foundation Report, Winter 2003: http://www.fordfound.org/publications/ff_report/view_ff_report_detail.cfm?report_index=382.
29 Drug Policy Alliance. *Whitner vs. the State of South Carolina.* DPA Statement. Last updated 23 June 2004: http://www.drugpolicy.org/law/womenpregnan/whitnervsth_/.
30 Drug Policy Alliance. *Ibid.*.
31 Talvi, Silja JA. Criminalizing Motherhood. *The Nation*, 11 Dec 2003, on: http://www.thenation.com/.
32 Beiser, Vince. Women who stand at the crossroads: Compassion or Punishment. *Shepherd Express Metro* (Milwaukee), vol 21, issue 32. 3 August 2000: http://www.shepherd-express.com/shepherd/21/32/cover_story.html.
33 Beiser, Vince, *Ibid.*
34 Drug Policy Alliance. *South Carolina v. McKnight.* DPA Statement. Last updated 23

June 2004: http://www.drugpolicy.org/law/womenpregnan/mcknight/.

35 Taylor, Diane, *op cit.*

36 Talvi, Silja JA, *op cit.*

37 Talvi, Silja JA, *Ibid.*

38 Goldenberg RL, Kirby R, Culhane JF. 'Stillbirth: a review'. *J Matern Fetal Neonatal Med* 2004;16(2):79-94.

39 *State v Kruzicki* 561 N.W.2d 729-49 (Wisconsin Supreme Ct 1997).

40 Beiser, Vince, *op cit.*

41 Wisconsin statute 48.133.

42 Morgan, John-David. 'Wisconsin at the Threshold'. *Shepherd Express Metro* (Milwaukee), vol 21, issue 32. 3 August 2000:
http://www.shepherd-express.com/shepherd/21/32/cover_story.html;Beiser, Vince, *op cit.*

43 *Matter of Fletcher* (1988), 533 N.Y.S.2d 241.

44 *In re Nassau County Deptartment of Social Services ex rel Dante M*, 87 N.Y.2d 73, 79 (1995).

45 *People v Morabito*, 151 Misc. 2d 259, 580 N.Y.S.2d 843 (Geneva City Ct. 1992), aff'd, slip op. (Ont. Cty. Ct. Sept. 24, 1992).

46 New York Civil Liberties Union - Reproductive Rights Project. *Court Rules New York State Child Endangering Law May Not Be Used To Punish Pregnant Woman for Health Problems. Charges against Stacey Gilligan dismissed.* NYCLU Statement, 9 April 2004: www.nyclu.org/rrp_gilligan_pr_040904.html.

47 *State of Hawaii v Tayshea Aiwohi.* IN THE CIRCUIT COURT OF THE FIRST CIRCUIT FC. CR. NO. 03-1-0036.

48 Barayuga, Debra. 'Ice' baby's mom pleads not guilty. *Honolulu Star-Bulletin*, Friday, October 17, 2003.

49 *State of Hawaii v Tayshea Aiwohi*, *op cit.*

50 *State of Hawaii v Tayshea Aiwohi*, *op cit.*

51 Talvi, Silja JA, *op cit.*

52 Cooper, Cynthia L, *op cit.*

53 Sage, Alexandria. 'Utah C-Section Mom Gets Probation'. *CBS News.com* 29 April 2004: http://www.cbsnews.com/stories/2004/03/12/national/main605537.shtml.

54 Taylor, Diane, *op cit.*

55 Johnson, Rebecca. 'C-Sections and the Real Crime'. *New York Times* 12 April 2004 (Rebecca Johnson is on the advisory board at the Sloane Hospital for Women at the Columbia University Medical Center).

56 National Advocates for Pregnant Women. Statement the day after Rowland's arrest, on: www.advocatesforpregnantwomen.org.

57 Minkoff H, Paltrow LM. 'Melissa Rowland and the rights of pregnant women'. *Obstet Gynecol* 2004;104:1234-6.

58 Udy, Pam. 'Legal system organizing against rights of pregnant women'. Guest Commentary, *Standard-Examiner* (Utah), 20 May 2004.

59 *In Re F (in utero)* (1988) TLR 5.2.88 : (1988) 2 AER 193 : (1988) 2 WLR 1288 : ILR 10.2.88 : (1988) FCR 529: (1988) 132 SJ 820 : (1988) 18 FAM LAW 337 : (1988) 138 NLJ 37 : (1988) 152 JPN 538 [Lawtel].

60 *Re MB* [1997] EWCA Civ 1361 (26th March, 1997) at 50.

61 per Balcombe LJ *Re F (In utero)* [1988] 2 All ER 193, at 143.

62 *In Re F (in utero)* [1988] 2 All ER 193.

63 Per May LJ: *In Re F (in utero)* [1988] Fam 122 at 135, 138.

64 Per Balcombe LJ: *Re F (In utero)* [1988] 2 All ER 193, at 144; per May LJ: *In Re F (in utero)* [1988] Fam 122 at 139.
65 *Paton v British Pregnancy Advisory Service Trustees* (1979) 1 QB 270.
66 *In Re F (in utero)* [1988] Fam 122 at 130 [my italics].
67 *In Re D (a minor)* sub nom *D (a minor) v Berkshire County Council* (1987) 1 AER 20 : ILR 5.12.86 : TLR 5.12.86 : (1986) 3 WLR 1080 : (1987) AC 317 : (1986) 151 JP 313 : (1986) 130 SJ 984 : (1987) 85 LGR 169 : (1987) 1 FLR 422 : (1987) 151 LG Rev 268 : (1987) 17 FAM LAW 202 : (1986) 136 NLJ 1184 : (1987) 151 JPN 190 : (1987) 84 LSG 574 ; 84 LSG 15 [Lawtel].
68 The subsequent legislation, the *Children Act 1989*, is considered *infra*.
69 Stein, Ellen J. 'Maternal-Fetal conflict: Reformulating the equation'. In: Grubb, Andrew (Ed). *Challenges in Medical Care*. John Wiley & Sons. Chichester 1992, 91-108, at p100.
70 Stein, Ellen J. *Ibid*, at pp 100, 104-5.
71 Department of Health Statistics Branch, personal communication.
72 In the year to 31 March 1999, of 4,400 care orders, 1,000 related to infants under one year of age, of which 900 were interim and 100 full care orders. Source: Department of Health, Children in Care Statistics, Table O: 'Children who started to be looked after during the year ending 31 March 1999 by legal status and age on starting'.
73 Department of Health Social Services Inspectorate, personal communication.
74 Except incidentally: for example, a media report of a drug addict convicted of murder noted in passing that he and his girlfriend had a 15-month-old son who had been taken into care at birth: Clough, Sue. 'Bag snatch driver guilty of murder.' *Daily Telegraph* 21 December 2001 at p4.
75 Mason JK, McCall Smith RA. *Law and Medical Ethics*. Butterworths London 1999, at p136.
76 Ondersma SJ, Simpson SM, Brestan EV, Ward M. 'Prenatal drug exposure and social policy: the search for an appropriate response.' *Child Maltreat* 2000 May;5(2):93-108.
77 Robertson J. 'Fetal abuse' (1989) 75 *American Bar Association* 38-9.
78 Eekelaar J. 'Does a mother have legal duties to her unborn child?' In: Byrne PA (Ed). *Health, Rights and Resources*: King's College Studies 1987-8. Oxford University Press, for King Edward's Hospital Fund, London 1988, pp55-75, at p65.
79 Robertson JA, Shulman JD. 'Pregnancy and prenatal harm: the case of mothers with PKU.' *Hastings Center Report* 17 (1987): 23-33.
80 Payne D. 'Couple has the right to refuse test on newborn baby.' *BMJ* 2001; 323: 1149 (News).
81 PKU is a genetic disorder in which the enzyme needed to metabolise phenylalanine in the diet is lacking, leading to a build-up of harmful chemicals in the bloodstream. These lead to progressive brain damage, mental retardation and other complications such as epilepsy unless a strict diet is followed from birth – hence most neonates are tested for PKU even though the condition is exceptionally rare.
82 *Re C (A Child) (HIV Testing)*; *sub nom*: *Re C (A Minor) (HIV Test)* [2000] Fam 48 : [2000] 2 WLR 270 : [1999] 3 FCR 289 : (1999) 50 BMLR 283.
83 Nicoll A, Peckham C. 'Reducing vertical transmission of HIV in the UK.' *BMJ* 1999; 319: 1211-12 (Editorial).
84 National Institutes of Health. 'Report of the NIH Panel to define principles of therapy of HIV infection.' *Morbidity and Mortality Weekly Report. Centers for Disease*

Control and Prevention 1998 (April 24), Vol 47, No. RR-5.

85 American College of Obstetricians and Gynecologists Committee on Obstetric Practice. 'ACOG committee opinion number 304, November 2004. Prenatal and perinatal human immunodeficiency virus testing: expanded recommendations'. *Obstet Gynecol* 2004;104(5 Pt 1):1119-24.

86 Minkoff H, O'Sullivan MJ. 'The case for rapid HIV testing during labor.' *JAMA* 1998; 279: 1743-4.

87 Sklar PA, Bathgate SL, Young HA, Parenti DM. 'Care of HIV-infected pregnant women in maternal-fetal medicine programs'. *Infect Dis Obstet Gynecol* 2001;9(2):81-7.

88 Cooper, Cynthia L, *op cit.*

89 Douglas, Gillian. *Law, Fertility and Reproduction.* Sweet & Maxwell 1991, at p 179.

90 Nair S, Morrison MF. 'The evaluation of maternal competency.' *Psychosomatics* 2000; 41(6): 523-30.

91 Anon. 'GP finds by chance a child who's not been immunised.' *Pulse* 17.6.00, at pp 68-73.

92 Menahem S, Halasz G. 'Parental non-compliance - a paediatric dilemma. A medical and psychodynamic perspective.' *Child Care Health Dev* 2000; 26(1):61-72.

93 Stone ML. 'Presidential Address'. *American College of Obstetricians and Gynecologists Newsletter*, 4 May 1979.

94 Oakley, Ann. *The Captured Womb.* Blackwell, London 1986, at p 219.

95 Research has repeatedly shown home birth to be as safe, if not safer, than hospital birth, see, for example: *BMJ* 1991; 303: 1517-9.

96 Cumberledge J. *Changing childbirth.* London: HMSO, 1993 [Cumberledge Report].

97 American Civil Liberties Union. *Reproductive Freedom: What's Wrong with Fetal Rights: A look at fetal protection statutes and wrongful death actions on behalf of fetuses.* American Civil Liberties Union 1997.
    www.aclu.org/issues/reproduct/fetal.html.

98 Chavkin, Wendy, professor of clinical public health at Columbia University, reported in: Cynthia L. Cooper. Pregnant and Punished. Ford Foundation Report, Winter 2003, on:
    http://www.fordfound.org/publications/ff_report/view_ff_report_detail.cfm?report _index=382.

99 Taylor, Diane. Does a foetus have more rights than its mother? *The Guardian*, Friday April 23, 2004.

100 Beiser, Vince. Women who stand at the crossroads, *op cit.*

101 Beiser, Vince, *Ibid.*

102 Paltrow LM. 'Punishing Women for Their Behavior During Pregnancy: An Approach That Undermines the Health of Women and Children.' In: Wetherington CL and Roman AB (Editors). *Drug Addiction Research and the Health of Women.* National Institute on Drug Abuse (DHHS), Bethesda, MD 1998, at pp. 467-501.

103 De Ville KA, Kopelman LM. 'Fetal protection in Wisconsin's revised child abuse law: right goal, wrong remedy'. *J Law Med Ethics.* 1999;27(4):332-42, 294.

104 Charo RA. 'Effect of the human genome initiative on women's rights and reproductive decisions'. *Fetal Diagn Ther* 1993;8 Suppl 1:148-59.

105 *Johnson v State* 1989, as cited in: American Civil Liberties Union. *Coercive and Punitive Governmental Responses to Women's Conduct During Pregnancy.* American Civil Liberties Union, September 1997, www.aclu.org/issues/reproduct/coercive.html.

106 American Civil Liberties Union. *Coercive and Punitive Governmental Responses to Women's Conduct During Pregnancy. Ibid.*

107 Stein, Ellen J. 'Maternal-Fetal conflict: Reformulating the equation,' *op cit*, at p102.

108 Per Blake J: *Ferguson v City of Charleston*, U.S. 4th Circuit Court of Appeals (1999) 186 F.3d 469.

109 Feinberg, Francine, drug treatment center director in Wisconsin, quoted in: Szalavitz, Maia. 'War On Drugs, War On Women.' *On The Issues*, Winter 1998.

110 American Civil Liberties Union. *Coercive and Punitive Governmental Responses to Women's Conduct During Pregnancy.* American Civil Liberties Union, September 1997, www.aclu.org/issues/reproduct/coercive.html.

111 *Johnson v State* 1989, cited in: American Civil Liberties Union. *Coercive and Punitive... Ibid.*

112 Talvi, Silja JA, *op cit.*

113 Paltrow, Lynn, director of National Advocates for Pregnant Women, quoted in: Beiser, Vince. Women who stand at the crossroads, *op cit.*

114 Chavkin, Wendy, quoted in Cooper, Cynthia L. Pregnant and Punished. *op cit.*

115 Court C. 'Child protection report urges more balance.' *BMJ* 1995; 311: 9 (News).

116 In: Aldgate J, Statham J. *The Children Act Now. Messages from Research. Studies in evaluating the Children Act 1989.* Stationery Office London 2001. Section 4, Working with Parents, pp64-81, at pp70-71.

117 Association for Improvement in Maternity Services. *False child abuse allegations are being made by NHS staff when mothers make complaints about maternity care, says maternity pressure group.* AIMS Press Release, 2 August 2004: www.aims.org.uk.

118 Robinson, Jean. 'Child protection system wilfully ignores principles of childcare' (letters). *Daily Telegraph* 5 August 2004, at p23.

119 per Jean Robinson, Honorary Research Officer of AIMS, retired Professor and lecturer in medical ethics and former member of the Ethics Committee of the Nursing and Midwifery Council, and of the General Medical Council's Professional Conduct Committee: AIMS Press Release, *Ibid.*

120 Eight-year-old Victoria Climbié was killed after a horrific catalogue of abuse while in the care of her great aunt and the aunt's boyfriend. The subsequent enquiry recommended, *inter alia*, greater coordination between departments concerned with children and families - Victoria died despite having come into contact with four social services departments, three housing departments, two specialist child protection teams of the Metropolitan Police, two hospitals and a families centre managed by the National Society for the Prevention of Cruelty to Children (NSPCC): Victoria Climbié Inquiry. *Victoria Climbié Report calls for radical change in the management of public services for children and families.* Statement, 28 January 2003: http://www.victoria-climbie-inquiry.org.uk.

121 Notwithstanding that, according to some commentators, in the case of Victoria Climbié, failure to identify the problem in time to save her arose from misunderstanding of the information available, not failure to share it: Action on Rights for Children. *Tracking children: a road to danger in the Children Bill?* 6 April 2004: www.arch-ed.co.uk.

122 House of Lords. Children Bill. HL Bill 35, 2004.

123 Action on Rights for Children. *Tracking children: a road to danger in the Children Bill?* 6 April 2004: www.arch-ed.co.uk.

124 'Statewatch News online. UK: Children Bill to introduce surveillance of every child and record 'concerns' about their parents'. *Statewatch* April 2004: http://www.statewatch.org/news/2004/apr/07children-bill.htm.

125 National Society for the Prevention of Cruelty to Children. *Children Bill media briefing*: www.nspcc.org.uk.

126 Cross, Michael. 'Eyes on the child'. *The Guardian*. 18 September 2003.

127 Arnott, Sarah. 'Ministers approve proposed database of all children in the UK'. *Computing* 8 December 2004.

128 Family & Youth Concern. 'Children Bill Update'. *Family Bulletin* No 116, Summer 2004.

129 Hague, Helen. 'Pupils urged to inform on problem parents'. *Daily Telegraph* 14 October 2002.

130 National Society for the Prevention of Cruelty to Children. *Children Bill media briefing*, *op cit*.

131 Watson M, Forshaw M. 'Child outpatient non-attendance may indicate welfare concerns.' *BMJ* 2002; 324:739.

132 Association for Improvement in Maternity Services. *AIMS journal* Summer 2002 vol 14 no 2: www.aims.org.uk.

133 National Commission of Enquiry into the Prevention of Child Abuse. *Childhood Matters. Report of the National Commission of Enquiry into the Prevention of Child Abuse*. Vols 1 and 2. Stationery Office. London 1996.

134 'We are aware of several cases where the courts have ordered children removed from the custody of their parents because of their apparent failure to eliminate [lice] infestations.': Pollack, Richard J. PhD. *Head lice: Information and Frequently Asked Questions*. Headlice Information, Laboratory of Public Health Entomology, Harvard School of Public Health.

135 Anon. 'US mother in court for sunburnt kids'. *BBC News*: Americas, 21 August 2002: http://news.bbc.co.uk/2/hi/americas/2207803.stm. (in this case the mother was arrested at a fairground and remained in jail for over a week awaiting a hearing).

136 *Grodin v Grodin*, 102 Mich. App. 396, 400-401, 301 N.W.2d 869 (Mich. Ct. App. 1980).

137 *Bonte v Bonte*, 136 N.H. 286, 289 (1992).

138 *Unger v Unger* 644 A.2d 691 (N.J. Sup. Ct. 1994).

139 Fenton, Ben. 'Court threat to "naked child" parents'. *Daily Telegraph* 11 July 2001.

140 Stanton AN. 'Sudden unexpected death in infancy associated with maltreatment: evidence from long term follow up of siblings'. *Arch Dis Child* 2003 Aug;88(8):699-701.

141 Carpenter RG, Waite A, Coombs RC *et al*. 'Repeat sudden unexpected and unexplained infant deaths: natural or unnatural?' *Lancet* 2005;365(9453):29-35.

142 http://www.sallyclark.org.uk.

143 Anon. 'Global experts slam cot death policy'. *BBC News*, published 20 January 2004 18:29:21 GMT: http://news.bbc.co.uk/go/pr/fr/-/1/hi/health/3412353.stm.

144 Anon. *BBC News*, published 6 October 2004 07:54:08 GMT: http://news.bbc.co.uk/go/pr/fr/-/1/hi/uk/3718862.stm.

145 Dyer C. 'Fewer care cases to be reopened than originally thought'. *BMJ* 2004; 328: 482 (News).

146 Hey E. 'Suspected child abuse: the potential for justice to miscarry'. *BMJ* 2003; 327: 299-300.

147 Alleyne, Richard. 'New guidelines for baby death trials'. *Daily Telegraph* 7 September 2004.

148 Fleming, Nic. 'Study finds 90pc double cot deaths are natural'. *Daily Telegraph* 31 December 2004.

149 Anon. Special report: House of Commons. 'Cannings case prompts concern'. *The Guardian*. 22 December 2004

150 Rozenberg, Joshua. 'Review of 300 child deaths identifies 28 "unsafe" cases'. *Daily Telegraph* 22 December 2004.

151 Rozenberg, Joshua and Jardine, Cassandra. 'Baby death mother to fight for jail pay-out'. *Daily Telegraph* 12 January 2005.

152 Per Dominic Grieve MP (Conservative), quoted in: Anon. Special report: House of Commons. 'Cannings case prompts concern'. *The Guardian*. 22 December 2004.

153 Blumenthal I. 'Shaken baby syndrome'. *Postgrad Med J* 2002;78(926):732-5.

154 Cory CZ, Jones BM. 'Can shaking alone cause fatal brain injury? A biomechanical assessment of the Duhaime shaken baby syndrome model'. *Med Sci Law* 2003;43(4):317-33.

155 Lantz PE, Sinal SH, Stanton CA, Weaver RG Jr. 'Perimacular retinal folds from childhood head trauma'. *BMJ* 2004;328:754–6.

156 Geddes JF, Plunkett J.. Editorial: 'The evidence base for the shaken baby syndrome'. *BMJ* 2004;328:719-20.

157 Lantz PE, personal communication.

158 See, for example: Punt J, Bonshek RE, Jaspan T, McConachie NS *et al*. 'The "unified hypothesis" of Geddes *et al* is not supported by the data'. *Pediatr Rehabil* 2004;7(3):173-84; Geddes JF, Tasker RC, Adams GG, Whitwell HL. 'Violence is not necessary to produce subdural and retinal haemorrhage: a reply to Punt *et al*'. *Pediatr Rehabil* 2004;7(4):261-5.

159 Talbert DG. 'Paroxysmal cough injury, vascular rupture and "shaken baby syndrome"'. *Med Hypotheses* 2005;64(1):8-13.

160 Munchausen's Syndrome is the fabrication of illness for attention-seeking purposes, named by a Dr Richard Asher in 1951, after a series of unlikely stories told by the fictional eighteenth century Baron von Munchausen in the book 'The Adventures of Baron Munchausen' by Rudolf Erich Raspe (1785) (according to the Oxford Reference Dictionary, the fictional Baron Munchausen was named after one Freiherr von Munchhausen, who fought against the Russians in the 1700s). In 1977 Professor Meadow adapted the term to apply to parents – almost always the mother – who fabricated illness in their children.

161 Le Fanu, James and Derbyshire, David. 'In the rush to protect children, "experts" use junk science to accuse innocent parents.' *Daily Telegraph* 13 December 2003, at p4.

162 Le Fanu, James and Derbyshire, David. 'Munchausen's by Proxy'. *Daily Telegraph* 13 December 2003.

163 Curtis, Tom. 'Torn apart by doctors' child abuse theory'. *Scotland on Sunday* 1 February 2004.

164 General Medical Council Professional Conduct Committee. Session beginning 7 June 2004: *New Case of Conduct - Professor David Patrick Southall*. GMC, Manchester 2004. Reported in full on: www.sallyclark.org.uk.

165 Dyer, Owen. 'Southall is barred for three years from child protection work'. *BMJ* 2004; 329: 366.

166 See, for example: Dyer, Clare. 'Father killed baby, high court rules'. *The Guardian* 11 December 2004.

167 McLean, Matilda. 'Mothers lose battle to be reunited with children'. *Daily Telegraph* 15 May 2004, at p10.

168 In *P v BW* (2003), the Family Division refused to entertain an application for a declaration that hearing family proceedings in private is incompatible with the Human Rights Convention, since the prohibition against publication was not absolute but left to the discretion of the court: hearing before Bennett J, 2 July 2003, reported *Daily Telegraph* Law Reports 10 July 2003, at p19.

169 Anon. 'Accused of abuse, but never tried'. *BBC News* 1 July 2003, 10:37 GMT 11:37 UK: www.bbc.co.uk.

170 Anon. 'Patel mother suffers child ban'. *BBC News* 13 June, 2003, 10:52 GMT 11:52 UK: www.bbc.co.uk.

171 Laville, Sandra. 'Mother cleared of killing baby fights to lift ban on her living with surviving child'. *Daily Telegraph* 15 December 2003, at p12.

172 Anon. 'False witness' (Editorial). *Daily Telegraph* 20 January 2004.

173 Dyer C. 'Fewer care cases to be reopened than originally thought'. *BMJ* 2004; 328: 482 (News).

174 Pook, Sally. 'Care order reviews offer little hope to parents'. *Daily Telegraph* 1 June 2004, at p2; Anon. 'Suffer the Parents' (Editorial). *Daily Telegraph* 1 June 2004.

175 Dyer, Clare. 'Falsely blamed mother asks law lords for right to sue'. *The Guardian* 21 June 2004.

176 Laville, Sandra. 'Parents cannot sue over child abuse errors'. *Daily Telegraph* 1 August 2003.

177 Dyer, C. 'Paediatricians did not have duty of care to patient's mother'. *BMJ* 2002; 325:1321.

178 Rozenberg, Joshua and Jardine, Cassandra. 'Baby death mother to fight for jail pay-out'. *Daily Telegraph* 12 January 2005.

179 Stephen Clark's statement after the GMC's investigation of his complaint against Professor Southall. August 2004: www.sallyclark.org.uk.

180 Dyer, Clare. 'The experts run for cover'. *The Guardian* 21 September 2004.

181 Kmietowicz, Zosia. 'Complaints against doctors in child protection work have increased fivefold'. *BMJ* 2004;328:601 (News).

182 Pragnell, Charles, 'Southall is just part of a much bigger problem'. Rapid responses to: Dyer, Owen. 'Southall is barred for three years from child protection work'. *BMJ* 2004; 329: 366. 17 August 2004: www.bmj.com.

183 Anon. 'Child protection system wilfully ignores principles of childcare' (letters). *Daily Telegraph* 5 August 2004, at p23.

184 British Association of Social Workers. Policy focus: 'Care or control?' *Professional Social Work* October 2004, at pp 18 – 19.

185 Hunt J, Macleod A, Thomas C. 'The Last Resort: Child Protection, the Courts and the 1989 Children Act.' In: Aldgate J, Statham J. *The Children Act Now. op cit*, pp198-201 (section 12), at p199.

186 Department of Health. *Framework for the Assessment of Children in Need and their Families*. Stationery Office, London 2000.

187 Anon. 'Working with Parents.' In: Aldgate J, Statham J. *The Children Act Now. op cit*, pp64-81 (Section 4), at p78.

188 Brophy J, Bates P, Brown L *et al*. 'Expert Evidence in Child Protection Litigation.' In: Aldgate J, Statham J. *The Children Act Now. op cit*, pp169-173 (Section 5) at 170.

189 In one recent case, the mother had been monitored daily during later pregnancy and the child protection order was enforced immediately upon delivery: Cramb, Auslan. 'Mother 'may have killed eight children''. *Daily Telegraph* 26 November 2001, at p 3; the baby was taken by police on delivery and the woman was reported to have been unaware of the surveillance programme: Scott, Kirsty. 'Baby taken from inquiry mother.' *The Guardian* 26 November 2001.

190 Association for Improvement in Maternity Services. *AIMS journal* Summer 2002 vol 14 no 2: www.aims.org.uk.

191 *In Re F (in utero)* (1988) TLR 5.2.88 : (1988) 2 AER 193 : (1988) 2 WLR 1288 : ILR 10.2.88 : (1988) FCR 529: (1988) 132 SJ 820 : (1988) 18 FAM LAW 337 : (1988) 138 NLJ 37 : (1988) 152 JPN 538 [Lawtel].

Chapter 6

Ongoing Challenges to Autonomy

Pressures promoting intervention in pregnancy are likely to intensify in future. In the US, the potential for invoking state interests to override maternal autonomy is very much alive. In the UK, there are multiple mechanisms, in addition to questioning competence or child welfare, by which women's compliance with medical advice might be secured. Whilst some of these concerns are, at present, purely speculative, it should be borne in mind that, repeatedly, throughout the sequence of British forced Caesarean cases, it appeared that no further such cases would arise: *In Re S*[1] was followed by Royal College of Obstetricians and Gynaecologists (RCOG) guidelines[2] which stated emphatically that judicial intervention was inappropriate, yet further cases followed.[3,4] Notwithstanding the guidance given in *Re MB*,[5] the *Collins* case[6] still occurred. Autonomy is, as yet, far from guaranteed, and there are numerous factors that may in the coming years create increased demands for control over pregnancy by parties other than the woman involved.

Pressures for a Swing in the Balance

Ever more extensive and sophisticated means for imaging and testing a foetus *in utero* are likely further to drive the current impetus towards 'quality control' of pregnancy outcome. Inevitably, this will intensify pressures on women to undergo such tests and, of course, to act upon the results – indeed, some commentators have argued that the advent of such technologies has not enhanced maternal choice at all.[7] Treatment options will increasingly become available, many of which may involve invasive procedures such as intra-uterine surgery – even the possibility of *in utero* heart transplant has been suggested.[8]

Extensive possibilities are being put forward for genetic testing in pregnancy; for example, a proposal for universal antenatal screening for the most common life-shortening single gene disorder, cystic fibrosis – for which one in 24 people in Britain is a carrier.[9] Feitshans has pointed out that, given the unfavourable chain of precedents regarding women's autonomy during pregnancy, the impact of new genetics technologies may require strong legislation to protect women's rights during pre-natal care, particularly regarding adequate information, rights of refusal and confidentiality of information about prenatal prognosis.[10]

Charo notes that social policies designed to serve the significant public interest in the size and makeup of populations are usually applied to women rather than to the population at large. So in future, increased knowledge about likely birth outcomes as a result of the Human Genome Initiative may result in women being held accountable by the public, their families, and any impaired children they may have for the size, health and demographic makeup of future generations. Moreover, women will be subjected to two conflicting pressures – that to avoid conceiving or bearing affected children, and that from the anti-abortion movement's attempts to restrict women's rights to decide to avoid such births.[11]

In this context, it is interesting to note the comments of one American court as early as 1980 in a case in which an infant was permitted to sue a medical laboratory for negligently permitting him to be born with Tay-Sachs disease, a rare genetic disorder. The court suggested that parents who made a conscious decision to proceed with a pregnancy despite knowledge of such an outcome could similarly be held liable:

> We see no sound public policy which should protect those parents from being answerable for the pain, suffering and misery which they have wrought upon their offspring.[12]

The already considerable pressure put upon women from health insurance companies, medical professionals and government agencies to undergo pre-natal tests is likely to increase as more tests become available and their reliability improves, perhaps accompanied by reduced invasiveness and greater potential for effective intra-uterine therapy.[13] Such developments are predicted to increase conflict between physicians and their pregnant patients,[14] and are likely also to have wider social and political implications. The current social climate is already perceived to stigmatise parents who refuse to abort 'low-quality' pregnancies[15] and, in circumstances of stretched health and social care financing – increasingly a phenomenon of global concern – tests to detect affected foetuses and 'avoid' their future high costs to society could well in future be viewed as legitimate targets for effective coercion.

Inevitably, such measures would also promote an atmosphere that would further 'encourage' pregnant women whose foetuses 'pass' the tests to maintain their high-quality product by recommended medical, dietary and lifestyle compliance. Such trends may be enhanced by current demographic changes leading towards smaller families, making children a scarcer, more precious resource. This, combined with several social trends such as reduced tolerance of even small degrees of risk or uncertainty, and increasing expectations of state intervention in family life, could promote the tendency to regard pre-natal duties towards the foetus increasingly as equating to those of parents towards born children. If, for example, parental smoking may justify giving child custody to the other parent,[16] why should a pregnant woman who smokes not be subject to checks or limitations, at least on birth?

As research increasingly yields knowledge of further potential harms and ever more delicate risks to the foetus, the range of issues – and the stage of pregnancy – that could be the focus for outside interest is likely also to expand. The scope of such concerns is potentially limitless – a recent animal study at Cambridge University suggested that a well-balanced diet in pregnancy resulted in healthier, longer-lived offspring; conversely, undernourishment while in the womb combined with a poor diet as an adult led to premature death.[17] This supports decades of research demonstrating that low birth weight babies are more likely to develop heart disease, stroke, hypertension and type II diabetes in later life,[18] suggesting that poor nutrition in the womb restricts normal foetal development and can cause permanent changes of physiology and metabolism – the 'foetal origins hypothesis'.

Nor need such issues be restricted to women who are obviously pregnant. In the Wisconsin case of *State v Kruzicki*,[19] discussed in Chapter 5, dissenting opinion from the American Medical Association during the original trial stated that 'the AMA believes that the detention of pregnant women [for treatment of drug or alcohol abuse] will be of limited value *since a considerable amount of damage could be done to the fetus before a woman even realized she was pregnant*'.[20]

In the US the scope as well as the frequency of attempted interventions in pregnant women's lifestyles is already expanding. Currently we have seen attempted compulsion, imposition of liability or punitive sanctions concerning abstinence from drug and alcohol use, use of prescription drugs (such as tetracycline and anti-retroviral drugs) and over-the-counter medicines (including Tylenol/codeine), choice of location for birth, method of delivery, failure to follow medical advice about sexual intercourse or bed rest during pregnancy, refusal to submit to medical examinations and delay in seeking medical assistance.

Some of the judiciary are using their own initiative as well as supporting medical recommendations. In January 2005 it was reported that a pregnant woman had been barred from getting a divorce until after her baby was born, even though the husband, who did not object, was not the father, was subject to a restraining order forbidding him to contact her, and was at the time in jail for beating her. The Washington state judge apparently commented that: 'It is the policy of the state that you cannot dissolve a marriage when one of the parties [*sic*] is pregnant.' Yet violence from male partners – including rape – commonly intensifies both during pregnancy and when the woman threatens to leave. As her attorney pointed out, the ruling was 'telling abusers that if you can get her pregnant you can keep her married to you.'[21] The notion that pregnancy may enable control of a woman's actions has also permeated the public consciousness. At least one husband has sought a court order arguing for visitation rights to his 'child' in the attempt to stop his estranged pregnant wife from leaving town until she gave birth – the application was denied.[22]

Another potential facet of policing pregnancy against a background of promoting only high-quality 'products' of gestation would be the attempted enforcement, by various possible measures, of health stipulations for pregnancy itself. For example, currently women are encouraged to take folic acid supplements *before* conceiving, to minimise the risk of neural tube defects among offspring, and this is particularly so among mothers who have already given birth to one affected child. If parents might be held liable for negligently permitting a child to be born with a genetic disorder about which they can do nothing, save avoiding or terminating the pregnancy, how much more readily might liability be imposed (or child abuse proceedings instituted, or criminal sanctions applied) for a foreseeable condition, with dire consequences for the child, that could have been averted altogether by the simple and non-invasive means of taking a daily dietary supplement for a few months? Similar considerations might, by extension, apply to women with conditions such as diabetes, or epilepsy, who are currently strongly advised to obtain preconceptual advice to ensure optimal treatment routines before contemplating pregnancy.

The logical next step could even be limitations on who may reproduce, either for those regarded as able to offer only a potentially hostile uterine environment, or for those of whose lifestyle choices society already disapproves. Already there is a private, and highly successful – though also highly controversial – organisation in the US dedicated to encouraging (voluntary) sterilisation of potential 'drug mothers'. Originally set up by Barbara Harris, the woman who, alongside a local conservative politician, attempted in the early 1990s to introduce legislation in California that would have made it a crime to give birth to a drug-damaged child,[23] the initiative now has chapters in 28 states. Formerly called 'Crack', for 'Children Requiring a Caring Kommunity' [*sic*], and now renamed 'Project Prevention' it claims that well over a thousand women have responded to its offer of a $200 inducement for being sterilised.

Inevitably, Project Prevention has attracted intense criticism, not least because a disproportionate number of those who have taken up the offer have been of black or Latino origin. Harris however can hardly be accused of racism: she is married to a black man and all her adoptive children are black, and the project has been greeted with approval in some quarters, including by some social workers, prison wardens and probation officers, a prominent African-American community activist in Los Angeles and a popular talk-radio host, as well as from the conservative right.[24,25]

Harris claims that Project Prevention is doing something positive, whereas there are few public policy initiatives making significant inroads into the problem. Moreover, the scheme is not that removed from official policies: notably sterilisation (unlike abortion or fertility treatment) is freely available through Medicaid (public funding) – indeed, most of those who have taken Project Prevention's dollars have been sterilised at public expense – and judges have on occasion ordered drug-using parents with children in care to have no more children until they are judged fit to parent those they already have.[26,27]

Increased neonatal testing is also likely and could have retrograde effects on attitudes to pregnant women, in terms of both increased prenatal surveillance and child welfare issues (see Chapter 5). There is significant potential for punitive actions if tests on the neonate – for which there are expanding possibilities[28] – reveal either drug use or mal-compliance with medical advice, especially in the presence of chronic disorders known to affect the foetus but amenable to treatment, for example, diabetes.

On the frontiers of technology, the continual pushing back of the threshold of possible viability outside the womb holds the potential for attempts to intervene progressively earlier in pregnancy, and is likely increasingly to blur the already imprecise viability distinction often drawn by courts, especially in the US. This could well promote the notion of foetal interests – especially in combination with increasing understanding of the sensory and sentient capabilities of the foetus – and may increase support for implying foetal 'personhood' or granting foetal rights at ever earlier stages of gestation. Such possibilities are likely to be seized upon with enthusiasm by opponents of abortion, and are unlikely to enhance pregnant women's autonomy for reasons extensively discussed in earlier chapters. On the other hand, predictions from research into artificial amniotic fluid and methods for supporting extra-uterine gestation suggest the further possibility that technology will continue to develop to the point where an unwilling woman will no longer need to gestate the foetus at all – possibly within as little as 15 years. Such developments may be expected both to enhance the view of the foetus as having independent interests and to diminish the respect given to a pregnant woman's autonomy and privacy rights if she is merely exercising an option to gestate inside her body, rather than undergoing the inevitable consequences of pregnancy.[29,30,31]

Diversity of Opinion and Approach

As has been noted, ethical and medico-legal viewpoints on maternal autonomy, foetal rights and the proper resolution of obstetric conflict are diverse. The currently prevailing view supporting maternal autonomy has vociferous opponents and could change, as might social and judicial attitudes.

Although the RCOG in the UK has from the beginning weighed in against using the courts to achieve obstetric coercion, cases that have occurred in Britain suggest that not all staff at 'grass roots' level agree. One obstetric team stated (albeit in the hypothetical context of a woman *preferring* a Caesarean delivery) that:

> *Unfortunately*, the law does not distinguish between the rights of a mentally competent but foolish (unwise) pregnant woman and other adults.[32]

In the US, patient autonomy does seem to have gained some ground within the medical profession. A national survey in 1987 reported that 46 per cent of leading maternal-foetal medicine specialists was in favour of detention for women refusing medical advice and thereby endangering the life of the foetus, and 47 per cent supported court orders for procedures such as intra-uterine transfusions.[33] Following the Carder case, the American Medical Association[34] and the American College of Obstetricians and Gynecologists[35] have stated firmly that forced intervention is inappropriate, as have numerous other medical, public health and other organisations in the course of various court cases (see Chapter 5). By 2002, only four per cent of directors of maternal-foetal medicine fellowship programmes believed that pregnant women should be forced to undergo potentially life-saving treatment for the sake of their foetus, and the number of requests for court orders in such cases had declined – although, some practitioners and some judges still supported them.[36]

However, whilst this apparently dramatic decline in the number of obstetricians favouring compulsion as regards obstetric procedures has been much cited, in a less-quoted study by researchers in Michigan in 2002 it was found that obstetricians, paediatricians, and family practice physicians were overwhelmingly in favour of involvement of the criminal justice system for drug and alcohol abuse during pregnancy. Almost all – 95 per cent – stated that pregnant women had a moral duty 'to ensure they had healthy babies', and well over half (59 per cent) felt that this should translate to a legal responsibility to do so.

The proportion of doctors approving of mandatory screening in pregnancy was 77 per cent as regards HIV testing, 61 to 75 per cent (depending on subspecialty) for alcohol abuse and, perhaps curiously, much lower – 43 to 55 per cent – for illicit drug use.[37] Many physicians recognised the futility of criminal action, with 61 per cent agreeing that fear of prosecution would deter pregnant drug users from seeking pre-natal care and, as the report put it, were generally 'opposed to criminal prosecution for either alcohol abuse or illicit drug use' during pregnancy. Nevertheless, it is noteworthy that nearly 40 per cent *did not* agree that fear of prosecution would deter women from seeking care (notwithstanding all the evidence that it does), and that there was still arguably an alarmingly high proportion in favour of prosecutions – 18 to 31 per cent as regards alcohol and 23 to 34 per cent for illicit drug use. It is also notable that these proportions are more or less equivalent, and that these doctors therefore favour prosecution as much for a legal as for an illegal activity – in the former case, effectively criminalising women for the fact of pregnancy itself.

Overall, rather than criminalising women for such activities however, many physicians would prefer to see their children removed: a majority agreed that existing laws regarding child abuse and neglect should be redefined to include alcohol (54 per cent in favour) and drug abuse (61 per cent in favour) during pregnancy, and 52 per cent approved of new laws to define drug or alcohol use during pregnancy as 'child abuse' for the purposes of removing that child from maternal custody. Around half of all physicians approved of the notion of court-ordered contraception for alcohol- and drug-abusing women (50 and 47 per cent respectively – interestingly, slightly higher for alcohol).[38] If over half of involved physicians in the US would like to see laws that enable children to be removed should the mother have used alcohol during pregnancy, this does not bode well for the future of pregnant women's autonomy.

In addition, as has been discussed, other legislation impacting on foetal status may have an influence on the degree to which pregnant women's autonomy is upheld. The approach of the courts in various jurisdictions to the question of whether a pregnant woman's refusal of medical treatment may be judicially overridden, either in her interests or those of the unborn child, 'has arguably been confused and contradictory'[39] and judicial comments reveal some ambivalence even in the UK. For example, even though the court in *In Re F (in utero)* noted that the only purpose of extending its jurisdiction to include a foetus was to enable the mother's actions to be controlled,[40] at least one judge clearly regretted that this was not possible. May LJ stated: 'this is a case in which, on its facts, I would exercise the jurisdiction if I had it'[41] and:

I have no doubt myself that if the court had power I would give leave to issue the necessary originating summons and make the unborn child a ward of court.[42]

Similarly, comments of the court in *Re MB* suggest that at least some of the judiciary are uncomfortable with the notion that the woman should not be called to account for an adverse pregnancy outcome if she has failed to follow medical advice:

> Although it might seem *illogical* that a child capable of being born alive is protected by the criminal law from intentional destruction, and by the Abortion Act from termination otherwise than as permitted by the Act, but is not protected from the (*irrational*) decision of a competent mother not to allow medical intervention to avert the risk of death, this appears to be the present state of the law.[43]

Indeed, there are some grounds for viewing the decisions of the higher courts in cases like *Collins*, in the UK, and *Re AC*, in the US, as anomalies – exceptions to the general rule of first instance decisions in which courts have almost always followed the line of medical argument (the practical difficulties in upholding autonomy at the level of the family court are discussed below). Thus the court in *Re MB* noted that the decision in *Re AC* revealed 'a significant change of view' in the American decisions but suggested that despite detecting in 'the most recent trend in appellate decisions a move towards the approach of the English courts', overall the US decisions were inconclusive.[44] This, in turn, suggests that the conclusion might readily swing the other way.

Are the Courts Resorting to Moral Arguments?

In this context it is worrying that the language used to describe women refusing interventions has been, at times, quite intemperate and that, at other times, courts have introduced factors which suggest more of a moral than a medical judgement.

For example, in *In Re F*[45], it was stated of the mother in court that 'her personal life and sexual relationships were... utterly chaotic'; she 'formed casual relationships with men' and had a 'strained relationship' with her own mother. In *Re MB*, the psychiatrist's opinion that the woman was 'naïve' and 'not very bright' was reiterated.[46] S in *Collins* was described as 'unusual, unreasonable';[47] her thinking process 'bizarre'; her refusal to accept treatment as 'intransigence',[48] and her decision to exercise her right to refuse as 'morally repugnant'.[49]

In the US, suggestions that a woman's refusal was religiously motivated have been used to undermine the validity of her decision. Ayesha Madyyun's treating physicians portrayed her wish to wait and attempt to deliver spontaneously before resorting to Caesarean section as an irrational religious objection to surgery.[50] By the time of the Marlowe case in Pennsylvania, merely suggesting that a woman's motives were religious – hospital lawyers stated that the woman adamantly refused to deliver by Caesarean section because of 'religious' beliefs –

seemed sufficient to impugn her motives; the claim was later denied by the woman.[51]

In contrast, the motives of those attempting to override pregnant women's wishes – even where there was compelling evidence of gross abuses of the power vested in them by the medical and legal systems – have, by and large, been upheld as pure, even noble.

In the *Collins* case, the Court stated variously:

> It is clear that everyone involved in the process which led to MS's admission ... was equally *motivated by a genuine desire to achieve what in their professional judgment was best* for MS herself and for her baby.[52]

> [On Louize Collins] Whatever our conclusion we *admire her courage* in reaching any decision at all in such difficult circumstances.[53]

> [On the (illegal) use of the 1983 Act] Even when used by *well-intentioned individuals* for what they believe to be *genuine and powerful reasons, perhaps shared by a large section of the community....*[54]

> [On the original *ex parte* application where the judge was 'told of some things which were not true (notably that S had been in labour for 24 hours) and was not told some other things which would have been highly material (that S was thought to have capacity to refuse treatment, that she had been in touch with a solicitor, and that she had not been told of the application)']: Those lapses, although *not involving any bad faith*, are highly regrettable.[55]

Thus the judiciary is sometimes hostile, in language if not in law, to the principle of a woman refusing what has been almost universally regarded as irrefutably correct medical advice; moreover, whilst upholding the law, there are indications of a certain ambivalence as to so doing. This is perhaps understandable while the judiciary places such faith in medical pronouncements. Lord Justice Thorpe has commented:

> *It is unnecessary to dwell on best interests in the context of cases involving Caesarean section. Obviously*, if the patient lacks capacity, the obstetrician proceeds towards the goal of successful delivery in the exercise of his clinical judgment. However, if the consultant is faced with a clinical choice between two possible procedures, in making that choice he should have regard to the circumstances and the patient's stated or presumed preference.[56]

This is an illuminating statement for the multiple interlinked linked assumptions it contains – all of which may seem perfectly reasonable without further knowledge of the shaky basis of some of the medical evidence underlying such decisions. It presupposes that successful delivery is indeed best achieved by Caesarean section once this has been recommended; that there are, in such cases, no other possible alternative procedures, and that best interests are automatically served by such intervention. Bearing in mind that in English law it is the *woman's* best interests that should be considered, not those of the foetus, this seems a question at least worthy of further examination by any future court asked to adjudicate.

Rights of Refusal

The possibilities for challenging the basis of refusals are amply illustrated by *In Re T*[57], in which T's refusal was vitiated in the initial interlocutory hearing by the judge's conclusion that 'because of her condition and the effect of the narcotic medication she had not been fully rational when she signed the refusal form'. At the subsequent hearing her capacity to make a rational decision was held unimpaired and, despite the influence of her mother, her refusal of transfusion was deemed voluntary – but she was found to have been 'lulled into a sense of false security by the hospital staff and ... misinformed as to the availability and effect of alternative procedures' and her refusal did not extend to the changed situation. On appeal by the Official Solicitor as guardian *ad litem*, it was held that 'in all the circumstances, including her mental and physical state when she signed the form, the pressure exerted on her by her mother and the misleading response to her inquiry as to alternative treatment, her refusal was not effective'.

This sequence demonstrates the range of factors (including their own misrepresentations) which doctors are invited to consider in determining, in their own clinical judgement, whether a patient's refusal may be valid. There is a potential for illicit drug use, too, to be advanced as a vitiating factor: Flagler and colleagues have commented[58] that many behaviours – such as addictions – that may ultimately harm a foetus cannot properly be described as choices, and one clinician has suggested that pregnant women 'imprisoned by their addiction' should not be abandoned without therapeutic intervention.[59] Whilst this is perfectly reasonable in terms of efforts to make (voluntary) addiction treatment more widely available to pregnant women, and to increase their practical access to it by suitable childcare provision, it is not hard to see how it could become a rationale for imposing forced treatment.

Moreover, whilst accepting that 'misinforming a patient, whether or not innocently, and the withholding of information which is expressly or impliedly sought by the patient may well vitiate either a consent or a refusal', the Court in *In Re T* noted that failure in performance of a doctor's (general) duty to give the patient appropriately full information sounds in negligence and does not, as such, vitiate a consent or refusal.[60] This demonstrates one reason why, in principle, the US concept of informed consent may be more protective of patient autonomy. In the UK, the implication is that consent remains valid even when a doctor fails to inform an unquestioning patient of relevant known risks, yet failure to inform (or mis-informing – even 'not innocently') a patient when specifically asked for information may override a refusal, which seems a somewhat skewed position.

The Court also considered the argument that 'informed refusal' should be required before a patient is allowed to dissent[61] and concluded that, since English law does not accept the concept of informed consent (although this is increasingly regarded as an ethical imperative for good medical practice),[62] it would reject any concept of 'informed refusal'.[63] However it is arguable, given the criteria in *Re C*[64] and, indeed, the stipulations in *In Re T* itself as to ensuring that the patient has full notice of the consequences of refusal, that a level of informed refusal is already required. Mason and McCall Smith note that the stipulation in *Re C*[65] that the patient must comprehend the information given does not require that the patient *can* understand but that the patient *does* understand – this places a paradoxical obligation on medical staff to ensure that understanding is reached, when 'staff might not want the patient to understand if they disagree with the nature of his or her decision'.[66] Clearly, there is room for manoeuvre here.

A further issue is the level of semantic confusion evident in various rulings as to the rationality of refusal decisions. British law affirms that a patient may make treatment decisions even when these might appear misguided, *irrational* or absurd, and that treatment may be refused even if the reasons are *rational*, *irrational*, unknown or non-existent.[67,68] To any lay person, equating 'irrational' with some flawed mental process, and knowing that the courts may intervene if a person's mental processing is inadequate, this might appear to contradict common sense.[69]

As the court in *Re MB* put it:

> Irrationality is here used to connote a decision which is so outrageous in its defiance of logic or of accepted moral standards that no sensible person who had applied his mind to the question to be decided it could have arrived at it.

Distinguishing this from a misperception, which is more readily accepted to be a disorder of the mind the court continued:

> Although it might be thought that irrationality sits uneasily with competence to decide, panic, indecisiveness and irrationality in themselves do not as such amount to incompetence, but they may be symptoms or evidence of incompetence.[70]

The various pronouncements in *In Re T*,[71] in which T's refusal was first held vitiated because she had 'not been fully rational', and then her capacity to make a 'rational decision' about her treatment was held unimpaired, suggest that the judiciary is not immune to the same level of confusion, and that acceptable reasons for refusal may not be impervious to future manipulation. Similarly, the Court in *Collins*, in ruling that the *Mental Health Act* could not be deployed to detain an individual against her will 'merely because her thinking process is unusual, even apparently bizarre and *irrational*...,' later in the same paragraph stated 'she may be perfectly *rational* and quite outside the ambit of the Act ...,'[72] as if rationality was at issue. Whilst this may appear to be semantic quibbling, if the courts are basing such weighty decisions on these definitions, they have a responsibility to be both precise and consistent.

A further possibility is that, were policy issues in such cases to come more to the fore (*vide infra*), the existence of public policy grounds for vitiating consent[73] suggests that policy considerations could also be taken into account in refusals of consent. Maclean comments

> If policy arguments can be used to vitiate a freely given consent where harm is likely to occur ... then public policy should at least be considered where refusal of consent may result in such harm.[74]

On a positive note, the *Mental Capacity Bill* expected to become law in the UK in 2007 (see Chapter 1) will, for the first time, allow the appointment of healthcare proxies in the UK, as well as giving legal backing to advance directives (living wills).[75] The law will give statutory force to the legal presumption that individuals have the capacity to take their own health care decisions, unless proved otherwise. Even if they cannot, where they have appointed a health care proxy to make decisions on their behalf, a doctor or hospital would have to apply to the court of protection to challenge any decision so made. Under the related *Mental Health Bill*, even individuals with mental illness should be helped to make their own decision or to participate in the decision, where possible. The proposed new legislation does not bar pregnant women from making advance treatment refusals, or appointing proxies; however some provisions introduce greater flexibility, which may be of concern in the light of the use of mental health legislation in past UK forced Caesarean cases. In particular, rather than allowing only treatment of benefit for the mental condition for which a patient is admitted, the new law requires that 'treatment is available which is appropriate in the patient's case'.[76] This may fill the current illogical lacuna as to treatment of unrelated conditions, but clearly allows greater scope for the imposition of treatments deemed by clinical judgement to be in the patient's best interests, which could conceivably include obstetric interventions.

Status of the Foetus

The 'novel problem of considerable legal and ethical complexity'[77] facing the courts in the case of treatment refusals by pregnant women is predicated on the significance of the presence of a foetus. In the US, as discussed in Chapter 1, foetal status may be a fluid concept, varying depending on the state and the statute involved. Many states have introduced specific foetal homicide laws, which cover a range of stages of development from conception to viability. In some cases, courts have held that the wording of existing homicide statutes could be taken to include a viable foetus[78,79,80,81] – demonstrating the potential for judicial willingness to reinterpret existing provisions that raises the issue of how else such semantic manoeuvring might be applied. The federal *Unborn Victims of Violence Act 2004 (UVVA)*[82] amends the federal criminal code to create a separate offence of causing death or bodily injury to an 'unborn child'; its provisions have been heavily criticised for, *inter alia*, not distinguishing stage of pregnancy – implying the possibility of charges for violence to a fertilised ovum, blastocyst or early embryo.[83] Of even more of concern as regards the pregnant woman are the rulings in some states, such as South Carolina, that have declared that a viable foetus is a person and so covered by state child abuse laws.[84]

Pressures for more foetal rights legislation are unlikely to subside in the US, and the anti-abortion agenda views any attempt to give the foetus 'personhood', even through legislation with entirely different aims, as positive progress towards its own goals. Notably, earlier attempts to enforce the right to extraordinary medical care for seriously handicapped neonates involved tactics such as pressing for state and federal legislation, gathering political support and promoting candidates empathic to their cause, courting the support of related organisations, seeking out legal test cases and timing campaigns to intercept court decisions[85] – similar to the tactics that the anti-abortion lobby now use to promote foetal homicide and drug mother laws as a means of enhancing the legal status of the foetus and so strengthening the case against abortion. The protection of 'unborn children' from uncooperative 'mothers' is not at odds with such goals.

At the start of 2005, conservative Christians were reported to be confident that they had 'gained a philosophical majority' in Congress and across America, and were awaiting the chance to press through legislation on several issues dear to the heart of the religious right.[86] Commentators as diverse as the US National Organization for Women (NOW)[87] and the British Medical Journal (BMJ)[88] expressed concerns that Bush's second term of office would promote regressive social policies underpinned by fundamentalist views on sexuality and family relationships, and that expected changes in the composition of the Supreme Court would facilitate a review of the legality of abortion.

Meanwhile, the boundaries formerly established by birth – and relying so heavily on a woman to provide the definition of humanity – are dissolving, thanks to medical technology. As briefly mentioned in Chapter 1, when the *Unborn Victims of Violence Act*[89] was under consideration in Congress, it was noted that 'the born alive rule has been rendered obsolete by progress in science and medicine'.[90] This rule developed at common law because pregnancy was difficult to determine, so live birth was the most reliable means of ensuring that a woman was with child and that the child was in fact a living being. As one comment had it, 'the historical basis of the born alive rule was developed out of a lack of sophisticated medical knowledge.'[91] The House of Representatives specifically noted that now: 'The use of ultrasound, fetal heart monitoring, in vitro fertilization, and fetoscopy has greatly enhanced our understanding of the development of unborn children,' [92] contributing to the trend in American law to abolish the born alive rule in such instances as wrongful death actions and foetal homicide laws in various states. In turn, 'such legislation further reflects the growing trend in American jurisdictions of recognizing greater legal protections for unborn children, a trend consistent with the advancements in medical knowledge and technology.' [93]

The House also cited the case of *People v Hall* (1990),[94] in which a court relied on advancements in medical technology to determine that a 28-week-old foetus removed from its mother's womb by Caesarean section and immediately placed on a ventilator was a 'person' under New York penal law. This implies that a foetus can go directly from life-support via the placenta to life-support via a ventilator without so much as an intervening breath and still count as a 'person' – making medical technology rather than the act of giving birth the definer of human status.

Even in the UK, foetal status and interests remain an emotive issue, with boundaries that are sometimes muddled, among both medical professionals and the judiciary. After *In Re L* (1996),[95] as previously noted, the chairman of the British Medical Association's Medical Ethics Committee queried the competence assessment. He was quoted as saying:

> The doctors were justified in seeking a ruling from the court because the mother's decision affected not just her own life but the life of her baby. I am, however, puzzled about the decision which cast doubt on the mother's mental competence...'[96]

This seems a curious statement – if disagreement with doctors is not to be deemed an indicator of incompetence, but nevertheless justifies seeking a ruling to override a woman's wishes, on what basis might such a declaration be given? The implication is that since the decision affected the life of the foetus, this ought to be reason to grant a declaration even in the case of a competent woman, a position completely at odds with the principles of English law since the foetus has no legal persona to justify setting its interests above the woman's right to refuse treatment.

English law does recognise at least the potential for public interest to override individual refusals of consent to medical treatment. As was said in a different context:

> The right to refuse consent to treatment is not abrogated even where the treatment is necessary to preserve life and *generally* the right will override the public interest in the preservation of life.[97]

Moreover, various judicial pronouncements suggest that the legal view of the foetus is not as uncomplicated as blunt statements about its lack of personhood or of legal rights until born alive might suggest. Notwithstanding the many recent developments in medical and legal approaches to the foetus, there is still no precise legal definition of what a foetus is and, in particular, whether it is to be regarded as a separate entity or as part of the mother. This is a crucial distinction for the purposes of obstetric conflict – if the foetus is part of the mother, arguably she could no more be charged for causing harm to it than she could for cutting her own finger, or hair.

Again, different approaches to this question are apparent between jurisdictions and purposes. While clearly the federal *UVVA* in the US, and several corresponding state homicide laws, define the foetus as a separate entity, this is not true in all states, nor necessarily for other types of legislation. In the Australian case discussed in Chapter 1 that led ultimately to loss of a foetus being embraced within the definition of grievous bodily harm in the *Crimes Act*, the court ruled that the close physical bond between mother and foetus justified its being regarded as part of the mother.[98] Notwithstanding the caveat that this change was for the purposes of crimes of violence, the approach is distinct from that taken so far by the English courts.

In *Attorney-General's Reference* (No. 3 of 1994)[99] (*vide infra*), the House of Lords explicitly rejected the view that the foetus was a mere part of the mother's body, Lord Mustill described:

> ... an intimate bond between the foetus and the mother ... two distinct organisms living symbiotically, not a single organism with two aspects ... the foetus ... is a unique organism.[100]

Similarly, Lord Hope of Craighead commented:

> It [the *Human Fertilisation and Embryology Act* 1990 (*HFEA* 1990)] serves to remind us that an embryo is in reality a separate organism from the mother from the moment of its conception. ... So the foetus cannot be regarded as an integral part of the mother ... notwithstanding its dependence upon the mother for its survival until birth.[101]

These statements were considered in *Collins*, where the Court commented:

> Accordingly the interests of the foetus cannot be disregarded on the basis that in refusing treatment which would benefit the foetus a mother is simply refusing treatment for herself.[102]

Moreover, Lord Craighead's comment referring to *HFEA* 1990 is particularly interesting in the light of a discussion by Stein, shortly after its coming into effect, of the potential effects of the Act. Stein postulated that the 24-week time limit introduced for terminations of pregnancy on 'normal' grounds[103] might alter the general view of the viable foetus; some commentators had even suggested that it could enable wardship of an unborn (but viable) foetus.[104] Stein suggested that the Act 'may encourage legal intervention parallel to the US practice of balancing the rights of the fetus versus those of the mother'.[105]

Whilst these concerns do not seem to have materialised, it is not difficult to envisage that the Act could have led to viable foetuses being regarded as deserving of enhanced protections.[106] This example illustrates how other legal changes affecting the foetus (which are not unlikely in the current climate of genetic testing, cloning, embryo research etcetera), could have a lateral impact on foetal status. Similarly, the imposition of any form of liability for third party acts that harm the foetus would seem likely in the UK to require a definition of a starting point at which liability commences – the most likely candidate for which is the point of viability.

Similar developments elsewhere also suggest that the global judicial climate is potentially flexible. For example, Queensland in Australia added foetal homicide and foetal harm offences to its criminal code in 1977.[107] In 2002, the Queensland Court of Appeal upheld a Supreme Court ruling that a mother has a duty of care to her unborn child when driving a motor vehicle. Although a driving case is arguably different from others in that the purpose of the action is generally driven by an insurance claim, the court's comment is worrying: 'That the foetus was within the driver is only incidentally relevant.'[108]

Even the most apparently authoritative court rulings may leave some scope for challenge. For example, although the European court ruled decisively in *Paton v United Kingdom*[109] that the foetus has no 'right to life' under Article 2(1) of the European Convention for the Protection of Human Rights and Fundamental Freedoms, in a subsequent abortion case the European Commission of Human Rights, while not expressing an opinion on the instant case, stated that it would not exclude that in certain circumstances Article 2 *does* offer such protection, though it did not indicate what those circumstances might be.[110]

Similarly, in another European case in which two German women challenged the then West German restrictions on abortion, the Commission also declined to decide whether the foetus has rights under Article 2 but commented that:

> Pregnancy cannot be said to pertain uniquely to the sphere of private life. Whenever a woman is pregnant, her private life becomes closely connected with the developing foetus.[111]

Notably, these were all abortion cases concerning early pregnancy – an obstetric conflict case concerning a viable foetus could prompt further consideration of the matter and possibly a change in approach.

Foetal Protection

Any change in foetal legal status in the UK would have immediate implications for foetal protection policies as have been implemented extensively in the US, where many states now enable the foetus to be taken into custody if it is endangered[112] (see Chapter 5). The American Civil Liberties Union, which has warned of the dangers of such foetal protection statutes, says it 'frequently opposes court orders to seeking to compel women to act according to doctors' advice as to place of birth or Caesarean section'.[113] In the US it has been argued extensively that pressures for foetal protection laws stem more from an anti-abortion agenda than from concern for child health.[114]

Many groups would like to lobby for similar laws in the UK and, as in the US, anti-abortion politics readily spill over into this arena too. For example, the final *Collins* ruling was described as 'perverse' by the anti-abortion charity 'Life', whose spokesman said: 'We feel strongly that the mother in that situation should have a Caesarean in order to save the child's life and also to preserve her own health'.[115] The incentive is clear – the more rights are given to the foetus and taken away from the mother, the higher the perceived chance of success in the goal of restricting abortion. The movement in the US has overtly stated that whilst, legislatively, 'full legal protection' for 'unborn children' is its long-term goal, it also supports more limited legislation, which can be passed more quickly, in an 'incremental strategy' that has encompassed parental notification laws (requiring that teenagers' parents be notified when they seek abortions), restrictions on public funding for abortion, banning so-called 'partial-birth' (late-term) abortion (usually carried out because of a threat to the mother's health or life), and requiring that 'women seeking abortions be given the facts about the development of unborn babies'.[116] One proposed measure, the *Unborn Child Pain Awareness Act*, would require doctors to inform women seeking abortions after 20 weeks' gestation of medical evidence that foetuses feel pain, and offer anaesthetic to minimise that pain[117] (somewhat ironic in a country that until recently circumcised a large proportion of its male neonates without anaesthetic at all – a practice that causes both short- and long-term changes in infant behaviours).[118,119]

In the UK Clarke, noting the dangers of moves towards policing pregnancy, suggests that indeed, any greater control over treatment of the foetus *in utero* would threaten abortion availability.[120] Whilst the UK would appear to offer solid legal protection against such actions, again, judicial pronouncements suggest a few windows though which changes might creep. For example, in *In Re T* it was stated:

> North American jurisprudence recognises a rare exception to the principle [of competent adults' right to refuse treatment] where treatment is necessary to prevent an innocent third party being harmed[121].... English jurisprudence *may not* recognise such an exception.[122]

As discussed, judicial attitudes in cases of forced Caesareans have leaned heavily towards safeguarding the foetus, and commentary even in those cases which have upheld autonomy has suggested that foetal protection has heavy emotive appeal. Even in *Collins*, the Court observed that the facts that S was heavily pregnant and adamantly refusing treatment were, at least potentially, of 'compelling importance' to any informed judgement, and that to require Louize Collins to make her judgement by ignoring this reality would be absurd.[123] Moreover, in considering assessment for sectioning, the Court said:

> ...her health and safety could not be assessed on the basis that she was not 36 weeks pregnant and not suffering from pre-eclampsia. Those responsible have to deal in realities, and MS was dangerously ill. Although the risks were caused by her pregnancy, *the potential damage could have fallen within section 2(2)(b)*.[124]

This latter statement is open to interpretation – s2(b) deals with detention in the interests of the patient's own health or safety or 'with a view to the protection of other persons' – but presumably implied, since the foetus does not in law qualify within the remit of 'other persons,' that if S was judged to be putting her own health at risk because of mental illness, the pregnancy being the incidental underlying cause of the 'damage', the sectioning might have been legal. This would not, however, obliterate the problem that treatment related to the pregnancy would not fall (*Tameside*[125] reasoning aside) under the definition of treatment of the mental condition (and in any case the application here was under s2). The reality which Collins faced – S's pregnancy-related illness – therefore could not have been solved in this manner even if S had qualified as sufficiently mentally ill to justify detention. The court's reasoning here seems to have gone slightly askew, since it had elsewhere criticised the failure to maintain the distinction between S's need for treatment arising from her pregnancy, and the separate question of whether her depression warranted her detention in hospital.[126] Hence whilst it may well have been 'absurd' to ignore the reality of S's pregnancy in terms of the emotional response to the situation, there was no legal justification for taking it into consideration in the context of the s2 application, as the Court elsewhere made crystal clear. Yet the tone of this passage suggests that the Court itself was not immune to this form of reasoning.

Mason and McCall Smith favour arriving at a 'humane' solution in such cases even if this is not the correct jurisprudential one. They compare the declaration given in *Re S*,[127] allowing forced Caesarean, with the final verdict in the US case of *Re AC*[128] (which vacated the previous order compelling Carder to have a Caesarean), supporting the former on the grounds that the mother would otherwise have died, and the latter on the grounds that maternal death could not have been avoided anyway[129] – 'the perfect example of circumstances altering the case'.[130] It would also seem to be an example of a risk-related standard applied to competent women that, unless the entire jurisprudential principle of adult autonomy is to be overturned, must – again – be predicated on the presence of a foetus. Again, a slippery slope comes into view.

Maternal Liability

The Court in *Collins* also commented that '... pregnancy increases the personal responsibilities of a woman ...'[131] Whilst the extent of these increased responsibilities was not specifically defined, the Court did dwell at length on the observations of Lord Mustill and Lord Hope in *Attorney-General's Reference* (No 3 of 1994) (1997),[132] in particular as regards the lack of common law penalties for harm to a child *en ventre sa mere*[133] compared with the position of the foetus once born alive, which '...may also carry with it the effect of things done to it before birth which, after birth, may prove to be harmful'.[134] As discussed (see Chapter 1), this Reference held that injuring a child *in utero* could create liability for manslaughter if the child was born alive but subsequently died, leaving open the question of maternal liability for grossly negligent actions during pregnancy. Maclean points out that if an unreasonable or irrational refusal (which all such refusals are likely to be argued to be) of Caesarean section could be considered gross negligence, and a woman who has so refused gives birth to a live child who subsequently dies, she may be guilty of manslaughter – a draconian and undesirable way of policing pregnancy, and a legal lacuna which the Court in *Collins* failed to address.[135]

There could indeed be extensive possibilities for such actions, which might both add to pre-natal pressures to comply with medical advice and create a climate in which women with adverse pregnancy outcomes became suspected of foetal abuse, as has happened in the US. Women in the *Charleston* case were suspected of drug use if there was, *inter alia*: unexplained intra-uterine growth retardation, pre-term labour, birth defects, abruptio placentae or intra-uterine foetal death. Yet many such features regarded as suspicious are, according to the *amicus* brief in the case, as much indicators of poverty as of cocaine use.[136]

Apart from objections on the grounds of maternal autonomy, such actions could well have adverse effects on the mother-child and intra-family relationships. As with the maternal exception under the *Congenital Disabilities (Civil Liability) Act 1976*, which precludes children having a right of action against their own mothers on the basis of concerns that such actions could have potentially deleterious effects on both child and family and might provoke intra-family disputes, such an exception might be deemed equally wise in the case of criminal prosecutions. It is also notable that the 1976 Act does not exclude the *father's* liability in negligence to his own child, yet – notwithstanding the damage which may be caused, *inter alia*, by partner violence against the mother in pregnancy (see Chapter 3) – this possibility in general has not attracted anything approaching the attention that has flowed to the prospect of maternal liability.

A further major objection to imposing liability on women for actions during pregnancy is the clear potential for unjust verdicts: how can a woman 'prove' that an adverse pregnancy outcome was *not* due to her behaviour, any more than obstetricians can 'prove' that their interventions will definitely reduce the risk of harm or, indeed, not cause further damage? Adverse outcomes happen even under obstetric supervision, and the doctors involved are rarely held accountable notwithstanding the lack of evidence, and the dangers, of some procedures. As discussed in Chapter 3, even in the arguably extreme situation of drug use during pregnancy, the assumption that the drug caused harm is often questionable. It cannot be right that a blanket assumption of maternal blame is so frequently accepted by the courts in such cases, whereas in the case of applications for forced interventions obstetricians and, even more remarkably, their advocates, have not had to back up their claims, either of predicted harm from failure to follow their preferred course, or of the alleged benefits of the unwanted intervention.

The day after Melissa Rowland's arrest in Utah on a charge of murder, when failing promptly to comply with obstetric advice was followed by the stillbirth of one of her twins[137] (see Chapter 5), Paltrow commented on the discrepancy with the case of Angela Carder, whose death was hastened by a court-ordered Caesarean section[138] – in the Carder case, 'no one suggested arresting the doctor or hospital officials for murder, in that case arguably a double homicide.'[139] As Annas commented before the appeal court verdict in Carder:

> They [the judge and the doctors] treated a live woman as though she were already dead, forced her to undergo an abortion, and then justified their brutal and unprincipled opinion on the basis that she was almost dead and her foetus's interests in life outweighed any interest she might have in her own life and health.[140]

Changing Constructions of Social Ethics

Further illumination as to the possible role of changes in social attitudes may come from comparing *Re AC* with a very different case indeed. In an intriguing analysis, Hasnas has compared the order granted by the lower court in the Carder case with the verdict in the infamous British case of *R v Dudley and Stevens*,[141] which scandalised Britain in 1884. In that case, three crew members of a dinghy adrift in the South Atlantic, who had run out of food and water, killed and ate Richard Parker, the cabin boy, who was dehydrated and near death. There was no doubt that without this action, all four would have perished before rescue, and the three survivors were surprised to be arrested and charged for murder on their return (only two actually went to trial). The High Court took the view that the men's actions were neither excused by self-defence nor justified by necessity, and found them guilty of murder (their death sentence was later commuted to six months' imprisonment), even though killing Parker was clearly the most rational way to preserve the maximum number of lives.

In the case of Carder, the details of which have been recounted many times previously, the court was presented with a very different situation, yet engaged in a similar balancing act: the life of the foetus could, possibly, be saved by the Caesarean, whereas it would otherwise certainly perish; AC, like Parker, was anyway doomed – she had, at best, two days of sedated life left. The lower court's decision that the Caesarean should go ahead was, again, the most rational way to preserve the maximum number of lives.

Thus in *Dudley and Stephens* the defendants were punished as murderers for taking the utilitarian course, whereas in *Re AC* the court itself ordered the doctors to proceed. The former, Hasnas suggests, demonstrates the 'classical' conception of legal rights as indefeasible, absolute, morally fundamental entities that protect individual autonomy, with the right to life taken very seriously indeed. Each man's right to life was absolute, so there was no morally acceptable justification for depriving Parker of his remaining hours, even under such dire circumstances.

In contrast, *Re AC* employed a 'contemporary' conception of rights as a means to the achievement of more fundamental moral interests; rights are accompanied by a welfare entitlement to things necessary to sustain life, and the right to life of individuals may compete. The proper resolution is the one that would result in the maximum preservation of life, a utilitarian balancing act that, incidentally, produces an identical course to the one that would be reached if no rights were involved at all. This is what happened when the court order was given ordering Angela Carder to undergo Caesarean even though it would hasten her death. The foetus was viewed as having competing, though not absolute, rights, and the resulting conflict was best resolved by taking the utilitarian course that best promoted the preservation of human life. In contrast, under the classical conception of rights, the fact that the Caesarean represented the best way to maximize the number of lives saved would not justify the court in depriving Carder of her remaining hours or days of life.

Hasnas sees these different approaches as representing a change in the general conception of rights over the century between the two cases. The classical conception of legal rights ensures that they fulfil their essential function of protecting individuals against the exercise of state power, he suggests. In contrast the contemporary interpretation does not take the right to life very seriously – a worrying shift that cannot be appropriate for a liberal legal regime.

Hasnas notes also that even though the decision in *Re AC* was reversed, the appeal court still did not rule out the balancing of rights as under the contemporary conception – it merely ruled that the trial judge improperly failed to determine whether Carder was competent and, if not, to apply a substituted judgement standard. The court still allowed that there may be 'extremely rare and truly exceptional' cases in which a 'conflicting state interest may be so compelling that the patient's wishes must yield;' implying that in some cases it may be proper to order a Caesarean for an unconsenting woman.[142]

This analysis offers the interesting idea that obstetric conflict may be one manifestation of a general tendency towards utilitarianism and moral relativism, and away from the concept of rights as absolute and the right to life as a moral imperative. It is also interesting to note that, under a classical conception of rights, while forced Caesareans would be impermissible, the question of abortion would depend ultimately on the extent to which the foetus was accorded personhood or rights (not to be killed).

Public Policy

However, whether or not individual rights may be balanced against those of others, they have always been subject to an extent to the interests of the State. In the case of obstetric conflict, this interest has been overt in the US, but little discussed in the UK.

Whilst emphatically supporting the woman's autonomy, the appeal court in the *Collins* case did note that in the US, when treatment had been forced on an unwilling woman, the rationale had been described as 'the unborn child's right to live' and 'the State's compelling interest in preserving the life of the foetus'[143] or 'the potentiality of human life'.[144] Yet, other than a few such asides, policy considerations have been largely ignored in UK cases of obstetric conflict. Notably, Lord Donaldson MR's much cited potential exception to the rights of competent adults to refuse treatment[145] was prompted by consideration of the conflict between the individual's right of refusal and society's interest in preserving life.

As noted previously, two judges in *Re F (In utero)* suggested that the issue of interference with a woman's liberty during pregnancy for the benefit of her foetus was a question for Parliament.[146] Balcombe LJ, with great foresight considering the possibility that the Court might be asked to order a Caesarean section, commented:

> It would be intolerable to place a judge in the position of having to make such a decision without any guidance ... If Parliament were to think it appropriate that a pregnant woman should be subject to control for the benefit of her unborn child, then doubtless it would stipulate the circumstances in which such controls may be applied and the safeguards appropriate for the mother's protection. In such a sensitive field, affecting as it does the liberty of the individual, it is not for the judiciary to extend the law.[147]

Maclean[148] points out that although the reasoning behind the decision in *Re S*[149] was not explained, the judge's reference to *Re T*[150] suggests that policy played a major role. He asserts that 'in the other caesarean section cases policy has been side-stepped by using the flexibility of the principle of competence' and notes that *Re MB*[151] has been criticised for, *inter alia*, failing to consider policy issues[152] and that the Court of Appeal in *Collins* also failed to consider any of the relevant interests and left open the question of public interest in the foetus. Yet:

> There is a distinction between the interests of the foetus and the public interest in preserving the life and well-being of the foetus .... Society must have an interest in the protection of both the mother and her unborn child. If the judges are unwilling, and maybe rightly so, to confront the policy arguments, then they need urgent consideration by Parliament.[153]

Again, he suggests that the omission of any real discussion of public policy leaves 'room for manoeuvre should a court in the future decide to introduce those issues into the equation'.[154] Lord Justice Thorpe similarly sees 'at least a distinct possibility that social pressures and changes will require further development of this most difficult legal territory, if not by case law, then by legislation', noting that: 'If the law were to be reviewed in Parliament, the debate would inevitably be wide ranging and passionate'.[155]

Coercion by Limiting Alternatives

As has been noted previously, in the UK women dependent on the National Health Service have a reduced range of options as to the type of maternity care they receive. In marked contrast to the situation in the US, the Government promotes their theoretical choice in this area up to and including that of home birth.[156] However in practice obstetric paternalism still flourishes, medical support for such options is often lacking and choice may be limited to what medical staff and hospitals deem it appropriate to provide, as well as circumscribed by the type of information they choose to impart.[157,158]

In modern obstetrics, as has been observed in Australia, 'inequalities in power and status in the maternity services have a greater influence on what happens to women giving birth than ... the choices they feel informed to make'.[159] Indeed, one British doctor has commented aptly that 'in the context of pregnancy care in the United Kingdom it is doubtful whether any decision is voluntary, given the attitudes and behaviour of some staff...'.[160] Moreover, the 'establishment' will often vigorously defend its position, including taking legal action against midwives, as well as mothers, who threaten it by pursuing a non-interventionist stance.[161]

Home births in particular may both threaten and create difficulties for a system now largely geared towards hospitalisation – in the UK obstetric 'flying squads' are no more; the number of general practitioners performing domiciliary obstetrics has fallen to negligible levels, yet staffing pressures have also resulted in a shortage of midwives so severe that it is reportedly regularly risking the lives of women giving birth in hospitals.[162] If women assume, as many do, that hospital birth is their only choice, health care personnel are unlikely to volunteer information about home birth even though they purport to support women who are already aware of this option.[163] Anecdotally, women have been told that they are 'high risk,' or that they have problems such as elevated blood pressure or urine glucose levels, in order to discourage home birth; some have even been told by medical staff that it is 'illegal' to give birth at home. Some women with booked home births are told when they call for assistance once labour has started that there are no midwives available and they will have to come into hospital.[164]

Once in hospital, as one British doctor has commented, 'patients are often not expected to make any decisions themselves but … are simply expected to comply with the policy of the obstetric unit, whatever that might be'.[165]

According to a report by the House of Commons Select Committee on Health in 2003, women still did not feel in control of their births and had high levels of interventions, with too little made of the optional nature of tests; moreover, 'testing and screening sometimes inhibit rational choice and sometimes encourage higher levels of interventions.' In general, there was little research available to support the effectiveness of the service provided. The Committee accepted that in many cases there was only an 'illusion of choice,' and suggested that maternity services led by acute general hospitals were over-medicalising birth, while the closure of small maternity units severely constrained local choice.[166] In response to evidence from AIMS concerning the tactics used towards the end of pregnancy to 'persuade' women to go into hospital, the Committee commented: 'We regard this treatment of women particularly at such an important stage of their pregnancy as wholly unacceptable.'[167]

In the USA similar trends are apparent, with non-interventionist, traditional midwifery even more under threat. In addition, a major focus of concern has been the pressures on women who have had a Caesarean to deliver by Caesarean in subsequent pregnancies – against such a high background rate of primary Caesarean, this represents a major contributor to the rising Caesarean rate[168] and is thought to be partly responsible for increases in maternal and infant mortality that have recently occurred in the US.[169,170] The traditional obstetric maxim 'once a Caesar, always a Caesar' no longer holds – in fact, the evidence from numerous studies suggests that elective repeat Caesarean section is more hazardous for the woman and no safer for the baby than vaginal birth after Caesarean section (VBAC),[171,172,173] even after two previous Caesareans.[174]

One large survey of over three hundred thousand Canadian women between 1988 and 2000 showed that although 'trial of labour' after previous

Caesarean was associated with an increased risk of uterine rupture, it significantly reduced the risk of maternal death compared with elective Caesarean section (1.6 versus 5.6 per 100,000).[175] Studies have shown that at least 70 per cent of women who are allowed to labour without undue restrictions will give birth vaginally, thus ending their exposure to the hazards of repeat Caesarean section.[176] In Canada, a policy statement by the Society of Obstetricians and Gynaecologists states that every hospital equipped for obstetric care should be able to offer VBAC and even twins and breech presentations are not excluded.[177]

Yet in the US there are still intense pressures put upon women to submit to repeat Caesarean – not only the type of scare tactics reported in Chapter 3, but also simply refusing to provide them with any alternative. Many hospitals have refused to provide for VBAC since a 1999 recommendation by the American College of Obstetricians and Gynecologists (ACOG) that VBAC should be attempted only in institutions equipped to respond to emergencies, with a surgeon, anaesthesiologist and operating personnel present and immediately available throughout the trial of labour to provide emergency care.[178]

As an aside, this rather begs the question as to the point for other women of a hospital birth in an institution not so equipped to respond to emergencies, since a dire situation could in theory arise suddenly in any birth, albeit with substantially lower frequency in pregnancies not complicated by previous Caesarean – indeed the possibility of unpredictable complications is often used to justify women's presence in hospital for birth.

The recommendation meant effectively that private obstetricians had to be in the hospital at all times when one of their patients was labouring, and that hospitals had to have staff and operating theatres available at all times in case emergency Caesarean was necessary – a requirement that many found too onerous. One study showed that in Maine VBAC rates declined from 30.1 per cent[179] to 13.1 per cent in the three years after the recommendation, with the most common reason for the decrease in VBAC being the inability of a hospital to meet ACOG guidelines. In the same period, Caesarean rates rose further from 19.4 per cent to 24.0 per cent.[180] The situation has worsened since a further ACOG recommendation in July 2004 that trial of labour should be limited to women with only one previous Caesarean.[181]

As an example of how this works in practice, one hospital in Santa Barbara reportedly stated that it now requires women who demand a VBAC do so against medical advice[182] – this could, in turn, threaten their health insurance coverage. In such a situation, women have little choice other than to take the risk of uterine rupture in a non-hospital setting, which is not reasonable (and which may in any case result in forcible removal to hospital).[183] Obstetricians have no need to resort to court orders in such situations, the combination of lack of provision of alternatives with withdrawal of financial cover being quite sufficient effectively to compel Caesarean without recourse to the law at all.

This is by no means an isolated instance. According to the International Cesarean Awareness Network, at least 250 hospitals nationwide have 'banned' VBACs and in rural areas where there are no other hospitals, women may have no choice – thousands are being forced into Caesareans that expose them and their babies to avoidable risk.[184,185]

A further hurdle that any pregnant woman may need to negotiate is that many obstetricians – on the advice of a former ACOG president[186] – simply refuse to accept as patients those who will not agree in advance to accept their recommendations, whatever these might turn out to be at the crucial time.

If hospitals simply refuse to provide for normal deliveries or health authorities to provide for home births, most woman have little *de facto* choice but to comply with 'recommendations'.

Obstetrics is a 'high risk' speciality and inevitably attitudes are affected by liability concerns, so there is no doubt that some of the restrictions on the choices offered to pregnant women, especially at the time of birth, are driven by 'defensive medicine'. For example, according to the Marlowes in Pennsylvania (see Chapter 3), a doctor insisted that Marlowe undergo a Caesarean, even though there were no problems with the foetus, because it was over 11lbs and 'the doctor didn't want a lawsuit'.[187] Tonya Jamois, President of the International Cesarean Awareness Network, has commented:

> We have yet to hear of a case where a hospital refuses to allow a woman to choose a Caesarean. Choice [is] honored as long as it is the 'right' choice. That usually means the choice that offers the physicians the lowest risk of liability – a primary concern today among doctors, hospitals and insurance companies.[188]

The lowest risk of liability however does not necessarily represent the lowest risk to the patient, or to the foetus. In the current obstetric climate in which the threshold for intervention has plummeted,[189] the obstetrician may be criticised for failing to act, and responsibility for adverse outcomes may appear to devolve accordingly; once intervention commences however, the obstetrician has done his or her best, the risks often become those of the birth or of the procedure itself and, short of negligence in performing the procedure, the obstetrician is thereby absolved.

In the UK, the House of Commons Select Committee Report on choice in maternity services commented: 'the defensive approach to medicine may particularly undermine giving women choice in maternity services.'[190] Currently it seems extremely unlikely that concerns over escalating litigation risks will lessen in the near future. However, possible reforms in the approaches to dealing with medical negligence, as proposed on both sides of the Atlantic, could have an impact on such concerns, especially if they involved limitations on the scale of medical liability for adverse birth outcomes.

Practical Difficulties in Upholding Autonomy

A final issue to be considered is whether the extensive deliberations of the higher courts are likely to hold sway at the level of the family court should the need for an urgent decision arise again. As presciently noted by Thorpe LJ before the *Collins* case:

> It is, perhaps, easier for an appellate court to discern principle than it is for a trial court to apply it in the face of judicial instinct, training and emotion. Applications in Caesarean cases are confined to judges of the Family Division. Those judges are dedicated to upholding child welfare. It is simply unrealistic to suppose that the preservation of each life will not be a matter of equal concern to the Family Division judge surveying the medical dilemma. ... Unless the recognition of this consideration is legitimated there is an obvious risk of strained reasoning, increased litigation ... and stress in interdisciplinary co-operation.[191]

After the case, he opined:

> [T]he resolution at which the Court of Appeal has emphatically arrived creates undoubted difficulty for the professionals, including the psychiatric social worker, the consultant psychiatrist, the obstetrician and the first-instance judge. ... It is also hard for the first-instance judge to suppress his every instinct to avert tragedy ... it may also be easier for judges to apply the principles retrospectively. Some may perceive the judges as more confident in defining the principle of autonomy than in applying it to a mother and fetus for whom death is at the door.'[192]

This, again, suggests that the issue may not yet be completely closed, particularly since it may also be difficult for a woman to find a lawyer with the necessary experience of such cases to represent her at the time of a first-instance decision, especially in an emergency. The Appeal Court in the Collins case noted that S would have been entitled to apply for *habeas corpus*,[193] though obviously this had not been suggested by her lawyer. Similarly in the US, Paltrow has noted that in the case of criminal prosecutions, typically related to drug use in pregnancy, most attorneys fail to challenge the validity of charges brought against pregnant women, despite the fact that such cases are usually brought under statutes never intended to be applied to a pregnant woman's behaviour. As a result, 'many women in America are serving jail terms or are on probation for non-existent crimes'.[194]

Similar considerations arise at the level of the obstetric ward. As Dame Elizabeth Butler-Sloss, President of the Family Division, has said in other circumstances:

> [T]he law is clear and easily to be understood by lawyers [but] its application to individual cases in the context of a general practitioner's surgery, a hospital ward and especially in an intensive care unit is infinitely more difficult to achieve.[195]

Several commentators have suggested that coercion may be ethically justifiable in exceptional situations with near-certain harm to the foetus, coupled with probable benefit to the woman.[196] Obstetricians have even attempted to provide ethical justification for emergency Caesarean delivery without a court order despite a pregnant woman's refusal,[197] on the basis of 'obligations to the at-term fetal patient'. The justification advanced supposes three criteria: reliable judgement that Caesarean delivery will prevent serious infant morbidity or mortality; lack of physical resistance, and insufficient time to consider a court order.

The requirement for lack of resistance, whilst clearly sensible on the grounds proposed (that resistance could significantly increase the risks of maternal or foetal harm), raises a number of ethical issues. Hewson too noted after *Re MB* that the Court of Appeal 'hinted' that if a patient were expected to put up stiff resistance, this might justify not seeking relief.[198] This suggests, variously, a tendency to pick on women who cannot or will not defend themselves, a (welcome) reluctance to impose medical decisions by physical force, and a willingness to back off if the fight seems likely to be a bloody one. What it does not suggest is a universal, needs-based standard of intervention based on sound legal (or medical) principles and applied with proper regard to the due processes of the law.

The criterion of insufficient time raises numerous dangers already considered. Furthermore, the obstetricians' conclusion that such actions are justified (only) when these three criteria are satisfied 'on a case-by-case basis' makes clear that in adopting this stance the ultimate decision, again, would rest with those who will carry out the treatment.

Moreover this is not merely a theoretical argument. It is not unknown for forced treatment decisions to be made without recourse to the courts. In the UK in 1997 a woman accepted an out-of-court settlement after claiming that she was forced to have a Caesarean section against her will (and that she was assaulted by a doctor who carried out an internal examination without her consent); at the time six other cases were said to be in the pipeline and it was reported that the case 'could open the doors to scores of copycat claims'.[199]

In the US, perhaps more alarmingly, in 1999 a court ruled in *Pemberton v Tallahassee Memorial Regional Medical Center* that a woman's federal constitutional rights were *not* violated when she was forced to have a Caesarean section against her will. Although the ruling was confined to the particular circumstances of the case – the state's interest in preserving the life of a full-term foetus when the woman was in active labour, had sought medical assistance and desired a live birth, and the birth was stated to be 'imminent' at the time that the surgery was commenced[200] – the potential implications for any woman who chooses to give birth in a hospital setting are considerable. It is obviously very much easier simply to proceed with surgery in the face of the woman's objections than to go to all the trouble of obtaining a court declaration, with the risk that it may be refused. How frequently such compulsion occurs remains unknown although incidents that result in subsequent law suits are almost certainly in the minority.

It could also be that in an emergency situation, expecting either doctors or family courts to use competency as the test of whether a pregnant woman may refuse treatment is simply too much to ask. In the UK, Lady Justice Hale, regarding the *Collins* ruling as an 'exception', has asked:

How many courts, and how many doctors, would find that a woman did have capacity to refuse emergency treatment which would save her own and her baby's life?[201]

Again, it may be easier for an appeal court to reach such a verdict after the event. Indeed, as Lady Hale points out, it could be argued that we are better off giving legal justification for imposing life-saving treatment in an emergency where death is imminent, and then allowing debate to take place in a calmer and more structured way later – but this, of course, might validate enforced Caesareans in every case where there was a credible risk to the mother's life. She concludes:

One has to question whether the concept of capacity is yet strong enough to bear the weight which the law lays upon it.[202]

Notes

1 *In Re S* (1992) ILR 14.10.92:TLR 16.10.92 3 WLR 806:4 AER 671; (1993) 4 Med LR 28 [Lawtel].
2 Royal College of Obstetricians and Gynaecologists. *A consideration of the law and ethics in relation to court-authorised obstetric intervention.* Ethics No. 1. RCOG. April 1994.
3 *Norfolk and Norwich Healthcare (NHS) Trust v W* (1996) 2 FLR 613 [Lawtel].
4 *Rochdale Healthcare (NHS) Trust v C* (1996) LTL 12/7/96 [Lawtel].
5 *Re MB* [1997] EWCA Civ 1361.
6 *St George's Healthcare National Health Service Trust v S : R v (1) Louize Collins (2) Pathfinder Mental Health Services Trust (3) St George's Healthcare NHS Trust, ex parte S (No.2)* (1998)LTL 7/5/98 : TLR 8/5/98 : ILR 12/5/98 : (1998) 2 FLR 728 [Lawtel].
7 See, for example: Rothman, Barbara Katz. *The Tentative Pregnancy* Pandora 1994; Lippman, Abby. 'The Genetic Construction of Prenatal Testing: Choice, Consent, or Conformity for Women?'. In: Rothenberg and Thomson (Editors). *Women and Prenatal Testing: Facing the Challenges of Genetic Technology.* Ohio State University Press, 1994.
8 Anon. 'Heart op fear for unborn baby.' *Guardian* 15 January 2001.
9 James Meek. 'Ethical grey areas: Genetic screening.' *Guardian* 26 June 2000.
10 Feitshans IL. 'Legislating to preserve women's autonomy during pregnancy.' *Med Law* 1995;14(5-6):397-412.
11 Charo RA. 'Effect of the human genome initiative on women's rights and reproductive decisions.' *Fetal Diagn Ther* 1993;8 Suppl 1:148-59.
12 *Curlander v Bio-Science Laboratories* 165 Cal. Rptr. 477 (1980).
13 Boss JA. 'First trimester prenatal diagnosis: earlier is not necessarily better.' *J Med Ethics* 1994; 20(3):146-51.
14 Swartz M. 'Pregnant Woman v Foetus: A Dilemma for Hospital Ethics Committees.' *Cambridge Quarterly Healthcare Ethics*;1992;1:51, at p53.
15 Sutton A. *Prenatal Diagnosis: Confronting the Ethical Issues.* The Linacre Centre, London 1990, at pp20-21.
16 *Unger v Unger* 644 A.2d 691 (N.J. Sup. Ct. 1994).

17 CBS News. 'Mom's Diet May Affect Baby's Life'. 28 January 2004: www.CBSNews.com.
18 See, for a recent example: Barker DJ. 'The developmental origins of well-being.' *Philos Trans R Soc Lond B Biol Sci* 2004;359(1449):1359-66.
19 *State v Kruzicki* 561 N.W.2d 729-49 (Wisconsin Supreme Ct 1997) (my italics).
20 *Angela M.W.* 197 Wis 2d at 503, n8 (1995).
21 Anon. 'A woman's interest competes against law protecting children. Battered pregnant woman denied divorce until after giving birth'. *CNN.com* 9 January 2005: www.cnn.com.
22 *In re Wilner* 601 N.Y.S.2d 518, 521 (Sup. Ct. 1993).
23 The attempt failed, partly due to questions as to its constitutionality.
24 Gumbel, Andrew. 'America's New Family Values'. *The Independent* 25 November 2003.
25 Paltrow, Lynn M, J.D. and Newman, Robert, M.D. 'Treatment, not sterilization, is the way to help addicted moms.' *Houston Chronicle* 30 January 2000, at p4C.
26 See, for example, Anon. *Judge Orders Addict to Stop Having Kids.* ABC News 4 January 2005: abcnews.go.com.
27 Santora, Marc. 'Negligent couple is told not to procreate'. *New York Times* May 2004.
28 For example, neonatal hair analysis is growing in popularity and may detect cocaine exposure not uncovered by maternal history and neonatal urinalysis: Koren G, Klein J, McMartin K. 'Diagnosing intrauterine exposure to cocaine by hair testing: six years of clinical use.' *Ther Drug Monit* 1998; 20(5): 478-80.
29 Unno, Nobuya. 'Development of an Artificial Placenta'. In: Stocker, Gerfried and Schoepf, Christine (Eds). *Next Sex: Ars Electronica 2000.* Springer Verlag, 2000 Wien, at p 252-3.
30 Powledge, Tabitha M. 'The Ultimate Baby Bottle'. *Scientific American* 1999; 10(3).
31 Hughes, James J, Ph.D. 'The Future of Death: Cryonics and the Telos of Liberal Individualism'. *J Evolution Technol* 2001, vol 6 (July 2001): http://jetpress.org/volume6/death.html.
32 Amu O, Rajendran S, Ibrahim I Bolaji II. 'Maternal choice alone should not determine method of delivery.' *BMJ* 1998; 317: 462-465 (my italics).
33 Kolder VE, Gallagher J, Parsons MT. 'Court-ordered obstetrical interventions.' *N Engl J Med* 1987 May 7;316(19):1192-6.
34 American Medical Association Board of Trustees. 'Legal Interventions During Pregnancy. Court-ordered medical treatments and legal penalties for potentially harmful behaviour by pregnant women'. *J Am Med Assoc* 1990; 264: 2663-70.
35 American College of Obstetricians and Gynecologists. Informed refusal. Committee Opinion No 237, June 2000.
36 Adams SF, Mahowald MB, Gallagher J. Refusal of treatment during pregnancy. *Clin Perinatol* 2003;30(1):127-40, vii-viii.
37 It may be, as with other figures in this survey, that physicians regard pregnant women who use alcohol – especially in the face of the multitude of warnings in the US that they should not do so – as somehow more culpable than drug users, who at least have the possibility of addiction to 'excuse' their failings.
38 Abel EL, Kruger M. 'Physician attitudes concerning legal coercion of pregnant alcohol and drug abusers'. *Am J Obstet Gynecol* 2002;186(4):768-72.
39 Rossiter GP. 'Contemporary transatlantic developments concerning compelled medical treatment of pregnant women.' *Aust N Z J Obstet Gynaecol* 1995 May;35(2):132-8.
40 Per Balcombe LJ: *Re F (in utero)* [1988] Fam 122 at 143.
41 Per May LJ: *In Re F (in utero)* [1988] Fam 122 at 138.

42 Per May LJ: *In Re F (in utero)* [1988] Fam 122 at 135.

43 *Re MB* [1997] EWCA Civ 1361 (my italics).

44 *Re MB* [1997] EWCA Civ 1361.

45 *In Re F (in utero)* [1988] Fam 122.

46 *Re MB* [1997] EWCA Civ 1361.

47 *In the matter of an application for judicial review: Queen v Louize Collins ; Pathfinder Mental Health Services Trust and St George's Healthcare NHS Trust, ex parte 'S'* [1998] EWHC Admin 490 (7th May, 1998), at 79.

48 *In the matter of an application for judicial review: Queen v Louize Collins & Ors, Ibid*, at 78.

49 (1) *St George's Healthcare National Health Service Trust* v S (1998) : (2) R v *Louize Collins , Pathfinder Mental Health Services Trust & St George's Healthcare NHS Trust, ex parte S* (NO.2)(1998) LTL 7/5/98 : TLR 8/5/98 : ILR 12/5/98 : (1998) 2 FLR 728.

50 *In re Madyyun,* 114 Daily Wash L Rptr 2233 (DC Super Ct 26 July 1986).

51 Weiss D. Court Delivers Controversy. *Times Leader Northeastern Pennsylvania* 16 January 2004.

52 *In the matter of an application for judicial review: Queen v Louize Collins & Ors, op cit*, at 77 (my italics).

53 *In the matter of an application for judicial review: Queen v Louize Collins & Ors, Ibid*, at 79 (my italics).

54 (1) *St George's Healthcare National Health Service Trust* v S (1998), *op cit* (my italics).

55 *In the matter of an application for judicial review: Queen v Louize Collins & Ors, op cit*, at 112 (my italics).

56 Thorpe MA. Consent for Caesarean Section: Part 2 - autonomy, capacity, best interests, reasonable force and procedural guidelines. *Clinical Risk* 2000;5:209-212 (my italics).

57 *In Re T* [1993] Fam 95.

58 Flagler E, Baylis F, Rodgers S. 'Bioethics for clinicians: 12. Ethical dilemmas that arise in the care of pregnant women: rethinking "maternal-fetal conflicts"'. *Canadian Med Assoc J* 1997 Jun 15;156(12):1729-32.

59 Chudley AE. 'Safe haven for addicted mothers'. *CMAJ* 1997; 157: 1201 (letter).

60 *In Re T* [1993] Fam 95 at 115.

61 The fact that this argument is phrased thus is telling, for it could alternatively be argued that if doctors are bound to seek informed consent they should also honour informed dissent.

62 General Medical Council. *Seeking Patients' Consent: The Ethical Considerations.* General Medical Council. London 1999.

63 *In Re T* [1993] Fam 95 at 115.

64 *Re C* [1994] 1 FLR 31.

65 *Re C (adult: refusal of medical treatment)* [1994] 1 All ER 819.

66 Mason JK, McCall Smith RA. *Law and Medical Ethics.* Butterworths London 1999 at p264.

67 *Sidaway v Board of Governors of the Bethlem Royal Hospital and the Maudsley Hospital* [1985] AC 871, at 904-905.

68 *In Re T* [1993] Fam 95 at 99, 102 (my italics).

69 Rational: endowed with reason, having sound judgement, *sane...*: Oxford English Dictionary on CD-ROM v 2.0. Oxford University Press Oxford 1999.

70 *Re MB* [1997] EWCA Civ 1361.

71 *In Re T* [1993] Fam 95.
72 *In the matter of an application for judicial review: Queen v Louize Collins & Ors, op cit,* at 73.
73 *R v Brown* [1993] 2 All ER 75, [1993] 2 WLR 556.
74 Alasdair R Maclean. 'Caesarean Sections, Competence and the Illusion of Autonomy.' *Web Journal of Current Legal Issues* (1999) 1 Web JCLI , 1/2/99 [Lawtel].
75 *Mental Capacity Bill.* HL Bill 13 House of Lords Session 2004 – 05.
76 Heginbotham, Christopher. 'Mental capacity bill will improve lives'. *The Guardian* 15 September 2004.
77 per Lord Donaldson: *In Re T* [1993] Fam 95 at 102.
78 *Commonwealth v Cass* 467 N.E.2d 1324 (Mass. 1984).
79 *Commonwealth v Lawrence* 536 N.E.2d 571 (Mass. 1989).
80 *State v Horne* 319 S.E.2d 703 (S.C. 1984).
81 *State v Ard* 505 S.E.2d 328 (S.C. 1998).
82 H.R. 1997.
83 Center for Reproductive Law and Policy. *The 'Unborn Victims of Violence Act'.* CRLP Factsheet F015, May 2001.
84 Macready N. 'US state rules that a viable fetus is a person.' *BMJ* 1997; 315: 1485-1488 (News).
85 Paige C, Karnofsky EB. 'The antiabortion movement and Baby Jane Doe.' *J Health Polit Policy Law* 1986;11(2):255-69.
86 Bjerga, Alan. 'Brownback sees "culture of life" prevailing in '05.' *Wichita Eagle* (Kansas), 3 January 2005.
87 Gandy, Kim. NOW Activists Stand Up to Bush Agenda, Protest Barriers to Legitimate Dissent on Inauguration Day: *Statement of NOW President Kim Gandy*, 20 January 2004: http://www.now.org/press/01-05/01-20.html.
88 McKee M, Foster S. 'George W Bush's second term' (Editorial). *BMJ* 2005; 330: 155-6.
89 H.R. 1997, Unborn Victims of Violence Act of 2004
90 House Rpt. 106-332 - Part 1 – Unborn Victims of Violence Act of 1999.
91 Leventhal, Cari L. Comment: 'The Crimes Against the Unborn Child Act: Recognizing Potential Human Life in Pennsylvania Criminal Law.' 103 *Dick. L. Rev.* 173, 175 (1998).
92 House Rpt. 106-332 - Part 1 – Unborn Victims of Violence Act of 1999.
93 House Rpt. 106-332, *Ibid.*
94 *People v Hall* 557 N.Y.S.2d 879 (N.Y. App. Div. 1990).
95 *In Re L* (1996) LTL 18/12/96 : TLR 1/1/97 : ILR 10/2/97 : (1997) 2 FLR 837 [Lawtel].
96 Hall, Celia. 'Judge forces mother to be injected to save baby.' *Daily Telegraph* 14 December 1996.
97 *In Re J. (A Minor) (Wardship: Medical Treatment)* [1991] Fam 33, at 44 (my italics).
98 Wallace, Natasha. New law to protect unborn as killer father jailed. *Sydney Morning Herald* 17 June 2004.
99 *Attorney-General's Reference* (No. 3 of 1994) [1997] 3 WLR 421.
100 *Attorney-General's Reference* (No. 3 of 1994) [1997] 3 WLR 421 at 428.
101 *Attorney-General's Reference* (No. 3 of 1994) [1997] 3 WLR 421, as cited in: *In the matter of an application for judicial review: Queen v Louize Collins & Ors, op cit,* at 54.
102 *In the matter of an application for judicial review: Queen v Louize Collins & Ors, op cit,* at 55.
103 Other than risk to the mother's life, permanent injury to her health, or foetal handicap.

104 Stein, Ellen J. 'Maternal-Fetal conflict: Reformulating the equation.' In: Grubb, Andrew (Ed). *Challenges in Medical Care*. John Wiley & Sons. Chichester 1992, 91-108, at p96-8.

105 Stein, Ellen J. *Ibid*, at p96-8.

106 As is the position in the US, where the stipulations in *Roe v Wade* ([1973] 410 US 113) define the limits of state intervention according to the trimester of pregnancy (of which the first third approximately corresponds with foetal viability).

107 s313 (2) Queensland Criminal Code.

108 *Bowditch v McEwan* [2002] QCA 172.

109 *Paton v United Kingdom* [1980] 3 EHRR 408.

110 *H v Norway* (1990) (N0 17004/90, unreported), as cited in *Re MB* [1997] EWCA Civ 1361.

111 *Bruggemann and Scheuten v Federal Republic of Germany* [1977] 3 EHRR 244.

112 For example the New Jersey statute NJ Stat Ann No. 30: 4C-11.

113 American Civil Liberties Union. *Reproductive Freedom: What's Wrong with Fetal Rights: A look at fetal protection statutes and wrongful death actions on behalf of fetuses*. American Civil Liberties Union 1997.
www.aclu.org/issues/reproduct/fetal.html.

114 See, for example: Marshall MF. 'Commentary: mal-intentioned illiteracy, willful ignorance, and fetal protection laws: is there a lexicologist in the house?' *J Law Med Ethics* 1999; 27(4):343-6, 294.

115 Dutter, Barbie. 'Caesarean forced on mother was unlawful.' *Daily Telegraph*, 8 May 1998.

116 St. Martin, Darla. 'Better to Save Some Lives Now than None at All, Ever.' From an editorial reproduced from the *National Catholic Register* by John Mark Ministries on: http://jmm.aaa.net.au/articles/978.htm (Darla St. Martin is the Associate Executive Director of the National Right to Life Committee in the USA).

117 Bjerga, Alan, *op cit*.

118 Taddio A. 'Pain management for neonatal circumcision.' *Paediatr Drugs* 2001;3(2):101-11.

119 Indeed, as recently as 1998, only around half of all neonates received analgesia or anaesthesia for circumcision – and although obstetricians were more likely to be performing regular circumcisions than paediatricians or family physicians, only 25 per cent of obstetricians used analgesia: Stang HJ, Snellman LW. 'Circumcision practice patterns in the United States.' *Pediatrics* 1998 Jun;101(6):E5.

120 Linda Clarke. 'Abortion: A rights issue?' In Robert Lee & Derek Morgan (eds). *Birthrights. Law and Ethics at the Beginning of Life*. Routlege London 1990, at p158-9.

121 *Conroy, In Re* (1985) 486 A.2d 1209, as cited in *In Re T (Adult: Refusal of Treatment)* [1993] Fam 95.

122 *In Re T (Adult: Refusal of Treatment)* [1993] Fam 95 (my italics).

123 *In the matter of an application for judicial review: Queen v Louize Collins ; Pathfinder Mental Health Services Trust and St George's Healthcare NHS Trust, ex parte 'S'* [1998] EWHC Admin 490 (7th May, 1998) at 85.

124 *In the matter of an application for judicial review: Queen v Louize Collins & Ors, Ibid*, at 90 (my italics).

125 *Tameside and Glossop Acute Services Trust v CH (a patient)* (1996) ILR 26/2/96: (1996) 1 FLR 762 [Lawtel].

126 *In the matter of an application for judicial review: Queen v Louize Collins & Ors, op cit*, at 92.

127 *In Re S* (1992) ILR 14.10.92:TLR 16.10.92 3 WLR 806:4 AER 671; (1993) 4 Med LR 28 [Lawtel].

128 *Re AC* (1990) 573 A 2d 1235 (DC Ct Appeals).

129 Carder was dying of cancer, and her death was probably hastened by the forced surgery. In both cases (this and *Re S*), the foetus died anyway.

130 Mason JK, McCall Smith RA. *Law and Medical Ethics*. Butterworths London 1999, at p 138.

131 *In the matter of an application for judicial review: Queen v Louize Collins & Ors, op cit*, at 72.

132 *Attorney-General's Reference* (No.3 of 1994) (1977) LTL 25/7/97 : TLR 25/7/97 : (1997) 3 WLR 421 : (1997) 3 AER 936 : ILR 1/10/97 : (1998) CAR 91 [Lawtel].

133 *In the matter of an application for judicial review: Queen v Louize Collins & Ors, op cit*, at 66.

134 As cited in: *In the matter of an application for judicial review: Queen v Louize Collins & Ors, op cit*, at 69.

135 Alasdair R Maclean. 'Caesarean Sections, Competence and the Illusion of Autonomy.' *Web Journal of Current Legal Issues* (1999) 1 Web JCLI , 1/2/99 [Lawtel].

136 *Ferguson v City of Charleston* [2001] 99-936 (Supreme Court of the United States).

137 Taylor, Diane. 'Does a foetus have more rights than its mother?' *The Guardian*, 23 April 2004.

138 *Re AC* (1990) 573 A 2d 1235 (DC Ct Appeals).

139 Lynn M Paltrow, Executive Director of National Advocates for Pregnant Women, on: www.advocatesforpregnantwomen.org.

140 Annas G. 'She's Going to Die: The Case of Angela C.' *Hastings Center Report* 1988; 18 (1): 25.

141 *R v Dudley & Stevens* (1884) 14 QBD 273.

142 Hasnas J. 'From cannibalism to Caesareans: Two conceptions of fundamental rights'. *Northwestern University Law Review* 1995;89: 900.

143 *In the matter of an application for judicial review: Queen v Louize Collins & Ors, op cit*, at 56 (citing *Jefferson v Griffin Spalding County Hospital Authority* [1981] 274 S 2d 457).

144 *In the matter of an application for judicial review: Queen v Louize Collins & Ors, op cit*, at 56 (citing *Re Madyyun* [1986] 573 A 2d 1259).

145 '...the only possible qualification is a case in which the choice may lead to the death of a viable foetus': *In Re T (adult - refusal of medical treatment)* [1992] 3 WLR 782 at 786.

146 Per Balcombe LJ: *Re F (In utero)* [1988] 2 All ER 193, at 144; per May LJ: *In Re F (in utero)* [1988] Fam 122 at 139.

147 Per Balcombe LJ: *Re F (In utero)* [1988] 2 All ER 193 at 144.

148 Maclean, Alasdair R. *op cit.*

149 *In Re S* (1992) ILR 14.10.92:TLR 16.10.92 3 WLR 806:4 AER 671; (1993) 4 Med LR 28 [Lawtel].

150 *Re T* [1992] 3 WLR 782.

151 *Re MB (An Adult: Medical Treatment)* [1997] 2 FCR 541, as cited in Maclean, *op cit.*

152 Stauch M. 'Court-Authorised Caesarians and the Principle of Patient Autonomy.' 6 *Nottingham Law Journal* 74 (1997), as cited in Maclean, *op cit.*

153 Maclean, Alasdair R. *op cit.*

154 Maclean, *Ibid.*
155 Thorpe MA. 'Consent for Caesarean Section: Part 2 - autonomy, capacity, best interests, reasonable force and procedural guidelines.' *Clinical Risk* 2000;5:209-212.
156 Cumberledge J. *Changing childbirth.* London: HMSO, 1993.
157 See, for example, Nicole Martin. 'Family doctors accused of steering mothers away from home births'. *Daily Telegraph,* 25 June 2001.
158 Edwards, Nadine. 'The choice is yours - or is it?' *AIMS Journal* Autumn 2003, Vol 15 No 3.
159 Vernon B, Tracy S, Reibel T. 'Compliance, coercion, and power have huge effect in maternity services'. *BMJ* 2002; 325:43.
160 Reeves D. 'Provision of information is only one component of informed choice'. *BMJ* 2002; 325:43.
161 See, for example: Kitzinger, Sheila. 'Midwives on Trial'. Sheila Kitzinger's Letter from Europe. September 1999 Vol. 26.3: http://www.sheilakitzinger.com/midwives%20on%20trial.htm.
162 Ashcroft B, Elstein M, Boreham N, Holm S. 'Prospective semistructured observational study to identify risk attributable to staff deployment, training, and updating opportunities for midwives'. *BMJ* 2003; 327:584.
163 Madi BC, Crow R. 'A qualitative study of information about available options for childbirth venue and pregnant women's preference for a place of delivery.' *Midwifery* 2003;19(4):328-36.
164 See numerous reports, and especially the 'home birth' section, on the Association for Improvement in Maternity Services website: www.aims.org.uk.
165 Reeves D, *op cit.*
166 House of Commons Health Committee. *Choice in Maternity Services:* Ninth Report of Session 2002-03. Stationery Office London 2003: www. parliament.the-stationery-office.co.uk/pa/ cm200203/cmselect/cmhealth/796/796.pdf.
167 Beech, Beverley Lawrence. 'Challenging the illusion of choice'. *AIMS Journal* Autumn 2003, Vol 15 No 3.
168 The overall Caesarean delivery rate is both directly associated with the primary Caesarean rate and inversely associated with the VBAC (vaginal birth after Caesarean section) rate: Centers for Disease Control and Prevention. 'Rates of Cesarean Delivery - United States, 1993.' *Morbidity and Mortality Weekly Report* 1995;44(15):303-307.
169 International Cesarean Awareness Network. ICAN press kit: background information, on: www.ican-online.org.
170 Anon. 'U.S. Infant Mortality Rises.' *CBS News* Atlanta 12 February 2004: www.CBSNews.com.
171 Mozurkewich EL, Hutton EK. 'Elective repeat cesarean delivery versus trial of labor: a meta-analysis of the literature from 1989 to 1999.' *Am J Obstet Gynecol* 2000:183:1187-97.
172 Rageth JC, Juzi C, Grossenbacher H. 'Delivery after previous cesarean: a risk evaluation. Swiss Working Group of Obstetric and Gynecologic Institutions.' *Obstet Gynecol* 1999;93(3):332-7.
173 Roberts RG, Bell HS, Wall EM *et al.* 'Trial of labor or repeated cesarean section: The woman's choice.' *Arch Fam Med* 1997;6:120-125.
174 Garg VK, Ekuma-Nkama EN. 'Vaginal birth following two cesarean deliveries - are the risks exaggerated?' *Ann Saudi Med* 2004 Jul-Aug;24(4):276-9.

Policing Pregnancy

175 Wen SW, Rusen ID, Walker M *et al*. Maternal Health Study Group, Canadian Perinatal Surveillance System. 'Comparison of maternal mortality and morbidity between trial of labor and elective cesarean section among women with previous cesarean delivery.' *Am J Obstet Gynecol* 2004;191:1263-9.
176 Goer H. *The Thinking Woman's Guide to a Better Birth*. Perigee Books, New York 1999, at p169.
177 Maternal/Fetal Medicine Committee of the Society of Obstetricians and Gynaecologists of Canada. *Clinical Practice Guidelines. Policy Statement 68*, December 1997.
178 American College of Obstetricians and Gynecologists. *Practice Bulletin Number 5*. ACOG 1999.
179 Roughly equivalent to the rate in England and Wales, which the UK National Caesarean Audit found to be 33 per cent: Thomas J, Paranjothy S. Royal College of Obstetricians and Gynaecologists Clinical Effectiveness Support Unit. National Sentinel Caesarean Section Audit Report. *RCOG Press*; 2001.
180 Pinette MG, Kahn J, Gross KL *et al*. 'Vaginal birth after Cesarean rates are declining rapidly in the rural state of Maine.' *J Matern Fetal Neonatal Med* 2004;16(1):37-43.
181 American College of Obstetricians and Gynecologists. *Practice Bulletin Number 54*. ACOG 2004.
182 Schultz, Thomas. 'Cottage C-section rule has some moms upset.' *Santa Barbara News Press* 25 June 2003.
183 See: *Pemberton v Tallahassee Memorial Regional Medical Center Inc*. (1999) 66 F.Supp.2d 1247 (N.D.Fla. 1999).
184 International Cesarean Awareness Network. *Statement on Melissa Rowland* ICAN E-News Line. Volume 17, 22 March 2004.
185 Jamois, Tonya. 'Women have right to refuse Caesarean.' *North County Times* (California). 13 April 2004 (Tonya Jamois is President of the International Cesarean Awareness Network).
186 Harer W Benson Jr. Scenario: Does an obstetrician always have to follow the patient's wishes? Patient, doctor should discuss delivery options. Ethics Forum. American Medical News, April 7, 2003.
187 Napersky, Lisa. 'Woman hits hospitals' stance that she agree to C-section.' *The Citizens' Voice*, Pennsylvania 17 January 2004.
188 Jamois, Tonya. 'Women have right to refuse Caesarean'. *North County Times* (California). 13 April 2004.
189 Leitch CR, Walker JJ. 'The rise in caesarean section rate: the same indications but a lower threshold'.*Br J Obstet Gynaecol* 1998;105(6):621-6.
190 House of Commons Health Committee. *Choice in Maternity Services*, Ninth Report of Session 2002-03, *op cit*.
191 Thorpe LJ. 'The Caesarean Section Debate.' 1997 *Family Law* 663.
192 Thorpe MA. Consent for Caesarean Section: Part 2 - autonomy, capacity, best interests, reasonable force and procedural guidelines. *Clinical Risk* 2000;5:209-212.
193 *In the matter of an application for judicial review: Queen v Louize Collins ; Pathfinder Mental Health Services Trust and St George's Healthcare NHS Trust, ex parte 'S'* [1998] EWHC Admin 490 (7th May, 1998).
194 Paltrow Lynn M. *Criminal Prosections Against Pregnant Women. National Update and Overview*. Reproductive Freedom Project, American Civil Liberties Union Foundation. April 1992.

195 *Re B (Adult: Refusal of Medical Treatment)* [2002] EWHC 429 (Fam), [2002] 2 All ER 449.

196 See, for example: Tauer CA. 'Lives at stake. How to respond to a woman's refusal of cesarean surgery when she risks losing her child or her life.' *Health Prog* 1992; 73(7): 18-27.

197 Chervenak FA, McCullough LB, Skupski DW. 'An ethical justification for emergency, coerced cesarean delivery.' *Obstet Gynecol* 1993; 82(6): 1029-35.

198 Hewson B. 'How to escape the surgeon's knife.' *New Law Journal* 23 May 1997 at p 752.

199 Knowsley J, Reid T. 'Payout for woman who was forced to have a caesarean.' *Sunday Telegraph* 1 June 1997.

200 *Pemberton v Tallahassee Memorial Regional Medical Center* 66 F. Supp. 2d 1247 at 1251 n.10 (N.D. Fla.1999).

201 Hale, The Right Honourable Lady Justice, DBE. *A Pretty Pass: When is there a right to die?* Fison Memorial Lecture at 'The Art of Dying' series, Kings College, University of London, 24 October 2002.
http://www.kcl.ac.uk/depsta/humanities/art_of_dying/ppass.doc.

202 Hale, The Right Honourable Lady Justice, DBE, *Ibid.*

Conclusions

The Current Position

Most pregnant women will willingly undergo considerable inconvenience and privation to do what they believe to be best for their foetus. Often their belief stems from advice they receive from health care providers, and often such advice is correct. However medical knowledge is not infallible and does change with time – at various stages in the past pregnant women have been advised by their doctors to have X-rays, to smoke, to rest in bed and to take drugs such as thalidomide.[1]

As discussed, many current recommendations are not evidence-based, and many are influenced by factors quite separate from any health risks to the pregnant woman or the foetus – including scheduling convenience, staffing availability, litigation fears and financial considerations, as well as prevailing medical dogma. There is some evidence that, because they fear malpractice suits, doctors are shifting their focus away from giving helpful advice and towards the 'foetal rights' debate.[2]

Many of the cases that have come to court suggest that women are being treated differently from other competent adults merely because of the fact of pregnancy. There is reason to believe that women may be blamed – scapegoated even – for adverse pregnancy outcomes, while other agents which pose an equal or greater threat to the foetus, but are perhaps less easy or more costly to target, are ignored. The concentration on women's behaviour and choices in pregnancy, and the concerted attempts to elevate 'foetal rights' often for other purposes, stand in marked and ironic contrast to the inattention and lack of support or resources given to mothers and young children.

Under these circumstances, it is particularly vital that women are not pressurised to undergo interventions known to pose additional risks, without reasonable certainty that these risks are outweighed by the benefit of such procedures – either for the woman herself or, if she is willing to incur the additional risk, for the foetus. Annas has aptly described use of the judiciary to enforce compliance over the objections of competent pregnant women as 'counterproductive, unprincipled, sexist, and repressive.'[3]

Unfortunately perhaps, the intervention that has been most subject to obstetric conflict and court scrutiny is Caesarean section, also one of the most invasive and the most contentious. Cases that have arisen well-illustrate the complex dilemmas involved, particularly for family courts, which may be faced with an urgent decision with potentially drastic consequences and must usually rely on the evidence presented by the medical representatives who seek the decision. If, in future, conflict arises based on new technology, as surely it must – intra-uterine surgery being one obvious candidate – the lessons learned from the Caesarean cases will be helpful, but additional complicating factors are likely to creep in. The risks and benefits to the foetus may be more specific and readily quantified; the potential harm to the woman, say from minimally invasive surgery or foetal transfusion, less serious; the differential costs to society greater. Any attempts to balance the avoidance of foetal harm against the risks to the woman could be perhaps even more difficult. Numerous, sometimes conflicting, social forces may be brought to bear on such decisions, which could have implications too for the care of neonates and infants, especially as regards influences like breastfeeding.

It is clear that although UK law ostensibly upholds pregnant women's rights to make their own decisions about medical care, provided they are judged competent, there remain serious questions about whether this theoretical support is likely to hold firm in practice, and whether alternative routes might be utilised to bypass autonomy. In the US, a variety of court-ordered interventions, pre-natal seizures and criminal sanctions applied to pregnant women continue to pose a threat to pregnant women's rights to bodily integrity, notwithstanding similar legal tenets upholding patient autonomy and the emphatic statements of professional bodies that pregnant women should not be subject to either forced treatment or criminal penalties for behaviour in pregnancy.

Pregnant women face a number of disadvantages in both medical and legal systems should their decisions, behaviours or lifestyles conflict with those regarded as appropriate. Involved professionals have strong incentives – likely to become more forceful in the coming years – to ensure their compliance with medical and behavioural recommendations. This impetus is supported by academic arguments for imposing control on women's behaviours and choices in pregnancy, and the threat is not ameliorated by judicial inconsistencies as to the significance of the presence of a foetus.

In the UK there remains significant potential for autonomy to be undermined by weak evidential requirements; 'emergency' exceptions allowing decisions in haste and without proper representation; undue flexibility of interpretation of competence assessment, and other legal lacunae; by sanctions applied post-birth, or by various other legal and ethical challenges. Moreover there is the continuing risk that women's decisions may be simply disregarded altogether by decisions taken under pressure 'at the coal face'.

Although very few cases have reached court in the UK, the implications of using legal compulsion to achieve medical aims have had wide-ranging – and largely negative – effects. In the US, there is the additional threat of criminal sanctions, with various high profile cases being played out under the glare of considerable media publicity, often involving emotive descriptions and including the most heinous accusations that modern society has to throw against the women involved: child abuse, drug addiction, homicide.

In the US, such challenges are much tied in both with political lobbying by anti-abortion activists as to foetal status, and with the 'war on drugs'; in both cases often involving the religious right, associated legislators and various lobby groups on all sides utilising emotive media portrayals and semantic manoeuvring to press their case. In some states – most notably South Carolina – such forces have increasingly threatened women's autonomy.

Tangential influences, such as foetal homicide laws, may assist attempts to impose unwanted interventions and specific lifestyle choices on pregnant women. In dissenting views during the passage of the federal *Unborn Victims of Violence Act* (*UVVA*), Representatives noted that even though the *UVVA* specifically excludes the pregnant woman from penalties, the fact that it gives the foetus a legal status equal to that of the woman could open the door to legal sanctions in future, and 'the rights of a pregnant women may be placed in direct conflict with, or subordinate to, those of her fetus'. It was suggested that a future statute might require a woman to be prosecuted for any act or 'error' in judgement during her pregnancy, such as for her consumption of wine or cigarettes, or for actions such as her decision to fly during pregnancy. Similarly, if child custody provisions may be expanded to cover foetuses, they could be used as a basis for allowing, say, a biological father awarded custody of the foetus to control the woman's behaviour or, in some cases, civilly commit a pregnant woman in order to 'protect' the foetus. They warned:

> The specter of the state arrogating to itself the right to control the fate of a fetus by exerting coercive control over a pregnant woman, even placing her in custody, reduces her to a mere vessel for the eventual delivery of the then fetus. [*sic*] Such governmental coercion is far from hypothetical. Several courts have exercised this extreme form of control.[4,5]

Women's Vulnerability

Every pregnant woman is affected by the willingness of those in a position of considerable power, at a time of heightened personal vulnerability, to pay due regard to autonomy and to respect a woman's decisions. Those few women who have had the resources – both personal and financial – and the inclination to pursue their cases in court are likely to be an exceptionally small and probably unrepresentative selection of pregnant women affected. For them, should initial forced treatment decisions be found to be in error, criminal charges or child abuse proceedings retracted, or treatment instituted without recourse to the courts at all, post-hoc judgments in the woman's favour represent a somewhat hollow victory. The majority of pregnant women will probably succumb to the powerful combination of medical authority, information control and selective availability of alternatives and, even for those who dissent, coercion by moral pressure is likely to succeed long before legal intervention is even contemplated.

Judicial rulings and ethical pronouncements on such cases undoubtedly influence prevailing medical mores and practice, even as they are influenced in reverse. Yet there is evidence not only that the sequelae of forced interventions are harmful for the vast majority of women and children who are their potential targets, but also that these high-profile conflicts have had repercussions in terms of both increasing assumptions of obstetric control and driving women away from obstetric care – spreading the net of conflict ever wider. The overall effects may be markedly detrimental to the very people whose 'best interests' are being fought over. In

England, the Association for Improvement in Maternity Services (AIMS) has reported that 'the small number of court cases has caused a few obstetricians to act in an increasingly authoritarian manner', and describes women becoming anxious if referral for an obstetric opinion is suggested, and being reluctant to enter hospital even for outpatient care. One woman with several risk factors stated that she had decided to conceal her pregnancy rather than run the risk of her rights not being respected; others have asked if they needed to go abroad to escape such potential threats.[6]

Women in the UK have no 'right' to abortion, little choice but to accept medical intervention at birth and, notwithstanding Government rhetoric, limited options as to their type of obstetric care within the National Health Service (NHS). Those on the other side of the Atlantic have a right to abortion before foetal viability, although this may be limited by access and financing, and may find their choices as to obstetric care even further restricted by the services that local hospitals and obstetricians – arguably more conservative and more swayed by litigation concerns in the US than in the UK – are willing to provide. Notably however, obstetric conflict has involved mainly non-paying patients, who are in a similar position in many ways to those in the NHS.

Respect for autonomy is even more important in any system where patients have little option as to the type of care offered or the personnel providing it, and where the medical profession is relatively homogenous in attitude. Yet as Cahill points out,[7] whilst court-ordered Caesareans represent 'an unusual extreme within contemporary maternity care', they bring into sharp relief some of the stereotypical assumptions about women that underlie much of current medical practice, and may compromise or disempower women in other ways during pregnancy and labour. Feitshans too has noted that women are often excluded from the process of medical decision-making during pregnancy, even though such decisions affect them personally and affect the future well-being of the foetus; she warns that the impact of new technologies for testing and treatment may further compromise their autonomy.[8]

Furthermore, forced and unnecessary Caesareans and other non-voluntary or unneeded interventions in pregnancy have been viewed as part of a continuum of female abuse and disempowerment, linking male violence and women's health on a spectrum that includes domestic violence during pregnancy, genital mutilation, forced sterilisation and psychiatric abuse of women deemed 'promiscuous'.[9]

Yet the judiciary has largely accepted without demur not only the medical evidence presented but also the underlying assumption that doctors have a greater claim to knowing, and safeguarding, the foetus' interests than does the mother herself. Legal rulings have been somewhat tainted by association, allowing interventions based on sometimes shaky medical evidence that has been largely accepted at face value, often with the usual standards of proof suspended, and side-stepping policy issues, whilst leaving a substantial quantum of discretion in the hands of the medical profession.

The issues arising from obstetric conflict potentially affect every sexually active, fertile woman. Accepting the burdens of 'quality control' of pregnancy outcome is seen as a woman's responsibility, and the woman carrying the child may be regarded as accountable for a 'faulty' outcome even though the 'blame' may lie elsewhere.

Medical Responses

Patient-physician conflicts may not be common, but they are not particularly rare either. Robertson postulates that mandatory Caesarean section is the most likely candidate for imposition.[10] In one US study, two per cent of patients undergoing non-elective caesarean section initially disagreed with the recommendation; these were exclusively clinic (non-paying) patients, and among this subgroup the rate of conflict was over six per cent. Although all ultimately agreed to surgery, afterwards 8.7 per cent indicated that they did not have adequate input in the decision.[11]

Recourse to legal intervention could be regarded as a short-cut to tackling failures of communication on the part of medical professionals – women's most consistent complaints about obstetric care are that they are given insufficient information and that they lack involvement in decisions about birth.[12]

Despite extensive discussions of maternal duty in such cases, there has been little attention paid to the question of medical duty in cases of obstetric conflict – and, in particular, whether doctors have fulfilled their duty by their behaviour in sometimes inadequate or even false presentation of evidence, or indeed in taking their patient to court at all, rather than attempting the more complicated and time-consuming option of communicating with her. If Melissa Rowland was as mentally disturbed as was so publicly alleged, her doctors' duty of care towards her surely could not be discharged by attempting, retrospectively, to have her charged with murder? Many of the cases of obstetric conflict that have arrived in court – often as an emergency – might have been avoided by giving more time and attention at an early stage and concentrating on problem-resolution within the clinical relationship, rather than resorting to the law to enforce the medical side of the argument. There is ample evidence from the cases of failures of communication, mistrust and sometimes outright hostility. Problems could often be identified earlier, allowing more time to arrive at a solution or, at least, more time for the woman too to obtain legal advice and if necessary to prepare her case.

In *Re MB*,[13] for example, it was clear from an early stage that the pregnant woman involved had a morbid fear of needles (see Chapter 2). Arguably, when she refused to have a blood sample taken at her first antenatal appointment, and certainly at the stage where Caesarean was contemplated, this should then have prompted formal psychiatric and competency assessment if her capacity to refuse was in any doubt, as well as attempts to deal with the problem by helping her – rather than, as occurred, resorting to legal action only when she went into labour.

As has been discussed, current obstetric practices are not always evidence-based. Discrimination has been apparent in some attempts at coercion in pregnancy. Conflicts have seemed often to be largely power-based even whilst being presented as primarily concerned with the best interests of the mother and/or the foetus. Resort to the courts has paralleled increasing criticism of the medicalisation of childbirth, as if obstetricians are employing legal reinforcement as their own power to impose their will by traditional paternalism has declined, in the face of increasing consumer choice and the natural childbirth movement. As Irwin and Jordan put it:

> A court-ordered cesarean section not only determines the authority of a particular doctor over a particular woman, it confirms medical authority in birthing.[14]

Many experts are now querying whether medical control of the birth process is, overall, a positive development, or whether in fact 'thousands of women and babies are put at avoidable risk', as some of those concerned with the increase in Caesarean section rates have claimed.[15] As Canadian obstetrician Dr Philip Hall has observed:

> Surely humans should be more evolving in the direction of reproductive success like all other species? Humans seem somehow to be the exception, where we are rescuing babies ... from one in five women in one of the healthiest countries in the world. It doesn't compute.[16]

Redressing the Balance

Women who question medical advice may well do so in the sincere belief that they are doing the best for their future child; moreover the medical profession is not always right. It has been argued that the motives – as well as the modus operandi – of those who would pursue forced interventions are not entirely beyond suspicion. Medical pronouncements as to urgency, prognosis and recommended treatment may not be evidence-based, and alternatives are rarely mentioned.

This suggests an urgent need for unbiased assessment in cases of obstetric conflict, a role that would ideally fall to the courts, yet in which the courts have been dually hampered by the alleged urgency of the need for a decision and by their unwillingness or inability to question medical evidence. It has been noted that the courts are averse to interfere in clinical matters, and it is striking that the court remained disinclined even to raise such issues when the *Collins* case went to appeal,[17] notwithstanding that the most blatantly obvious clinical fact – whether or not S was in labour – was known to have been wrong.

In this context too, the flexibility allowed in competency assessments in the UK, discussed in Chapter 4, is a further area in urgent need of address. Although the *Collins* guidelines recommend that in future cases, if competence is in question, it should be assessed by an approved psychiatrist,[18] multiple such assessments proved little safeguard in *Collins* itself. Competence is a legal test, albeit one that tends to be placed in the hands of medical professionals; moreover, even leaving aside the issue of whether medical professionals might tend towards similar attitudes towards medical interventions, if the psychiatrist involved is working for the same organisation (such as an NHS trust) applying for the intervention, this must inevitably raise questions about the independence of the judgement.

The evidence presented here suggests that the courts have erred in taking medical pronouncements at face value. Indeed Lord Chief Justice Woolf recently stated that English courts had been 'excessively deferential' to doctors.[19] Although his pronouncements were in a different context,[20] many of his comments are applicable to the present analysis. In particular, referring to the series of well-publicised recent scandals in the UK that have dented the 'automatic presumption of beneficence' that the courts had in the past accorded doctors, he said:

> I cannot help believing that the behaviour of those involved ... betrays a lack of appreciation of the limits of their responsibility. They were not motivated by personal gain but they had lost sight of the limits of their powers and authority. They acted as though they were able to take any action they thought desirable irrespective of the views of others.[21]

This is a pretty damning indictment. Lord Woolf's conclusion, that it is 'unwise to place any profession or other body providing services to the public on a pedestal where their actions cannot be subject to close scrutiny', is commended.

Recommendations for the Law

It seems also unwise to pass any judgment, or enact any legislation, that sets the rights and interests of the foetus not only above those of the woman in whose womb it is carried, but also above those possessed by a born child. The ultimate implication of such laws is that attempts should be made to preserve the foetus, perhaps irrespective of its gestational stage or prognosis, in preference to the interests of the woman (think of the case of Angela Carder)[22] and, further, that such attempts may logically be reduced once the foetus is actually born (as may be the case with handicapped neonates – see Chapter 4).

For the multiple reasons discussed, such measures pose dire dangers to the civil rights of women as a whole; to the well-being of pregnant women, foetuses and children in general, and often even to the particular individuals whose interests are in question in cases of obstetric conflict.

In the US particularly, the various attempts to inveigle foetal status into a range of statutes irrespective of the actual consequences for women and children represent wilful political manoeuvring, as does the perverse semantic wrangling attempting to substitute phrases such as 'unborn child' for foetus, in the attempt to make them interchangeable – when, in fact, the former is misleading insofar as it has no legal or medical meaning.[23]

The separate issues of obstetric conflict (and perhaps 'foetal homicide'), on the one hand, and abortion, on the other, need to be clearly demarcated to avoid the former becoming dragged further into religious or political conflict.

The law must address, as a matter of some urgency, the exact definition and status of a foetus, against the background of current medical and technological capacity. The issue does not have to devolve into a contest between regarding the entity discussed as a 'foetus' (with no rights under common law) or an 'unborn child' (entitled to be treated as if it were an actual child in waiting). Clearly, a foetus is a living biological entity; however it is not the same as a child, being incapable of independent life and exclusively dependent on the body of a woman for its continued existence. It is a potential human-in-being but not yet an actual one, just as the woman carrying the foetus is a potential mother,[24] but not yet an actual one.

It would be useful for the law to come to some conclusion as to whether the foetus is therefore to be regarded as a separate entity, or as part of the mother, or as something in-between. However, even if the verdict of such an analysis were to regard the foetus as a separate entity, it does not follow that the foetus – even the near-term foetus – should be accorded 'personhood' and equated with a citizen, with all the full human rights that such status implies, and it certainly does not follow that that anyone is entitled therefore to compromise the pregnant woman's autonomy. Further again, even if the foetus, at least after a certain stage of gestation, were to be regarded as a 'person', this still does mean that it has rights to demand the sacrifice of bodily integrity from its mother, any more than a born child could demand that she be cut open to donate her kidney, or force her to donate a pint (or even a thimbleful) of blood or, for that matter, to abstain from alcohol, or from trampolining, or to take an antibiotic, or a dietary supplement.

In resolving the underlying ethical debates stemming from this analysis, Hasnas's exposition of the 'classical conception' of human rights, in which the right to life is absolute and cannot be balanced against the rights of others, is potentially helpful. In any return to the classical conception – which may be also desirable on other grounds – the woman's rights (to life and, in parallel, to bodily integrity) are absolute and, whatever purported rights may be attributed to the foetus, they do not entitle it to compromise the woman's rights by demanding obstetric (or any other) intervention, even for proven benefit. As discussed in Chapter 6, this concept is one that leaves open the question of abortion, whilst clearly distinguishing it from issues of obstetric conflict, thus enabling resolution of the latter on both legal and ethical grounds without getting drawn into the moral tangle of the former. Such resolution has much to commend it.

It is interesting to note that under this conception, the issue of obstetric conflict also becomes clearly distinguishable from that of prohibitions against women's actions that may positively harm the foetus, such as drug or alcohol use. Again, to separate out these issues – if necessary to continue the debate on the latter – may be useful in terms of resolving at least issues of 'pure' obstetric conflict and avoiding their entanglement in 'foetal rights' issues.

In the case of such prohibitions, again, the question is left open by this analysis; as with abortion, it is dependent on the rights given to the foetus. However, even if the foetus were to be deemed to have certain rights, this would not entitle it to demand *any* behavioural intervention that might be deemed appropriate in pregnancy. The foetus's rights may not be balanced against those of the woman; rather, it has an absolute right not to be harmed, and so might require the pregnant woman to abstain from drugs, or alcohol, or smoking or, come to that, bungee jumping – but those rights would not entitle anyone to require the mother positively to act, for example by taking a nutritional supplement or undergoing a medical test.

Clearly this analysis still leaves problems – in particular, if the foetus were to be granted full 'personhood' rights, what of the situation where the woman, say, needed a drug that might damage the foetus, or wished to engage in sporting activity, or even drive a car? These examples may, indeed, militate against giving the foetus full rights.

In any event, to take the most emotive case, there is sufficient evidence of the harms of punitive actions against drug-using pregnant women, and sufficient grounds to believe that alternative approaches are much more productive (*vide infra*), that there is a good case to be made separately against such measures. Again, an ethical duty to refrain from drug use, which many commentators agree already exists, does not necessarily translate into a legal duty. An alternative approach is to argue that *society* has an ethical duty to offer the addicted woman appropriate treatment, just as it may offer (though not compel), medical or dental treatment, or pre-natal vitamin supplements, or financial assistance.

In terms of 'foetal homicide' laws, it is possible similarly to give recognition both to the wrong done to the woman by interruption of a wanted pregnancy (or even an unwanted one, given that there may be future reproductive or health consequences of traumatic termination of pregnancy or miscarriage) and to the wrong of halting the development of the foetus towards personhood – arguably a greater wrong the more progress the foetus has made – without drawing in concepts of 'unborn children' designed to undermine abortion rights. It may be right that penalties be imposed upon anyone who violates the potentiality of either: that of the woman to become a mother, or that of the foetus to be born and thereby attain legal personhood. However, most such laws already rightly recognise that these two potentialities are irrevocably intertwined. Therefore, their sanctions cannot ethically be applied against the woman, whose own bodily effort and sacrifice are a pre-requisite for the potentiality of the foetus, which attains its ultimate status only through the mother duly bringing it to term and giving birth – any more than sanctions could be applied against the foetus for any failure in enabling the woman to attain motherhood or, indeed, for causing the woman's death during the process of childbirth.

A foetus may be amply protected from third party interference (excepting, perhaps, that of medical professionals – also generally excluded under foetal homicide laws) in and as itself – as is the case with the foetal homicide law in, say, California – without needing to resort to the obfuscating terminology of the *UVAA* and allow further unwarranted implications to be drawn from this. The California law and the few others like it are to be commended on this account.

Policy Considerations

In the light of its negative sequelae, the UK would do well to resist the US trend towards further coerced interventions during pregnancy; there is a better focus for improving maternal and child outcome overall (*vide infra*). Therefore, any suggestion of expansion in the scope of interference in pregnancy should be a question of public policy for widespread discussion and Parliamentary debate as to the extent of society's legitimate interest in such questions; such discussion, if it ever arises – and particularly any professional advice given to ministers – should not only encompass the complex considerations discussed here but also allow room for women's views to be aired, especially regarding the quality of their obstetric experiences, their preferences and their priorities within the context of their lives as a whole.

Until and unless such intervention is given public and Parliamentary approval, and given the loopholes in the current law that have been discussed, it is unfortunately the case that existing safeguards may be insufficient to ensure pregnant women's autonomy (and thus, in the view presented here, the overall well-being of women and their foetuses and future children). One proposal – echoing Lord Woolf's suggestions in reference to medical negligence, 'to clarify the responsibility of health care professionals to their patients' – is that as soon as an apparent conflict arises, health care professionals should, like solicitors, have a duty to advise their clients to seek independent advice.[25] That this immediately throws into sharp relief the difficulties of implementing such a patient safeguard within a system such as the NHS, in which patients have little choice of health care provider, arguably merely further demonstrates the flaws within the present health care system in terms of disempowering patients.

Ideally, one result of such a change would be to promote a greater spirit of cooperation in the face of issues that could turn into potential conflicts – many of which are obvious, or could be predicted with adequate initial discussions, and at least some of which could be perhaps resolved at an earlier stage given greater effort towards communication, negotiation and exploration of possible alternatives that could satisfy both parties.

Next, many of the problems that have occurred at the law-medicine interface reveal the difficulty of trying to resolve clinical dilemmas in the courtroom and suggest the need for an alternative source of readily accessible expert advice for the courts in cases where patients and doctors are in conflict. The recent decision (in a case of compulsory treatment of a mental patient)[26] that the court was entitled to review the merits of a medical decision on treatment without consent, and that in such a case the patient was entitled to require the attendance of medical witnesses for cross-examination, made clear that with the coming into force of the *Human Rights Act 1998*, the court's need to investigate and resolve medical issues in such cases has become even plainer. As discussed, the role of the official solicitor does not seem to offer patients unbiased advocacy within a system heavily weighted against them, and there are few grounds for supposing that an equivalent 'official doctor' would be any more impartial. This may be a further arena requiring a dually-trained advocate, as recently recommended to meet the need for expert witnesses to 'reach agreement on the limits of medical probability, rather than score points off each other...';[27] it could also be an ideal role for a medical ethicist trained to look at the wider picture including the medico-legal and ethical implications.

Moreover, if an adversarial legal system is deemed suitable to deal with such conflicts, its safeguards should at least be allowed time to come into play.

Therefore, mechanisms should be set in place in the UK to ensure beyond doubt that should any future cases of conflict arise, pregnant women are assured – even in an emergency – of independent competency assessments, representation and unbiased evaluation of evidence. Should a woman be genuinely incapable of making her own decision, she should be assured of independent assessment of her best interests or perhaps, given the difficulties discussed on the part of both medical profession and judiciary of separating out maternal and foetal interests, substituted judgement where possible as to what she would have preferred.

Furthermore, to ensure that there can be no hint of the courts acting to legitimate medical autocracy, the party making the application should never be the party ultimately to decide on or carry out the treatment. Given the relatively vulnerable position of the woman and the power wielded by medical professionals in such cases, this dual involvement is potentially a dire subversion of natural justice. Also, if a woman is deemed incompetent, the court could consider the appointment of a disinterested party to take decisions on her behalf, rather than allowing the doctors with whom the woman has been in conflict simply to treat her according to their view of her best interests.

One potential mechanism for this is illustrated by US practices – for example, in *In the Matter of Alice Hughes*,[28] a surrogate was appointed when the woman's advance refusal of blood transfusions was held not to apply to the circumstances that actually arose (because her doctor had led her to believe that transfusion would not be necessary during a hysterectomy, and had not discussed what she would want should an emergency arise). Assuming independence of the surrogate, this would avoid the possibility of a court order being used as a weapon in possible power struggles between a woman and her obstetric advisers. It is interesting to note in this context that in the reverse situation, where the *woman* took action to compel doctors to stop treating her against her will – in a recent British case in which a terminally ill woman dependent on a ventilator succeeded in petitioning the court for the right to have the ventilator switched off[29] – the doctors involved were entitled to step back, and she was transferred to another hospital for treatment to be discontinued. This would seem an excellent policy in cases of obstetric conflict, unless the woman herself expressed a preference for treatment at the original institution.

It is further recommended that similar safeguards for independence of both assessment and implementation be instituted in the case of any attempts to remove a child at or shortly after birth based on medical concerns arising during pregnancy or in the neonatal period. As far as potential drug exposure is concerned, a woman's ability to parent her child should be assessed as such, and not based solely on results of toxicology screening without evidence of harm.

It has been noted that one of the stimuli for increased obstetric intervention is the threat of litigation, which may make it 'safer' for the professional (though not necessarily the mother or foetus) to intervene. A similar scenario obtains in the case of potential child abuse – if a child, like Victoria Climbié, dies because gross abuse is missed, there will be consequences, quite likely including a public enquiry and possible pillorying in the media. However, mistakenly removing a child, or taking out an unnecessary care order, is usually a private tragedy for the child and family, rarely followed by any consequences for doctors, social workers or other professionals involved. This is so even in high profile cases such as the mistakenly-convicted 'cot death' mothers discussed in Chapter 5. It was the expert witness who was called to account not, for example, the social workers imposing restrictions on Trupti Patel's access to her surviving child, even after she was acquitted in court. The same is true of cases in which subsequent babies were removed from women who had been suspected of such killings on the basis of similarly flawed evidence.

Some greater level of accountability for decisions that, if made in error, may wreck the lives of women, children and their families is warranted. The Women's Aid Federation of England, commenting on the cases described in Chapter 3 in which fathers killed their own children after court-ordered contact arrangements, pointed out that there is nothing to indicate that any court professionals were held accountable. It recommends:

> Mechanisms are required for holding family court professionals accountable for decisions that result in children being killed or seriously harmed. If found to be responsible, professionals (judges, magistrates, barristers, solicitors, expert witness or family court adviser) should lose their right to adjudicate, represent parties, provide evidence or report to the court in family proceedings.[30]

Such accountability would be well-extended to cases in which professionals – doctors, social workers, expert witnesses, lawyers and judges – are responsible for children being wrongly removed from their homes and families. Arguably to make false or malicious allegations concerning child welfare issues should be a criminal offence, as it already is in many other countries.[31] At the very least, such actions might prompt educative efforts towards greater understanding of the possible life-long harms that may flow from family disruption, analogous to the 'parenting education' that many women are forced to undergo to retain access to their children.

Moreover, those who are responsible for unwarranted obstetric interventions, whether court-ordered or not, might similarly be barred from involvement in comparable cases in future.

Alternative Approaches

Arguably however, in terms of obstetric conflict such safeguards of independence and accountability are needed only because the current climate is one in which pregnant women are still regarded as legitimate targets for paternalistic interference, and in which both the medical profession and the law have deemed it appropriate to attempt to intervene. Other than situations in which a pregnant woman is genuinely incapable of deciding for herself, in most cases of obstetric conflict the assumption of the need for intervention is predicated on the presence of a foetus and thereby, inevitably, treats the pregnant woman as having fewer rights than any other adult. The ultimate question is whether the law should place itself as arbiter between a woman's decision and the views of those who 'know better'.

Ideally, of course, women would not need safeguards to protect them from their doctors. The court cases that have arisen on both sides of the Atlantic, as well as academic views that treat women as little more than foetal containers, have greatly enhanced the atmosphere of conflict already apparent in obstetrics as professionals and mothers vie for control of pregnancy and birth. Labelling women as deviant, incompetent or criminal should not be a substitute for provision of good medical care – which does not and, arguably, cannot occur in the courtroom – nor should coercion be used in place of collaborative efforts to find solutions. It is to be hoped that in future – having perhaps, by overruling women's decisions, encouraged obstetric paternalism to its last flourish – the law will now help to promote a new attitude of collaboration.

Harris has proposed an alternative model, moving law and policy away from criminalisation and toward prevention of pre-natal harm. This encourages obstetricians to focus on the mutual needs of pregnant women and foetuses, rather than on their mutually exclusive needs, and recommends that when faced with ethical dilemmas they should attempt to understand pregnant women and their decisions within their broad social networks and communities, as well as examining their own standpoint and asking whether their own ethical formulations reduce or enhance existing gender, class, or racial inequality.[32] Similarly, midwives have been advised that a crisis intervention approach to maternal-foetal conflicts fosters an adversarial view of the relationship between the pregnant woman and her foetus, which can be divisive and counterproductive, and a better approach emphasises mutually held goals rather than countervailing rights.[33]

Such approaches are consistent with suggestions that, rather than adopt coercive measures which may reflect retrograde assumptions about women's role and which, paradoxically, may encourage some women to avoid beneficial medical and social services, a better focus is upon promoting women's health *and* their rights[34,35] including improving education and drug treatment programmes[36], particularly to address the lack of services specific to the needs of women with children.[37,38] Adverse neonatal outcomes are associated with homelessness, physical and sexual abuse and sexually transmitted infections in pregnancy, as well as with more obviously controllable factors such as smoking and alcohol use, and fragmented health care over the course of women's reproductive lives has been identified as a predominant theme in such cases, leading researchers to conclude that the focus of maternal and child health care should shift to a model which addresses the chronicity of social and clinical risks.[39]

There is ample evidence of the effectiveness of more positive interventions in 'high risk' women in improving not only perinatal[40,41,42,43] but also longer-term outcomes.[44,45] In particular, measures such as providing child care, parenting classes, nutritional education and vocational training significantly improve abstinence among drug-using pregnant women[46] and outcome in drug-exposed infants,[47] suggesting that addressing social barriers to 'good' maternal behaviour is effective.

Moreover, most women addicted to drugs have other psychosocial risk factors for poor obstetric outcome, such as poverty and single motherhood,[48] and the multiple medical and social risk factors associated with long-term poverty have powerful, compromising effects on children's outcomes which may overshadow any specific effects of pre-natal cocaine exposure.[49] Addressing other high risk conditions such as domestic violence, known to be associated with drug use in pregnancy[50] and a significant factor in adverse pregnancy outcomes such as low birthweight[51] and pre-term delivery[52,53], has also been recommended. Whereas the US prevalence of pre-natal illicit drug use is about 5 per cent overall,[54] violence from a husband or partner occurs in at least 2.4 per cent to 5.6 per cent of pregnancies,[55] and up to 20 per cent in some studies,[56] and is often accompanied by sexual[57] or emotional and verbal abuse,[58] which are also associated with detrimental outcomes.

It could also be argued that concentrating pejorative comments and punitive responses on a few extreme cases with emotive appeal deflects attention from the urgent need to improve the social conditions of women and children generally, as well as raising standards of – and choices in – obstetric care and providing better access to drug treatment services with facilities for women and children.

In 1993, the Canadian Royal Commission on New Reproductive Technologies produced an unequivocal report[59] whose conclusions are here commended for adoption in both the UK and US. These recommend that:

- Medical treatment never be imposed upon a pregnant woman against her wishes
- Criminal law, or any other law, never be used to confine or imprison a pregnant woman in the interest of her fetus
- The conduct of a pregnant woman in relation to her fetus not be criminalized
- Child welfare or other legislation never be used to control a woman's behaviour during pregnancy
- Civil liability never be imposed upon a woman for harm done to her fetus during pregnancy.

Meanwhile it has been amply demonstrated that, despite the apparent theoretical primacy of a pregnant woman's decision in the UK at least, the current legal position may still encourage doctors to override autonomy – although it may have altered the manner in which this may be done and/or the stated justifications for it. In the US, women are clearly vulnerable to attempts to override their decisions or to penalise them for adverse neonatal outcomes, and such interventions are often initiated by third parties with a variety of ulterior motives.

The court in *Collins* referred to a passage of Lord Reid holding that:

> English law goes to great lengths to protect a person of full age and capacity from interference with his personal liberty. We have too often seen freedom disappear in other countries ... by gradual erosion; and often it is the first step that counts. So it would be unwise to make even minor concessions.[60]

In the court's view, and in the view of this author, the importance of that salutary warning remains undiminished.

Notes

1 Indeed, recent evidence suggests that doctors were largely to blame for the thalidomide tragedy, in which the drug was prescribed to thousands of pregnant women to treat morning sickness, causing babies to be born with malformations, especially missing limbs. According to one eminent medical historian, the disaster occurred because the medical establishment was affected by a kind of 'mass denial', sticking rigidly to the then-prevailing belief that dangerous substances were unable to pass through the placenta and therefore could not affect the foetus – despite abundant evidence to the contrary: Dally A. 'Thalidomide: was the tragedy preventable?' *Lancet.* 1998;351(9110):1197-9; Fletcher, David. 'Doctors "to blame for thalidomide disaster"'. *Daily Telegraph* 18 April 1998, at p4.

2 Johnsen D. 'A new threat to pregnant women's autonomy'. *Hastings Cent Rep* 1987;17(4):33-40.

3 Annas GJ. 'Foreclosing the use of force: A.C. reversed'. *Hastings Cent Rep* 1990;20(4):27-9.

4 Conyers J, Jr., Berman HL, Boucher R and nine other Representatives. *Dissenting Views to H.R. 1997, 'Unborn Victims of Violence Act of 2003.'* Washington, 2004: http://www.house.gov/judiciary_democrats/hr1997dissenting108cong.pdf.

5 The potential for such issues to be drawn into the often bitter disputes among separating couples is clear. For example, already in two cases in the UK, the court has ruled in favour of estranged, unmarried fathers' applications to immunise their children with the controversial MMR vaccine against the wishes of mothers with sole custody – even though in one case the father had delayed for years before making the application and his ten-year-old daughter had said she did not want the immunisation: Waterhouse, Rosie. 'Mothers lose court fight to stop MMR jabs'. *Daily Telegraph* 31 July 2003, at p3; Anon. 'Mothers lose MMR appeal'. *BMJ* 2003; 327: 306 (News).

6 Beech BAL. 'Court ordered caesarean sections are discouraging women from seeking obstetric care.' *BMJ* 1997;314:1908 (letter).

7 Cahill H. 'An Orwellian scenario: court ordered caesarean section and women's autonomy.' *Nurs Ethics* 1999; 6(6): 494-505 [Medline].

8 Feitshans IL. 'Legislating to preserve women's autonomy during pregnancy.' *Med Law* 1995;14(5-6):397-412.

9 Heise LL. 'Reproductive freedom and violence against women: where are the intersections?' *J Law Med Ethics* 1993;21:206-16.

10 Robertson, John A. *Children of Choice. Freedom and the new reproductive technologies.* Princeton University Press, New Jersey 1994, at p 189.

11 Lescale KB, Inglis SR, Eddleman KA et al. 'Conflicts between physicians and patients in non-elective cesarean delivery: incidence and the adequacy of informed consent.' *Am J Perinatol* 1996;13(3):171-6 [Medline].

12 Hall, Celia. 'Doctors told to check on need for Caesareans.' *Daily Telegraph,* 19 March 1997.

13 *Re MB* [1997] EWCA Civ 1361.

14 Irwin S, Jordan B. 'Knowledge, Practice, and Power: Court-Ordered Cesarean Sections.' *Medical Anthropology Quarterly*; 1987: 1(3):319-334.

15 From: International Cesarean Awareness Network. 'Statement on Melissa Rowland'. *ICAN E-News Line* Volume 17, 22 March 2004.

16 Cited in: International Cesarean Awareness Network. 'Statement on Melissa Rowland', *Ibid.*

17 *In the matter of an application for judicial review: Queen v Louize Collins; Pathfinder Mental Health Services Trust and St George's Healthcare NHS Trust, ex parte 'S'* [1998] EWHC Admin 490 (7th May, 1998).

18 *In the matter of an application for judicial review: Queen v Louize Collins & Ors, op cit,* at 122 (ii).

19 Reported in: Dyer C. 'Courts too deferential to doctors, says judge.' *BMJ* 2001; 322: 129 (News).

20 Lord Woolf was referring to negligence actions - where, he said, it had become clear to the courts that the hospitals and the medical professions could not be relied on to resolve justified complaints justly. Arguably, doctors have been examined in such cases in greater detail, and with greater leisure, than has been the case in most instances of obstetric conflict, making his observations even more pertinent to the latter.

21 Reported in: Dyer C. 'Courts too deferential to doctors, says judge,' *op cit.*

22 *Re AC* (1990) 573 A 2d 1235 (DC Ct Appeals).

23 Conyers J, Jr., Berman HL, Boucher R and nine other Representatives. Dissenting Views to H.R. 1997, 'Unborn Victims of Violence Act of 2003.' Washington, 2004: http://www.house.gov/judiciary_democrats/hr1997dissenting108cong.pdf.

24 As neatly recognised in the quaint old phrase 'mother-to-be'.

25 Burn, Suzanne (Secretary, Civil Litigation Committee, The Law Society). 'Access to civil justice: Lord Woolf's visionary new landscape.' *BMJ* 1996;313:242-243 (Editorial) (commenting on: Woolf H. *Access to Justice: final report to the Lord Chancellor on the civil justice system in England and Wales.* London HMSO 1996).

26 *R (Wilkinson) v Broadmoor Hospital and Others* (2001) TLR 22/10/01.

27 Richards P, Kennedy IM, Woolf H. 'Managing medical mishaps.' *BMJ* 1996;313:243-244 (Editorial).

28 *In the Matter of Alice Hughes* (1992) 611 A 2d 1148 (NJ SC App Div).

29 *Ms B v An NHS Hospital Trust.* [2002] EWHC 429 (Fam).

30 Saunders, Hilary. *Twenty-nine child homicides: Lessons still to be learnt on domestic violence and child protection.* Women's Aid, London 2004: www.womensaid.org.uk.

31 Robinson, Jean. 'Child protection system wilfully ignores principles of childcare' (letters). *Daily Telegraph* 5 August 2004, at p 23.

32 Harris LH. 'Rethinking maternal-fetal conflict: gender and equality in perinatal ethics.' *Obstet Gynecol* 2000 Nov; 96(5 Pt 1): 786-91.

33 King NM. 'Maternal-fetal conflicts. Ethical and legal implications for nurse-midwives.' *J Nurse Midwifery* 1991; 36(6): 361-5.

34 Roth R. 'At women's expense: the costs of fetal rights.' In: Merrick, Janna C and Blank, Robert H. *The politics of pregnancy: policy dilemmas in the maternal-fetal relationship.* Harrington Park Press, Binghamton, New York, 1993: pp 117-135 (my italics).

35 McCloskey L, Plough AL, Power KL *et al.* 'A community-wide infant mortality review: findings and implications.' *Public Health Rep* 1999; 114(2): 165-77.

36 DeVille KA, Kopelman LM. 'Moral and social issues regarding pregnant women who use and abuse drugs.' *Obstet Gynecol Clin North Am* 1998; 25(1): 237-54.

37 Byrd RS, Neistadt AM, Howard CR *et al*. 'Why screen newborns for cocaine: service patterns and social outcomes at age one year.' *Child Abuse Negl* 1999; 23(6): 523-30.

38 Howell EM, Chasnoff IJ. 'Perinatal substance abuse treatment. Findings from focus groups with clients and providers.' *J Subst Abuse Treat* 1999; 17(1-2): 139-48.

39 McCloskey L, Plough AL, Power KL *et al*, *op cit*.

40 Kukko H, Halmesmaki E. 'Prenatal care and counseling of female drug-abusers: effects on drug abuse and perinatal outcome.' *Acta Obstet Gynecol Scand* 1999; 78(1): 22-6.

41 Corse SJ, Smith M. 'Reducing substance abuse during pregnancy. Discriminating among levels of response in a prenatal setting.' *J Subst Abuse Treat* 1998; 15(5): 457-67.

42 Burkett G, Gomez-Marin O, Yasin SY, Martinez M. 'Prenatal care in cocaine-exposed pregnancies.' *Obstet Gynecol* 1998; 92(2): 193-200.

43 Kaltenbach K, Finnegan L. 'Prevention and treatment issues for pregnant cocaine-dependent women and their infants.' *Ann N Y Acad Sci* 1998; 846: 329-34.

44 Berkowitz G, Brindis C, Peterson S. 'Substance use and social outcomes among participants in perinatal alcohol and drug treatment.' *Womens Health* 1998; 4(3): 231-54.

45 Olds D, Henderson CR Jr, Cole R *et al*. 'Long-term effects of nurse home visitation on children's criminal and antisocial behavior: 15-year follow-up of a randomized controlled trial.' *JAMA* 1998; 280(14): 1238-44.

46 Howell EM, Heiser N, Harrington M. 'A review of recent findings on substance abuse treatment for pregnant women.' *J Subst Abuse Treat* 1999; 16(3): 195-219.

47 Mahony DL, Murphy JM. 'Neonatal drug exposure: assessing a specific population and services provided by visiting nurses.' *Pediatr Nurs* 1999; 25(1): 27-34, 108.

48 Bishai R, Koren G. 'Maternal and obstetric effects of prenatal drug exposure.' *Clin Perinatol* 1999; 26(1): 75-86.

49 Tronick EZ, Beeghly M. 'Prenatal cocaine exposure, child development, and the compromising effects of cumulative risk.' *Clin Perinatol* 1999; 26(1): 151-71.

50 Hans SL. 'Demographic and psychosocial characteristics of substance-abusing pregnant women.' *Clin Perinatol* 1999; 26(1): 55-74.

51 Campbell J, Torres S, Ryan J *et al*. 'Physical and nonphysical partner abuse and other risk factors for low birth weight among full term and preterm babies: a multiethnic case-control study.' *Am J Epidemiol* 1999; 150(7): 714-26.

52 Fernandez FM, Krueger PM. 'Domestic violence: effect on pregnancy outcome.' *J Am Osteopath Assoc* 1999; 99(5): 254-6.

53 Shumway J, O'Campo P, Gielen A *et al*. 'Preterm labor, placental abruption, and premature rupture of membranes in relation to maternal violence or verbal abuse.' *J Matern Fetal Med* 1999; 8(3): 76-80.

54 Howell EM, Heiser N, Harrington M, *op cit*.

55 Colley GBJ, Johnson CH, Morrow B *et al*. 'Prevalence of selected maternal and infant characteristics, Pregnancy Risk Assessment Monitoring System (PRAMS), 1997.' *Mor Mortal Wkly Rep CDC Surveill Summ* 1999; 48(5): 1-37.

56 Fernandez FM, Krueger PM. 'Domestic violence: effect on pregnancy outcome,' *op cit*.

57 Martin SL, Matza LS, Kupper LL et al. 'Domestic violence and sexually transmitted diseases: the experience of prenatal care patients.' *Public Health Rep* 1999; 114(3): 262-8.

58 Hedin LW, Janson PO. 'The invisible wounds: the occurrence of psychological abuse and anxiety compared with previous experience of physical abuse during the childbearing year.' *J Psychosom Obstet Gynaecol* 1999; 20(3): 136-44.

59 Royal Commission on New Reproductive Technologies. *Proceed with care: Final Report of the Royal Commission on New Reproductive Technologies.* Vol 2. Ottawa: Minister of Government Services; 1993: 964-65.

60 Per Lord Reid in *S v McC : W v W* (1972) AC 25, as cited in: *In the matter of an application for judicial review: Queen v Louize Collins & Ors, op cit,* at 48.

Bibliography

Abel E.L., Kruger M., 'Physician attitudes concerning legal coercion of pregnant alcohol and drug abusers'. *Am J Obstet Gynecol* 2002;186(4):768-72.

Action on Rights for Children. *Tracking children: a road to danger in the Children Bill?* 6 April 2004: www.arch-ed.co.uk.

Adams, S.F., Mahowald MB, Gallagher J. Refusal of treatment during pregnancy. *Clin Perinatol* 2003;30(1):127-40, vii-viii.

Albers, L.L., Savitz D.A. 'Hospital setting for birth and use of medical procedures in low-risk women.' *J Nurse-Midwifery* 1991; 36: 327-33.

Akkad, A., Jackson, C., Kenyon, S. *et al.* 'Informed consent for elective and emergency surgery: questionnaire study.' *Br J Obstet Gynaecol* 2004 Oct;111(10):1133-8.

Aksoy, Sahin. 'Antenatal screening and its possible meaning from unborn baby's perspective.' *BioMed Central Medical Ethics* 2001 2: 3.

Aldgate, J., Statham J. *The Children Act Now. Messages from Research. Studies in evaluating the Children Act 1989.* Stationery Office London 2001.

Alleyne, Richard. 'New guidelines for baby death trials'. *Daily Telegraph* 7 September 2004.

American Academy of Pediatrics. Committee on Substance Abuse. 'Tobacco, alcohol, and other drugs: the role of the pediatrician in prevention and management of substance abuse.' *Pediatrics* 1998 Jan; 101(1 Pt 1): 125-8.

American Civil Liberties Union. *ACLU, Center for Reproductive Rights, and Florida NOW Fight Efforts to Interfere With Care of Severely Disabled Rape Victim.* ACLU Press Release June 17, 2003: www.aclu.org.

American Civil Liberties Union. *ACLU Letter to the Senate Urging Opposition to S. 146/S. 1019, 'The Unborn Victims of Violence Act'.* 24 March 2004: http://www.aclu.org.

American Civil Liberties Union. *Coercive and Punitive Governmental Responses to Women's Conduct During Pregnancy.* American Civil Liberties Union, September 1997: www.aclu.org/issues/reproduct/coercive.html.

American Civil Liberties Union. *Legislative Analysis of The Unborn Victims Of Violence Act.* ACLU, 18 February 2000: URL: http://www.aclu.org/ReproductiveRights/ReproductiveRights.cfm?ID=90 13&c=144

American Civil Liberties Union. *Reproductive Freedom: What's Wrong with Fetal Rights: A look at fetal protection statutes and wrongful death actions on behalf of fetuses.* American Civil Liberties Union 1997. www.aclu.org/issues/reproduct/fetal.html.

American College of Obstetricians and Gynecologists. *Evaluation of Cesarean Delivery.* ACOG. Washington, DC, 2000.

American College of Obstetricians and Gynecologists. *Informed refusal. Committee Opinion No 237*, June 2000.

American College of Obstetricians and Gynecologists. 'Patient Testing.' In: *Ethics in Obstetrics and Gynecology.* 2ⁿᵈ Ed. ACOG, Washington DC 2004, pp26-28.

American College of Obstetricians and Gynecologists. *Placenta accreta. Committee Opinion No. 266*, ACOG, Jan 2002.

American College of Obstetricians and Gynecologists. *Practice Bulletin Number 5.* ACOG 1999.

American College of Obstetricians and Gynecologists. *Practice Bulletin Number 54.* ACOG 2004.

American College of Obstetricians and Gynecologists. *Weighing the Pros and Cons of Cesarean Delivery.* ACOG Press release, 31 July 2003.

American College of Obstetricians and Gynecologists Committee on Obstetric Practice. 'ACOG committee opinion number 304, November 2004. Prenatal and perinatal human immunodeficiency virus testing: expanded recommendations'. *Obstet Gynecol* 2004; 104(5 Pt 1):1119-24.

American College of Nurse-Midwives. *Soaring Cesarean Section Rates Cause for Alarm.* ACNM statement, 13 January 2003.

American Medical Association Board of Trustees. 'Legal Interventions During Pregnancy. Court-ordered medical treatments and legal penalties for potentially harmful behaviour by pregnant women'. *J Am Med Assoc* 1990; 264: 2663-70.

Amu, O., Rajendran S., Bolaji I.I. 'Maternal choice alone should not determine method of delivery.' *BMJ* 1998; 317: 462-465 (letter).

Ananth, C.V., Smulian, J.C. Vintzileos, A.M. 'The association of placenta previa with history of cesarean delivery and abortion: a metaanalysis.' *Am J Obstet Gynecol* 1997; 177(5):1071-8.

Andres, R.L., Day, M.C., Larrabee, K. 'Recent cocaine use is not associated with fetal acidemia or other manifestations of intrapartum fetal distress.' *Am J Perinatol* 2000; 17(2): 63-7.

Annas, G.J. 'Forced cesareans: the most unkindest cut of all.' *Hastings Cent Rep* 1982; 12(3):16-7, 45.

Annas, G.J. 'Foreclosing the use of force: A.C. reversed'. *Hastings Cent Rep* 1990;20(4):27-9.

Annas, George. *Judging Medicine.* Human Press 1988.

Annas, G. 'Protecting the liberty of pregnant patients.' *New Engl J Med* 1987; 316: 1213-4.

Annas, G. 'She's Going to Die: The Case of Angela C.' *Hastings Center Report* 1988; 18 (1): 25.

Annibale, D.J. *et al.* 'Comparative neonatal morbidity of abdominal and vaginal deliveries after uncomplicated pregnancies.' *Arch Pediatr Adolesc Med* 1995; 149(8): 862-7.

Anon. 'A woman's interest competes against law protecting children. Battered pregnant woman denied divorce until after giving birth'. *CNN.com* 9 January 2005: www.cnn.com.

Anon. 'Accused of abuse, but never tried'. *BBC News*. 1 July 2003, 10:37 GMT 11:37 UK: www.bbc.co.uk.

Anon. *BBC News*, published 6 October 2004 07:54:08 GMT: http://news.bbc.co.uk/go/pr/fr/-/1/hi/uk/3718862.stm.

Anon. Case Comment, Constitutional Law. 'Transfusions Ordered for Dying Woman over Religious Objections'. 113 *U Pa L Rev* 290, 294 (1964).

Anon. 'Cesarean Birth Associated with Adult Asthma.' *Ob Gyn News* Vol 36, No. 12, 15 June 2001.

Anon. 'Child protection system wilfully ignores principles of childcare' (letters). *Daily Telegraph* 5 August 2004, at p23.

Anon. 'Diagnosis and Management of Placental Percreta.' *Continuing Medical Education* 1998; 53 (8) (Review Article).

Anon. 'False witness' (Editorial). *Daily Telegraph* 20 January 2004.

Anon. 'Global experts slam cot death policy'. *BBC News*, published 20 January 2004 18:29:21 GMT:
http://news.bbc.co.uk/go/pr/fr/-/1/hi/health/3412353.stm.

Anon. 'GP finds by chance a child who's not been immunised.' *Pulse* 17.6.00, at pp 68-73.

Anon. 'In America: Hidden Agendas.' *New York Times*, 14 June 1998.

Anon. *Judge Orders Addict to Stop Having Kids*. ABC News 4 January 2005: abcnews.go.com.

Anon. 'Justices: Fetus is Not a Person.' *The Houston Chronicle*, 30 August 2004: http://www.chron.com/cs/CDA/printstory.mpl/front/2767852.

Anon. *Milton v Cary Medical Center*, 22 February 1988. United States. Maine. Supreme Judicial Court. *Annu Rev Popul Law*. 1988;15:48-9.

Anon. 'Mom's Diet May Affect Baby's Life'. *CBS News* 28 January 2004: www.CBSNews.com.

Anon. 'Mothers lose MMR appeal'. *BMJ* 2003; 327: 306 (News).

Anon. 'Order in the Piazzi case. Georgia. Superior Court, Richmond County.' *Issues Law Med* 1987;2(5):415-8.

Anon. 'Patel mother suffers child ban'. *BBC News* 13 June, 2003, 10:52 GMT 11:52 UK: www.bbc.co.uk.

Anon. 'Placenta Previa, C-section History Ups Accreta Risk.' *Ob.Gyn. News* 15 Sept 2001, Vol 36, No 18.

Anon. 'Pregnant drinkers face a crackdown.' *New York Times*, 24 May 1998.

Anon. *Pregnant Woman Being Forced Into Custody at a State Medical Facility in Massachusetts to Ensure That Her Baby is Born Safely*. National Public Radio 14 September 2000.

Anon. 'S. Dakota to enforce treatment of pregnant moms who drink.' *CNN*, 24 May 1998: http://www.cnn.com/HEALTH/9805/24/fetal.syndrome/.

Anon. Special report: House of Commons. 'Cannings case prompts concern'. *The Guardian*. 22 December 2004

Anon. 'Suffer the Parents' (Editorial). *Daily Telegraph* 1 June 2004.

Anon. Tristate News Summary. *The Cincinnati Enquirer.* 5 April 2000.

Anon. 'U.S. Infant Mortality Rises.' *CBS News* Atlanta 12 February 2004: www.CBSNews.com.

Anon. 'US mother in court for sunburnt kids'. *BBC News*: Americas, 21 August 2002: http://news.bbc.co.uk/2/hi/americas/2207803.stm. (in this case the mother was arrested at a fairground and remained in jail for over a week awaiting a hearing).

Anon. 'Working with Parents.' In: Aldgate J., Statham J. *The Children Act Now. Messages from Research. Studies in evaluating the Children Act 1989.* Stationery Office London 2001, pp64-81 (Section 4).

Armstrong, E.M. 'Diagnosing moral disorder: the discovery and evolution of fetal alcohol syndrome.' *Soc Sci Med* 1998 Dec; 47(12): 2025-42.

Armstrong, E.M., Abel, E.L. 'Fetal alcohol syndrome: the origins of a moral panic.' *Alcohol* 2000; 35(3): 276-82.

Arnott, Sarah. 'Ministers approve proposed database of all children in the UK'. *Computing* 8 December 2004.

Asakura, H. and Myers, S.A. 'More than one previous cesarean delivery: a 5-year experience with 435 patients.' *Obstet Gynecol* 1995; 85(6): 924-9.

Ashcroft, B., Elstein, M., Boreham, N., Holm, S. 'Prospective semistructured observational study to identify risk attributable to staff deployment, training, and updating opportunities for midwives'. *BMJ* 2003; 327:584.

Association for Improvement in Maternity Services. *AIMS journal* Summer 2002 vol 14 no 2: www.aims.org.uk.

Association for Improvement in Maternity Services. *False child abuse allegations are being made by NHS staff when mothers make complaints about maternity care, says maternity pressure group.* AIMS Press release, 2 August 2004: www.aims.org.uk.

Atkins, A.F.C., Hey, E.N. 'The Northern Regional Fetal Abnormality Survey.' In: Drife JO, Donnai D (Eds). *Antenatal Diagnosis of Fetal Abnormalities.* Springer-Verlag, London 1991, at pp13-34.

Bager, P., Melbye, M., Rostgaard, K. et al. 'Mode of delivery and risk of allergic rhinitis and asthma.' *J Allergy Clin Immunol* 2003; 111: 51-6.

Bahl, R., Strachan, B., Murphy, D.J. 'Outcome of subsequent pregnancy three years after previous operative delivery in the second stage of labour: cohort study.' *BMJ* 2004; 328: 311.

Bailit, J.L., Love TE, Mercer B. 'Rising cesarean rates: are patients sicker?' *Am J Obstet Gynecol* 2004; 191: 800-3.

Barayuga, Debra. 'Ice' baby's mom pleads not guilty. *Honolulu Star-Bulletin*, Friday, October 17, 2003.

Barker, D.J. 'The developmental origins of well-being.' *Philos Trans R Soc Lond B Biol Sci* 2004; 359(1449): 1359-66.

Barth, R.P. 'Research outcomes of prenatal substance exposure and the need to review policies and procedures regarding child abuse reporting.' *Child Welfare* 2001; 80(2): 275-96.

Beauchamp, T.L., Childress JF. *Principles of Biomedical Ethics*. Oxford University Press, New York 1994, 4th edition, at 135.

Beech, B.A.L. 'Court ordered caesarean sections are discouraging women from seeking obstetric care.' *BMJ* 1997; 314: 1908 (Letter).

Beech, Beverley Lawrence. 'Challenging the illusion of choice'. *AIMS Journal* Autumn 2003, Vol 15 No 3.

Behnke, M., Eyler, F.D., Garvan, C.W., Wobie, K. 'The search for congenital malformations in newborns with fetal cocaine exposure.' *Pediatrics* 2001 May; 107(5): E74.

Beiser, Vince. Women who stand at the crossroads: Compassion or Punishment. *Shepherd Express Metro* (Milwaukee), vol 21, issue 32. 3 August 2000: http://www.shepherd-express.com/shepherd/21/32/cover_story.html.

Bell, J.S., Campbell, D.M., Graham, W.J. *et al.* 'Do obstetric complications explain high caesarean section rates among women over 30? A retrospective analysis'. *BMJ* 2001; 322: 894-895.

Benshoof, J. 'Beyond Roe, after Casey: the present and future of a "fundamental" right'. *Womens Health Issues* 1993;3(3):162-70.

Berkowitz, G., Brindis, C., Peterson, S. 'Substance use and social outcomes among participants in perinatal alcohol and drug treatment.' *Womens Health* 1998; 4(3): 231-54.

Bishai, R., Koren, G. 'Maternal and obstetric effects of prenatal drug exposure.' *Clin Perinatol* 1999; 26(1): 75-86.

Biskupic, Joan. '"Crack Babies" And Rights'. *Washington Post*. 29 Feb 2000.

Bjerga, Alan. 'Brownback sees "culture of life" prevailing in '05.' *Wichita Eagle* (Kansas), 3 January 2005.

Blumenthal, I. 'Shaken baby syndrome'. *Postgrad Med J* 2002;78(926):732-5.

Boss, J.A. 'First trimester prenatal diagnosis: earlier is not necessarily better.' *J Med Ethics* 1994; 20(3):146-51.

Boy, A., Salihu, H.M. 'Intimate partner violence and birth outcomes: a systematic review.' *Int J Fertil Women's Med* 2004;49(4):159-64.

Brazier, Margaret. *Medicine, Patients and the Law*. Penguin, London 1992.

Bricker, L., Neilson, J.P. 'Routine doppler ultrasound in pregnancy.' *Cochrane Database Syst Rev* 2000; 2: CD001450.

Bright, H.L. 'Safe havens for addicted mothers.' *CMAJ* 1997; 157: 1201 (letter).

British Association of Social Workers. Policy focus: 'Care or control?' *Professional Social Work* October 2004, at pp 18 – 19.

Brock, D.W., Wartman, S.A. 'When competent patients make irrational choices.' *N Engl J Med* 1990; 322: 1595-9.

Brophy, J., Bates, P., Brown, L. *et al.* 'Expert Evidence in Child Protection Litigation.' In: Aldgate J., Statham J. *The Children Act Now. Messages from Research. Studies in evaluating the Children Act 1989*. Stationery Office London 2001, pp169-173 (Section 5).

Browne, A. 'Midwife crisis puts home births at risk.' *Observer*, 7 May 2000.

Burkett, G., Gomez-Marin, O., Yasin, S.Y., Martinez, M. 'Prenatal care in cocaine-exposed pregnancies.' *Obstet Gynecol* 1998; 92(2): 193-200.

Burn, S. 'Access to civil justice: Lord Woolf's visionary new landscape.' *BMJ* 1996; 313: 242-243 (Editorial).

Burrows, J. 'The parturient woman: can there be room for more than "one person with full and equal rights inside a single human skin"'? *J Adv Nurs* 2001; 33(5):689-95.

Byrd, R.S., Neistadt, A.M., Howard, C.R. *et al.* 'Why screen newborns for cocaine: service patterns and social outcomes at age one year.'*Child Abuse Negl* 1999; 23(6): 523-30.

Byrne, P.A. (Ed). *Health, Rights and Resources: King's College Studies 1987-8.* Oxford University Press, for King Edward's Hospital Fund, London 1988.

Cahill, H. 'An Orwellian scenario: court ordered caesarean section and women's autonomy.' *Nurs Ethics* 1999; 6(6): 494-505.

Campbell, J., Torres, S., Ryan J *et al.* 'Physical and nonphysical partner abuse and other risk factors for low birth weight among full term and preterm babies: a multiethnic case-control study.' *Am J Epidemiol* 1999; 150(7): 714-26.

Campbell, J.C., Webster, D., Koziol-McLain J *et al.* 'Risk factors for femicide in abusive relationships: results from a multisite case control study.' *Am J Public Health* 2003; 93: 1089-97.

Capen, Karen. 'Mother's rights can't be infringed to protect fetus, Supreme Court's landmark ruling states.' *Canadian Med Assoc J* 1997;157 (11):1586-7.

Carpenter, R.G., Waite, A., Coombs, R.C. *et al.* 'Repeat sudden unexpected and unexplained infant deaths: natural or unnatural?' *Lancet* 2005; 365(9453): 29-35.

Caruso, David B. 'Court cases revive debate about rights of mothers during childbirth'. *Boston Globe* 19 May 2005.

Center for Reproductive Law and Policy. *Florida Court Refuses to Appoint Guardian for a Fetus.* CRLP Press Release 9 January 2004: http://www.crlp.org/pr_04_0109JDS.html.

Center for Reproductive Law and Policy. *Women Mistreated by Hospital, Police Ask Supreme Court for a Hearing.* CRLP Press Release. Washington DC, 1 December 1999.

Center for Reproductive Law and Policy. *The 'Unborn Victims of Violence Act'.* CRLP Factsheet F015, May 2001.

Centers for Disease Control. *National Hospital Discharge Survey of the National Center for Health Statistics*, Table 1, 1990.

Centers for Disease Control and Prevention. 'Rates of Cesarean Delivery - United States, 1993.' *Morbidity and Mortality Weekly Report* 1995;44(15):303-307.

Centers for Disease Control and Prevention, National Institute of Justice. *Extent, Nature, and Consequences of Intimate Partner Violence*, July 2000. (National Violence Against Women Survey)

Chamber, E. 'Dead Baby's Mother Faces Criminal Charge on Acts in Pregnancy'. *New York Times*, 9 October 1986, p A22.

Chambliss, L.R., Bay, R.C., Jones RF 3rd. 'Domestic violence: an educational imperative?' *Am J Obstet Gynecol* 1995;172(3):1035-8.

Charo, R.A. 'Effect of the human genome initiative on women's rights and reproductive decisions'. *Fetal Diagn Ther* 1993;8 Suppl 1:148-59.

Chasnoff, I.J., Landress, H.J., Barrett, M.E. 'The Prevalence of Illicit-Drug or Alcohol Use During Pregnancy and Discrepancies in Mandatory Reporting in Pinellas County, Florida'. *New Eng. L Med.* 1990; 322: 1202-6.

Chervenak, F.A., McCullough, L.B., Skupski D.W. 'An ethical justification for emergency, coerced cesarean delivery.' *Obstet Gynecol* 1993; 82(6): 1029-35.

Childhood Matters. Report of the National Commission of Enquiry into the Prevention of Child Abuse. Vols 1 and 2. Stationery Office. London 1996.

Chudley, A.E. 'Safe haven for addicted mothers.' *CMAJ* 1997; 157: 1201 (letter).

Ciolli, P., Caserta D., Giordanelli E., Russo R. 'Cesarean section and spontaneous birth: clinical aspects and maternal psychodynamic impact.' *Minerva Ginecol* 1995; 47(6): 263-7.

Clarke, The Hon. David. *Unborn victims of violence.* New South Wales Legislative Coalition for Improving Maternity Services: www.motherfriendly.org.

Clough, Sue. 'Bag snatch driver guilty of murder.' *Daily Telegraph* 21 December 2001. Council. Hansard 17 March 2004, at p7411.

Colb, Sherry F. 'Governor Jeb Bush Sends Lawyers to Represent a Fetus: Targeting A Mentally Retarded Pregnant Woman for Pro-Life Intervention'. *FindLaw* 27 August 2003: www.findlaw.com.

Coid, J. *Domestic Violence. A Health Response.* Working in a Wider Partnership Conference Report, Department of Health, London 2000, at p41.

Colley, G.B.J., Johnson, C.H., Morrow, B. *et al.* 'Prevalence of selected maternal and infant characteristics, Pregnancy Risk Assessment Monitoring System (PRAMS), 1997.' *Mor Mortal Wkly Rep CDC Surveill Summ* 1999; 48(5): 1-37.

Commonwealth Fund. *Health Concerns Across a Woman's Lifespan: 1998 Survey of Women's Health.* Commonwealth Fund, May 1999.

Conyers, J., Jr., Berman, H.L., Boucher, R. and nine other Representatives. *Dissenting Views to H.R. 1997, 'Unborn Victims of Violence Act of 2003.'* Washington, 2004: http://www.house.gov/judiciary_democrats/hr1997dissenting108cong.pdf.

Cooper, Cynthia L. *Pregnant and Punished.* Ford Foundation Report, Winter 2003: http://www.fordfound.org/publications/ff_report/view_ff_report_detail.cf m?report_index=382.

Corse, S..J., Smith, M. 'Reducing substance abuse during pregnancy. Discriminating among levels of response in a prenatal setting.' *J Subst Abuse Treat* 1998; 15(5): 457-67.

Cory, C.Z., Jones, B.M. 'Can shaking alone cause fatal brain injury? A biomechanical assessment of the Duhaime shaken baby syndrome model'. *Med Sci Law* 2003; 43(4): 317-33.

Court, C. 'Child protection report urges more balance.' *BMJ* 1995; 311: 9 (News).

Coverdale, J.H., McCullough L.B., Chervenak F.A. et al. 'Clinical implications of respect for autonomy in the psychiatric treatment of pregnant patients with depression.' *Psychiatr Serv* 1997; 48(2): 209-12.

Cox, J., Bota, G.W., Carter, M. *et al*. 'Domestic Violence, Incidence and prevalence in a northern emergency department.' *Canadian Family Physician* 2004; 50: 90 – 97.

Cramb, Auslan. 'Mother "may have killed eight children"'. *Daily Telegraph* 26 November 2001, at p 3.

Crane, J.M., van den Hof, M.C., Dodds L *et al*. 'Neonatal outcomes with placenta previa.' *Obstet Gynecol* 1999; 93(4): 541-4.

Cross, Michael. 'Eyes on the child'. *The Guardian* 18 September 2003.

Cumberledge, J. *Changing childbirth*. London: HMSO, 1993.

Curtis, Tom. 'Torn apart by doctors' child abuse theory'. *Scotland on Sunday* 1 February 2004.

Dally, A. 'Thalidomide: was the tragedy preventable?' *Lancet*. 1998; 351(9110): 1197-9.

Davis, L.G., Riedmann, G.L., Sapiro, M. *et al*. 'Cesarean section rates in low-risk private patients managed by certified nurse-midwives and obstetricians.' *J Nurse Midwifery* 1994; 39(2): 91-7.

DeBettencourt, Kathleen B. 'The wisdom of Solomon: cutting the cord that harms - children and crack exposure.' *Children Today*, July-August 1990.

Debus, Bob. *Questions Without Notice. Unborn victims of violence legislation*. NSW Legislative Assembly. Hansard 7 December 2004, at p13390.

Declercq, E.R., Sakala, C., Corry, M.P. *Listening to Mothers: Report of the First National U.S. Survey of Women's Childbearing Experiences*. Maternity Center Association. New York, October 2002.

Department of Health. *Framework for the Assessment of Children in Need and their Families*. Stationery Office, London 2000.

Department of Health. *The Children Act Report 2000*. DoH, London 2001.

Department of Health and Social Services. *Reducing the Risk: Safer Pregnancy and Childbirth*. HMSO London, 1977

Dessole, S., Cosmi, E., Balata, A. *et al*. 'Accidental fetal lacerations during cesarean delivery: experience in an Italian level III university hospital.' *Am J Obstet Gynecol* 2004; 191: 1673-7.

De Ville K.A., Kopelman, L.M. 'Fetal protection in Wisconsin's revised child abuse law: right goal, wrong remedy'. *J Law Med Ethics*. 1999; 27(4): 332-42, 294.

De Ville, K.A., Kopelman, L.M. 'Moral and social issues regarding pregnant women who use and abuse drugs.' *Obstet Gynecol Clin North Am* 1998; 25(1): 237-54.

Dillon, W.P., Lee, R.V., Tronolone MJ, *et al*: 'Life support and maternal death during pregnancy.' *JAMA* 1982; 248: 1089-91.

DiMatteo, M.R., Morton, S.C., Lepper, H.S. *et al*. 'Cesarean childbirth and psychosocial outcomes: a meta-analysis'. *Health Psychol* 1996; 15(4): 303-14.

DeMeo, James PhD. 'Why are American boys so Aggressive?' *Ashville magazine*: www.newfrontier.com/asheville/American-boys.htm.

Dobson, R. 'Caesarean section rate in England and Wales hits 21.' *BMJ* 2001; 323: 951.

Dolan, B., Parker, C. 'Caesarean section: a treatment for mental disorder?' *BMJ* 1997; 314: 1183.

Dornin, Rusty. 'Jury recommends death for Peterson'. *CNN.com*. 14 December 2004: www.cnn.com/2004/LAW/12/13/peterson.case/.

Douglas, Gillian. *Law, Fertility and Reproduction*. Sweet & Maxwell 1991.

Dr Foster's Case Notes. 'Social class and elective caesareans in the English NHS.' *BMJ* 2004; 328:1399.

Drife, J.O., Donnai, D. (Eds). *Antenatal Diagnosis of Fetal Abnormalities*. Springer-Verlag, London 1991.

Drug Policy Alliance. *South Carolina v. McKnight*. DPA Statement. Last updated 23 June 2004: http://www.drugpolicy.org/law/womenpregnan/mcknight/.

Drug Policy Alliance. *Whitner vs. the State of South Carolina*. DPA Statement. Last updated 23 June 2004:
  http://www.drugpolicy.org/law/womenpregnan/whitnervsth_/.

Dutter, Barbie. 'Caesarean forced on mother was unlawful.' *Daily Telegraph,* 8 May 1998.

Dyer, C. 'Court case may clarify law on caesarean sections.' *BMJ* 1997; 314: 623 (News).

Dyer, C. 'Courts too deferential to doctors, says judge.' *BMJ* 2001; 322: 129 (News).

Dyer, Clare. 'Falsely blamed mother asks law lords for right to sue'. *The Guardian* 21 June 2004.

Dyer, Clare. 'Father killed baby, high court rules'. *The Guardian* 11 December 2004.

Dyer, C. 'Fewer care cases to be reopened than originally thought'. *BMJ* 2004; 328: 482 (News).

Dyer, C. Mental capacity bill to punish abusers. *The Guardian*, 19 June 2004.

Dyer, C. 'Paediatricians did not have duty of care to patient's mother'. *BMJ* 2002; 325:1321.

Dyer, Clare. 'The experts run for cover'. *The Guardian* 21 September 2004.

Dyer, Owen. 'Southall is barred for three years from child protection work'. *BMJ* 2004; 329: 366.

Edwards, Nadine. 'The choice is yours - or is it?' *AIMS Journal* Autumn 2003, Vol 15 No 3.

Eekelaar, J. 'Does a mother have legal duties to her unborn child?' In: Byrne PA (Ed). *Health, Rights and Resources*: King's College Studies 1987-8. Oxford University Press, for King Edward's Hospital Fund, London 1988, pp 55-75.

Esposito, M.A., DeLony, R., Goldstein, P.J. 'Postmortem cesarean section with infant survival: a case report of an HIV-infected patient.' *Md Med J* 1997;46(9):467-70.

Evans, M., Richardson, D., Sholl, J., Johnson, B. 'Caesarean section: Assessment of the convenience factor.' *J Reprod Med* 1984; 29: 670-3.

Family & Youth Concern. 'Children Bill Update'. *Family Bulletin* No 116, Summer 2004.

Farrant, W. 'Who's for Amniocentesis?: The Politics of Prenatal Screening.' In: Homans H (Ed). *The Sexual Politics of Reproduction*. Gower Publishing Hampshire 1985, at 96-122.

Faundes, A. 'The risk of urinary incontinence of parous women who delivered only by cesarean section'. *Int J Gyn Ob* 2001; 72: 41-46.

Fazzone, P.A., Holton, J.K., Reed, B.G. *Substance Abuse Treatment and Domestic Violence.* Treatment Improvement Protocol (TIP) Series 25. U.S. Department of Health and Human Services, Maryland 1997. (DHHS Publication No. (SMA) 97-3163).

Feitshans, I.L. 'Legislating to preserve women's autonomy during pregnancy.' *Med Law* 1995; 14(5-6): 397-412.

Fenton, Ben. 'Court threat to "naked child" parents'. *Daily Telegraph* 11 July 2001.

Fernandez, F.M., Krueger P.M. 'Domestic violence: effect on pregnancy outcome.' *J Am Osteopath Assoc* 1999; 99(5): 254-6.

Finamore, E.P. 'Jefferson v Griffin Spalding County Hospital Authority: court-ordered surgery to protect the life of an unborn child.' *Am J Law Med* 1983; 9(1): 83-101.

Finnerty, J.F., Fuerst, C.W., Karns, L.B., Pinkerton, J.V. 'End-of-life discussions for the primary care obstetrician/gynecologist.' *Am J Obstet Gynecol* 2002;187(2):296-301.

Flagler, E., Baylis, F., Rodgers, S. 'Bioethics for clinicians: 12. Ethical dilemmas that arise in the care of pregnant women: rethinking "maternal-fetal conflicts"'. *CMAJ* 1997 Jun 15;156(12):1729-32.

Fleming, Nic. 'Study finds 90pc double cot deaths are natural'. *Daily Telegraph* 31 December 2004.

Fletcher, David. 'Doctors "to blame for thalidomide disaster"'. *Daily Telegraph* 18 April 1998, at p4.

Frank, D.A., Augustyn, M., Knight W.G., Pell, T., Zuckerman B. 'Growth, development, and behavior in early childhood following prenatal cocaine exposure: a systematic review.' *JAMA* 2001; 285(12): 1613-25.

Frye, V. 'Examining Homicide's Contribution to Pregnancy-Associated Deaths.' *JAMA* 2001; 285: 1510-1.

Gandy, Kim. NOW Activists Stand Up to Bush Agenda, Protest Barriers to Legitimate Dissent on Inauguration Day: *Statement of NOW President Kim Gandy*, 20 January 2004: http://www.now.org/press/01-05/01-20.html.

Garg, V.K., Ekuma-Nkama EN. 'Vaginal birth following two cesarean deliveries - are the risks exaggerated?' *Ann Saudi Med* 2004 Jul-Aug; 24(4): 276-9.

Geddes, J.F., Plunkett, J. Editorial: 'The evidence base for the shaken baby syndrome'. *BMJ* 2004; 328: 719-20.

Geddes, J.F., Tasker, R.C., Adams, G.G., Whitwell, H.L. 'Violence is not necessary to produce subdural and retinal haemorrhage: a reply to Punt *et al*'. *Pediatr Rehabil* 2004; 7(4): 261-5.

General Medical Council. *Good Medical Practice*. General Medical Council. London 2001.

General Medical Council. *Seeking Patients' Consent: The Ethical Considerations*. General Medical Council. London 1999.

General Medical Council Professional Conduct Committee. Session beginning 7 June 2004: *New Case of Conduct - Professor David Patrick Southall*. GMC, Manchester 2004. Reported in full on: www.sallyclark.org.uk.

Gessert, C.E., Forbes, S., Bern-Klug, M. 'Planning end-of-life care for patients with dementia: Roles of families and health professionals.' *J Death Dying* 2000-2001; 42(4): 273-291.

Goer, H. *The Thinking Woman's Guide to a Better Birth*. Perigee Books, New York 1999, at p169.

Goldbeck-Wood, S. 'Women's autonomy in childbirth: We may advise and persuade, but never coerce.' *BMJ* 1997; 314: 1143 (Editorial).

Goldenberg, R.L., Kirby, R., Culhane, J.F. 'Stillbirth: a review'. *J Matern Fetal Neonatal Med* 2004; 16(2): 79-94.

Goldman, S.M., Wagner, L.K. 'Radiologic ABCs of Maternal and Fetal Survival after Trauma: When Minutes May Count.' *Radiographics* 1999; 19: 1349-1357.

Goodman, Ellen. 'Inconceivable cynicism'. *Boston Globe* 7 February 2002, at A19.

Goodwin, T., Breen, M. 'Pregnancy outcome and fetomaternal haemorrhage after noncatastrophic trauma.' *Am J Obstet Gynecol* 1990; 162: 665-71.

Gould, D.A., Butler-Manuel, A.S., Turner, M.J., Carter, P.G. 'Emergency obstetric hysterectomy - an increasing incidence.' *J Obstet Gynaecol* 1999; 19: 580-583.

Gould, J.B., Qin, C., Marks, A.R., Chavez, G. 'Neonatal Mortality in Weekend vs Weekday Births.' *J Am Med Assoc* 2003; 289: 2958-2962.

Greenlaw. J.L. 'Treatment refusal, noncompliance, and substance abuse in pregnancy: legal and ethical issues.' *Birth* 1990; 17(3):152-6.

Grossman, N.B. 'Blunt trauma in pregnancy.' *Am Fam Physician* 2004; 70(7):1303-10.

Grubb, Andrew (ed.) *Challenges in Medical Care*. John Wiley & Sons. Chichester 1992.

Guidance for Doctors and Lawyers on the Assessment of Mental Capacity. Law Society and BMJ Publishing, London 1995.

Gumbel, Andrew. 'America's New Family Values'. *The Independent* 25 November 2003.

Hague, Helen. 'Pupils urged to inform on problem parents'. *Daily Telegraph* 14 October 2002.

Hakansson, S., Kallen, K. 'Caesarean section increases the risk of hospital care in childhood for asthma and gastroenteritis.' *Clin Exp Allergy*. 2003; 33: 757-64.

Hale, The Right Honourable Lady Justice, DBE. *A Pretty Pass: When is there a right to die?* Fison Memorial Lecture at 'The Art of Dying' series, Kings College, University of London, 24 October 2002.
http://www.kcl.ac.uk/depsta/humanities/art_of_dying/ppass.doc.

Hall, Celia. 'Judge forces mother to be injected to save baby.' *Daily Telegraph*, 14 December 1996.

Hall, Celia. 'Doctors told to check on need for Caesareans.' *Daily Telegraph*, 19 March 1997.

Hall, M.H. 'Commentary: confidential enquiry into maternal death.' *Br J Obstet Gynaecol* 1990; 97:752-3.

Hall, S. 'Under what circumstances can you ask to die?' *The Guardian*, 15 December 2004.

Hannah, M.E., Hannah W.J., Hellman J. *et al*. 'Induction of labor as compared with serial antenatal monitoring in post-term pregnancy.' *N Engl J Med* 1992; 326: 1587-92.

Hans, S.L. 'Demographic and psychosocial characteristics of substance-abusing pregnant women.' *Clin Perinatol* 1999; 26(1): 55-74.

Harer, W.B. 'Patient, doctor should discuss delivery options. Scenario: Does an obstetrician always have to follow the patient's wishes?' Ethics Forum. *American Medical News* April 7, 2003: www.ama-assn.org/amednews/2003/04/07/prca0407.htm.

Harris, L.H. 'Rethinking maternal-fetal conflict: gender and equality in perinatal ethics.' *Obstet Gynecol* 2000 Nov; 96(5 Pt 1): 786-91.

Hasnas, J. 'From cannibalism to Caesareans: Two conceptions of fundamental rights'. *Northwestern University Law Review* 1995;89: 900.

Health Grades Report for 2003, cited in: International Cesarean Awareness Network. ICAN press kit: background information, on: www.ican-online.org.

Hedin, L.W., Janson P.O. 'The invisible wounds: the occurrence of psychological abuse and anxiety compared with previous experience of physical abuse during the childbearing year.' *J Psychosom Obstet Gynaecol* 1999; 20(3): 136-44

Heginbotham, Christopher. 'Mental capacity bill will improve lives'. *The Guardian* 15 September 2004.

Heikkinen, J.E., Rinne, R.I., Alahuhta, S.M. *et al.* 'Life support for 10 weeks with successful fetal outcome after fatal maternal brain damage.' *Br Med J* 1985; 290: 1237-8.

Heise, L.L. 'Reproductive freedom and violence against women: where are the intersections?' *J Law Med Ethics* 1993; 21: 206-16.

Hemminki, E., Merilainen, J. 'Long-term effects of caesarean section: ectopic pregnancies and placental problems.' *Am J Obstet Gynaecol* 1996; 174: 1569-1574.

Hewson, B. 'How to escape the surgeon's knife.' *New Law Journal* 23 May 1997, at p 752.

Hewson, B. 'Could the High Court order you to have an operation?' (1998) 115 *Living Marxism* 24.

Hey, E. 'Suspected child abuse: the potential for justice to miscarry'. *BMJ* 2003; 327: 299-300.

Hilder, L., Costeloe, K., Thilaganathan, B. 'Prolonged pregnancy: evaluating gestation specific risks of fetal and infant mortality.' *Br J Obstet Gynaecol* 1998; 105: 169-173.

Hill, Amelia. 'Scans "may damage babies"'. *Observer* 9 December 2001.

Hiscock, John. 'Waiters sacked over drink and babies warning.'*Daily Telegraph.* 1 April 1991, at p5.

Hnat, M.D., Sibai, B.M., Kovilam, O. 'An initial Glasgow score of 4 and Apgar scores of 9 and 9: a case report of a pregnant comatose woman.' *Am J Obstet Gynecol* 2003; 89(3): 877-9.

Horon, I.L., Cheng, D. 'Enhanced Surveillance for Pregnancy-Associated Mortality - Maryland, 1993 – 1998.' *JAMA* 2001; 285(11): 1455-9.

House of Commons Health Committee. *Choice in Maternity Services*: Ninth Report of Session 2002-03. Stationery Office London 2003: www. parliament.the-stationery-office.co.uk/pa/ cm200203/cmselect/cmhealth/796/796.pdf.

Howell, E.M., Chasnoff, I.J. 'Perinatal substance abuse treatment. Findings from focus groups with clients and providers.' *J Subst Abuse Treat* 1999; 17(1-2): 139-48.

Howell, E.M., Heiser, N., Harrington, M. 'A review of recent findings on substance abuse treatment for pregnant women.' *J Subst Abuse Treat* 1999; 16(3): 195-219.

Hughes, James J, Ph.D. 'The Future of Death: Cryonics and the Telos of Liberal Individualism'. *J Evolution Technol* 2001, vol 6 (July 2001): http://jetpress.org/volume6/death.html.

Hunt, J., Macleod, A., Thomas, C. 'The Last Resort: Child Protection, the Courts and the 1989 Children Act.' In: Aldgate J., Statham J. *The Children Act Now. Messages from Research. Studies in evaluating the Children Act 1989*. Stationery Office London 2001, pp198-201 (section 12)

International Cesarean Awareness Network. 'Statement on Melissa Rowland'. *ICAN E-News Line*, Volume 17, 22 March 2004.

Irwin, S., Jordan, B. 'Knowledge, Practice, and Power: Court-Ordered Cesarean Sections.' *Medical Anthropology Quarterly*; 1987: 1(3):319-334.

Jacobson B., Nyberg, K., Gršnbladh, L. *et al.* 'Opiate addiction in adult offspring through possible imprinting after obstetric treatment.' *Br Med J* 1990; 301: 1067-70.

Jamois, Tonya. 'Women have right to refuse Caesarean.' *North County Times* (California), 13 April 2004.

Johnsen, D. 'A new threat to pregnant women's autonomy.' *Hastings Cent Rep* 1987; 7(4): 33-40.

Johnson, J.K., Haider, F., Ellis, K. *et al.* 'The prevalence of domestic violence in pregnant women.' *Br J Obstet Gynecol* 2003; 110(3): 272-5.

Johnson, Rebecca. 'C-Sections and the Real Crime'. *New York Times* 12 April 2004.

Jolly, J. Walker, J., Bhabra, K. 'Subsequent obstetric performance related to primary mode of delivery.' *Br J Obstet Gynaecol* 1999; 106(3): 227-32.

Joyce, R., Webb, R., Peacock, J. 'Predictors of obstetric intervention rates: case mix, staffing levels and organizational factors of hospital of birth.' *J Obstet Gynecol* 2002; 22: 618-25.

Justin, R.G., Rosner, F. 'Maternal/fetal rights: two views.' *J Am Med Womens Assoc* 1989; 44(3): 90-5.

Kaiser, G. 'Do electronic fetal heart rate monitors improve delivery outcomes?' *J Fla Med Assoc* 1991; 78: 303-7.

Kalish, R.B., McCullough, L., Gupta, M. *et al.* 'Intrapartum elective cesarean delivery: a previously unrecognized clinical entity.' *Obstet Gynecol* 2004; 103: 1137-41.

Kaltenbach K., Finnegan L. 'Prevention and treatment issues for pregnant cocaine-dependent women and their infants.' *Ann N Y Acad Sci* 1998; 846: 329-34.

Kelly, G.D., Blunt, C., Moore, P.A., Lewis, M. 'Consent for regional anaesthesia in the United Kingdom: what is material risk?' *Int J Obstet Anesth* 2004;13:71-4.

Kelly, R., Zatzick, D., Anders, T. 'The detection and treatment of psychiatric disorders and substance use among pregnant women cared for in obstetrics.' *Am J Psychiat* 2001; 158(2): 213-9.

King, N.M. 'Maternal-fetal conflicts. Ethical and legal implications for nurse-midwives.' *J Nurse Midwifery* 1991; 36(6): 361-5.

Kitzinger, Sheila. 'Midwives on Trial'. Sheila Kitzinger's Letter from Europe. September 1999 Vol. 26.3: http://www.sheilakitzinger.com/midwives%20on%20trial.htm.

Kluge, E.H. 'When caesarean section operations imposed by a court are justified.' *J Med Ethics* 1988; 4(4): 206-11.

Kmietowicz, Zosia. 'Complaints against doctors in child protection work have increased fivefold'. *BMJ* 2004;328:601 (News).

Knowsley, J., Reid T. 'Payout for woman who was forced to have a caesarean.' *Sunday Telegraph,* 1 June 1997.

Kolder, V.E.B., Gallagher, J., Parsons, M.T. 'Court-ordered obstetrical interventions'. *N Engl J Med* 1987; 316: 1192-6.

Koren, G., Klein, J., McMartin, K. 'Diagnosing intrauterine exposure to cocaine by hair testing: six years of clinical use.' *Ther Drug Monit* 1998; 20(5): 478-80.

Kowalski, S.L. 'Looking for a Solution: Determining Fetal Status for Prenatal Drug Abuse Prosecutions.' *Santa Clara Law Review* 1998; 38(4): 1255-1292.

Kravitz, R.L., Krackhardt, D., Melnikow, J. *et al.* 'Networked for change? Identifying obstetric opinion leaders and assessing their opinions on caesarean delivery.' *Soc Sci Med* 2003; 57(12): 2423-34.

Kukko, H., Halmesmaki, E. 'Prenatal care and counseling of female drug-abusers: effects on drug abuse and perinatal outcome.' *Acta Obstet Gynecol Scand* 1999; 78(1): 22-6.

Lane, A, Westbrook, A., Grady, D. *et al.* 'Maternal brain death: medical, ethical and legal issues.' *Intensive Care Med* 2004; 30(7):1484-6.

Lantz, P.E., Sinal, S.H., Stanton, C.A., Weaver, R.G. Jr. 'Perimacular retinal folds from childhood head trauma'. *BMJ* 2004; 328: 754-6.

Laubereau, B., Filipiak-Pittroff, B., von Berg, A. *et al.* 'Caesarean section and gastrointestinal symptoms, atopic dermatitis, and sensitisation during the first year of life.' *Arch Dis Child* 2004;89:993-7.

Laville, Sandra. 'Mother cleared of killing baby fights to lift ban on her living with surviving child'. *Daily Telegraph* 15 December 2003, at p12.

Laville, Sandra. 'Parents cannot sue over child abuse errors'. *Daily Telegraph* 1 August 2003.

Law Commission Report No 60, Cmnd 5709.

Le Fanu, James and Derbyshire, David. 'In the rush to protect children, "experts" use junk science to accuse innocent parents.' *Daily Telegraph* 13 December 2003, at p4.

Le Fanu, James and Derbyshire, David. 'Munchausen's by Proxy'. *Daily Telegraph* 13 December 2003.

Lee, Robert and Morgan, Derek (Eds). *Birthrights. Law and Ethics at the Beginning of Life*. Routlege London 1990.

Leitch, C.R., Walker, J.J. 'The rise in caesarean section rate: the same indications but a lower threshold'.*Br J Obstet Gynaecol* 1998; 105(6): 621-6.

Lent, M. 'The medical and legal risks of the electronic fetal monitor.' *Stanford Law Rev* 1999; 51(4): 807-37.

Lescale, K.B., Inglis, S.R., Eddleman, K.A. *et al.* 'Conflicts between physicians and patients in non-elective cesarean delivery: incidence and the adequacy of informed consent.' *Am J Perinatol* 1996; 13(3): 171-6.

Leventhal, Cari L. Comment: 'The Crimes Against the Unborn Child Act: Recognizing Potential Human Life in Pennsylvania Criminal Law.' 103 *Dick. L. Rev.* 173, 175 (1998).

Levine, E.M., Ghai, V., Barton, J.J., Strom, C.M. 'Mode of delivery and risk of respiratory diseases in newborns.' *Obstet Gynecol* 2001; 97(3): 439-42.

Lewis, G. Chapter 14: 'Coincidental (Fortuitous) deaths.' In: Lewis G, Drife J, editors. *Why Mothers Die 1997–1999. Fifth Report of the Confidential Enquiries into Maternal Deaths.* London: RCOG Press; 2001, at pp 225–30; 241–51.

Lieberman, E., Ernst, E.K., Rooks, J.P. *et al.* 'Results of the national study of vaginal birth after cesarean in birth centers.' *Obstet Gynecol* 2004; 104(5 Pt 1): 933-42.

Lin, H.C., Sheen, T.C., Tang, C.H., Kao, S. 'Association between maternal age and the likelihood of a cesarean section: a population-based multivariate logistic regression analysis.' *Acta Obstet Gynecol Scand* 2004; 83(12): 1178-83.

Loewy, E.H. 'The pregnant brain dead and the fetus: must we always try to wrest life from death?' *Am J Obstet Gynecol* 1987; 157: 1097-101.

Losco, J., Shublack, M. 'Paternal-fetal conflict: an examination of paternal responsibilities to the fetus.' *Polit Life Sci* 1994; 13(1): 63-75.

Louis, J.M., Ehrenberg, H.M., Collin, M.F., Mercer, B.M. 'Perinatal intervention and neonatal outcomes near the limit of viability.' *Am J Obstet Gynecol* 2004; 191(4): 1398-402.

Love, C.D., Wallace, E.M. 'Pregnancies complicated by placenta praevia: what is appropriate management?' *Br J Obstet Gynaecol* 1996; 103(9): 864-7.

Luckas, M., Buckett, W., Alfirevic, Z. 'Comparison of outcomes in uncomplicated term and post-term pregnancy following spontaneous labor.' *J Perinat Med* 1998; 26(6): 475-9.

Lydon-Rochelle, M.T., Holt, V.L., Martin, D.P. 'Association between method of delivery and maternal rehospitalization.' *JAMA* 2000; 283:2411-6.

Lydon-Rochelle, M.T., Holt, V.L., Martin, D.P. 'Delivery method and self-reported postpartum general health status among primiparous women.' *Paediatric Perinatal Epidemiology* 2001; 15: 232-40.

Lydon-Rochelle, M. *et al.* 'First-birth cesarean and placental abruption or previa at second birth.' *Obstet Gynecol* 2001; 97(5 Pt 1):765-9.

Lyon, Deborah MD. 'Perimortem Cesarean Delivery.' *E-medicine*, last updated October 6, 2004. http://www.emedicine.com/med/topic3398.htm.

Macfarlane, A.I. 'Day of birth.' *Lancet* 1984; Sept 27: 695.

Mackenzie, T.B., Nagel, T.C., Rothman, B.J.K. 'When a Pregnant Woman Endangers Her Foetus'. *Hastings Center Report* 1986; 16(1): 24-25.

Maclean, Alasdair R. 'Caesarean Sections, Competence and the Illusion of Autonomy.' *Web Journal of Current Legal Issues* (1999) 1 Web JCLI , 1/2/99.

Macready, N. 'US state rules that a viable fetus is a person.' *BMJ* 1997; 315: 1485-1488 (News).

Madi, B.C., Crow, R. 'A qualitative study of information about available options for childbirth venue and pregnant women's preference for a place of delivery.' *Midwifery* 2003; 19(4): 328-36.

Mahony, D.L., Murphy, J.M. 'Neonatal drug exposure: assessing a specific population and services provided by visiting nurses.' *Pediatr Nurs* 1999; 25(1): 27-34, 108.

Marshall, M.F. 'Commentary: mal-intentioned illiteracy, willful ignorance, and fetal protection laws: is there a lexicologist in the house?' *J Law Med Ethics* 1999; 27(4): 343-6, 294.

Marteau, T.M., Johnston, M., Plenicar, M. *et al.* 'Development of A Self-administered Questionnaire To Measure Women's Knowledge of Prenatal Screening and Diagnostic Tests.' *J Psychosomatic Research* 1988; 32: 403-8.

Martin, J.A., Hamilton, B.E., Ventura, S.J. *et al.* 'Births: final data for 2001.' *Natl Vital Stat Rep* 2002; 51(2): 1-102.

Martin, S.L., Matza, L.S., Kupper, L.L. et al. 'Domestic violence and sexually transmitted diseases: the experience of prenatal care patients.' *Public Health Rep* 1999; 114(3): 262-8.

Martin, Nicole. 'Family doctors accused of steering mothers away from home births.' *Daily Telegraph,* 25 June 2001.

Martin, S.L., Matza, L.S., Kupper, L.L. et al. 'Domestic violence and sexually transmitted diseases: the experience of prenatal care patients.' *Public Health Rep* 1999; 114(3): 262-8.

Mason, J.K., McCall Smith, R.A. *Law and Medical Ethics.* Butterworths London 1999 (fifth edition).

Maternal/Fetal Medicine Committee of the Society of Obstetricians and Gynaecologists of Canada. *Clinical Practice Guidelines. Policy Statement 68*, December 1997.

Mattingly, S.S. 'The maternal-fetal dyad. Exploring the two-patient obstetric model.' *Hastings Cent Rep* 1992 Jan-Feb; 22(1): 13-8.

McLean, Matilda. 'Mothers lose battle to be reunited with children'. *Daily Telegraph* 15 May 2004, at p10.

McCloskey, L., Plough, A.L., Power, K.L. et al. 'A community-wide infant mortality review: findings and implications.' *Public Health Rep* 1999; 114(2): 165-77.

McKee, M., Foster, S. 'George W Bush's second term' (Editorial). *BMJ* 2005; 330: 155-6.

McWilliams, M., McKiernan, J. 'Bringing It All Out Into The Open: Domestic Violence in Northern Ireland.' HMSO, Belfast 1993.

Medical Research Council. *Report by the Working Group on Screening for Neural Tube Defects.* DHSS, London 1979, at p28.

Menahem, S., Halasz, G. 'Parental non-compliance - a paediatric dilemma. A medical and psychodynamic perspective.' *Child Care Health Dev* 2000; 26(1): 61-72.

Merrick, Janna C. and Blank, Robert H. *The politics of pregnancy: policy dilemmas in the maternal-fetal relationship.* Harrington Park Press, Binghamton, New York, 1993

Mezey, G.C. 'Domestic violence in pregnancy.' Bewley S *et al.* In: *Violence Against Women.* RCOG, London 1997.

Michalowski, Sabine. 'Court-authorised Caesarean Sections - The end of a trend?' 1999 *MLR* 62 (1): 115-127.

Miles, S.H., August A. 'Courts, Gender and "The Right to Die."' *Law, Medicine and Health Care* 1990; 18: 85-95.

Mill, John Stuart. *On Liberty and Representative Government*. Second edition, chapter 1, 1859.

Minkoff, H., O'Sullivan M.J. 'The case for rapid HIV testing during labor.' *JAMA* 1998; 279: 1743-4.

Minkoff, H., Paltrow, L.M. 'Melissa Rowland and the rights of pregnant women'. *Obstet Gynecol* 2004; 104: 1234-6.

Miovich, S.M. et al. 'Major concerns of women after cesarean delivery.' *J Obstet Gynecol Neonatal Nurs* 1994; 23(1): 53-9.

Mohaupt, S.M., Sharma, K.K. 'Forensic implications and medical-legal dilemmas of maternal versus fetal rights.' *J Forensic Sci* 1998 Sep; 43(5): 985-92.

Morgan, John-David. 'Wisconsin at the Threshold'. *Shepherd Express Metro* (Milwaukee), vol 21, issue 32. 3 August 2000: http://www.shepherd-express.com/shepherd/21/32/cover_story.html.

Moyes, Gordon. *Victory for unborn child protection*. Christian Democratic Party Media Release, Wednesday, 25 June 2003, on: www.cdp.org.au.

Mozurkewich, E.L., Hutton, E.K. 'Elective repeat cesarean delivery versus trial of labor: a meta-analysis of the literature from 1989 to 1999.' *Am J Obstet Gynecol* 2000: 83: 1187-97.

Mukherjee, S., Shah, A. 'Capacity to consent: issues and controversies.' *Hosp Med* 2001; 62(6): 351-4.

Murphy, D.J. 'Commentary: Obstetric morbidity data and the need to evaluate thromboembolic disease.' *BMJ* 2001; 322: 1093-4.

Murphy, D.J., Pope, C., Frost, J., Liebling, R.E. 'Women's views on the impact of operative delivery in the second stage of labour: qualitative interview study.' *BMJ* 2003; 327: 1132-35.

Mutryn, C. 'Psychosocial impact of cesarean section on the family: a literature review.' *Soc Sci Med* 1993; 37(10): 1271-81.

Nair, S., Morrison, M.F. 'The evaluation of maternal competency.' *Psychosomatics* 2000; 41(6): 523-30.

Nannini, A., Weiss, J., Goldstein, R., Fogerty, S. 'Pregnancy-Associated Mortality at the End of the Twentieth Century: Massachusetts, 1990 – 1999.' *J Am Med Women's Assoc* 2002; 57(23): 140-3.

Napersky, Lisa. 'Woman hits hospitals' stance that she agree to C-section.' *The Citizens' Voice*, Pennsylvania 17 January 2004.

National Advocates for Pregnant Women. *Commentary on 42 C.F.R. Part 457*. http://www.advocatesforpregnantwomen.org/issues/finalcommentonCHIP.htm.

National Commission of Enquiry into the Prevention of Child Abuse. *Childhood Matters. Report of the National Commission of Enquiry into the Prevention of Child Abuse*. Vols 1 and 2. Stationery Office. London 1996.

National Institutes of Health. 'Report of the NIH Panel to define principles of therapy of HIV infection.' *Morbidity and Mortality Weekly Report. Centers for Disease Control and Prevention* 1998 (April 24), Vol 47, No. RR-5.

National Right-to-Life Committee. *President Bush Signs Unborn Victims of Violence Act Into Law, After Dramatic One-vote Win in Senate.* NRLC news release, April 6, 2004.

National Right to Life Committee. *What supporters of legal abortion say about "fetal homicide" laws.* NRLC February 2, 2004: www.nrlc.org.

National Society for the Prevention of Cruelty to Children. *Children Bill media briefing*: www.nspcc.org.uk.

Nelson, K.B., Dambrosia, J.M., Ting, T.Y., Grether, J.K. 'Uncertain Value of Electronic Fetal Monitoring in Predicting Cerebral Palsy.' *New Engl J Med* 1996; 334: 613-8.

Neumann, P.G., Valladares, L. 'The emergence of maternal-fetal conflict policies.' *Health Care Law News* 1991; 6(12): 3-7.

New York Civil Liberties Union. *Legislative Memo: Crimes of Violence Against a Fetus. S. 57-B/A.6681-A – An Act to amend the penal law, in relation to unborn victims of violence.* NYCLU 2003.

New York Civil Liberties Union - Reproductive Rights Project. *Court Rules New York State Child Endangering Law May Not Be Used To Punish Pregnant Woman for Health Problems. Charges against Stacey Gilligan dismissed.* NYCLU Statement, 9 April 2004: www.nyclu.org/rrp_gilligan_pr_040904.html.

Nicoll, A., Peckham, C. 'Reducing vertical transmission of HIV in the UK.' *BMJ* 1999; 319: 1211-12 (Editorial).

Nyberg, K., Allebeck, P., Eklund, G., Jacobson, B. 'Socio-economic versus obstetric risk factors for drug addiction in offspring.' *Br J Addict* 1992; 87(12): 1669-76.

Nyberg, K. *et al.* 'Perintal medication as a potential risk factor for adult drug abuse in a North American cohort'. *Epidemiology* 2000: 11: 715-6.

Oakley, Ann. *The Captured Womb.* Blackwell, London 1986.

Oates, Laurence (official solicitor to Supreme Court). 'The courts' role in decisions about medical treatment.' *BMJ* 2000; 321: 1282-1284.

O'Brien, J.M., Barton, J.R., Donaldson, E.S. 'The management of placenta percreta: conservative and operative strategies.' *Am J Obstet Gynecol* 1996; 175(6): 1632-8.

O'Connor, T.G., Heron, J., Beveridge, M., Glover, V. 'Maternal antenatal anxiety and children's behavioural/emotional problems at 4 years. Report from the Avon Longitudinal Study of Parents and Children.' *Br J Psychiatry* 2002; 180: 502-508.

Olds, D., Henderson, C.R. Jr, Cole, R. *et al.* 'Long-term effects of nurse home visitation on children's criminal and antisocial behavior: 15-year follow-up of a randomized controlled trial.' *JAMA* 1998; 280(14): 1238-44.

Olshan, A.F., Teschke, K., Baird, P.A. 'Paternal occupation and congenital anomalies in offspring.' *Am J Ind Med* 1991; 20: 447-75.

Ondersma, S.J., Simpson, S.M., Brestan, E.V., Ward, M. 'Prenatal drug exposure and social policy: the search for an appropriate response.' *Child Maltreat* 2000; 5(2): 93-108.

Ostrea, E.M. Jr, Matias, O., Keane, C. *et al.* 'Spectrum of gestational exposure to illicit drugs and other xenobiotic agents in newborn infants by meconium analysis.' *J Pediatr* 1998; 133(4): 513-5.

Oxford English Dictionary on CD-ROM v 2.0. Oxford University Press, Oxford, 1999.

Paige, C, Karnofsky, E.B. 'The antiabortion movement and Baby Jane Doe.' *J Health Polit Policy Law* 1986;11(2):255-69.

Pajulo, M., Savonlahti, E., Sourander, A., Helenius, H., Piha, J. 'Antenatal depression, substance dependency and social support.' *J Affect Disord* 2001 Jun; 65(1): 9-17.

Paltrow, Lynn M. *Criminal Prosections Against Pregnant Women. National Update and Overview.* Reproductive Freedom Project, American Civil Liberties Union Foundation. April 1992.

Paltrow, L.M. 'Do Pregnant Women Have Rights?' *Alternet*, 22 April 2004. http://www.alternet.org/story/18493.

Paltrow, L.M. 'Punishing Women for Their Behavior During Pregnancy: An Approach That Undermines the Health of Women and Children.' In: Wetherington, C.L. and Roman A.B. (Editors). *Drug Addiction Research and the Health of Women.* National Institute on Drug Abuse (DHHS), Bethesda, MD, 1998.

Paltrow, Lynn M, J.D. and Newman, Robert, M.D. 'Treatment, not sterilization, is the way to help addicted moms.' *Houston Chronicle* 30 January 2000, at p4C.

Pan American Health Organization (regional office of the World Health Organization), Washington DC. Program on Women, Health and Development. Factsheet: *Domestic violence during pregnancy*.

Partnership for Caring. *Women and End-of-Life Decisions.* February 2001. ww.partnershipforcaring.org.

Paterson-Brown, S. 'Should doctors perform an elective caesarean section on request? Yes, as long as the woman is fully informed.' *BMJ* 1998; 317: 462-465 (letter).

Payne, D. 'Couple has the right to refuse test on newborn baby.' *BMJ* 2001; 323: 1149 (News).

Peerzada, J.M., Richardson, D.K., Burns, J.P. 'Delivery room decision-making at the threshold of viability.' *J Pediatr* 2004; 145(4): 492-8.

Peipert, J.F., Bracken, M. 'Maternal age: an independent risk factor for cesarean delivery.' *Obstet Gynecol* 1993; 81: 200-5.

Pinette, M.G., Kahn, J., Gross, K.L. *et al.* 'Vaginal birth after Cesarean rates are declining rapidly in the rural state of Maine.' *J Matern Fetal Neonatal Med* 2004; 16(1):37-43.

Plaat, F., McGlennan, A. 'Women in the 21st century deserve more information: disclosure of material risk in obstetric anaesthesia.' *Int J Obstet Anesth* 2004; 13:69-70.

Plichta, S.B. 'Intimate partner violence and physical health consequences: policy and practice implications.' *J Interpers Violence* 2004; 19(11): 1296-323.

Pollack, Richard J. PhD. *Head lice: Information and Frequently Asked Questions.* Headlice Information, Laboratory of Public Health Entomology, Harvard School of Public Health.

Pollard, I. 'Substance abuse and parenthood: biological mechanisms - bioethical challenges.' *Women Health* 2000; 30(3): 1-24.

Pollitt, K. 'Fetal rights: a new assault on feminism.' *The Nation*, Mar 26, 1990.

Pollitt, Katha. *Reasonable Creatures: Essays on Women and Feminism.* Vintage 1995, at p182.

Pook, Sally. 'Care order reviews offer little hope to parents'. *Daily Telegraph* 1 June 2004, at p2.

Powledge, Tabitha M. 'The Ultimate Baby Bottle'. *Scientific American* 1999; 10(3).

Powner, D.J., Bernstein. I.M. 'Extended somatic support for pregnant women after brain death.' *Crit Care Med* 2003;31(4):1241-9.

Pragnell, Charles, 'Southall is just part of a much bigger problem'. Rapid responses to: Dyer, Owen. 'Southall is barred for three years from child protection work'. *BMJ* 2004; 329: 366. 17 August 2004: www.bmj.com.

Prentice, A., Lind, T. 'Fetal heart rate monitoring during labour - too frequent intervention, too little benefit?' *Lancet* 1987; 8572: 1375-7.

Punt, J., Bonshek, R.E., Jaspan, T., McConachie, N.S. *et al.* 'The "unified hypothesis" of Geddes *et al* is not supported by the data'. *Pediatr Rehabil* 2004; 7(3): 173-84.

Pursley-Crotteau, S., Kemp, V.H. 'Intervening With Prenatal Crack Cocaine Users.' *Nurs Clin N America* 1998; 33(1): 15-27.

Rachana, C., Suraiya, K., Hisham, A.S. *et al.* 'Prevalence and complications of physical violence during pregnancy.' *Eur J Obstet Gynecol Reprod Biol* 2002; 103(1): 26-9.

Radestad, I., Rubertsson, C., Ebeling, M., Hildingsson, I. 'What factors in early pregnancy indicate that the mother will be hit by her partner during the year after childbirth? A nationwide Swedish survey.' *Birth.* 2004; 31(2): 84-92.

Rageth, J.C., Juzi, C., Grossenbacher, H. 'Delivery after previous cesarean: a risk evaluation.' Swiss Working Group of Obstetric and Gynecologic Institutions. *Obstet Gynecol* 1999;93(3):332-7.

Reardon, David C. 'Report misses association of violence with pregnancy.' *BMJ* 2003; 326: 104 (letter).

Reeves, D. 'Provision of information is only one component of informed choice'. *BMJ* 2002; 325: 43.

Reich, W.T. (Ed). *Encyclopedia of Bioethics.* Vol 3. Simon & Schuster MacMillan, New York 1995.

Report of the NIH Panel to define principles of therapy of HIV infection. *Morbidity and Mortality Weekly Report. Centers for Disease Control and Prevention* 1998 (April 24), Vol 47, No. RR-5.

Richards, P., Kennedy, I.M., Woolf, H. 'Managing medical mishaps.'*BMJ* 1996;313:243-244 (Editorial).

Richman, S. 'Patient, doctor should discuss delivery options. Scenario: Does an obstetrician always have to follow the patient's wishes?' Ethics Forum. 7 April 2003. *American Medical News*: www.ama-assn.org/amednews/2003/04/07/prca0407.htm.

Roberts, R.G., Bell, H.S., Wall, E.M. *et al.* 'Trial of labor or repeated cesarean section: The woman's choice.'*Arch Fam Med* 1997;6:120-125.

Robertson, Geoffrey. *Freedom, the Individual and the Law*. Penguin, London, 1993.

Robertson, J. 'Legal issues in prenatal therapy.' *Clin Obstet Gynecol* 1986; 29(3): 603-11.

Robertson, J. 'Fetal abuse.' (1989) 75 *American Bar Association* 38.

Robertson, John A. *Children of Choice. Freedom and the new reproductive technologies*. Princeton University Press, New Jersey 1994.

Robertson, J.A., Shulman, J.D. 'Pregnancy and prenatal harm: the case of mothers with PKU.' *Hastings Center Report* 17 (1987): 23-33.

Robinson, Jean. 'Child protection system wilfully ignores principles of childcare' (letters). *Daily Telegraph* 5 August 2004, at p23.

Robinson, J. 'Post traumatic disorder - a consumer view.' In: MacLean A, Neilson J. *Maternal Morbidity and Mortality*. RCOG Press 2002, at pp 313-22.

Rosenfield, A. 'Women's reproductive health'. *Am J Obstet Gynecol* 1993; 169(1): 128-33.

Rossiter, G.P. 'Contemporary transatlantic developments concerning compelled medical treatment of pregnant women.' *Aust N Z J Obstet Gynaecol* 1995; 35(2): 132-8.

Roth, R. 'At women's expense: the costs of fetal rights.' In: Merrick, Janna C and Blank, Robert H. *The politics of pregnancy: policy dilemmas in the maternal-fetal relationship*. Harrington Park Press, Binghamton, New York, 1993, pp 117-135.

Rothenberg and Thomson (Editors). *Women and Prenatal Testing: Facing the Challenges of Genetic Technology*. Ohio State University Press, 1994.

Rothman, B. *The Tentative Pregnancy: Prenatal Diagnosis and the Future of Motherhood*. Viking Penguin, New York 1986.

Rothman, Barbara Katz. *The Tentative Pregnancy* Pandora 1994.

Royal College of Obstetricians and Gynaecologists. *A consideration of the law and ethics in relation to court-authorised obstetric intervention*. Ethics No. 1. RCOG. April 1994.

Royal College of Obstetricians and Gynaecologists. *National Sentinel Caesarean Section Audit Published*. RCOG press release, 26 October 2001.

Royal College of Physicians: *Prenatal Diagnosis and Genetic Screening: Community and Service Implications.* RCP, London 1989.

Royal Commission on New Reproductive Technologies. *Proceed with care: Final Report of the Royal Commission on New Reproductive Technologies.* Vol 2. Ottawa (Canada): Minister of Government Services; 1993: 964-65.

Rozenberg, Joshua. 'Review of 300 child deaths identifies 28 "unsafe" cases'. *Daily Telegraph* 22 December 2004.

Rozenberg, Joshua and Jardine, Cassandra. 'Baby death mother to fight for jail pay-out'. *Daily Telegraph* 12 January 2005.

Ryding, E.L., Persson, A., Onell C., Kvist L. 'An evaluation of midwives' counselling of pregnant women in fear of childbirth.' *Acta Obstet Gynecol Scand* 2003; 82: 10-7.

Ryding, E.L., Wiren, E., Johansson, G. *et al.* 'Group counseling for mothers after emergency cesarean section: a randomized controlled trial of intervention.' *Birth.* 2004 Dec; 31(4): 247-53.

Sabrine, N. 'Elective caesarean can increase the risk to the foetus.' *BMJ* 2000; 320: 1072 (letter).

Sage, Alexandria. 'Utah C-Section Mom Gets Probation'. *CBS News.com* 29 April 2004: http://www.cbsnews.com/stories/2004/03/12/national/main605537.shtml.

St. Martin, Darla. 'Better to Save Some Lives Now than None at All, Ever.' From an editorial reproduced from the *National Catholic Register* by John Mark Ministries on: http://jmm.aaa.net.au/articles/978.htm.

Sakala, C. 'Medically unnecessary cesarean section births: introduction to a symposium.' *Soc Sci Med* 1993 Nov; 37(10): 1177-98.

Sampson, M.B., Petersen, L.P. 'Post-traumatic coma during pregnancy.' *Obstet Gynecol* 1979 Mar; 53(3 Suppl): 2S-3S.

Santora, Marc. 'Negligent couple is told not to procreate'. *New York Times* May 2004.

Saunders, Hilary. *Twenty-nine child homicides: Lessons still to be learnt on domestic violence and child protection.* Women's Aid, London 2004: www.womensaid.org.uk.

Schoeman, J., Grove, D.V., Odendaal, H.J. 'Are Domestic Violence and the Excessive Use of Alcohol Risk Factors for Preterm Birth?' *J Trop Pediatr* 2004; 15 December.

Schuitemaker, N. et al. 'Maternal mortality after cesarean in The Netherlands.' *Acta Obstet Gynecol Scand* 1997; 76(4):332-4.

Schultz, Thomas. 'Cottage C-section rule has some moms upset.' *Santa Barbara News Press* 25 June 2003.

Scott, Kirsty. 'Baby taken from inquiry mother.' *The Guardian* 26 November 2001.

Shaw, M. 'Preconception and parental torts.' In: Milunsky A, Annas G (eds). *Genetics and the Law* II, 1980, at p 228.

Shearer, E.L. 'Cesarean section: medical benefits and costs.' *Soc Sci Med* 1993;37(10):1223-31.

Sheikh, A.A., Cusack, D.A. 'Maternal brain death, pregnancy and the foetus: the medico-legal implications for Ireland.' *Med Law* 2004; 23(2): 237-50.

Shumway, J., O'Campo, P., Gielen, A. *et al.* 'Preterm labor, placental abruption, and premature rupture of membranes in relation to maternal violence or verbal abuse.' *J Matern Fetal Med* 1999; 8(3): 76-80.

Siefert, K., Pimlott, S. 'Improving pregnancy outcome during imprisonment: a model residential care program.' *Soc Work* 2001; 46(2): 125-34.

Silverman, J.G., Mesh, C.M., Cuthbert, C.V. *et al.* 'Child custody determinations in cases involving intimate partner violence: a human rights analysis.' *Am J Public Health* 2004; 94(6): 951-7.

Sjogren, B., Uddenberg, N. 'Decision Making During the Prenatal Diagnostic Procedure. A Questionnaire and Interview Study of 211 Women Participating in Prenatal Diagnosis.' *Prenatal Diagnosis* 1988; 8: 263-73.

Skla, P.A., Bathgate, S.L., Young, H.A., Parenti, D.M. 'Care of HIV-infected pregnant women in maternal-fetal medicine programs'. *Infect Dis Obstet Gynecol* 2001; 9(2): 81-7.

Smith, Elmer. 'Regina McKnight: The Baby Drug War'. *Philadelphia Daily News* 8 October 2003.

Smith, G.C., Pell, J.P., Dobbie, R. 'Caesarean section and risk of unexplained stillbirth in subsequent pregnancy.' *Lancet.* 2003;362:1779-84.

Smith, J.C. and Hogan, Brian. *Criminal Law.* Butterworths, London 1992.

Smith, S. 'The role of the court in ethical decision making.' *Clin Med* 2001; 1(5): 371-3.

Soet, J.E., Brack, G.A., Dilorio, C. 'Prevalence and predictors of women's experience of psychological trauma during childbirth.' *Birth* 2003;30(1):3 6-46.

Spinelli, M.G. 'Antepartum and postpartum depression.' *J Gend Specif Med* 1998; 1(2): 33-6.

Stang, H.J., Snellman, L.W. 'Circumcision practice patterns in the United States.' *Pediatrics* 1998 Jun: 101(6):E5.

Stanton, A.N. 'Sudden unexpected death in infancy associated with maltreatment: evidence from long term follow up of siblings'. *Arch Dis Child* 2003 Aug;88(8): 699-701.

Statewatch News online. UK: Children Bill to introduce surveillance of every child and record 'concerns' about their parents'. *Statewatch* April 2004: http://www.statewatch.org/news/2004/apr/07children-bill.htm.

Stein, Ellen J. 'Maternal-Fetal conflict: Reformulating the equation'. In: Grubb, Andrew (Ed). *Challenges in Medical Care.* John Wiley & Sons. Chichester 1992, 91-108.

Steinbock, Bonnie. *Life Before Birth: The moral and legal status of embryos and fetuses.* Oxford University Press, Oxford 1996 (paperback edition).

Steinbock, B. 'Maternal-fetal conflict and *in utero* fetal therapy.' (1994) 57 *Albany Law Rev* 781.

Stephenson, P.A., Wagner, M.G. 'Reproductive rights and the medical care system: a plea for rational health policy.' *J Public Health Policy* 1993;14(2): 174-82.

Stevens, Kathy. Fetal-drug prosecution ignites debate in S.C. State stands alone in arresting women who engage in risky behavior during pregnancy. *The Post and Courier* (South Carolina), February 23, 2003.

Stone, M.L. 'Presidential Address'. *American College of Obstetricians and Gynecologists Newsletter,* 4 May 1979.

Stout, David. 'Supreme Court to Discuss Legality of Drug Tests of Pregnant Women.' *New York Times,* 28 Feb 2000.

Sultan, A.H., Stanton, S.L. 'Preserving the pelvic floor and perineum during childbirth: elective caesarean section?' *Br J Obstet Gynaecol* 1996; 103: 731-734.

Sutherland, E., McCall Smith, R.A. *Family Rights: Family Law and Medical Advance.* Edinburgh University Press 1990.

Sutton, A. *Prenatal Diagnosis: Confronting the Ethical Issues.* The Linacre Centre, London 1990, at pp 20-21.

Swahnberg, K., Wijma, B., Wingren, G. *et al.* 'Women's perceived experiences of abuse in the health care system: their relationship to childhood abuse'. *Br J Obstet Gynaecol* 2004;111(12):1429-36.

Swartz, M. 'Pregnant Woman v Foetus: A Dilemma for Hospital Ethics Committees.' *Cambridge Quarterly Healthcare Ethics*;1992;1:51, at p53.

Szalavitz, Maia. 'War On Drugs, War On Women.' *On The Issues*, New York, Winter 1998.

Taddio, A. 'Pain management for neonatal circumcision.' *Paediatr Drugs* 2001; 3(2): 101-11.

Talbert, D.G. 'Paroxysmal cough injury, vascular rupture and "shaken baby syndrome"'. *Med Hypotheses* 2005;64(1): 8-13.

Talvi, Silja J.A. 'Criminalizing Motherhood'. *The Nation*, 11 Dec 2003: http://www.thenation.com/.

Tamminen ,T., Verronen, P., Saarikoski, S. et al. 'The influence of perinatal factors on breast feeding.' *Acta Paediatr Scand* 1983; 72(1): 9-12.

Tauer, C.A. 'Lives at stake. How to respond to a woman's refusal of cesarean surgery when she risks losing her child or her life.' *Health Prog* 1992; 73(7): 18-27.

Tauer, C.A. 'When pregnant patients refuse interventions.' *AWHONNS Clin Issues Perinat Womens Health Nurs* 1993;4(4):596-605.

Taylor, Diane. 'Does a foetus have more rights than its mother?' *The Guardian*, Friday April 23, 2004.

Tew, Marjorie. 'Do obstetric intranatal interventions make birth safer?' *Br J Obstet Gynaecol* 1986; 93: 659-74, at p671.

Tew, Marjorie. *Safer Childbirth? A Critical History of Maternity Care.* First edition. Chapman & Hall 1990; also third edition, Free Association Books, London 1998.

Thomas, J., Paranjothy, S. 'Royal College of Obstetricians and Gynaecologists Clinical Effectiveness Support Unit. National Sentinel Caesarean Section Audit Report.' *RCOG Press*, 2001.

Thomas, Karen. 'Parents pressured to put kids on Ritalin. N.Y. court orders use of medicine.' *USA Today*. 8 August 2000.

Thornton, T.E., Paltrow, L. 'The Rights of Pregnant Patients. Carder Case Brings Bold Policy Initiatives'. *HealthSpan* 1991; 8(5).

Thorpe, L.J. 'The Caesarean Section Debate.' 1997 *Family Law* 663.

Thorpe, M.A. 'Consent for Caesarean Section: Part 1 - development of the law.' *Clinical Risk* 2000;5:173-176.

Thorpe, M.A. 'Consent for Caesarean Section: Part 2 - autonomy, capacity, best interests, reasonable force and procedural guidelines.' *Clinical Risk* 2000;5:209-212.

Tronick, E.Z., Beeghly, M. 'Prenatal cocaine exposure, child development, and the compromising effects of cumulative risk.' *Clin Perinatol* 1999; 26(1): 151-71.

Tucker, J.S., Hall, M.H., Howie, P.W. *et al.* Should obstetricians see women with normal pregnancies? A multicentre randomised controlled trial of routine antenatal care by general practitioners and midwives compared with shared care led by obstetricians. *BMJ* 1996;312:554-9.

Tuohey, J.F. 'Terminal care and the pregnant woman: ethical reflections on In Re: A.C.' *Pediatrics* 1991;88(6):1268-73.

Tuzovic, L., Djelmis, J., Ilijic, M. 'Obstetric risk factors associated with placenta previa development: case-control study. *Croat Med J* 2003;44:728-33.

Udy, Pam. 'Legal system organizing against rights of pregnant women'. *Standard-Examiner* (Utah) 20 May 2004.

Unno, Nobuya. 'Development of an Artificial Placenta'. In: Stocker, Gerfried and Schoepf, Christine (Eds). *Next Sex: Ars Electronica 2000*. Springer Verlag, 2000 Wien, at p 252-3.

Ussher, Jane. *Women's Madness: Misogyny or mental illness?* Harvester Wheatsheaf, Hemel Hempstead, 1991.

Usta, I.M., Mercer, B.M., Sibai, B.M. 'Current obstetrical practice and umbilical cord prolapse.' *Am J Perinatol* 1999;16(9):479-84.

van Ham, M.A., van Dongen, P.W., Mulder, J. 'Maternal consequences of caesarean section. A retrospective study of intraoperative and postoperative maternal complications of cesarean section during a 10-year period.' *Eur J Obstet Gynecol Reprod Biol* 1997;74(1):1-6.

Varawalla, N., Settatree, R. 'Does the attending obstetrician influence the mode of delivery in the standard nullipara?' *J Ob Gyn* 1988; 18: 520-3.

Ventura, S.J., Martin, J.A., Curtin, S.C., Mathews, T.J. 'Births: Final Data for 1997.' *National Vital Statistics Reports* 1999, Volume 47, Number 18.

Vernon, B., Tracy, S., Reibel, T. 'Compliance, coercion, and power have huge effect in maternity services'. *BMJ* 2002; 325:43.

Victoria Climbié Inquiry. *Victoria Climbié Report calls for radical change in the management of public services for children and families.* Statement, 28 January 2003: http://www.victoria-climbie-inquiry.org.uk.

Vintzileos, A.M., Nochimson, D.J., Guzman, E.R. *et al.* 'Intrapartum electronic fetal heart rate monitoring versus intermittent auscultation: a meta-analysis.' *Obstet Gynecol* 1995; 85:149-55.

Voltaire, Francois M. *Candide or Optimism.* Penguin Classics, London 1990.

Wagner, Marsden. 'Bad Habits.' *AIMS Journal*, Winter 1999/2000 Vol 11, No.4.

Wallace, Natasha. New law to protect unborn as killer father jailed. *Sydney Morning Herald* June 17, 2004.

Waterhouse, Rosie. 'Mothers lose court fight to stop MMR jabs'. *Daily Telegraph* 31 July 2003, at p3.

Watson, M., Forshaw, M. 'Child outpatient non-attendance may indicate welfare concerns.' *BMJ* 2002; 324:739.

Wax, J.R., Cartin, A., Pinette, M.G., Blackstone, J. 'Patient choice cesarean: an evidence-based review.' *Obstet Gynecol Surv* 2004;59(8): 601-16.

Weiss, D. 'Court Delivers Controversy.' *Times Leader Northeastern Pennsylvania*, 16 January 2004.

Wen, S.W., Rusen, I.D., Walker, M. *et al.* Maternal Health Study Group, Canadian Perinatal Surveillance System. 'Comparison of maternal mortality and morbidity between trial of labor and elective cesarean section among women with previous cesarean delivery.' *Am J Obstet Gynecol* 2004; 191:1263-9.

Wetherington, C.L. and Roman A.B. (Editors). *Drug Addiction Research and the Health of Women.* National Institute on Drug Abuse (DHHS), Bethesda, MD 1998.

Wick, Alison. 'Choosing to have your baby at home is set to become less of a battle.' *Daily Telegraph,* 18 January 1997.

Williams, L. 'Religious restrictions and the trauma patient.' *Certified Registered Nurse Anaesthetist* 1997; 8(1): 40-4.

Wolf, Naomi. *Misconceptions. Truth, Lies and the Unexpected on the Journey to Motherhood.* Doubleday Books New York 2001.

Woolf, H. *Access to Justice: final report to the Lord Chancellor on the civil justice system in England and Wales.* London HMSO 1996

Women's Law Project. 'In re guardianship of JDS'. *Women's Law Project Newsletter*. Fall 2003. Philadelphia Pa: www.womenslawproject.org.

World Health Organization. 'Appropriate technology for birth.' *Lancet* 1985;2(8452): 436-437.

Zdeb, M.S., Therriault G.D., Logrillo V.M. 'Frequency, spacing, and outcome of pregnancies subsequent to primary cesarean childbirth.' *Am J Obstet Gynecol* 1984; 150(2): 205-12.

Index